PRAISE FOR SEVEN ZONES FOR LEADERSHIP

"Penetrating insights into the dynamics of human and organizational leadership, examining process and structure, and offering predictability, action alternatives, and, above all, wisdom."

James V. Toscano, Executive Vice President, Park Nicollet Institute

"This is the book we've been waiting for! It offers a comprehensive guide to help us understand which leadership interventions are best in particular contexts. *Seven Zones for Leadership* is both an impressive intellectual achievement and a practical guide to action."

Barbara C. Crosby, Senior Fellow, Humphrey Institute of Public Affairs; author, *Leadership for the Common Good* and *Leadership for Global Citizenship*

"Bob Terry has created a virtual road map for use in the journey toward becoming an authentic leader. He even has developed signposts along the way that help identify dangerous curves in the road, one-way trails, rest stops, places to yield, green lights, and literal stop signs. This book is an excellent tool for anyone concerned about being a leader who serves people and stewards resources."

Timothy N. Gibson, Executive Director, World Servants

"Bob Terry is one of the most insightful persons who have studied the concepts of leadership. For executives, managers, and people who lead organizations, *Seven Zones for Leadership* is immensely helpful."

Kevin S. Burke, Chief Judge, Hennepin County (MN) District Court

"This book puts leadership theories in perspective by providing a context for analysis and application. Bob Terry does a great service to anyone interested in creating successful leaders—from CEOs to human resource practitioners."

Margery L. Pabst, President, MLP Enterprises; author, *A Moving Experience*

"Bob Terry has the unique capacity to synthesize, quantify, and reframe massive amounts of information into a workable scheme for the rest of us. A very helpful book for anyone interested in leadership and organizational development at a time when the culture is moving back and forth from stability to chaos."

Jack Fortin, Executive Director, Center for Lifelong Learning, Luther Seminary

"The winds of change will fill your sails and try your soul. Bob Terry's wisdom will help you navigate with authentic strength."

David Tiede, President, Luther Seminary

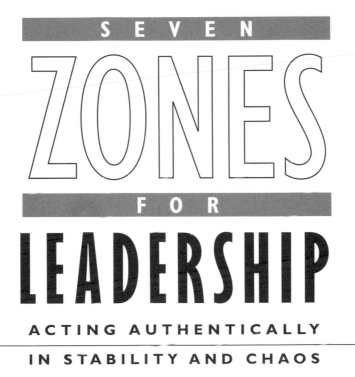

SEVEN ZONES FOR LEADERSHIP

ACTING AUTHENTICALLY
IN STABILITY AND CHAOS

ROBERT W. TERRY

DAVIES-BLACK PUBLISHING
Palo Alto, California

Published by Davies-Black Publishing, an imprint of Consulting Psychologists Press, Inc., 3803 East Bayshore Road, Palo Alto, CA 94303; 1-800-624-1765.

Special discounts on bulk quantities of Davies-Black books are available to corporations, professional associations, and other organizations. For details, contact the Director of Book Sales at Davies-Black Publishing, an imprint of Consulting Psychologists Press, Inc., 3803 East Bayshore Road, Palo Alto, CA 94303; 650-691-9123; Fax 650-623-9271.

Visit the Davies-Black Publishing web site at www.daviesblack.com.

05 04 03 02 01   10 9 8 7 6 5 4 3 2 1
Printed in the United States of America

Library of Congress Cataloging-in-Publication Data

Terry, Robert W.
  Seven zones for leadership : acting authentically in stability and chaos/
  Robert W. Terry.—1st ed.
      p. cm.
  Includes bibliographical references and index.
  ISBN 0-89106-158-4
  1. Leadership. 2. Title.

  HD57.7 .T464 2001
  658.4′092—dc21

                                                    2001028574

FIRST EDITION
First printing 2001

To my mother, Lillian Pendelton Terry,
and to Janet and George Odell
and Nan Carnes, my treasured relatives

CONTENTS

FOREWORD

Fasten your seat belt. This book, like its author, is so unusual as to be extraordinary.

Bob Terry has long been a wise, witty, and very popular lecturer on leadership. A product of the University of Chicago's unusual Ph.D. in social ethics program, he became a thoughtful activist on the many puzzles of America's social diversity and wrote a book on race relations, *For Whites Only*, that sold more than a quarter million copies.

During the decade of the 1980s, he directed one of the earliest university-based efforts to marry theory and practice to do what we then called "bringing people together in organizations to make something different happen." This was, and is, the Center for Reflective Leadership at the University of Minnesota's Hubert H. Humphrey Institute of Public Affairs—where, as a close colleague and collaborator, I enjoyed Bob's engaging personality and admired his probing mind. Thereafter, in the midst of an active life as a successful consultant, Bob authored *Authentic Leadership: Courage in Action* (1993) and began the long think that led to this remarkable writing.

Bob Terry has read widely in the fast-growing literature about leadership. And he has, between these two covers,

- Created a map of the whole field of leadership studies

- Framed personal development, professional development, and organizational development as linked parts of a whole

- Placed the myriad kinds of leadership actions in their multiple contexts, broadening the term *leadership* way beyond the actions and attitudes of people in "leadership positions"

- Explored the role of spirituality in the practice of leadership

- Rediscovered the old truth that, as a leader, *who you are* is even more important than *what you do*

For those of us who grew up before and during World War II, the word *leader* (in German, *der Führer*) was not quite an obscenity, but it was often a conversation stopper. It carried at worst the baggage of dictatorship, oppression, and genocide. At best, it connoted hierarchy and positional authority, leaving very little room for leadership by indirection, brainy expertise, or moral authority.

The writer E. B. White, a philosopher disguised as a humorist, posed long ago (in a *New Yorker* story) a question that has intrigued me for most of my life: "Have you ever considered how complicated things can get, what with one thing always leading to another?"

Public affairs and other kinds of organized activity—business, education, science, art, communication, and all the components of "civil society"—have become so intermeshed, interactive, and international that complexity clearly has a bright future. Bob Terry has taken the trouble to understand chaos and complexity theory—and found in it creative juices that can help reflective leaders lead.

He has pondered the complex polarities and paradoxes of organizational life in our time, and reflected deeply on the way men and women—and the organizations they create—develop in response to them.

In the twilight of hierarchy, he now thinks, "leadership is less doing than being." The practice of leadership is not merely, or even mostly, tactics and technique; it engages the whole person.

Taking this idea seriously leads the author, and the reader, through zone after zone of the leadership experience, from Serving the Past—which can't be changed, but can only be lived up to or lived down—to Living the Promise of what hasn't happened yet—which can't ever be a straight-line extrapolation from the past because it depends so much on who leads and how and toward what, from now on.

This inquiry ultimately leads the author—and the reader—into profound reflection on the nature of evil and the quality of "authentic wisdom." Most writings in this field, whether by scholars or practitioners, stop well short of trying to bring *spirituality* and *leadership* together between the covers of a single book. Bob Terry manages to venture onto this sensitive terrain without trying to sell either a philosophical doctrine or a theological dogma—because he writes as a truth seeker still seeking, not as a salesman selling what he already knows you should believe.

So this book is part erudition, part exploration—the erudition lightened by the author's breezy personal style, the exploration reinforced by a lifetime of lively "thought leading to action."

Harlan Cleveland
President Emeritus
World Academy of Art and Science

Professor Emeritus and founding Dean
Hubert H. Humphrey Institute of Public Affairs
University of Minnesota

PREFACE

Have you ever experienced any of the following situations?

- Positional leaders are preoccupied with worker participation when the infrastructure is crumbling.

- The workforce knows that person X is the wrong person in the job, yet that person is promoted and the situation gets worse.

- A team leader is preoccupied with results and the situation actually requires that the team's energy be engaged because changing conditions have blurred organizational goals.

- Lower and middle managers want to be heard; they want a voice. In response, upper management recommends, or even demands, that they take a training course to improve skills. The situation deteriorates.

- An executive returns from a seminar excited about a consultant's program. The consultant is hired, the plan is implemented, the consultant leaves, and the plan fizzles.

Two economists on National Public Radio (May 5, 1998, Morning Edition), reflecting on corporate mergers, reported that two-thirds of mergers failed to deliver on their anticipated results. In the 1950s and 1960s restructuring hit about every seven years. Now it seems continuous. Yet Hamel and Prahalad (1994) tell us that "masquerading under names like refocusing, delayering, decluttering, and right-sizing (one is tempted to ask why the 'right' size is always smaller), restructuring always has the same result: fewer employees. . . . Restructuring seldom results in fundamental improvement of the business. At best, it buys time. One study of sixteen large U.S. companies with at least three years of restructuring experience found that although restructuring usually did improve a firm's share price, the improvement was almost always temporary" (p. 11). Of reengineering along with restructuring they observe, "Far from being a tribute to senior management's steely resolve or farsightedness, a large restructuring and reengineering charge is simply the penalty that a company must pay for not having anticipated the future" (pp. 13–14).

Questions are being raised even about the sacred cow of quality. As one CEO told me, "Quality will no longer create a competitive advantage. It will be the floor, the foundation. Without world-class products, effective and efficient production processes, and superb customer service, we will not even be in the game." And the popular phrase "delight the customer" is being challenged. What if customers are a drag on your business? Don't delight them; get rid of them or charge them more (Brooks, 1999).

Whole-system change, currently a very hot organizational technology, is being challenged for lack of follow-through. In whole-system change events, large numbers of people—in the hundreds or even over a thousand—traverse a participatory process to address organizational issues. Evaluations of these methods are just now being collected and assessed. I have participated in many whole-system change events. Some work, some do not.

I have talked with cynical executives who want to collect all the strategic visions and interventions and flush them down the toilet. Organizational players and consultants alike propose and engage in thousands of fix-it activities:

- Personal profile seminars
- 360-degree performance reviews
- Team building (including outdoor exercises)

- Strategic vision statements
- Project task forces
- Total quality management
- Quality award goals

- Transformation visioning
- Diversity training
- Cultural change projects
- Core value identification
- Shared-value surveys
- Mission definition

- Customer-focus programs
- Reenergizing systems
- Reengineering, restructuring
- Mergers, partnerships
- Downsizing

Not to mention large-scale interventions:

- Alignment processes
- Futuring
- Follow-up task forces
- Breakthrough teams
- Strategic planning

- Long-range planning
- Creativity seminars
- Humor seminars
- Market redefinition

The list goes on and on.

The less-than-hoped-for results from these fix-it strategies are causing weariness and cynicism. Who captures today's cynicism with organizational life better than Scott Adams in his comic strip *Dilbert*®? *Dilbert* casts a laser beam on the disconnect between strategies and reality, the inauthenticity in many organizations.

Now we are seeing new books on polarities, paradoxes, shadows, complexity theory, and spirituality in leadership and organizational life. The more I consult with clients who lead organizations, the more the complexity and proliferation of options for leadership action overwhelm me. The more I read and the more I experience organizational life, the deeper the puzzles. I have come to believe that it is crucial to propose and test a comprehensive theory or map that can orient and guide us.

I am not only a leadership educator. I am also an executive advisor and organizational consultant. Over the years I have become increasingly wary of the fact that formal and informal leaders at all levels have so many alternatives to choose from in defining their leadership role and yet are expected to select and focus on only one. I have longed for a diagnostic model of organizational development so I could more wisely offer sound advice—advice about selecting leadership actions in relationship to the great variety of real-world situations. Strategies abound. Yet there are few blueprints to place them in context so people can make *wise* and *adept* decisions about how to understand them and when to employ them.

What choices should we make? Are the choices dictated by the contextual realities of the organization, community group, or agency? Or are the interventions so good as to be valued and utilized regardless of the context and conditions? Intervention options are often discussed as though each one can be applied in a great range of situations, and the issue then becomes which one is best overall. What if that is not the case? What if in fact there is no single best intervention? What if there are *many* effective interventions, and the real issues are the context and how well an intervention fits it? Then we have to start asking what are the expectations from the intervention, and how are they grounded in an appropriate understanding of the context—what is *really* going on within the organization and outside it. If, for example, the world five to ten years from now is unknowable, what sense does it make to use methods of intervention that presuppose predictability, market share, and customer loyalty? We also have to ask how we move from intervention to intervention.

If we had a map of different leadership contexts, or worlds, so that we could figure out what leadership choices best fit each world, wouldn't we experience the reverse of the situation I just described? Leadership actions would work wonderfully. Crumbling infrastructure is repaired and then worker participation is built upon a solid foundation. The right people are in the right jobs doing the right thing at the right time for the right reason. Preoccupation with results is set aside to allow the team to become engaged in setting new goals and then organizing themselves to accomplish those goals. Forums are offered for dialogue. Consultant fixes are carefully assessed to ensure they fit organizational realities; processes are implemented and include follow-through.

The purpose of this book is to offer such a map. It matches possible leadership actions to seven zones, each zone representing a different reality ranging from the world where we know what is really going on inside and outside our organization to the world in which everything seems unknowable. The zones describe stages of leadership in that later zones rest on earlier ones, yet none of the zones ever becomes unimportant. In this model, leadership accumulates competencies so it can ultimately function in all the zones. The zones reflect the history of leadership and organizational theories and practices, yet no zone ever becomes the past. While leadership action differs in each zone, there are constants shaping that action. Ethical principles and standards for authenticity are always at work. The matching of action to reality is not a mechanical task. It involves seeking to grasp what is happening in the world that requires a different understanding of leadership action.

IS THIS BOOK FOR YOU?

If you are a truth seeker, this book is for you. You might be an executive looking to define your organization's condition; a manager or employee seeking to lead from the middle or the bottom of your organization; a community member, board member, or committee or task force participant; or an individual personally or professionally intrigued by the subject of leadership. This book also speaks to leadership educators.

It is not for those looking for a quick fix, simple solutions, or easy skill training. Leadership is not taught over lunch or in a daylong seminar. It can take a lifetime to understand how to connect leadership practice and theory. This book invites you into a reflective inquiry, both playful and serious, that can help you learn leadership as you live it.

OVERVIEW OF THE CHAPTERS

The Introduction lays out the foundations, major themes, and challenges for this book. The book's thirteen chapters are organized into three parts.

Part One (Chapters One and Two) welcomes you to view and walk around in the leadership landscape. Chapter One offers a leadership debate over eight pairs of leadership choices, allowing you to determine your current overall view of leadership. For example, after reading arguments favoring a view that leaders are born and arguments favoring the view that leaders are made, you will be invited to indicate which view you lean toward. In Chapter Two, I lay out the seven leadership zones, discussing them in terms of the action wheel from my 1993 book *Authentic Leadership* and in terms of worlds shifting from knowable and fixable to unknowable and unfixable. All the choices you make in Chapter One will match some part of the worldly map I draw in Chapter Two. Each zone connects leadership, worldly context, and strategic actions. The independent variable in this linkage is the world. As it changes, our understanding of leadership and appropriate strategies and interventions changes.

Part Two (Chapters Three through Ten) presents the first six zones. (Zones 3 and 5 are each divided into two subzones, so each of these zones is discussed over two chapters.) I begin the view of each zone or subzone with a story that illustrates the main point of the zone. This is followed by an analysis of the core ideas of the zone and a discussion of the application of the ideas in practice. Next you have an opportunity to answer a series of questions that will help you figure out how well your organization functions in the zone, where your organization is currently focusing its attention, and how prepared you are to exhibit leadership in the zone. The examination of each zone concludes with a zone summary and samplings of what I call negative and positive stirrings—thoughts and feelings that may either trap people in the zone or quicken movement into the next zone in accord with the changing reality.

Part Three (Chapters Eleven through Thirteen) explores Zone 7 and leadership actions and ideas that apply across all the zones. Zone 7 has three subzones. Chapter Eleven looks at what it means to be wise and adept in making choices for leadership action. In Chapter Twelve, I address in some detail some of the larger ideas about leadership raised by an examination of the zones and the worlds the zones correspond to, delving into leadership's response to chaos and complexity theory, polarities and paradoxes, and the organizational shadow (or informal organization), and discussing the zone leadership map as leadership development theory. In Chapter Thirteen, I push the boundaries of the leadership field as I address the provocative themes of spirituality and authenticity in leadership and propose a link between leadership and certain deeper aspects of spirituality that go beyond where the field goes.

The ideas that inform most of the content of this book come from pivotal thinkers and theorists in the field, practitioners who live the material every day, educators, and consultants, as well as my own lived experiences. As the inclusiveness of the mapping should make apparent, I am convinced that all the ideas and theories I mention add value. I do raise questions about what zone each leadership view fits best, and I describe the problems that occur when a view is applied beyond the zone where it fits. This should not be taken to mean that I am questioning the essential validity of any view. Indeed, this map rests on the idea that many views are valid. Its strength comes from the strength of many. You will meet the contributors as the zones unfold.

ACKNOWLEDGMENTS

I may sit alone when I write; however, colleagues and friends are ever present to support, offer feedback, do research, share materials, or just be there. One person stands out from the rest: Judie Ramsey. She is the key administrator for Zobius Leadership International, formerly known as The Terry Group. She contributed endless hours of editing and feedback during the writing process. Judie actually created the new name of our firm, linking Zones to the Mobius loop—Zobius. Without her, this book would not exist.

Many others offered ideas, reviewed early texts, and added wisdom. They include: Mo Fahnestock, Warren Hoffman, Cathy Polanski, Tom Heuerman, David Tiede, Jack Fortin, Tom Fiutak, Barbara Crosby, Harlan Cleveland, Dan Little, Jim Emrich, Bruce Gibb, Tim Gibson, Carl Holmstrom, Bill Mills, David O'Fallon, Jim Toscano, Larry Shelton, Rob and Mark Stevenson, Wendell Willis, Glenda Eoyang, Stefan Botes, Jim LaRue, Dick Broholm, Marilyn Nelson, Patrick Kiefert, Donna Rae Scheffert, Linda Giesen, and George Callendine. There were many others, in my classes and seminars, who offered comments and insight that affected this text.

Still others had the courage to build these ideas into their organizations. They include: Eric Jackson, Gary Cerney, John Remes, Sue Reimer, Patti Wilder, Craig Halverson, Richard O'Dell, Bruce

Nicholson, Bill Scheurer, Joyce Kaser, Carol Bonosaro, John Euler, John Brandl, Paul Terry, Jim Hawley, Frank Klisanich, John Bryson, Lisa Carlson, Bill Chilton, Lisa Dinndorf, Louise Ninneman, Andy Frost, Diana Jones, Mark Jenner, and Rick Becker, as well as heads of professional associations who used the materials in their seminars.

Also deserving of special attention are the editors. Linda Rening did the first, very helpful, complete edit prior to offering the text to a publisher. Copyeditor Elspeth MacHattie greatly strengthened this book, as she did my last one. Alan Shrader, as overall editor, proved again to be a great professional editor and wonderful person with whom to work.

What a wonderful guild of friends. Without you there would be no book. Thank you.

Robert Terry, President of Zobius Leadership International, formerly The Terry Group, is a leadership architect, executive mentor, author, public speaker and seminar conductor, and peer advisor to leadership educators in the Minneapolis area. As Director of the Reflective Leadership Center at the Hubert H. Humphrey Institute at the University of Minnesota and scholar in leadership studies, plus having led and currently leading a for-profit organization, he is positioned uniquely as a leadership educator.

With an undergraduate degree in sociology from Cornell University, a master in divinity degree from Colgate Rochester Divinity School, and master's and doctoral degrees in social ethics from the University of Chicago Divinity School, Terry is uniquely equipped for intellectual exploration. He delights in boundary pushing as he challenges leadership studies. As a creator of a social movement to fight racism, and a hands-on practitioner in both running a firm and consulting with hundreds of for-profit and not-for-profit firms nationally and globally, he brings reflective practice to the table. He delights as well in contributing to real, live hands-on situations.

In 1984, the University of Minnesota awarded Terry the Gordon Starr Faculty and Staff Outstanding Contribution Award. In 1994, he received The Ethical Leadership Award from the University of Minnesota University YMCA. And in 1998, he received The Ted

Kern Award, the highest honor bestowed on senior executives in the federal government by the Senior Executive Association. He was made an honoree member of government in order to receive the award.

Terry is known for his depth of content, sense of humor, passion for the subject matter of authenticity and leadership, and total engagement with his audiences, clients, and customers.

———————

Zobius Leadership International, a guild of seasoned leadership architects and educators, partners with for-profit and not-for-profit organizations, co-creating and delivering a full array of leadership programs. These comprise mostly long-term programs inside organizations, along with coaching, mentoring, and organizational assessment and follow-through that links personal, professional, and organizational realities grounded in research, professional experience, tested success, and authentically grounded significance.

THE CHALLENGES
OF LEADERSHIP

One of the most useless statements I hear in organizations today is "We need more leadership around here." One of the most useful statements I hear in organizations today is "We need more leadership around here." What makes the statement useless is a lack of serious and shared meaning embodied in the term *leadership*. What makes it useful is that it triggers an occasion to engage in a lively and informed discussion about leadership.

The overall purpose of this book is to engage in that discussion: to deepen and broaden our understanding of the content of leadership; guide us in figuring out the current characteristics of external reality, the world around us; and give us ways to make wise, adept choices. In the course of this discussion I map the different worlds around us, which I call *zones*. Then I match appropriate leadership strategies and interventions to each of those different worlds.

Theory without practice is irrelevant, soaring into empty skies; practice without theory is meaningless, acting on ignorance, chance, and guesswork. This book couples theory and practice. Does it deal with competencies and skills? Yes, it does. You will become more skillful as you move through the zones. However, leadership is not reducible to competencies. Unless you know what leadership is and recognize what external reality is inviting it, you cannot figure out what competencies to use.

As a result of our journey through leadership theory and practice in this book,

1. You will know what you believe leadership is.

2. You will have a map of the leadership zones to use for organizational and personal leadership assessment.

3. You will gain insights about leadership action and authenticity in each zone.

4. You will sharpen your senses to hear and assess underlying thoughts and beliefs and informal relationships (shadows, or stirrings) in your organization. These stirrings will help you find a path through the map. You will grow in anticipatory wisdom.

5. You will know the critical issues shaping discussion in the field of leadership so you can be a more astute reader in the field, listener in seminars, and assessor of people you might hire to help you figure things out.

6. You will be invited to go where other thinkers in leadership do not as you gain an additional perspective on reality.

I have partly built and partly discovered the foundation for this discussion of leadership over many years. This Introduction offers an overview of that foundation and the major themes it supports, of the genesis of this book, and of the book's basic organization. I begin with two of the most important elements in the foundation: the concepts of action and authenticity.

ACTION AND AUTHENTICITY IN LEADERSHIP

For as long as I can remember, one concept and one question have haunted and guided my life. The concept is authenticity, and the question is, What is really going on? What is really going on both inside of us and outside of us (in the world)? The struggle to find out, fully understand, and see clearly what is true and real in the world and in myself has shaped me personally and professionally. No matter what I do, I cannot escape the inquiry. Authenticity hovers over me like a palpable presence, demanding that I probe for the truth of a situation, challenging me to go deeper, ask more questions, live more profoundly in the truths I have discovered. Truth even grabs me, from time time to time.

When I was hired to be the first director of the Reflective Leadership Center at the Hubert H. Humphrey Institute of Public Affairs at the University of Minnesota in the early 1980s, authenticity took over as it had before in my life, and I found myself asking, What is really going on in the field of leadership?

During my ten-year term, I and some colleagues struggled mightily over that question. If we were going to teach leadership, it might be good to know what it is—or at least know what people think it is. So we read books, discussed, designed curricula, tested our ideas in practice, interviewed titular leaders, and tried to make sense of the vast and rich subject matter. Three books resulted from our inquiry: John Bryson and Barbara Crosby's *Leadership for the Common Good* (1992), Barbara Crosby's *Leadership for Global Citizenship* (1999), and my *Authentic Leadership: Courage in Action* (1993). In that book I map the leadership field. I cluster schools of leadership into twelve camps, arguing that the camps are not mutually exclusive. Instead, I show how each is necessary and that none of the perspectives alone can cover the breadth of the field.

I also describe how the human universes of *action* and *authenticity* embrace and position all leadership perspectives. I discuss how the history of the term *leadership* relates to the idea of action and how leadership conceived as action resolves many of the apparent conflicts among the various theories of leadership that have evolved during the twentieth century, and among the roles played by leaders' skills, personal abilities, and values. The universe of action gives us a conceptual space within which we can see that many aspects of leadership relate to specific features of action. The model I offer for this universe of action is the *action wheel* (see Figure 1 on the next page), which divides any human action into seven features, or components. These features seem the most basic elements that can be used to explain human action. They are distinct from one another yet also related to one another; are easy to apply to actual leadership situations; can offer insight into an action; and, taken all together, produce an understanding of leadership.

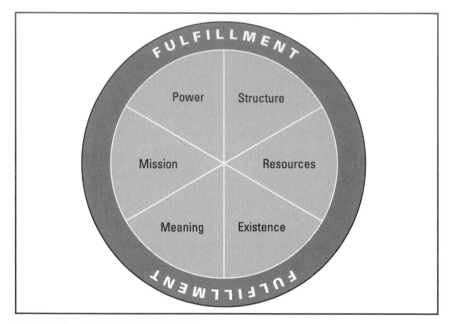

FIGURE 1 • THE ACTION WHEEL

- Existence—the history that limits and launches what we do

- Resources—the things that we use in what we do

- Structure—the form and processes that support and sustain what we do

- Power—the commitment and passion that energize what we do

- Mission—the aim and priority that give direction to what we do

- Meaning—the justification and significance that tell us why or for what we do what we do

- Fulfillment—the completed action that embraces existence, resources, structure, power, mission, and meaning

This is a simplified version of the action wheel, showing what is essential for an understanding of the leadership zones I describe later. The action wheel is a way to frame any issue, to begin to see how your journey as a leader through an issue might look. Each feature guides leaders to ask a question that will help them answer that larger leadership question, What is really going on (Terry, 1993, p. 61)?

What is the history of this event or situation? (Existence)

What are the central resources? (Resources)

What are the plans and processes? (Structure)

What is the stakeholders' level of commitment? (Power)

What is the direction? (Mission)

What is at stake? (Meaning)

What is the event in its completed action? (Fulfillment)

The action wheel also helps leaders identify the most important feature of a problem in order to answer questions such as whether the issue they are facing is a meaning problem, a resources problem, or something else entirely.

In this book I pour new content into the features of action. Each leadership zone embodies all of the first six features. Only one feature is the driver, defining the zone. I will suggest ways for us to accurately name the zone in which we find ourselves and thus determine which aspect of action is central for leadership in that zone.

Although leadership occurs in the universe of human action, as I pointed out in *Authentic Leadership*, not all action is leadership. *Action* is a broader term since some action is inauthentic. Leadership resides in the universe of authenticity (Terry, 1993, p. 107). It is authentic action. Part of my purpose in this book is to define what authenticity looks like in each of the leadership zones.

What is authenticity in general? Authenticity entails action that is both *true* and *real* in ourselves and in the world. We are authentic when we discern, seek, and live into truth (Terry, 1993, pp. 111–12). One particularly helpful way I and others have found for thinking about authenticity is to distinguish it from sincerity. Sincerity, as Mike Martin (1986) tells us, "Frequently . . . retains the positive connotation of purity derived from its Latin root *sincerus*, which means unadulterated," whereas authenticity "is captured by the idea of genuineness rather than purity. The authentic is the bona fide (insurance policy), real (Chinese tapestry), official (commemorative stamp), or authoritative (executive order), as opposed to the fake, imitative, unofficial, or unauthorized. . . . An authentic compliment is one that succeeds in praising someone, in contrast to a sincere compliment, which need only be intended to express feelings of admiration" (pp. 68–69). In addition, sincerity explores the self but not the world. Authenticity asks us what is really going on inside and outside of ourselves. Sincerity asks us only to be true to ourselves.

Finally, authenticity is genuineness and a refusal to engage in self-deception. An authentic action is one that succeeds in accomplishing its mission (Terry, 1993, p. 128). Authenticity matters for leadership because without it we cannot define with the necessary clarity the issues we and our organizations face, and we cannot find the answers that offer true and real solutions to those issues. (Although the significance of action and authenticity are discussed further in this book, those who are interested in the use of the action wheel and the in-depth arguments for focusing on action and authenticity as embracing all types of leadership are invited to read *Authentic Leadership*.)

FROM THE ACTION WHEEL
TO LEADERSHIP ZONES

In 1996 I conducted leadership seminars for a large South African banking organization in which I portrayed the debates in the field so that each person in the audience could identify his or her own perspective on leadership (as you will have a chance to do later in this book). At the same time, I was introduced to Ralph Stacey's works on creativity and complexity in organizational life, including *Complexity and Creativity in Organizations* (1995).

I had never read a book more comprehensive or more focused on organizations than Stacey's. He triggered *Seven Zones for Leadership*. For the first time I could see a way to set my *Authentic Leadership* materials in a worldly context. Stacey stressed that one had to know what was going on in the organization. That knowledge, he suggested, had direct bearing on what leadership and management actions to take. He also offered a framework that liberated my thinking. We will explore that framework soon.

A new map showed up in my mind. In *Authentic Leadership* I had mapped the field of leadership studies from *within* the field. I had created a workable framework. However, it had no inherent boundaries or context for application. People employed the action wheel model as though it were a kaleidoscope. In effect, they looked out at the world through it, and as they turned the wheel, the lens would open different framing opportunities. The model did not give them an independent sense of the world that informed the lens. I was focusing on leadership perspectives rather than stepping out of the framework to focus on the situations that could help leaders assess what perspectives to employ and under what circumstances.

My earlier book gave the world a way to map leadership. Now I saw I could give leadership a way to map the world. *World* is the word I have chosen, after some struggle, to describe external reality. External reality refers to any aspect of life outside of who or whatever is viewing life. If I am on a team or in a group, external reality describes the aspects of life outside of the team or group. If I am on my own, external reality is anything outside of me. In other words, before there can be an outside, a world, there must be an inside, something viewing that world (and vice versa); the two are forever intimately connected.

After this breakthrough, I saw a comprehensive picture of multiple worlds, each requiring a different mode of engagement. The world is the context for action. As worlds shift, so too will leadership. In this context, the world will be relative to whatever aspect of action is being examined. With a map of these different realities, a worldly map, I could both clarify the choices people make when they define leadership and figure out how leadership varies depending on external conditions. Furthermore, I could offer a meaningful way to assess the vast array of organizational interventions that dominate the leadership literature. I could figure out the *fit* between the world and leadership action. I now had both an internal sense of the leadership field, based on and sorted by the action wheel, and an external context to which to apply these ideas. This volume presents that external context.

In all, I have identified seven external realities, worlds, or zones. A great sports anecdote can frame the dimensions of these zones for us. Three baseball umpires are sitting in a bar reminiscing, talking about balls and strikes and what it's like making the calls. One of the umpires says, "Let me tell you how it works. I call 'em the way they are." The second umpire says, "That ain't true. I call 'em the way I see 'em." The third umpire smiles. "Let me tell you how it really

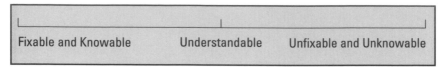

FIGURE 2 • THREE WORLDS

works. The way I call 'em is the way they are, and they ain't nothing till I call 'em" (slightly modified from Anderson, 1990, p. 75).

This story tells us about a great deal more than baseball. It captures three views of the world. Look at the line in Figure 2 that goes from left to right. On the left end of the line is a world that is knowable and fixable. In the center of the line is a world that is interpretable and understandable. On the right end of the line is a world that is unknowable and unfixable. Does leadership look different in each of those three worlds? What if we relied on what we could know or fix in a situation that was actually incomprehensible? Would the mismatch of leadership actions and real-world needs cause disaster? The seven zones mapped in this book are spread out along this line, and we must be able to identify each one when we face it, so we will know what actions are likely to accomplish our goals.

Each of the three umpires was right, given the right world. When your world is fixable and knowable, call 'em the way they are. When your world is understandable, call 'em the way you see 'em. And when your world is unknowable and unfixable, the way you call 'em creates 'em. Moreover, if we seek authenticity, we cannot accept that the three umpires encompass all possible realities. We have to ask another question: Is that all there is? Maybe there is another perspective, not overtly discussed yet but stirring in the neighborhood. A fourth umpire may just be waiting to be invited to the bar for a conversation and a drink.

MAJOR THEMES

On page 2, I listed six sets of insights and practices you will gain from the discussion in this book. Each reflects a major theme in this book and a purpose within its overall purpose. The first theme is addressed mainly in the first chapter. The remaining themes run throughout the discussion of the leadership zones.

The Leadership Debate: Identifying Your Own View

I find that most people I deal with in leadership seminars around the world are not aware of the choices they make when discussing and defining leadership. They either assume everyone thinks of leadership exactly the way they do or they dismiss the distinction in leadership definitions as rhetorical and therefore a waste of time to discuss. "Leadership cannot be defined," they may even say. "I know it when I see it."

At the same time, over the years I have spent consulting in organizations, working at the University of Minnesota, and listening to social and political commentary through the media, I have heard endless references to leadership. Often they sound like this: "We've got some serious problems around here [around this company, this country, this world]. We need more leadership." Likewise, the businesses that invite me to conduct leadership seminars tell me that management is not their problem. It is leadership that is lacking. Yet despite all the clamor on the airwaves and in organizations of all kinds, it is my experience that when people are pressed to define the term *leadership* or when a group is asked to clarify what kind of content it wants in a leadership seminar, assumed clarity flies from the room and vagaries abound. For that matter, recall your own last performance appraisal. Was leadership mentioned? If so, was it defined? And if it was, was a rationale offered for including or excluding particular categories and content? Is leadership a concept much discussed in your organization? If your organization needs more of it, why not include it in meaningful ways in the performance appraisal process?

Perhaps you have attended a leadership seminar in which the instructor asks participants to distinguish management from leadership. Everybody places vision in the leadership column. Management claims terms like *operations* and *making things happen*. As each group reports out, you wonder to yourself: "Is this just some word game? What difference does it make anyway? Managers have vision, too, and leaders have to make things happen." Our sometimes murky understanding and definition of leadership may have been compounded by such seminars in another way. Each seminar usually presents only one view of leadership. Go to a bookstore, and you will be amazed at the number of volumes asserting "leadership is this" or "no, leadership is that." Each author argues that his or her view is based in fact, never considering that perhaps it is a reflective choice, based in some cases on research or theory and in other cases on gut feel.

I am glad there are debates. My concern is that seldom is anyone challenged to construct her or his own perspective. Much of leadership inquiry is disturbingly parochial and apparently oblivious to the breadth of the field of leadership studies. It attempts to define leadership by limitation. A single view, one small cup, fails to hold the wonderfully rich variety of tastes available to us. We need many cups to sample many flavors. Think of understanding leadership as a wine-tasting or dessert-sampling event. The menu is expansive and enticing. Try it all before choosing what to add to your collection at home.

My first reason for writing this book is to offer you that opportunity, to show you that you have leadership choices and to help you determine which you prefer. None of us comes as a blank tablet to the topic of leadership. The first challenge of authenticity is to figure out and own your personal view. Once that is clear to you, you will be better equipped for engaging with the remaining purposes of this book.

The Wisdom to Make the Right Leadership Choice in the Proper Context

Once you are aware of your personal view and choices about leadership, another challenge surfaces. What choices should you make in the real world? It is one thing to know your preferences, and quite another to know which preferences are most effective under what conditions. It is to give you that wisdom that I map the differing worlds, each requiring different leadership choices.

Each of us has to learn how to understand all the umpires' worldviews I described earlier. As I have suggested, leadership will express itself very differently when the world is knowable and fixable than when it is unknowable and unfixable. And it will face great variety in between these extremes. Each leadership choice of action is valid when matched to an appropriate world. Leadership wisdom is getting the choice right.

The seven zones that I use to map the various worlds and provide the context for leadership are sorted by two variables that encompass fixability and knowability: how much agreement there is on direction and how certain is the outcome. Are all of us in the organization sure we are going in the same direction? Do we know the outcome of our chosen action? Shared direction and certainty of outcome set the boundaries for the first two zones, those that partake of a fixable and knowable world. As people in an organization face worlds that are understandable but unfixable or unknowable, they also move toward less shared direction and less certainty of outcome. Now they are working in the third and fourth zones. Finally, when they face the unfixable and the unknowable, they also have little shared direction and certainty of outcome. The first two zones reflect the first umpire's world, the second two that of the umpire who calls 'em the way he sees 'em, and the third two align with the third umpire's assertion that reality is what we say it is (see Figure 3 on the next page). And, yes, there is a fourth umpire waiting for an invitation to the table.

In this book, the major players are mapped in the field of leadership studies as I discuss the zones, affirm their contributions, and demonstrate how each type of leadership is necessary to some zone or zones but not sufficient to explain leadership throughout the whole worldly map. All the views add value. Properly understood and placed in a worldly map, they set foundations for others to build upon. I stress *properly understood* because if the platform is shaky, the whole edifice crumbles. Integrating the current leadership discussions into the map brings us to the third purpose of this book.

Figuring Out What Kind of Action Is Appropriate

It is crucial to know your choices. It takes wisdom to read the world and respond in fitting ways. My third purpose in this book is to help you answer the questions, What are fitting responses? What actions should we take?

As observed in the Preface, leadership literature is peppered with menus of strategic leadership actions, actions that can seriously impact people's lives as they change the organizations, communities, societies, and environment in which we all live. Increasingly we are hearing reports that these action and education strategies are producing the opposite results from those intended. Although the strategies' advocates deny these failures, organizational insiders and also

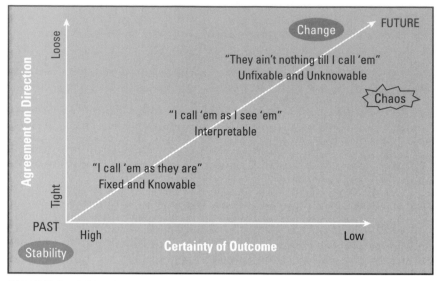

FIGURE 3 • ZONE LEADERSHIP

researchers and consultants seem increasingly of the opinion that fix-it strategies proposed and enacted regardless of context only compound problems. They waste money and time, jerk systems around inappropriately, damage morale, blur priorities, and evoke cynicism. It's not that the intervention itself was inherently wrong; it's just that the intervention didn't fit the reality of the situation to which it was applied.

Think about criteria that can help you evaluate what strategies fit what zones. When should restructuring be mandatory? And when is it a waste of time, money, and energy? Under what conditions does it make sense to bring a thousand employees or citizens into one room for three days to wrestle with and own organizational or community solutions? And when would that be a disaster? Authenticity must be at work in these choices. It is one thing to believe sincerely in the value of a strategy. It is quite another to have the integrity and courage to recommend that it not be applied under certain circumstances.

To know what is really going on in practice, one has to probe deeply into theory. Theory informs and directs practice; practice embodies and carries forward theory. This fact raises the fourth purpose of this volume.

Understanding and Connecting Theories That Matter to Leaders

As we explore the zones and through them the threefold intersection of leadership, world, and actions, we will confront (especially in Chapters Twelve and Thirteen) some provocative and sometimes puzzling concepts of which leaders are increasingly expected to have knowledge: chaos and complexity theory, polarity and paradox, organizational shadow, and leadership development theory.

Chaos and Complexity Theory

When external reality is unknowable and/or unfixable, we would expect chaos and complexity to be features of that world, and it also seems logical that leaders in that world should have an understanding of chaos and complexity theory. Popularized by Margaret Wheatley in *Leadership and the New Science* (1992), this relatively new body of thought is now addressed in numerous books and articles and is being embraced by consultants around the world. Chaos and complexity theory posits the necessity of seeing the world as an organic framework or living system, with the continual change and uncertainty that implies, rather than taking a mechanical or Newtonian worldview.

Consultants are increasingly bringing this framework to the table. It is worthy of serious thought, and as we progress through the zones we will increasingly observe leadership facing chaos and complexity. However, we will also see that chaos and complexity theory does not explain all that we encounter as the world becomes less and less knowable. In particular, it does not tell us what leadership does in the face of real chaos, even gross tragedy.

Polarity and Paradox

The theory that leaders must be able to operate effectively in the face of unresolvable paradoxes and polarities is also fast becoming part of the leadership literature. Some organizations no longer feel they must have a single major identity. Must an organization be in business primarily to serve its customers, to build a great organization for the long term, *or* to make a profit or steadily increasing return on investment? Or can it have and live a paradoxical identity? Can it see *all* these things as its primary identity, even though they pull in different directions and require different leadership actions? Can a mission statement have multiple focuses? Can a job title be paradoxical? Can there be more than one bottom line? Once we decide that we can accept paradoxes and the polarities they embrace, and that they are aspects of life that do not go away, the action implications are profound. What does it mean to lead through paradox and polarity? If, for example, the individual and the team are the two halves of a polarity, what are the implications for leadership if one wants to build a team *and* focus on the individual? If, as a team slogan has it, "There is no *I* in *team*," how do we fully embrace both individual and team without collapsing one into the other? Individual and team never disconnect. As we concentrate on one side of the polarity, the other side is always present.

Shadow

In his pioneering theories, psychologist and psychiatrist Carl Jung used the idea of shadow to refer to dimensions of life just below the conscious surface, tugging, pressing, and informing personal behavior. Thus, when shadow has been discussed in leadership studies, it has often been linked to the hidden, fear-based side of individuals' personalities. Now, however, theorists are focusing on the shadow, or hidden, parts of organizational life that affect the course of its overt life. Moreover, it is being argued that organizational shadows can be both positive and negative or even only positive. In either case, shadow analysis opens new doors to the understanding of creativity and change. If the dimensions lurking in the semidarkness of personal and organizational life are positive, then leadership needs to take on the task of treasuring, releasing, and celebrating their presence. They may offer wisdom that allows those struggling to make sense of a particular organizational or personnel situation to anticipate the future and to design a fitting leadership strategy.

The shadows in each zone are represented by what I call stirrings. As the world changes it causes changes in our personal and organizational understanding of leadership and appropriate strategies and interventions. These changes often are acknowledged first in the organizational shadow, with its acute awareness of chaos, complexity, polarities, paradoxes, spirituality, and authenticity. Stirrings, new thoughts and beliefs, positive and negative, arise from the shadow.

Leadership listens to these stirrings; the stirrings provoke the movement from zone to zone.

Leadership Development

Finally, as we look at the zones and the different leadership responses they require, it will be logical to ask whether leadership is developmental. Are there identifiable stages of leadership maturation? As far as I know, there are very few developmental frameworks in the leadership literature. Typically, advocates of one perspective on leadership contrast their view with the other views, usually one view at a time, largely in order to critique the others. They do not envision their view taking its place in an array of leadership options, an overarching developmental edifice. To build such a model, one would have to determine what categories would capture the essence of leadership orientations and what order to put them in. Is the sequence linear? Spiral? Some other, more dynamic, format? Is it hierarchical, with each new state of development superior to the last one?

If we had a developmental process outlined for leadership, we could plot where an organization is on the map and figure out the next stage of leadership and organizational action. We could also frame and then plot many of the leadership debates now occurring in the field. I am now ready to jump into the developmental quicksand. In discussing Zone 7, I propose a developmental scheme for leadership. In the process of examining how leadership might develop, I bring in the fifth major theme of this book: spirituality in leadership.

Going Where Others Have Not Gone—Beyond Spirituality

Is leadership inherently spiritual? If so, what does spirituality add to the concept of leadership? Examining these questions is a fifth purpose of this book. Books like *The Heart Aroused* (Whyte, 1994) and *Leading with Soul* (Bolman and Deal, 1995) have identified spiritual dimensions of leadership. Titles like *The Stirring of Soul in the Workplace* (Briskin, 1998) and *The New Bottom Line: Bringing Heart and Soul to Business* (Renesch and DeFoore, 1998) suggest a popular interest in spiritual dialogue that is persistent and poignant.

The key tasks will be to define spirituality as it might apply to leadership, considering what kinds of differences can be said to exist among spirituality, religion, and theology. Some worry that spirituality in leadership and the workplace may result in a focus on a particular religion, as we see in books such as *Jesus as CEO* (Jones, 1995), *The Leadership Wisdom of Jesus* (Manz, 1998), *The Tao of Leadership* (Heider, 1985), and *The Leadership Lessons of Jesus* (Briner and Pritchard, 1997).

Once into the subject, there are difficult questions to consider. Is there evil? What is evil? What implications does the existence of evil have for leadership? On what or in whom can we place our ultimate trust? What do we do with our own and others' cynicism? What generates hope? Is it enough to believe, as chaos and complexity theory does, that there is order in chaos? Can there be order with no grounded meaning? Are we called to live a faithful life on a trusted promise of redemption? Do these kinds of questions push leadership reflection beyond appropriate boundaries? What about those who are secular humanists, atheists, or skeptics or who are overtly hostile to such inquiry? Is there not the profound danger of trundling one's religious baggage into a topic that does not require it?

A Foundation for Whatever Happens—Authenticity

All of these complex issues push the discussion of leadership to the deepest place I find it can go—authenticity, the sixth major theme of this volume. Few writers were using the term *authenticity* when it was introduced as the centerpiece of my work in 1993. Since then the term and its surrogates are appearing everywhere. Concepts like credibility, trust, believability, transparency, sincerity, and integrity are now filling the leadership literature. John MacArthur's *The Power of Integrity* (1997), Diane Dreher's *The Tao of Personal Leadership* (1996), and Thomas Cleary's *The Book of Leadership and Strategy: Lessons of the Chinese Master* (1992), for example, implicitly concentrate on what is authentic in life and thus in leadership. Among the writers who use the term authenticity itself are Eric Harvey and Alexander Lucia (*144 Ways to Walk the Talk*, 1997), who open insights to personal authenticity, and Kevin Cashman (*Leadership from the Inside Out*, 1998), who defines leadership as "authentic self-expression that creates value" (p. 20).

Even so there is still much exploring ahead of us. So, in addition to defining how authenticity looks in each of the zones, I offer some thoughts about what authenticity has to do with chaos and complexity theory and its role in leadership development and spirituality. And I try to answer this question: Is authenticity an adequate, comprehensive, and compelling enough idea and experience to provide the profound meaning and grounding necessary for carrying out leadership, facing the world, and choosing fitting action?

GETTING STARTED

When we hear someone say, "We need more leadership around here," they do not usually follow it with, "And this is what I mean by leadership. . . ." People assume we are on the same page when we are not. Couple this conceptual ambiguity with the increased complexity of organizational and social life, driven in part by the speed of change. What a context for a serious inquiry into crucial subject matter. This is not a trivial task.

It is time to move beyond the partial, incomplete, and at times shallow understanding of leadership that has grown out of dealing with leadership theory and practice one view at a time. *Leadership* is not a simple term, nor is leadership itself easily understood and practiced. Definitions come and go. Wisdom endures. The provocative question is, What counts for wisdom in this area? This book offers a comprehensive framework of leadership that has the potential to assist us all to become wiser in how we understand the concept and live the reality, with the ultimate goal of being participants in robust and enduring organizations and communities.

This book will be most helpful to you if you keep your own organization in mind as you read and reflect. As you explore the text, figure out what zone your organization is currently in. What are your leadership challenges? What intervention strategies are working and which ones are not? Why are they working? Why aren't they working? Any organization can and should be able to work effectively in all the zones. To be stuck in one zone limits overall long-term endurance. All seven zones form a comprehensive map of leadership reality and action, allowing you to locate your current situation and anticipate future developmental challenges. If you can make this map work for you, you will enhance your current reading of reality, make better use of the lessons of the past, and develop a sense of what awaits you in the future.

For those of us committed to leaving significant, lasting footprints in our world, leadership offers one avenue into an engagement with the deepest inquiries of the human condition. Journeying deep into leadership theory and practice entices us to explore the most profound hopes and fears of human existence and to offer contributions to life that endure as lasting gifts.

Please join me as a member of a community of inquiry in exploring zone leadership.

PART ONE

LEADERSHIP CHOICES

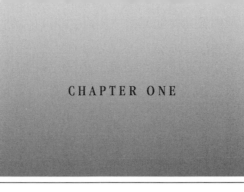

CHAPTER ONE

DECIDING WHAT YOU BELIEVE

Check the business section of any major bookstore, and you will find thousands of pages devoted to the topic of leadership, each volume espousing a different view. Check the mailbox of any manager in the public or private sector, and you will probably find at least one glossy brochure for a seminar that teaches a popular style of leadership. Check the Web, and you will find a multitude of sites explaining varied leadership approaches and offering endless opinions about what leadership looks like.

Definitions of leadership, argued with great conviction, are all over the place. They make a rich and intriguing field for inquiry. All these pages of text and speakers and workshops also suggest that we don't really understand leadership yet. The lack of agreement among researchers, professors, and consultants is astounding, exciting, and a little frightening. Moreover, they have been so busy arguing, asserting, and pontificating that no one in this field has paused long enough to ask those who must actually practice leadership, "What do *you* think leadership is?" They are told "the answer," not invited and challenged to figure it out for themselves.

All those who write and teach about leadership make consequential choices as they define and explore its character and operation; however, they rarely tell their audiences the details or the reasons for these choices. There is much assertion but little invitation to reflect and choose. In this chapter you will have the opportunity to construct your own perspective. It will be meaningful to you in all situations because you've figured it out for yourself. This is a foundational inquiry for you. Welcome to truth seeking.

After you complete this inquiry you may feel surprised and also intrigued about all the choices inherent in defining leadership. You will realize the choices you have already made—possibly without even knowing they were choices.

To warm up your brain synapses, here is a brief set of questions. Note that in this inquiry no modifiers are used with the term *leadership*. I am talking only about leadership—not effective, hoped-for, creative, good, bad, or ugly leadership, just leadership. To answer these questions, just check off *Yes* or *No* following the question.

1. Is it possible to have leaders who do not exhibit leadership?
   Yes___ No___

2. Is it possible to have bosses who do not exhibit leadership?
   Yes___ No___

3. Is it possible for an organization to be "leaderless"?
   Yes___ No___

4. Was Hitler a leader? Yes___ No___

5. Did Hitler exhibit leadership? Yes___ No___

6. Are leadership and management essentially different?
   Yes___ No___

7. Does your organization build leadership into performance reviews? Yes___ No__

8. Is leadership precisely defined in the performance review document? Yes___ No___

9. Is leadership essentially spiritual? Yes___ No___

All your answers represent choices you have already made. You will refer back to this quick exercise as you examine your choices in the rest of the chapter. You may want to reconsider your answers here once your options are more clearly defined.

In the remainder of this chapter I debate eight contrasting pairs of leadership views. For each pair, I argue first for one view then for the other. The debate will be passionate and spirited, at times even outrageous, as I solidify a case on one side or the other. Then I invite you to vote, to indicate the degree to which you agree with one view over the other. You vote by marking a scale like the following, with one leadership view on the left and the other on the right.

```
10 |  |  |  |  |  |  |  |  |  |  0  |  |  |  |  |  |  |  |  |  | 10
Leadership View                                      Leadership View
```

Was your choice: Easy____ Hard____?

Just place a mark on the line to indicate where you stand on the issue. It is better not to vote at zero, in the center. People get more out of the inquiry by forcing themselves to tilt one way or the other. If you strongly favor one side, vote farther away from the center. Even if you think both sides are quite true, if you think a little further you will probably determine that one view is a little more important than the other. In a couple of cases, one side already represents a combination of the views.

Each scale is followed by another question that asks whether you found making the choice *easy* or *hard*. Check the word that applies, and later I will share an educational strategy with you that makes use of your answers to this question.

Although the debates are very brief summaries of many arguments from many sources listened to and read over the years, I do mention a few key authors. For those interested in following up on particular views, the discussion of the zones names more of the works of specific authors with specific views.

Now, let us begin. Enjoy making your choices.

1. BORN OR MADE?

Leadership Is Born

How often have you experienced this scenario? Somebody is assigned to run a group. Somebody else in the group just takes charge and makes things happen. The person who's assigned doesn't have a clue what's going on and is totally ineffective. The reason many of us have seen this happening is that leadership is born.

People just have *certain natural gifts*. Do you have more than one child? Do you ever notice how one leads the other? Sometimes it's not always the older leading the younger; sometimes it's the younger leading the older, and you wonder, "How can she do that? She hasn't even had a course yet!" Where did she learn it? Leadership is born.

This is called *trait theory*. Trait theory dominated leadership in the 1960s. It faded in the last decade. It is now back. Jim Collins's (2001) new research, reported in "Level 5 Leadership," discovered that leaders who led organizations to greatness lived a paradox every day—*humility and fierce resolve*. While not entirely sure how these leaders developed, Collins wrote, "My preliminary hypothesis is that there are two categories of people: those who don't have the Level 5 seed within them and those who do" (p. 75). A different view, popular in the 1980s, argued that everybody can lead, and different types of people lead differently. Do you know the *Myers-Briggs Type Indicator®* (MBTI®) instrument—the personality assessment tool that identifies your personal preferences? All of us have preferences. They do not determine our actions. Just as we can all write our name with our nonpreferred hand, we can all do lots of different kinds of things. We just prefer not to. When it comes to leadership, some of us prefer to be visionary, some lean toward troubleshooting, some are inclined to be catalysts, and some are "get-it-done" folks. Leadership differs by preference. All of us are potential leaders. We lead differently when we act from our preferences.

In either case, whether we think leadership is trait or type, we bring natural talents, natural gifts, to the table. Everybody does. Leadership is born.

Leadership Is Made

That is the dumbest thing I've ever heard. Leadership is not born. It is made! It is learned from experience. The reason I like to work with adults is that most of us are wounded. As we get out in the world and battle around, we get beaten up. We can become perpetual victims or we can learn from these painful experiences, deepen our understanding of things, and master new insights and skills.

Here is the problem with the "born" argument of leadership: Guess what all the natural-born leaders look like? White, male, tall, and right-handed! When we see so-called traits in people, it's really because those traits are already present in our conceptual framework. If they weren't in our heads already, how would we see them? And as far as type theory goes, I may have a preference for left-handedness and yet be able to write with my right hand, but what difference does that preference really make? Whichever hand I write with, I still have to learn how to write.

I have no doubt that leadership can be taught. We learn from experience. That's what maturity is about. In my view leadership is made.

What do you think? Put a mark on the line to indicate your choice.

| 10 | | | | | | | | | | | | 0 | | | | | | | | | | | 10 |
| Born | | | | | | | | | | | | | | | | | | | | | | | Made |

Was your choice: Easy___ Hard___?

2. INDIVIDUAL OR RELATIONAL (TEAM)?

Leadership Focuses on the Individual

I don't really care if leadership is born or made. It doesn't make any difference to me. The important thing in leadership is a focus on the individual. There is all this talk today about team, team, team—yucko! Some organizations even have "team" as a core value. That is crazy!

Team is not a value. A team should be a mechanism for getting work done. In fact, teams don't work half the time and nothing really gets accomplished because no one is accountable. I have yet to see a whole team stand up and say in unison, "We screwed up." What they say is, "*He* screwed up; he was our leader." That's the good news and the bad news of leadership. A leader has to be accountable. In this team mania, nobody's accountable! There's a great book called *No More Teams* (Michael Schrage, 1995). I love that book.

The point is to target the individual. Individuals run teams. Think about *self-directed work teams*. I hate that term. Don't they get created by some boss? And isn't that boss the *individual* ultimately accountable? Leadership is focused on an individual. Leader equals leadership.

Leadership Focuses on the Relationship (Team)

Individual!! Individual!! I've had it up to here with this Western individualism. Don't we understand that that's seventeenth-century Newtonian physics that eventually led to microeconomics? And right into Milton Friedman? I mean, get a grip here. Individualists don't have a clue about life. Life is relational. Just like the new quantum physics, where everything exists in an adaptive relationship with everything else.

Try to describe yourself in nonrelational terms. I'm a father. Isn't that a statement of relationship? You might be a mother, a son, an aunt. It's all relational! Life is relational. The view argued by the individualists presupposes that life is a machine. It has discrete parts. Fix the part, or at least understand the causal connections of the parts, and you will be able to predict what the whole is going to do. Individualists also think that people's emotions get in the way. That's why one might do a cost-benefit analysis based on individual well-being. Don't buy it.

I advocate emotional intelligence, which tells us that life is not an entity; it is a relationship. It involves the people skills that connect and build effective relationships. Individualists want efficiency; I want effectiveness.

A term I just love is *self-directed work team*. These teams are like an improvisational jazz group. Who's this group's leader? It doesn't have one, except maybe the music itself. Each member of the group plays off and with the others. Together group members invent. They have great discipline, and they create wonderful music. Jazz is a wonderful metaphor for leadership.

This choice is profound. You are choosing a philosophy of life. Is life an entity to be fixed or is it a set of relationships to engage? Joseph Rost (1991), Kevin Frieberg and Jackie Frieberg (1998), and I know that leadership is a relational term. It is not just the leader who is accountable. All the members of a group or team are accountable. Challenge the individualism of the West. Go deeper. Understand that we are all part of the web of life. Leadership is relational.

What do you think? Put a mark on the line to indicate your choice.

```
10 |  |  |  |  |  |  |  |  |  |  0  |  |  |  |  |  |  |  |  |  10
Individual                                                Relational
```

Was your choice: Easy___ Hard___?

3. POSITIONAL OR EVERYWHERE?

Leadership Is Positional

One of the first, if not the first, uses of the term *leadership* surfaced in the late 1700s in England. It referred to the "head of the House of Commons." It meant "headship." The words *lead* and *leaders* have long histories. The word *leadership* is relatively new.

As a matter of fact, it entered the English language at about the same time as the word *responsibility*. That widely used ethical category does not have a long history either. In contrast to *love* and *justice*, *responsibility* and *leadership* are new creations to cope with a new world.

Although the word *leadership* is recent in our history, our now-common use of it to refer to the person in charge shows that leadership is positional. Leadership equals headship.

Military organizations think this way. Each organizational function has the same leadership hierarchy, with role responsibilities shifting as one moves up in the system. It's so easy to teach leadership with this model. Just keep teaching people the skills and knowledge of the next level up from the one they now occupy. This is the way the University of Minnesota's Carlson School of Management Executive Development Center organizes most of its courses. It has the Minnesota Management Academy for supervisors, the Minnesota Management Institute for midlevel people, and the Minnesota Executive Program for senior persons. Finally, it offers the Advanced Leadership Program (my leadership program) for very senior people. In this course, they learn improvisational theater skills! We bring in

Bob Wells, owner of Chicken Lips, a comedy theater in Denver, to teach improvisational skills. These executives say, "Thank you, that's what we're doing anyway. Anyone who thinks we know exactly what we're doing is deluded. We're guessing, playing off each other, and hoping that we have the collective wisdom to make good decisions."

How do you get to these top positions? A lot of ways—election, appointment, inheritance, tribal affiliation, whom you know. You can get there by unethical means—bribery, sexual seduction, coercion. In the U.S. most people in private organizations move up by promotion. So keep working. Make sure you're always stretching to reach the next level. Leadership is positional.

Leadership Is Everywhere

How many of you know bosses who retired early and forgot to send out the notice and head for home? They're leaders by position, but they have no idea what leadership is. They're just there, sitting in the chair. Can people in management positions exhibit leadership? Absolutely. Is it guaranteed because they have the position? Absolutely not.

Many organizations go under because they are led by positional fakes who do not have any idea what they're doing. These people are the opposite of the leaders we really need.

The other problem with those who see leadership as headship is that they're a bunch of elitists. And if you work in any organization like that, certain neck muscles are developed—*sucking-up* neck muscles. "I love the way you run this place." "You are really doing a fine job." Suck up, suck up, suck up.

What's really true is that leadership is all over the place and can come from anywhere. Case in point: In Minnesota, the Department of Transportation always used to build and repair roads during the daytime. Communities rose up and said, "Work on them at night. Get a light!" The top transportation executive said, "We can't do that; it's too expensive." Guess when they build and repair roads now in Minnesota? Mainly at night. Where did the leadership come from? The community. Leadership is potentially everywhere.

What do you think? Put a mark on the line to indicate your choice.

```
10 |  |  |  |  |  |  |  |  |  |  0 |  |  |  |  |  |  |  |  |  |  10
Positional                                          Everywhere
```

Was your choice: Easy___ Hard___?

4. RESULTS OR ENGAGEMENT AND INTENT?

Leadership Gets Results

You've all heard this: "Our leadership is failing; we are not getting the results we promised. We need more leadership around here." Invite in Peter Drucker, that brilliant managerial consultant (*The Leader of the Future*, 1996, p. xii). He and I agree that leadership is about making a difference. It's about results, results, results.

You have to make something happen! Who gets better marks for results, President Carter or President Reagan? From polls of the U.S. population, it is always Reagan. You may hate everything he stood for or love everything he stood for. That's not the issue. The question is, Who made the biggest difference? That's exhibiting leadership.

Whom do you follow in the workplace or the community? I follow someone who can deliver on her or his promises. The rhetoric of good intentions has sometimes seduced me, but too often those intentions have been unfulfilled. I have finally learned to go for results. Make it happen. Leave your footprint. Make a difference. Leadership is about results.

Leadership Is Engagement and Intent

Well, that's an interesting definition of management. It doesn't have anything to do with leadership. Don't get me wrong, I'm all for results. You manage for results. That's why we have project teams. That's why we have bureaucracies. But in answering the questions at the beginning of this chapter, you most likely said that leadership and management are different. That's what I think, too.

What leadership is all about is engaging people, quickening their spirit, so they can come up with something worthy of action. When people are engaged, they know what result to go after. As they get energized, they'll deliver the results!

I once had a four-star general and many other starred officers of the U.S. Army in Europe in a seminar on leadership. I took them through the same process you're going through now. Given the choice of leadership as results or engagement, guess which one the general chose? Engagement. The Berlin Wall had just come down, and the U.S. Army in Europe had no enemy. The leaders didn't know what they were there to do. You can't have results if you don't know what you're there for. There's nothing to measure! It's leadership that defines what's worth going after.

It is possible to have overwhelming failure and still have exhibited leadership. A case in point involved David Scott, who put a team together to be the first to get to the South Pole. Do you remember what happened to him and his team? They got there second, beaten by Amundsen. Do you remember what happened on the return trip? They all died! Following is a brief newspaper account of the event (Browne, 1996):

> . . . for one thing, while Scott had refused to acknowledge that he was in a race at all, Amundsen showed an iron determination to win. For another, Amundsen and his party used their sled dogs as food, as one dog after another tired to exhaustion. Amundsen returned triumphant from the pole, without any goods left, but with all his men.
>
> Scott, by contrast, disdained the use of sled dogs on his final attempt on the pole, using the pulling power of ponies and human beings instead. In the end, Scott and his men ate the ponies and he and his four companions all died of exposure, starvation, bad luck, and inadequate planning on the way back from the pole. (p. A22)

Scott's approach shows wonderful leadership—courageous, engaged, forward-looking. It also shows terrible management—poor planning and execution.

Leadership is engagement.

What do you think? Put a mark by the line to indicate your choice.

10 | | | | | | | | | | 0 | | | | | | | | | | 10
Results   Engagement

Was your choice: Easy___ Hard___?

5. COERCIVE AND NONCOERCIVE
OR ONLY NONCOERCIVE?

Leadership Is Both Coercive and Noncoercive

If you don't kill a couple of followers, you won't keep everyone else's attention. Have you ever noticed that? People do stupid things. You've got to discipline them and set boundaries for them, or they may hurt themselves or somebody else. Leadership is mostly non-coercive. It also has to be coercive.

In a dangerous situation like a fire, you don't have time to sit around and discuss the meaning of heat. You just move people. If they won't go you pick them up and drag them outside. That's coercive: getting people to do something against their will that's for their benefit. If you have too much of that, you're a tyrant, but that's not what I'm talking about. I'm not talking a Machiavellian belief in abuse. I'm talking about power—not influence, *power. Influence* is such a wimpy term. Come on! Get serious. Let's quit avoiding power; face it, own it, and use it.

Suppose you are a police sergeant cruising in your squad car, and you get a call that your troops are in an explosive situation. You speed to the scene, and when you arrive you see officers throwing passengers out of a van and beating them up. You quickly assess the situation, draw your gun, and arrest—whom? You arrest the police. They are abusing power. Does this take courage? Absolutely. They have guns too, and you know that if they do not get even with you today, they may tomorrow when you are not looking. I told this story to a police department. They didn't like it, yet they admitted they had to use coercion on some of their own people when they were out of control.

Leadership is both coercive and noncoercive. Remember, leadership is mostly noncoercive; it is not tyranny.

Leadership Is Only Noncoercive

As soon as you are coercive, there is no more leadership. If you use a little bit of coercion, that's called *management*: hiring, firing, disciplining. We have a whole set of carefully crafted processes for handling all kinds of situations. When you have to manage difficult cases, practice your finely tuned managerial skills. However, we are not talking management here; we are discussing leadership.

The essence of leadership is voluntary, noncoercive, and respectful relationships. James MacGregor Burns pioneered this view in 1978. Leadership is not fear driven. People follow somebody because they're excited about where that person is going. They don't follow a person with a gun because that person is leading them! If followers wander off someplace else, let them go. They're no longer part of your crowd. Remember, leaders never choose their followers; followers choose their leaders. Bosses can fire employees; leaders cannot fire followers.

When someone is assigned to an executive position, managerial responsibility is in place; leadership is not. Leadership has to be earned, over time, as credibility is built. It is no accident that when Kouzes and Posner (1993) reported what characteristics followers wanted in their leaders, coercive was not on the list—honest, forward-looking, inspiring, and competent were.

As in the engagement-versus-results argument, you can agree that coercion (properly directed and applied with restraint—according to a police manual of procedures, for example) is sometimes necessary and yet agree with me that leadership is noncoercive. I am not talking about the necessity of management, which uses coercion appropriately. I'm defining leadership. Leadership is only noncoercive.

What do you think? Put a mark on the line to indicate your choice.

10 | | | | | | | | | | | 0 | | | | | | | | | | 10
Coercive and Noncoercive   Only Coercive

Was your choice: Easy___ Hard___?

6. VISION OR FRAMING?

Leadership Constructs the Vision

While I hope this has been a fascinating discussion for you, we have only now arrived at the heart of the matter. When I ask people in seminars to distinguish leadership from management, most people, about 70 percent, put "vision" on the leadership side. They are wise and right. The essence of leadership is vision.

Vision is a sense of direction, a sure feeling of where we're going. Peter Senge (1990) uses a compelling image to illustrate vision. Imagine vision as a rubber band stretched between the index fingers of your two hands. If a vision is too dreamlike, too disconnected from reality, it is too expansive. A vision out of control stretches and breaks. If the vision is too loose, it holds nothing together. It's not really a vision because current reality is too much of a player in the process.

A vision extends us and keeps us focused. You can tell that you're dealing with vision when you get both excited and stretched. Vision takes you to places you otherwise would not visit. Can you look at Bosnia and see ethnic harmony? Or look out over the United States and see racial harmony? That's vision. What makes it a vision rather than a dream? It's that you can experience it as workable, not just as idle speculation. Martin Luther King Jr. went to the other side of the mountain and experienced the reality of the vision he saw.

We hear a lot of talk today about organizational vision statements. Organizations that heed this talk are on to something very important. Leadership is vision.

Leadership Is Framing

I am so tired of *vision, vision, vision.* What if that's not the problem? What if the problem is lack of courage? Visionaries sit on the porch chatting with each other, and they're not doing anything. They're not engaged in life; they're not taking any kind of action to move the vision forward. Vision doesn't necessarily get you off the porch.

Leadership figures out what is really going on and frames reality from multiple perspectives. If more vision seems to be needed, crank out another one. You may have read Bolman and Deal's *Reframing Organizations* (1991). They are brilliant! They use four frames to figure out what is going on: structural, human resource, political, and symbolic. When you look at things through these different lenses you become much more adept and wise. You're asking the fundamental question, what the heck is really going on here? If you don't know what's really going on, who cares if you have another vision?

Most leadership instruments are created and administered by the vision crowd. There is one that explores framing and helps you determine what is really going on and what your leadership actions should be. It's called the *Dimensions of Leadership Profile* (Kragness, 1994). Vision is only one of the activities of leadership. What if your vision is viable but then the world shifts on you? Now your vision is irrelevant. Leadership frames, and only one of the frames is vision.

Organizations have secrets, things they deny. When you frame, rich insights enter the room and denial leaves the room. I used to think the biblical prophets like Isaiah and Jeremiah were visionaries. Now I think they're framers. They were not saying, "Set your destination." They were saying, "We're not faithful. We're denying God." They were going to the heart of the people's betrayal of faith. That's scary. Leadership is profoundly about framing. Frame, then focus— not the reverse.

What do you think? Put a mark on the line to indicate your choice.

10 | | | | | | | | | | 0 | | | | | | | | | | 10
Vision   Framing

Was your choice: Easy___ Hard___?

7. ETHICAL AND UNETHICAL OR ONLY ETHICAL?

Leadership Is Both Ethical and Unethical

I think Hitler exhibited leadership. It doesn't mean I liked what he did or approved of it; as a matter of fact, I despised it. Nevertheless, no matter how evil it was, Hitler exhibited leadership. When I ask in seminars how many people think Hitler did not exhibit leadership and how many think Hitler was ethical, no one raises a hand for either question. So if Hitler was unethical and he exhibited leadership, it is possible to have unethical leadership.

Personally, I believe in the necessity of ethical leadership. I know, though, that it's possible to have unethical leadership, and Hitler is the example. The point is, you can have both. And that's the hard fact. If we try to say leadership is *inherently* ethical, we then have to decide whose ethics we are talking about, whose values we are talking about. Even if we aim for shared values, do you really think we could agree on a set of collective values? No, we can't get into the ethics issue by saying that leadership is inherently ethical.

Now, this in no way says ethics are not important. Keep your highest ethical principles, and acknowledge that leadership is both ethical and unethical.

Leadership Is Only Ethical

If something is unethical, it is *not* leadership. Hitler did not exhibit leadership. Hitler was a tyrant. He was about to destroy the globe. He lowered people's level of moral reasoning. James MacGregor Burns (*Leadership*, 1978), Barbara Crosby (*Leadership for Global Citizenship*, 1999), and I all know this. What are we called in life to be? Aren't we called to be our better selves? So how can leadership take us to our worst place? It makes no sense!

Burns has an answer for whose ethics we should use. The Friebergs define leadership as a "dynamic relationship based on mutual influence and common purpose between leaders and collaborators in which both are moved to higher levels of motivation and moral development as they effect real, intended change" (1998, p. 298). Their idea of moral development came directly from Burns, who took it from Lawrence Kohlberg, a theorist who defined this hierarchy of values in individual moral development (see Munsey, 1980):

Level one: avoid pain—This is the lowest level. The goal is to move on from here. Children begin here.

Level two: immediate benefit—Now the individual wants a perk, an immediate payoff for good action.

Level three: peer, boss, and significant others' approval—Now the individual becomes relational and sees the importance of inclusion and belonging.

Level four: it's the law—This is a major shift; now the person understands that law is not just an inconvenience but essential for civil society.

Level five: long-term benefit—No pain, no gain. The person accepts that short-term sacrifice is needed for long-term ethical incarnation.

Level six: it's right—Through careful thought the person concludes the issue is right regardless of the consequences.

Leadership takes us higher in the hierarchy. Hitler went the other
way. Or maybe you like Abraham Maslow's hierarchy (see Burns,
1978, p. 66), which moves from fulfillment of physiological needs to
self-actualization as a pattern of leadership development. This does
not mean leadership lives only at the highest level of either hierarchy.
Leadership moves upward from wherever it starts. It invites us to
higher levels of moral development.

Suppose you are uncomfortable with moral development
schemes, especially those developed by men. Suppose you distinguish
moral from ethical, the former referring to linking rules or codes of
conduct to behavior and the latter referring to using broad principles
that justify and guide moral development. You can still live here with
me. Maybe there is no universal ethic. Maybe we are all in disagreement on profound issues—we can still act on our highest principles
and believe leadership is inherently ethical. We can still deeply
respect each other because we know the complexity of profound ethical inquiry. We can be fundamentally different and still find common
ground. So to the extent former President Clinton practiced his
ethics, he was exhibiting leadership. To the extent he violated those
principles, he did not. Clinton was a positional leader as long as he
was in office. That does not mean that he always exhibited leadership. Leadership is only ethical.

What do you think? Put a mark on the line to indicate your choice.

10 | | | | | | | | | | 0 | | | | | | | | | | 10
Ethical and Unethical   Only Ethical

Was your choice: Easy___ Hard___?

8. SECULAR OR SPIRITUAL?

Leadership Is Secular

Tom Peters (*The New Bottom Line*, 1998) and I agree. Be nervous
about discussions of spirituality, especially in the workplace. Some-

body's religious or secular sensibilities will be violated. Lawyers will have a field day. Workplaces are gathering spots for diverse people where religious and spiritual matters should remain private.

At a major South African banking organization, employees are encouraged to participate in a journey retreat for alignment and leadership development. On this journey, participants watch the film *Jesus from Montreal.* When it was first shown, it infuriated the Roman Catholics. Participants were also taught holotropic breathing. This discipline asks you to lie on your back on a mat on the floor and rapidly breathe in through your nose and out through your mouth for four hours. Four hours! A small group of conservative Christians rose up and protested that the retreat covertly advocated Buddhism. In addition, people suspected that rejecting retreat content and methods would negatively impact their careers. They feared that promotion depended on participation and belief.

Do you see the danger? "Spiritual" means so many things to so many people. It is vague and diverse. There are equal opportunity issues here. There are discrimination issues. And, if you think about it more deeply, what does spirituality have to do with leadership? What substance does it add? I am not opposed to discussions of spirituality. They just don't belong in the workplace. Do you want spiritual growth? Go to church, go to synagogue, go to a mosque. Go home. Go to Boulder and sit on a mountain with a crystal. Don't take everyone else with you. Especially not your co-workers.

Lately, I have heard rumblings about theology and leadership. Holy cow! God-talk linked to leadership talk. Does this mean that one has to believe in a particular view of God to practice leadership? This really is bordering on a new form of religious oppression. The secular gives room to all to pursue their own beliefs. Spiritual and theological loyalties will divide us. If leadership challenges us to find common ground, different views of the spiritual will erode any ground we find. Leadership is secular.

Leadership Is Spiritual

Shallow, shallow, shallow. Tom Peters is shallow. In contrast, Bill George, the CEO of Medtronic, is deep. He knows that spirituality is at the heart of life; therefore it is the heart of everything we do, including leadership. It is not hidden Lutheranism, Buddhism, Catholicism, or some other thinly disguised religious belief. The heart of life is making meaning together out of the unknown, such as crises of relationships or illness that make no sense.

I think there is so much interest in spirituality in the workplace today because of the *in*authenticity of people's experience. Do you know the bestselling book in the business community in 1996? *The Dilbert Principles*. What makes Dilbert so popular? We resonate with the tragicomedy. The workplace situations are comedy because they're so funny, and they're tragedy because they're true. It is that disconnect that people experience in the workplace every day. In this time of merger mania, downsizing, reengineering, and reorganizing, corporate loyalty and job security are at risk. It is no wonder attention is being given to spirituality in the workplace given all the chaos and insecurity that people experience.

Don't you know wonderfully gifted and ethical people who are also cynical? Ethics does not guarantee hope. When you're being bashed and beaten up, from where do you get your hope? It's not enough to do the right thing. You have to find some kind of a home for yourself that provides meaning and a sense of faith and possibility that allows you to remain engaged in life. Cynicism disengages us from life. Leadership engages us. Hope comes from our deepest quest for significance in life. It is the foundation that sustains us.

One of the best introductory books connecting leadership and spirituality is *Leading with Soul* by Bolman and Deal (1995), a story about an executive who has had a lot of success in his external life but has lost his soul and lost his way in his internal life. The guidance he receives from a spiritual guru eventually reawakens his own spirituality. We're both external and internal. You can't have one without the other. The secret of leadership is not to get caught in your external self. It is to discover your heart, your spiritual core.

I have not affirmed any particular religious tradition, and I don't plan to. Here is the deeper dilemma in accepting spirituality. If I know meaning is a serious issue for me, and I also know I create meaning, does that meaning have any grounding other than my making it up? That's where talk about God enters into leadership studies. Is there a reality behind and within our experiences of life, calling us to a deeper authenticity? On the horizon, I anticipate attending, participating in, and conducting seminars on theology, spirituality, and leadership. Controversial? Of course. Requiring courage? Of course. Necessary? Of course. Potentially divisive? Of course. I'm not sure individual enlightenment is sufficient to face a world increasingly living at the edge of, and in, real chaos. Leadership is profoundly spiritual, even theological.

What do you think? Put a mark on the line to indicate your choice.

```
10 |  |  |  |  |  |  |  |  |  |  0  |  |  |  |  |  |  |  |  |  10
Secular                                                    Spiritual
```

Was your choice: Easy___ Hard___?

ASSESSING AND USING YOUR CHOICES

You now know more than 99.9 percent of the world's population does about the subject of leadership. You have figured out your own view and have gained some understanding of other views. There is much riding on the choices you and your organization make. Selection, promotion, organizational assessment, and futuring are all affected by what you mean by leadership. So the next time someone says, "You know, we need more leadership around here," you can reply, "Yes, I think that's true. Let's discuss what we mean by *leadership* so we can do a better job of figuring out how to proceed. Are you interested?" If he or she says no, you have not lost anything by engaging. If the answer is yes, you are prepared to engage in a provocative inquiry.

So far I have attempted to challenge you to discern your own perspective on leadership. There is great inherent value in that process, even if we were to stop right here. You have a picture of the types of leadership you choose to use. And now I will give you that educational strategy mentioned earlier. Please add up your *easy* votes and then your *hard* votes. Write your totals here:

Easy_____ Hard_____

To mature in your leadership wisdom, do you think you should work harder on understanding the easy or the hard choices? Most people say, "Work on the hard choices." My advice is to work more on the easy ones. They may have been too easy. Truth is waiting for you on the other side. All the choices are worthy of serious inquiry. All are hard. Do not take any for granted.

And there is more ahead to investigate. Remember the three umpires and their three views of the world. Our leadership choices should change as we move from a world that is knowable and fixable to a world that is unknowable and unfixable. Those who practice leadership must develop the wisdom to read the shifting worlds and to bring the appropriate skills and knowledge to bear. All the choices you have just made are important. The challenge is to figure out where each one fits.

In the next chapter I will begin identifying zones for leadership that include all the choices you just made, and will show where those choices fit. Join me now in a discussion of zone leadership.

CHAPTER TWO

CONSTRUCTING A LEADERSHIP MAP

Working in organizations, I find that individuals and groups considering new leadership strategies and actions often lack a comprehensive perspective from which to assess them. They have no map against which they can plot whether an action makes any sense. These questions often do not surface, yet are present in people's minds: Under what conditions should total quality management (TQM) be introduced and implemented? When does it make organizational sense to clarify vision, values, and mission? When does that make no sense? What signals the need to redesign or restructure? When are those leadership actions inappropriate, causing more problems than they solve? What about vision and framing? When should an organization choose vision, and when should it choose framing? When is it justifiable to judge leadership as ethical or unethical?

As discussed in the Preface, many organizations are learning that leadership actions that were supposed to fix their deepest problems have not succeeded. Leadership wisdom is much more than possessing appropriate skills and strategies. It is knowing what to do, when to do it, and for what reason. Leadership is never just one thing or one set of choices. So far you have identified your own leadership preferences by choosing among eight alternatives. It is very important for you to know your personal inclinations independent of context. Now that we are about to discuss context, your choices will reveal what you bring to the discussion based on your own thinking, experience, and the arguments you have just heard.

The central problem in the field of leadership practice and theory is—no map! We have had no guide to what to do, when to do it, and for what reason. There is so much focus on the parts of the field that we are not attending to the need for an overall view. Because leadership has been reduced to many narrow niches, each defended by passionate champions, few thinkers propose a comprehensive leadership framework or theory to connect the disparate niches to each other.

What is happening in leadership theory and practice parallels what has been happening in the sciences, vividly described by B. K. Forscher (1963). Forscher laments that science has been too committed to facts (bricks) and has failed to construct frameworks or theories (edifices) to link and assess these facts. One needs excellent bricks to build a sturdy edifice, and at first the builders (senior scientists) made their own, manufacturing only those needed for a particular project. Then junior scientists were brought in to be brick makers. They became obsessed with brick construction itself, manufacturing all kinds of bricks, often independently of larger projects. When reminded that the ultimate mission was a building, the brick makers replied that with so many different bricks available, the builders could choose among them and still construct great buildings. Brick storage places were organized (journals). However, locating the right bricks amid the flood of them taxed even the best builders. Sadly, "sometimes no effort was made even to maintain the distinction between a pile of bricks and a true edifice" (p. 143).

Those in the field of leadership also have fallen into the pattern of creating many bricks and few edifices. Worse, they often throw their bricks at each other rather than seeking to cement them together. I propose to sort out the existing leadership bricks. I will map organizational life by leadership zones in order to figure out what kind of leadership is required under differing conditions. Where do we place Peter Senge's brick, or the bricks of Margaret Wheatley, Peter Block, Peter Vaill, Barbara Kellerman, and the hundreds of others in the brick-building business? Together we can determine whether we can construct an edifice we would like to inhabit from all the bricks littering the landscape of leadership studies.

In this chapter I look at the overall universe (the various dimensions) of the map I will present over the course of this book. Then I briefly sketch the leadership zones, connect them with the action wheel, and discuss how they are depicted on the map. Finally, I suggest how the zones in general address leadership development, authenticity, metaphors that provide insight, ethical values, polarities, and stirrings.

THE UNIVERSE OF THE MAP

Although maps are exceedingly diverse in how much they reveal and how carefully they reveal it, every map is a visual representation of some aspect of reality. It may be geographic, but it can also lay out ideas, actions, or any other notions that require an orientation and perspective. Despite the fact that a map is always once removed from what it describes, it helps us connect things. If we are lost it can suggest a way out of a confusing, difficult, or even dangerous situation. It may even suggest how unexplored or unexplorable territory is likely to appear.

Boundaries

Let's begin our examination of leadership zones by looking further at the map's outer limits, outlined in the Introduction. The very nature of a map requires that it have boundaries of some sort. In the early 1990s, I had no such sense of what might set such a context. It was Ralph Stacey's *Strategic Management and Organisational Dynamics* (1993, p. 47) and *Complexity and Creativity in Organizations* (1996, p. 284) that provided two breakthrough concepts for constructing this map for leadership development and appropriate action in the real world—*certainty* and *agreement*. *Certainty* focuses on our confidence in the predictability of the outcomes and consequences of our actions. *Agreement* attends to the extent of alignment on where we are headed, on the direction toward which we are aiming. It might also address why we are going there or the significance of the mission.

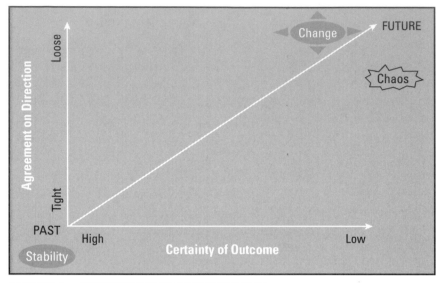

FIGURE 4 • DIMENSIONS OF THE ZONE MAP

Certainty and agreement can both be displayed on continua. Certainty can be spread from high to low. Agreement moves from tight to loose. When they are positioned in relation to each other on the map (see Figure 4), the lower left-hand corner marks stability rooted in the past. When the people in an organization or group have unified or tight agreement and high certainty, the result is great steadfastness and stability. Leadership and action in the external world are grounded in history and experience. As the context in which we are acting moves toward the upper right of the map, with less certainty and less agreement, the future looms as increasingly random, changing, and chaotic.

These two boundaries define different worlds. As explained in the Introduction, I use *world* to refer to any aspect of life outside of whatever is referencing it. If I talk about the world, I am referring to what is outside of me. If a team talks about a world, it is referring to whatever is outside of it. And so on. World is half of the polarity inside/outside. And using the story of the three umpires, I defined three worlds that exist along a continuum of reality, ranging from a world that is knowable and fixable ("I call 'em the way they are") through a world that is interpretable and understandable ("I call 'em the way I see 'em") to a world that is unknowable and unfixable ("the way I call 'em is the way they are").

As we shall see later, in Chapter Twelve, some writers, especially advocates of chaos and complexity theory, do not think constructing a map that includes the unknowable and unfixable is possible. They equate mapping with Newtonian science and the first umpire. A map calls 'em the way they are. Nevertheless, I am going to construct a map that includes all three umpires' perspectives and then adds a fourth. Some parts of the map will consist of the map that only the viewer can supply ("the way I call 'em is the way they are").

Have you had the experience of going to work with confidence that you would accomplish your goals for the day, then quickly realizing that the day you are actually experiencing was not the day on your schedule? You were challenged to act on entirely different demands than those you had anticipated.

Sometimes leadership is a foul-weather activity. Leadership, like everything else, only occurs in the present. The past is behind us; the future is in front of us. All we ever have is the present. Yet the realities of the past and anticipations for the future never cease to inform our response to what is happening in the immediacy of life.

Time

Some people hold on to the past as a reference; others argue it should be let go. Some suggest boldly dreaming of the future; still others consider that idle wishful thinking, unreal, a waste of time. How can one map embrace the full dimension of time? Stacey offers useful reflections. Even when people are considering the past and the present, their certainty and agreement occur *in the present*. Listen to Stacey (1993) on the subject of certainty: "An organization is close to certainty when its members face closed and contained change, that is, when they face repetitions of what has happened before. This makes it possible for them to make a useful forecast of what is likely to happen for at least a short time ahead; past experience is sufficient to enable some reasonably clear link between cause and effect to be identified." Organizational members are "far from certainty" when they "face open-ended change situations, that is, when they must act in unique circumstances that they have never before encountered. Without the benefit of similar past experience they are not able to make reliable connections between cause and effect and, therefore, they cannot predict the outcome of their actions over the long term" (p. 26).

Agreement also appears to occur in the present. Stacey observes that "unified agreement exists when members of an organization are moving in a shared direction, whether with a shared vision, mission or set of tested principles and procedures. Diverse agreement exists when there is scant alignment of objectives, direction, goals, processes or principles" (p. 26).

Though the future and past have direct bearing on our present experience, all actions occur in the present. The challenge then is to construct a map that illustrates how many different leadership zones can be present at the same time, even though we might be exploring only one given our current perception of reality. The worlds that form the continuum on which the zones exist can be *simultaneous* and *sequential*. On any given day, external reality may come at us seven different ways; we may be not be wise enough to recognize them and adeptly lead in their midst.

Chaos: Apparent or Real?

The worlds and the leadership zones progress from stability to change and chaos, and in these days chaos needs some explanation. Our traditional definition of chaos, a world of ever-present arbitrariness and capriciousness, is no longer the only definition. In the new science, chaos does not mean unresolved randomness or arbitrariness. Within chaos is an order that surrounds, bounds, and contains its apparent disorder. There are discernible and measurable patterns. *Low-dimensional chaos* reflects a structure but is unpredictable over the long view. *High-dimensional chaos* is generated "by a set of many rules and it displays very little structure; it is close to randomness and thus closer in meaning to the normal usage of the term *chaos*" (Stacey, 1996, p. 284). James Gleick, in *Chaos: Making a New Science* (1987), points out that chaos theory has been important in a gargantuan change in our understanding of our world, as signaled in a change of metaphor. Instead of taking a reductionist view that sees the natural world as a machine running according to implacable laws and yielding predictable results, we now tend to picture life as a complex system, a living organism, a body. This image suggests a very high degree of complexity that appears random on many levels yet nonetheless has some organization.

Ultimately, I believe chaos is both apparent and real. In anticipation, it often seems real; on reflection it often seems apparent. However, in the unknown and unfixable world, even though good things can happen here and surprise gifts do show up, I think that chaos is real, even when we are reflecting back on it. In this world, we experience randomness and unpredictability—being without apparent pattern, sense, or meaning. We do not have any power to guarantee an outcome or any assurance that we are all moving in the same direction. And even if some order emerges, it is insufficient to comfort us or to make meaning of events. As reality shifts from organized to unorganized (see Figure 5), chaos will be more palpable, will be more scary, and will require deeper inquiry into what is worth holding on to for action.

It is no accident that we spend much of our lives trying to minimize chaos. Insurance policies, police departments, airport security checks, bureaucracies, and our own comforting rituals all aim to reduce or control randomness. Yet it is also the case that some of our most creative moments occur when old forms break away and newness emerges. So while chaos frightens us, it also quickens us when we act in proximity to it or in its midst. This map will enable us to explore what leadership is both at the edge and in the midst of chaos.

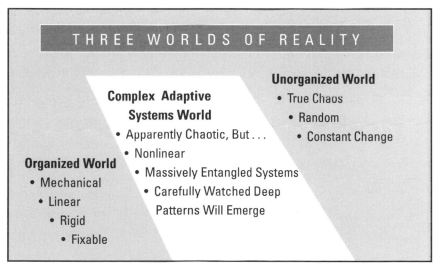

FIGURE 5 • THREE WORLDS OF REALITY

SEVEN LEADERSHIP ZONES

With the dimensions of action in front of us as a focus for each zone, we can now build the zone map. Within this universe bounded by agreement (tight to loose) and certainty (high to low) and stretching from the past and stability to the future and chaos and change, the seven leadership zones come into existence. It's time to name them and sketch their content. Three of the zones cover particularly broad areas, and so I have subdivided these discussions. However, the subdivisions are not shown on the map, which focuses on the zones as wholes.

In defining these zones, I was rolling out the action wheel (Figure 1 in the Introduction, p. 4) in the context of the map, pouring fresh leadership and organizational content into the authentic leadership model. Let's review the seven dimensions of the action wheel, showing again how they are the means of distinguishing the seven zones. The seven features of action are the following:

- Existence—the *from which* of action: our history, past, and memories in which the action is rooted or from which it arises (Zone 1)

- Resources—the *with which* of action: valued items, both tangible and intangible, that we use in the action (Zone 2)

- Structure—the *through which* of action: how processes and procedures are designed and implemented to get the action accomplished (Zone 3)

- Power—the *by which* of action: the energy or spirit that infuses the action (Zone 4)

- Mission—the *toward which* of action: the direction of the action (Zone 5)

- Meaning—the *for which* of action: the significance and rationale of the action (Zone 6)

- Fulfillment—the *into which* of action: the completed action (Zone 7)

Zone 1: *Serving the Past.* In this zone, the past as it links to the present sets the context for leadership. Leadership examines what that past means for leadership practice. What do we preserve and what do we release? Leadership in this zone roots itself in the heritage of the community, the organization, or the person. History is both good and terrible, yet it sets the ultimate platform for action. If one denies and distorts the past, as revisionists do, those actions will haunt whatever happens. If one assesses and owns the past, it can and will launch leadership into a world full of promise. Leadership serves the past as it launches into the future.

Zone 2: *Building Core Competencies.* In this zone, the focus shifts to resources. Leadership explores necessary skills (bricks for building). What are the core competencies required to address a fixable world? In this zone, leadership focuses on matching the right people to the right jobs and ensuring they are doing the right tasks at the right time with the right skills and information for the right pay and perks to get the job done consistently, efficiently, and reliably. Leadership ensures that the skills are built and maintained for reliable delivery of products and service.

Zone 3: *Systems Thinking.* This zone has two parts. They both attempt to structure its form and dynamic. Leadership has two primary functions.

Zone 3a: *Designing Sustainable Systems.* Leadership assesses what infrastructures are needed to craft the organizational foundation for system-based development. This involves mastering systems thinking, and building an edifice that can connect and order the competencies in Zone 2. What does it require to build sustainable systems? Teams, groups, communication, and linkage are critical. All human beings are islands, that is, unique outcroppings from a common land mass. That land must be firm yet flexible as a platform for any other action. We are all part of the same body. Leadership crafts systems for future growth.

Zone 3b: *Affirming Shared Identity.* Zone 3b shifts attention within the structural focus. Instead of examining the form of the structure, the world invents a more dynamic, living-systems approach. Leadership is thus challenged not just to craft systems. It must find a way to lead a more lively system.

Thus, leadership confronts the issue of identity. It is not where we are going; it is who we are. When the identity is secure and shared, workers and employees feel they are members. They know who they are and what their work is every day. Mission, value, and vision statements transform into identity affirmations and embodiment. Growing the identity is the glue of organizational life. Stakeholders—comprising customers, communities, employees, and shareholders—link to and grow with the organization as it creates its own long-term sustainability. Leadership grows the living-systems identity to include all significant players, adapting to each without selling out to any.

Zone 4: *Creating Ownership.* This zone attends to power—to all the voices speaking up and wanting to be heard. Leadership, therefore, is concerned with its power options. It asks, What uses of power make sense when the world offers less certainty of outcome and less agreement about direction? Leadership shifts from positional to potentially everywhere. People empower themselves and, together with other voices that are heard and heeded, codetermine the future of the company or community. New organizational and community strategies emerge so that workers become real members and the theme of buy-in shifts to the theme of ownership.

Zone 5: *Focusing on the Future.* This zone attends to the future. It has two parts. The first concentrates on the desired destination because shared direction is lacking. The second part explores the trip. The world is unpredictable and requires anticipation.

Zone 5a: *Setting Direction.* Leadership engages in futuring, focusing on the destination of the journey. Through participatory methods, the preferred future is created and plans devised to achieve it. Strategic planning transforms into strategic intent where priorities, once identified, serve as the locus of attention. Leadership sets direction.

Zone 5b: *Anticipating Change.* Leadership addresses a world that is unknown yet can be anticipated. Scanning, futuring, focusing less on the destination and more on the journey, scenario writing, and shifting from market share to opportunity share dominate this zone. An organization practices for events that might occur in the future, trying to position itself in a world on the brink of permanent and increasingly rapid change. It asks, how can it ensure that it is prepared for the new, which may be just up the street or corridor?

Zone 6: *Creating Meaning in Chaos.* As the world becomes more unknowable and unfixable, as shared meaning is wrenched apart, leadership shifts again. In this zone, leadership lives in the midst of chaos. Events occur that were not anticipated, were not on anyone's radarscope. "Permanent white water" (Vaill, 1996) is ever present, requiring process wisdom and improvisational skills. No one is in charge. Together, in the present, people co-create the means with no certainty of the outcome. Fear is rampant as people try to make meaning out of events that do not readily yield to sense making. How does leadership address a chaotic world?

Zone 7: *Serving the Promise of Authenticity.* At least in Zone 6, one could concentrate on a particular event or process. Even though it shatters old patterns and questions beliefs, this approach does not necessarily invite a broad overview of relevant questions. Fulfillment is at stake. The world of Zone 7 challenges leadership to make comprehensive choices, ask comprehensive questions, and face the most devastating aspects of human life. Leadership takes on three orientations in this zone.

Zone 7a: *Making Wise Choices.* Leadership assesses the worldly situation, listens to the stirrings, and makes wise choices that fit both what is external and what is internal to the context. Behind wise choice floats a leadership skill—adeptness. The choices made in the debate are matched to the zones. All the choices are necessary. They work only if they are matched authentically. In this zone, leadership asks such questions as: What does wise, adept action look like? How do I know I have it right? Do I hear the stirrings? Am I adept? What is the difference between leadership and management? Leadership chooses what the authenticity promise requires.

Zone 7b: *Probing Deeper.* Leadership probes deeply into some of the most difficult issues, into puzzles, in order to better inform practice. In this zone, leadership asks such questions as: What is really going on in chaos and complexity theory? Is it worthy of serious attention? What role does shadow (the stirrings) play in organizational and community life? How do I lead by addressing polarities and paradoxes when issues are not fixable? What theories support the zone leadership model? Leadership probes what the authenticity promise intellectually challenges.

Zone 7c: *Living the Promise.* Leadership lives hope and courage by addressing the issues of spirituality, evil, and theology. In this zone, leadership asks such questions as: What is spirituality? What are the differing perspectives? What is evil, and what does leadership mean in the most devastating situations known to human beings? How is theology different from religion, and what is its relevance to leadership? Is leadership really worthy of our deepest investment? In what should we ground our hope so that we continue to be engaged in life? Leadership lives the promise of authenticity every day, everywhere.

Of course, the zones, like the features of actions, are dynamic, not static. In this framework, each zone is simultaneously a whole and a part. In order for leadership to use the zones one at a time, to progress through each zone and on to the next, and finally to see leadership working within the scope of the entire map, each zone must be functional both as a self-contained whole that makes sense within itself and as a part that contributes to and makes sense within the larger whole. Each zone must be a secure foundation for the next one, which builds upon it. If a zone is shaky, it will collapse back onto the zone that supports it. One goal, then, in using the framework is to ensure that leadership in each zone is vibrant and robust so it can launch into the next zone.

In addition, all seven aspects of action are implicit in each zone; however, only one aspect is the focus of attention. As the action wheel rolls out, the leadership focus of attention shifts. So in the lower left, it begins with existence, then moves to resources and on out to meaning. Fulfillment occurs when a zone completes itself and prepares to stretch to the next zone.

To communicate the security of stability and the excitement of change, the sense of impending chaos as one looks to the future and of order when one views the past, in the move from Zone 1 to Zone 7, I vary the shape of the zones. Figure 6, for example, places Zone 1 on the map. The wavy shape around the zone represents the sense of chaos leadership must initially deal with in a new zone. In this zone, it is apparent chaos.

As the leadership focus shifts to Zone 2, that zone resides in apparent chaos while Zone 1 transforms into a more firmly bounded

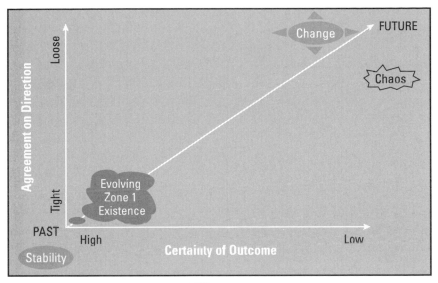

FIGURE 6 · ZONE MAP WITH ZONE 1

circle, taking on the shape and showing the features of the action wheel (see Figure 7). The same process continues throughout the mapping of the zones. However, in the later zones, especially 6 and 7, there is another change in the way the zones appear. They get larger, representing the increased difficulty of making sense of each new zone as the world becomes more unknowable and unfixable. The farther out to the upper right the zone is, the greater the experience of confusion, bewilderment, and nervousness (see Figure 8).

The arrow represents the time frame from past to future. Whatever zone you are in or attending to, anything in front of you (toward the upper right) directs you to the future, and anything behind you is in the past. In part, this is the sequential developmental framework that connects and orients the action players on the map.

As you look back on Zone 1 from Zone 2, the implicit chaos you felt in Zone 1 will appear orderly. You were in fact on the edge of chaos. The same dynamic will occur as you look back from each zone you are currently living in. Up to a point, there is order in chaos that we can perceive once we gain a more inclusive perspective. This is not true in Zones 6 and 7. New sets of questions emerge. The issue is not whether there is order in chaos. The question now shifts to meaning. Even if there is order, what difference does it make? And

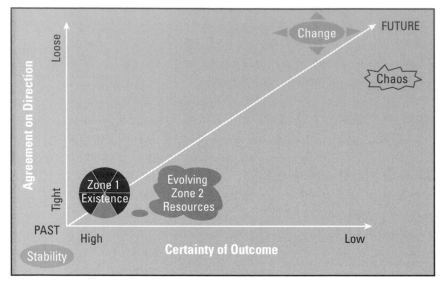

FIGURE 7 • ZONE MAP WITH ZONES 1 AND 2

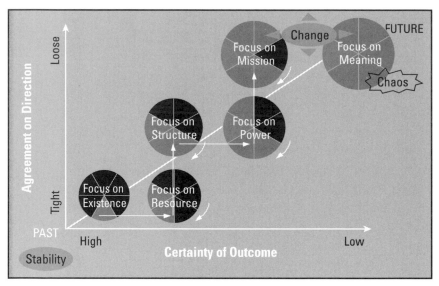

FIGURE 8 • ZONE MAP WITH ZONES 1 THROUGH 6

maybe there is no discernible order present that makes any sense, no matter how broad the perspective. These zones probe the most difficult human questions of evil and theology. Zone 7, representing fulfillment and the leadership action of Serving the Promise of Authenticity, embraces all the zones, as shown in Figure 9.

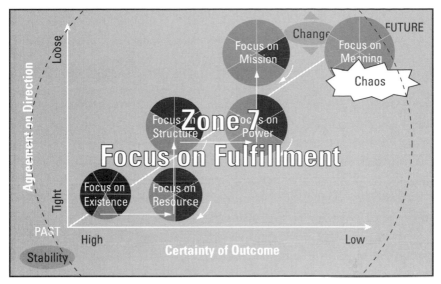

FIGURE 9 • ZONE MAP WITH ALL THE ZONES

THE MAP AS A DEVELOPMENTAL MODEL

Because it encompasses all the essential features of leadership action, relates them to the range of increasingly unknowable and unfixable realities, and thus guides people to an incremental and expanding understanding of leadership, the map of leadership zones is also a map of leadership development. This developmental model differs from both typical developmental models and standard theories of change.

As far as I know, only one other such framework has ever been assembled, by B. Hall and B. Ledig (1990, pp. 144–45). Hall and Ledig's framework, rooted in value-cluster identification, describes the following sequence of human cycles and leadership expressions:

- Safety/Security Cycle—Dictatorial Leader

- Security/Family Cycle—Benevolent Leader

- Family/Institutional Cycle—Manager Leader

- Institutional/Vocation Cycle—Enabling Leader

- Vocation/New Order Cycle—Collaborative Leader

- New Order/Wisdom Cycle—Servant Leader

- Wisdom/World Order Cycle—Visionary Leader

The world in which these cycles and types of leadership occur is a shifting one with four manifestations: a mystery over which one has no control, a problem with which one must cope, a project in which one wants to participate, and a mystery one cares about on a global scale. Maturity thus takes leadership from providing safety and security through supporting family and institutions and through supporting vocation and a new order to enabling wisdom and world order.

However, this leadership model embodies an evaluative progression. The goal is to move from one stage or cycle to the next, and each stage is somehow better or adds some value not found in the previous stage. The earlier stages are not treasured; they are only necessary steps to arrive at full maturity. Dictatorial leaders are not treasured in this framework. The goal is to move leaders away from earlier stages and toward wisdom and world order. Such evaluative progression also appears in many individual development models, including those of such thinkers as Hagberg and Guelich (1989) and Kohlberg (see Burns, 1978). Consider the levels in Kohlberg's hierarchy of moral development, listed on pages 35–36. Kohlberg's model certainly does not advocate that a person remain at the lowest level of moral reasoning—avoiding pain. In this model, maturity moves us up the hierarchy of moral reasoning from pain avoidance through stages of receiving immediate benefit and peer approval and toward long-term utility and moral rightness. To revert on this scale is to regress. The lower stages are not platforms to be used again but steps along the way to be left behind.

Conversely, because the map of leadership zones sees each zone as necessarily and continuously supporting the next zone, the developmental model embedded in the map sees the development in that zone as necessarily and continuously supporting the development in the next zone.

Now, to the second uniqueness of the zone model—change. Development is a kind of change, and very generally speaking, there have been two opposing views of how change occurs and new realities unfold and emerge. One camp is reductionist. Everything is explained by what precedes it. This is the mode of science; as Edward

O. Wilson (1998) says: "Complexity is what interests scientists in the end, not simplicity. Reductionism is the way to understand it. The love of complexity without reductionism makes art; the love of complexity with reductionism makes science" (p. 59). In the reductionist approach, the smaller parts explain the larger and knowing the laws of nature predicts the future. The alternative approach to understanding change reverses this order. It sees a deep purpose in the universe calling the universe toward it. Some call this force God, others teleology, others the infinite. Houston Smith (1989), for example, argues that science deals with only half of the reality of life. For him, the alternatives to "objectivity, prediction, control, and number are subjectivity, surprise, surrender, and words" (p. 105).

Again, the zone developmental model differs. It is neither reductionist nor teleological. Knowing the past does not explain or predict the future, yet the past is a necessary foundation upon which to build. Nor does the model seek to describe the future as a certain outcome or to downplay one stage as obsolete as the next stage emerges.

In short, in focusing simultaneously on the strengths inherent in a particular zone and the strengths of prior zones as required foundations to support the action in that zone, the developmental model I propose differs from other approaches by embodying a part/whole polarity. Leadership must deal with both poles.

A scenario offered by consultant Charles Bates in a personal conversation with me (1984) explains this puzzle well. Imagine that you own a house with a number of rooms. At first you live in just one room, and you find that room totally strange. But as you explore it and become familiar with it, what was initially strange becomes a comfortable set of stable reference points. You eventually take the pictures, lamps, and carpet as the givens of life. There is also a door. Every time you try to open it, it resists. So you go about other aspects of living in the room. However, periodically, you are drawn to the door. It still resists opening.

Curiosity persists. You try the door again. It opens! What a shock! Surprise, even joy, consumes you. Then you feel a touch of trepidation. You open the door ever so gently and peek inside. Nothing looks familiar. You shut the door. However, curiosity overcomes resistance and you open the door again. This time you enter, ever so briefly, just to get a look. It is still strange yet inviting. And still a bit scary. You want to go all the way in but feel reluctant. What will happen if you enter? Is it safe, like your present room? What does the future hold?

The brief visit appeared safe. So you enter more boldly, and this time in touring the room you pick up an object or two to take back to your first room, your "home"—objects you have never seen before. When you get back to the familiarity of your current lodging you discover that the objects do not fit. They are odd and out of place. So on your next visit to the new room, you return the objects, spend more time there, and began the exciting and challenging task of exploring the new setting. And guess what? There is another door. And the process of development continues. Eventually, you build more rooms onto your house.

Learning and moving on among the zones is like living in these rooms. As you look to the past, the rooms you are already living in are familiar; as you look to the future, the new room is scary yet intriguing.

Building on this building metaphor, you can determine your level of development, your zone, by your level of bewilderment. Whichever zone makes no sense or seems irrelevant is most likely the zone you are in right now because you are currently working on that zone's issue and struggling with it on a very deep level.

Thus far, we have seen how zone leadership offers an alternative to development and change. Now we come to the third issue—the relationship among personal and professional roles, organizational realities, and leadership. In this model, leadership is not reduced to a person, profession, or occupation, nor is it reduced to adapting to organizational/worldly realities. Leadership resides in the intersection of persons, their professional roles and functions, and organizations/communities. Zone leadership is not personal or professional or organizational development. It is leadership development that unites the three realities.

To put it another way, no human being exhibits leadership every day, and organizations and communities define leadership by roles and responsibilities, not necessarily by actions. So one can be a positional leader and not exhibit leadership. Role is no guarantee of leadership practice. In zone leadership, leadership changes its character, actions, and competencies by zone. Each person has to decide if she or he is prepared for leadership challenges as the zones shift. I agree with Rost's (1991) suggestion that leadership is episodic.

As the requirements for leadership shift due to differing contexts, any potential leader must figure out whether leadership makes sense for him or her within that context. Even though events may seem to demand leadership, there is no guarantee that any particular person, even with the best of intentions, will exhibit leadership well if he or she is not prepared intentionally, intellectually, and skillfully for leadership in that zone. Leadership thus lives at the intersection of personal, professional, and organizational realities.

KEY WAYS OF DEFINING ZONES

Each zone, as I have mentioned, is defined at its core by its focus on one feature of the action wheel. Of course leadership must deal with all the features of an action in each zone, but only one feature organizes the center of each zone. In addition, zones are defined by different authenticity criteria, metaphors, and polarities, all of which stir movement from one zone to another. I discussed some of these ideas as general themes in the Introduction. Now we can look at them as characteristics of zones.

Authenticity Criteria

What is *really* going on? That is the essential question of authentic leadership. The word *really* is especially critical. It suggests going beyond the obvious, the superficial. If we do not know what is *really* happening, we will act unwisely. Truth seekers are driven by this question. It travels both inward and outward. Looking inward, the person, team, or group looks at itself, its own sense of identity, character, choices, and leadership skills. Looking outward, the person, team, or group must figure out the nature of events and what action is required for authentic engagement. Moreover, in this looking—both inward and outward—they must be involved with the true and the real. In other words, authenticity embraces four dimensions that make up two polarities. *To live authentically is to be true and real, inside and outside.*

One polarity is the distinction between true and real. *True* describes that which needs no correction. That which is true meets many standards or criteria, such as correspondence, consistency, and coherence. No one criterion or standard exhausts the term and the reality to which it refers and which it describes. *Real* implies embodiment. Authenticity, as described in the Introduction, goes beyond sincerity in that sincerity means good intentions, while authenticity means genuineness, living the truth every day. This dimension of authenticity translates into integrity, embodying truth in whatever we do or say.

We have seen the inside/outside polarity before in the discussion of the different worlds across which leadership takes place. *Inside* refers to a single person or a unit of analysis like a team or division. *Outside* refers to a larger whole in relation to the inside, like a large team from which smaller teams come, a department, an organization, or the world at large. In the inside dimension, truth expresses itself as sincerity. That is, whatever is claimed as true is deeply believed by the individual or group. However, for this authenticity to be fully expressed, sincerity must translate into integrity as the claimed truth is lived every day. In the outside dimension, truth expresses itself as knowledge. One knows what is really going on in the world and in oneself. That knowledge becomes real, however, only when the actor, be it a person, team, or group, acts with wisdom. To know a lot does not guarantee wisdom. Knowledge plus reflection on current and historical experiences equals wisdom. The matrix in Figure 10 illustrates these dimensions and polarities in authenticity.

The polarities are often overlooked in the popular use of the term *authenticity*. How often have you heard someone say, "So-and-so is authentic; she walks her talk"? As mentioned earlier, an exclusive inner focus is inadequate. You can walk the talk *off a cliff*. Sincerity and integrity do not necessarily mean you grasp how the world is really operating or how you are really operating. You can sincerely believe you are telling the truth and simultaneously live in denial and fear. You can be ethically committed to a cause and fail to see the ramifications of your commitment on the welfare and well-being of others or on the global economy or ecology. In these cases, on reflection, knowledge is not wise. It turns out to be based on a distorted perspective that is self-serving. These kinds of inauthenticity are illustrated in Figure 11. Inauthentic truth claims result in distortion, which translates into hypocrisy when embodied. In the external world, this internal distortion becomes duplicity, disguising what is really going on. This behavior derails authenticity.

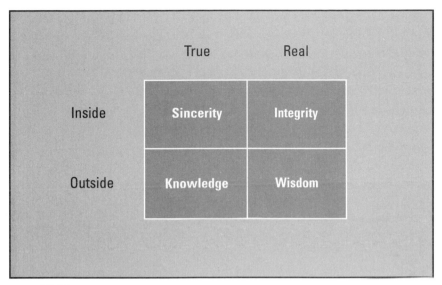

FIGURE 10 • AUTHENTICITY

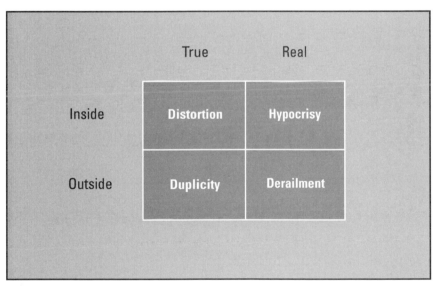

FIGURE 11 • INAUTHENTICITY

Many of my colleagues coach and mentor executives. Stories abound about inauthenticity. That is why executives need a coach/ mentor. One executive had no clue that his employees thought he was totally self-serving, dominating, and obnoxious. His self-perspective was one of openness, fairness, and collaborative problem solving. The 360-degree feedback was devastating. He never knew himself or the world he was supposedly leading. Employees experience this hypocrisy and derailment every day.

The aspect of authenticity that varies from zone to zone is the criterion for truth. What is true will, of course, reverberate across all the dimensions of authenticity. In the first zone, for example, the primary criterion for truth is *correspondence*. The world is knowable, so there should be a correspondence, an essential fit, between facts about the world and the way leadership is acting. Zone 2, building on Zone 1, shifts its truth entry to *consistency*. Now, delivering a reliable product or service sets the standard for authenticity.

Metaphors

Each zone is also distinguished by a metaphor, a comparison that identifies one thing with another, sometimes seemingly dissimilar thing. Metaphors can be mental or cultural lenses to focus our attention on some aspects of life and play down others. If I say marriage is warfare, some of you will say, "He's got that right. You have to dig in, hold your ground, fight to the bitter end, etc." Others will not find it revealing to look through that metaphorical lens. But you may be intrigued by the idea that marriage is poetry. Looking through that metaphorical lens may remind you or reveal to you that marriage is creative, playful, thoughtful, discerning, etc.

My intention in offering a metaphor for each zone is to deepen our insight into the zone, to allow us to use our intuition to go beyond literal meaning. (Six of these metaphors are discussed in detail in chapter 8 of *Authentic Leadership*.) Moreover, I suggest that leadership will do well to make adept choices of metaphor in response to particular stirrings. If we think in terms of an inappropriate metaphor as we feel negative and positive stirrings in our selves and our organizations, we may miss the depth and scope of what these stirrings signify, and our leadership may be less than adept.

Ethical Principles

Different ethical criteria also distinguish zones. Each zone embodies a core ethical principle that creates the outer boundary of the zone and is inherent and implicit in the guiding metaphor. In other words, the metaphors are not ethically neutral or value neutral.

The zones also concern core values, shared values, and universal principles that matter to leadership. Different zones will address these notions differently yet in a connected sequence. Values are hot topics in business today. Often what is not clear is what they are, who decides them, and what we do with them once they are identified and clarified. The discussion of the zones will address each of these questions.

Polarities

Each zone reflects a different polarity, a tension between concepts, things, or forces that is not resolvable by leadership. This polarity frames a dynamic pattern and ongoing movement inside the zone. A polarity such as part/whole, form/dynamic, or inside/outside further defines the uniqueness of each zone.

Stirrings

Movement from zone to zone cannot be explained totally by past events pushing us ahead or by some force pulling us into the future. Something is going on in the present (Wilber, 1996). Implicit in each zone is its own stirring. Something inside leads to something outside.

Stirrings, those events and intuitions that signal restiveness in a current zone, quicken authenticity into action. Each zone is defined in part by its characteristic stirrings. Negative and positive, they emerge from events, issues, and questions that leadership in the current zone cannot answer.

New truth expresses itself in these stirrings, inviting us to new awareness and understanding. Do we always want to go there? No; it can be scary. Yet the lure of inquiry stirs us in turn to confront ourselves, and the world, with hard questions. And this new truth challenges us to act in new ways, with new content in new zones. Being awake and aware challenges us to understand and act wisely. Escape, denial, and avoidance are certainly part of life, yet stirrings can question and probe these defenses that we have constructed.

Both negative and positive stirrings can impel appropriate movements to the next zone. Negative stirrings identify worldly and personal experiences of inauthenticity. Positive stirrings call forth authentic action that moves us to the next zone. In part, leadership in the zone framework is understood as responding to inauthenticity in life and moving to address it with authentic action. Therefore, when stirrings begin in a zone, they indicate that the current authenticity criterion is not adequate to grasp what is really going on. The next criterion, added to the old one, will be more inclusive or focused and will offer insights about the emerging world.

New truths often build on old ones rather than refute them. Quantum physics didn't replace Newtonian physics; it contributed a complementary view. Strategic planning didn't replace organizational development; it raised new system questions. Of course, some former truth claims are no longer believed. We now know that the earth is not flat and is not the center of the universe. However, *inquiry* never closes down. As we will see, what is true and real in one zone may be inadequate in other zones.

THE STRUCTURE OF THE ZONE DISCUSSIONS

The discussion of each zone follows the same organization. Each zone (except 7b) begins with a story that suggests the zone's focus. (The stories should not, however, be taken to imply that the persons or organizations mentioned are limited to the zone in which their story appears.) Next we'll examine the *core ideas* of the zone, describing the metaphor, the core ethical principle and other values, the authenticity criterion, and other central ideas in the zone. These ideas are the meanings that give identity to the zones.

The third section deals with *application* and demonstrates what the ideas look like when translated into action. More stories and examples identify the core skills and knowledge base necessary to exhibit leadership in the zone.

Next, I offer three *zone identification and leadership questions*, so you can assess how your organization or community is handling the zone:

1. How sturdy is my organization or community in this zone?

2. Where is my organization or community currently focusing its leadership attention?

3. Am I prepared to lead in this zone?

Each question is followed by a series of subquestions to help you frame your answer and diagnose which zones need leadership attention and what leadership development is needed. Answers are marked on a scale, as in Chapter Two. In Chapter Eleven you will have the opportunity to summarize your scores and your diagnostic wisdom.

Near the end of each zone, a *zone summary* reviews the defining characteristics of the zone and the leadership skills and interventions that are appropriate.

As the last item in each zone I present the typical *stirrings* encountered in each zone: the negative stirrings pointing to the worrisome face of reality and suggesting a retreat to the apparent security of this and earlier zones; the positive stirrings inviting movement to the next zone and into a new, potentially chaotic reality.

Armed with this broad picture of the map of the leadership zones, the important concepts addressed in the zones, and your own leadership choices, let's now go deeply into each zone, trying to figure out what the world calls us to do and be and what it takes to make wise, authentic, and adept choices. What is leadership in different worlds? What should leadership do in those different worlds? My hope is that the framework I have created will add to our appreciation of the rich diversity in leadership, and will help leadership live within and transcend complex realities in the real world and in our professional and personal being.

PART TWO

LEADERSHIP ZONES

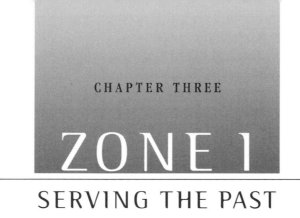

CHAPTER THREE

ZONE 1

SERVING THE PAST

PRESERVE THE BEST; OWN THE REST.

The old round-top trunk sits firmly against her office wall. Imprinted on it is a range of dates spanning fifty years—clearly visible and clearly important. This is the trunk her father, founder of the company, had passed on to her in a symbolic transfer of power and responsibility when she became CEO. Several thousand people attended the huge gala that marked this transfer of power. It honored the organization's past and signaled its transition to new positional leadership, leadership that would face a marketplace that offered both hope and unknown challenges.

Consider the metaphors this trunk suggests. If we are packing a trunk for an adventure there are questions about what to bring, what to leave home, what will be needed along the way, and what the destination will require. Suppose we end up in a different place than we intended?

What made the gesture particularly poignant was the founder's mixed reputation. His daughter honored many of her father's accomplishments; she also differed strongly with much of his leadership style and the organizational consequences. That is, this trunk came already packed, and she would have to repack it, choosing what to keep and what to replace.

The father's well-known approach—top-down, command-and-control—differed dramatically from the daughter's more participatory and inclusive manner and beliefs. Her challenge would be to preserve the best of the past without denying or dodging parts of the history that were no longer appropriate. In her speeches the daughter frequently praised her father's gifts of entrepreneurship, innovation, and creativity. All these reflections corresponded accurately with the facts of his legacy. She acknowledged that her challenge was to live the legacy, be a steward of the best of the company's collective history, and not pack the entire past for the next portion of the trip.

CORE IDEAS

In leadership Zone 1, at the intersection of high certainty about outcomes and tight agreement among the members of the organization or community about direction, the past closely accompanies the present (Figure 12). Leadership in this zone serves the past, using it as a platform from which the organization can launch into the future.

Since we live literally only in the present, our history moves into and out of our consciousness, yet it is ever a part of us. Past and present are never totally separable though the emphasis will shift from time to time. At times, events challenge us to address and rethink the past. That past may be the history of the world around us or our personal history, the history inside us. Again, the two are not entirely separable, and we can focus on outward and inward almost simultaneously. Thus leadership may be outward or inward. The woman in the above story focused outward, acknowledging what is involved in shifting formal power when there is much historical baggage. Inward focus addresses our personal memories, decisions, and values rooted in the past. In either case, leadership as Serving the Past brings the past as an immediate presence into the present moment. It seeks to *preserve the best; own the rest.*

Normal human responses to the past cover a range of options, from denying and scapegoating to affirming and embracing. We have certainty of outcome in this zone because the outcome is already with us. Agreement on direction is high because it, too, comes from the past, and to avoid and deny the past only intensifies the pressure to take it seriously. Still, when we are leading in this zone, the action

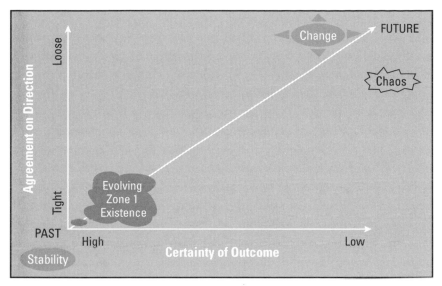

FIGURE 12 • ZONE 1: SERVING THE PAST

depicted on the map with the wavy line indicates unease. All is not clear yet; however, the potential for control and change is palpable. A fix-it mentality is justified.

The leadership challenge in this zone is to focus attention on the past in particular ways, by building on the best in the organizational or community history. What is important to a person, group, community, organization, or nation varies so widely that to insist on a focus on any particular set of significant facts is likely to sidetrack the necessary fundamental discussion. Whatever the context, we need to preserve the best and own the rest. Pick your own issues and passions and bring intentionality and inquiry to that aspect of your life.

To get at the core ideas in this zone, we can consider history as hard facts, as gifts, and as a foundation on which we can build.

Hard Facts

As we all know, the past is subject to widely differing interpretations. Nevertheless, there are fundamental givens in life that are nonnegotiable. There is a tough, unyielding stubbornness to rudimentary existence. Because of this hard-fact base, the action feature for this zone, *correspondence*, is the zone's authenticity criterion. What counts seriously here is evidence. The world is knowable through investigation, study, and reflection. In this zone, there is a forceful objectivity to existence, a *correspondence between fact and life*. Facts make a difference. All of life is not reduced to opinion. Facts can be tested, checked, and confirmed.

History grounds leadership in the past. The good news is the grounding is worthy of preserving. The bad news is the past can haunt and limit future actions of persons engaged in leadership.

Of late, there have been efforts to measure and assess umpires' calls with cameras. This already happens in football with the replay that allows referees to review camera shots of the plays in order to check the accuracy of the call. The first umpire was right. In this zone, "call 'em the way they are."

The hard facts will tell us when there are situations that require us to preserve the past and pass it on to the next generation. They will also tell us when there are situations that require us to face a past that should not be preserved in action and to squarely own up to that fact. In either case we ignore the past at our peril. Even so, denial and avoidance are a constant danger in this zone. Most histories contain events that we might rather not acknowledge, that tempt us to deny them and avoid them.

Gifts

These hard facts from the past can also be viewed as a bag of gifts, and the metaphor that I suggest for this zone is *life is a gift*. Sometimes we desire and delight in a particular gift; sometimes we hate it and want to toss it in the trash. In either case, the gift shows up and we are challenged to receive, understand, and embrace it. This challenge is constant. Leadership neither ignores nor adapts to the hard realities. It accepts them. They just are. At a deep level, leadership says, "Thank you." We have to choose what we are going to do with them.

Remember when some psychologists argued that individuals are born as blank tablets? Not so. We bring our DNA and whatever interpretation of the past is current in our being. From these fundamentals, we engage the world from birth through life. And if we have children, we pass it on as their genetic legacy. If we have other family members, we become part of their existence. The gifts persist.

Building on the Past

As I said, there is good news and bad about the past. The good news is that the past launches our actions, providing stability for engagement. The bad news is that the past limits our actions, locking us into the status quo and capturing our engagement. Leadership that serves the past emerges when the world stirs us to preserve the part of the past we consider worthy of taking into the future. Leadership also emerges when persistent events call us to acknowledge and own the part of the past that we would rather deny and escape as individuals, communities, or organizations. Serving the past confronts the impulse to run.

Stepping into the future, we remain stewards of the past. We carry history forward. It is almost as if we back into the future, informed, enriched, threatened, and frightened about the past and its implications for tomorrow.

Very few authors in leadership studies address Serving the Past as I define it here. The most straightforward affirmation of it, not by name but by concept, can be found in *Built to Last: Successful Habits of Visionary Companies* by Collins and Porras (1994). In their research, which is detailed more fully on page 155, they discovered that companies that endure for the long term as significant players in their field do so for three reasons. First, they know what business they are in and that that business has not changed over time. Second, they have values tied to the business. And third, they live those values "in their toes." Because they have stability anchored in core values, their prospects for change explode dramatically. The more secure their foundation, the more radical their BHAGs (big, hairy, audacious goals). The more sure their sense of themselves, the more these great companies risk.

Just to make sure the idea of core values is clear, let me distinguish core values from shared values. Core values are tied to the business; shared values are held in common. President Clinton's impeachment was argued from this distinction. The Republicans argued the impeachable issue was not sex; it was lying under oath. That was a violation of a core value undermining government credibility and trustworthiness and worthy of impeachment. The Democrats argued it was about sex, an affair, and the President should be disciplined. He should not be impeached. He violated a shared value—affairs are wrong—not a core value. Government was not under threat.

Furthermore, great results can happen even though the companies' core values may, upon reflection, not be ethical. Consider Philip Morris. Given the controversy surrounding the tobacco industry, many would find that company's ideology unethical. As Collins and Porras point out, from the point of view of the values' effectiveness for the company, "it doesn't matter whether or not you like or agree with the Philip Morris ideology—not unless you work for Philip Morris. . . . We concluded that the critical issue is not whether a company has the 'right' core ideology or a 'likeable' core ideology, but rather whether it *has* a core ideology—likeable or not—that gives guidance and inspiration to people *inside that company*" (p. 88).

With these findings Collins and Porras add a substantial brick to the leadership edifice and suggest the core ethical principle and the polarity for this zone. The core ethical principle is to have a focused personal and communal history, or sacred history. The polarity is stability/change. They are closely linked because the history provides the stability.

Often definitions of leadership involve dealing with change. Rost (1991), for example, argues that leadership "intends real change," and he makes no reference to stability. Rost employs the term *change* as if it were an isolated entity. As I examine in Chapter Twelve, change is always one half of a polarity; it exists only in relationship to that which is not changing, that which is stable or still. Understanding this polarity is essential to leadership.

Tom Atkinson, a senior vice president of the Forum Group, a training and consulting firm based in Boston, has this understanding: "I don't 'thrive' on chaos. I don't 'embrace' change. And I have no idea how to replace the engine on a 747 jet while it's in mid-flight" (1995, p. 106). For there to be change, there must be stability. For Atkinson a sense of direction, core values, ways to work together, and continuous growth and learning are "home bases" for change.

I wonder what it would be like to have organizations offer stability management seminars along with change management? Ironically, it might shake up the place!

APPLICATION

What, then, does Serving the Past look like when embodied? The past is always open to reinterpretation and rewriting; this is a never-ending process. Some even picture the past as alive and open rather than dead and closed. Even so, there are significant constants that ground reflection and launch action. Typically, these heavyweight parts of the past are solidified in some icon, ceremony, or other type of symbol that even when broadly interpreted acts as a concrete reference point. In families, this constant may be sacred memories passed on from generation to generation. In religious groups, it is often sacred texts. The Bible, the Torah, the Koran, and other written or oral traditions tie past to present and anchor action.

For citizens of the United States, the Declaration of Independence and the U.S. Constitution formally ground national self-understanding. These documents, despite great disagreements in interpretation, still constitute the facts of our existence, the focal point from which we move forward. The speech in which Martin Luther King Jr. told us "I have a dream" did not offer a new vision for America. He called us to live the vision already grounded in the Declaration of Independence and the Constitution. To be authentic as a nation, we have to live equality and justice in our toes. Our racism derails the best of our sacred history. It embodies the worst. To negate, abuse, or betray these historic texts directly is to commit the most heinous of crimes—treason. Traitors and terrorists attack the sacred history of their countries' founders.

To remember and reinforce the fundamentals in their past, organizations, communities, and nation-states of all kinds practice rituals and remembrances. Funerals, weddings, holidays, swearing-in ceremonies, masses or other liturgical expressions of faith, parades, costumes and native dress, flags, and other icons all reference the past and become the taproots for the present. We also establish organizations whose primary mission is to evoke and perpetuate public memory. Old buildings, museums, art galleries, and other public spaces invite historical reflection, triggered by objects that embody historical significance. Many are there to be celebrated—not all. The Holocaust Museum, for example, confronts us with a part of the past that deserves to be remembered, not celebrated.

I had the privilege of attending a profound organizational service to the past event in the late fall of 1998. Once a year, near the Christmas and Hanukkah season, the Medtronic Corporation holds its annual celebration event. Medtronic is a Minnesota company that pioneered the use of pacemakers and that "applies biomedical engineering in the research, design, manufacture, and sale of instruments or appliances that alleviate pain, restore health, and extend life." (This is part of Medtronic's mission statement, written boldly on the wall of the main headquarters for all to see.)

At this event, patients who have been restored to health by Medtronic inventions share their stories with the people who produce these lifesaving devices. It is indeed a joyous occasion. In the room where 2,500 employees met this day was the mural that is prominently reproduced in Medtronic printed materials. It depicts a human body lying on its back. In sequential images, the body lifts itself up and begins to walk, restored to health and vitality. The image is an anchor icon, capturing the spirit of the firm and the commitment of the workforce.

In his opening remarks, CEO Bill George affirmed the mission of the organization, avowing that it had not changed for almost fifty years and never would as long as he was in charge. Company founder Earl Bakken added that the employees now knew why he could retire so comfortably. The business was in good hands, the identity secure.

Diversity manifested itself. An employee rehearsed the history of Dutch Christmas traditions, linked to the States through what was once New Amsterdam and is now New York City. The choir performed "Hanukkah Tonight."

Then the stories began. A doctor would describe a patient's illness, and the patient would then recount in very personal terms the shift from debilitation to vibrancy, from lying on his or her back to walking forthrightly into a promising future. One was an eighty-five-year-old man who showed up wearing swimming medals he had recently won. Another was an eleven-year-old boy whose heart rhythm was now being managed with an implant. In all, six patients told their stories, with passion and thankfulness for the employees of Medtronic. Without the Medtronic devices, these people would not be alive.

The ceremony made it clear that leadership as stewardship was truly alive and well in Medtronic.

Personal Texts

Think for a moment about your own sacred objects or texts. What things do you have that link you to the past in ways that quicken, guide, and propel your actions in the future? I have two. One is my father's retirement plaque, honoring thirty-five years as fireman and engineer on the Long Island Railroad. It reminds me of persistence, hard work, and the power of engines to move people and goods down the tracks, both literally and metaphorically. It also offers an unintended reminder. My father's first name was Isaac; on the plaque it is spelled *Issac*. It is a gentle reminder that organizations are imperfect, and that we must remember to give care and attention to detail. Another sacred object is a letter from a dying friend that brings me both sadness and deep joy because his friendship was a gift to my life.

When I conduct leadership seminars, I often ask participants to bring their sacred objects and share them. I recommend that you share the significance of yours with a friend or colleague. When people share such objects, laden with meaning, they invoke memories that can launch them into the future with greater insight and wisdom. The farther we can look back with honesty, the farther we can see forward with anticipation and possibility.

We Have No Real Escape from Serving the Past

Often as we seek to preserve the best and own the rest, we deny parts of our past, we rationalize, we blame and shame others, making them the scapegoats for our own actions. That is, we try to refuse the leadership challenge of this zone. Ultimately we cannot escape this challenge because Serving the Past is the necessary foundation of all the rest of our leadership. There is certainty of outcome—the past has already happened—and there is agreement on direction—carry the past forward. The only choice is how thoughtfully and carefully we do it. The thoughtfulness and care—the authenticity of addressing what is true and real rather than self-serving and trumped up—distinguish the gift of the received past from the gift of the preserved past. The gift of the received past is not always welcome or initiated; it may include a life-threatening accident or an organizational crisis. Embracing this gift, assessing it, owning it, and learning from it turns it into part of the preserved past that we can build on.

Blacks and whites continued to address issues as the Truth and Reconciliation Commission concluded its work in South Africa. In the 1970s, many whites served the past as they defended apartheid and connected its oppression to historical stories of white efforts to settle the land. Blacks were stewards of their own past, linking their history to the land and their terrifying experiences of apartheid. Each claimed truth, each distorted, although whites were more in denial of the facts of their history than blacks. No one group ever has the whole truth, though some will be seen to be closer than others as hard facts are revealed and become part of public consciousness. The intention of the Truth and Reconciliation Commission was to bring to the surface as much hard truth as possible, mostly about white participation in apartheid. However, black involvement was reviewed as well. Although it is too early to tell whether this particular effort at leadership will help heal the nation and offer the possibility of forgiveness and new beginnings, one thing I am sure of is some successful effort at leadership will be necessary for ultimate success. However, Serving the Past alone will not be sufficient for ultimate conclusion. All the leadership zones must come into play for total authentic action.

One can come to terms with the past and go nowhere with the encounter. Hence, the stirrings. Reality is always more complex than what is captured by one zone. For long-term healing and progress, other leadership choices will be, and have been, made. Life is never reducible to one simple reality. Having been in South Africa during apartheid and after the revolution, I know that the multiple worlds requiring attention abound. The U.S. Congress struggled with issues in this zone when it apologized to the Japanese Americans for the way the government treated them during World War II, making financial compensation to demonstrate the seriousness of the reconciliation effort.

Americans who are not Native Americans continue to struggle with the history of the United States in relation to Native American bands and tribes, lacking full appreciation of what it means to indigenous Americans that whites continually made and broke treaties. White denial still exists about the tragedy of Native Americans in this country. I have attended too many seminars on racism to ignore the naiveté, rationalizations, and excuses for white oppression. Also, bands still wrestle with issues of tribal nationhood and the implications for law and life of both whites and tribal members.

American school students still study U.S. history from east to west, tracking the path of "Manifest Destiny." What would it be like to trace history from south to north, and face the nation's connections to Mexico?

The auto industry currently struggles in this zone. In 2000, Ford and Firestone had to confront their past—tire failures—and own the errors. Political dynamics emerged. Ford distanced itself from Firestone, and both companies engaged in some measure of denial. The past never totally leaves. It will haunt the reputations of both companies' products.

Mitsubishi Motors Corp. reshuffled management personnel in early September 2000 in an effort to regain credibility, blasted by revelations of a cover-up of auto defects extending over the previous two decades. Katsuhiko Kawasoe, president of Mitsubishi Motors Corp., came under intense pressure to resign after the reports surfaced, prompting a recall of 620,000 vehicles as well as a police investigation. IBM is also struggling to face its past with the Holocaust. Edwin Black (2001) offers a gripping account of the connections in *IBM and the Holocaust*. The past never totally goes away.

If one completely ignores or avoids the past, particularly if that past is heavily loaded with terrible baggage or consequences, the past will haunt and reemerge. Ford played down some information from the past about accidents, claiming the numbers were within the boundaries of normal tire patterns. As the numbers grew, and other agencies and voices were heard, the reasons were interpreted as rationalizations. Now, the tire company and the auto company have a new set of issues to address and lead through.

We cannot escape being stewards of the past. Leadership that serves the past expresses itself when we are willing to be intentional, thoughtful, and persistent in understanding history. It also pushes us beyond the past by going through it, not around it. Serving the Past lays the foundation for the next stages of leadership and builds on that foundation without negating it.

A DIFFERENT KIND OF ASSESSMENT

Almost all leadership assessment instruments identify an individual's traits, gifts, and talents by means of a set of questions, answered on a sheet and tabulated relatively quickly by oneself or a machine that scans the answers. The profile that emerges is fed back personally or in a seminar. Thousands of such instruments exist, some with a great database like the *Myers-Briggs Type Indicator* (MBTI) instrument, and others backed by questionable research.

Then there is *Motivated Abilities Pattern,* or MAP. Developed by Arthur F. Miller in the late 1950s, this approach is totally different. There is no set of questions, no formatted answer sheet with spots for check-offs, and no set number of types as with the MBTI instrument. Instead, you write down stories from your past that describe experiences that were very satisfying and/or successful for you. Starting with your earliest memories, you record narratives up to the present, sorted by age categories. It takes a fair amount of time to complete the stories—it took me six hours.

The stories are turned over to a person at a People Management International, Ltd., near you, part of a national partner franchise located around the world. Skilled and trained readers scan your stories. You are then interviewed. Themes are discerned in your stories by means of the language you use to describe success and satisfaction. The goal is to figure out your core being, your essence, the base that has guided your life from birth. And it works. Not limited by type categories, it is broader than the MBTI assessment, more targeted to you as an individual, and richer in content. I was stunned by the results and profoundly affected by the insights, and took home a deep sense of the core being that has in fact guided my life since birth. The match to Zone 1 is total. This world is knowable. (For more information, see Miller, 1999).

No one comes to the table for leadership neutral, blank, or empty. What is from the past presents itself in the present. Without knowing it, I was living my existence from the past every day. PMI connected that wired past to my present life. Is leadership born or made? Here, in this zone, the arguments often tilt to the "born" side. It is no accident that Collins's hypothesis was that Level 5 Leadership, living the paradox of humility and ferocious will, was born more than bred. Just as core values endure from the past, so, too, does the seeding. Collins is a strong advocate of Zone 1 reality.

The problem that will always confront leadership is the never-ending challenge to grow in wisdom and maturity while figuring out what to hold on to and what to let go of. We all have to pack our bags, and not just once. We do it over and over again. And we make mistakes. The leadership challenge of preserving the best and owning the rest never leaves us. It is personal, professional, and organizational.

ZONE IDENTIFICATION AND LEADERSHIP QUESTIONS

The following questions will guide you and your organization or community in determining whether Serving the Past is your leadership challenge now or if it is likely to be in the future.

1. How sturdy is my organization or community in this zone?

   - Are there issues from the past that still require attention?

   - How effectively have we addressed issues from the past?

   - Do we currently focus on preserving the best from our past?

   - Do we celebrate, honor, and remember the past as an integral aspect of our community or organizational life?

   - What are our core values?

   - Have we designed and implemented processes to carry our core values forward?

   - Is our foundation in our past stable enough that we can launch into a world increasingly requiring change?

```
10 |  |  |  |  |  |  |  |  | 0 |  |  |  |  |  |  |  |  | 10
Very Sturdy                                          Shaky
```

2. Where is my organization or community currently focusing its leadership attention?

   - Is it attending to the right zone?

   - Does it exhibit collective denials of important issues?

- Is its attention focused elsewhere, perhaps as a strategy to avoid the realities of this zone?

```
10 |  |  |  |  |  |  |  |  |  |  0  |  |  |  |  |  |  |  |  |  |  10
Excellent Fit                                                    Misfit
```

3. Am I prepared to serve the past?

- Have I reflected seriously on my own history in relation to my work?

- Are some issues from my own past haunting me today?

- Is my past an anchor that keeps me stuck in the mud or a sea anchor that I can take on travels in storm-tossed waters?

- What are my own core beliefs?

- What are my sacred texts?

- Do I have the knowledge and skills to be a steward?

- What am I currently doing or planning to do to ensure my foundation in this zone is solid?

```
10 |  |  |  |  |  |  |  |  |  |  0  |  |  |  |  |  |  |  |  |  |  10
Ready to Exhibit Leadership                     Not Prepared at All
```

ZONE SUMMARY

Leadership in Zone 1 concentrates on the past as the foundation for long-term authentic action. The past is critical because it provides the fundamental character for all that follows. Avoidance or denial of the past distorts any future action, shaping it in profound ways that are rarely understood or expected. Only by wrestling with and understanding history can one move past it.

Authenticity in this zone is grounded in facts—ideas, events, and actions—that are true and real. They just are. They are not made up.

They are extremely secure and stable. If eradicated, they take with them part of our sense of identity and our roots. They constitute our existence. Leadership cannot exist if no one and no thing shows up from the past and engages us. We are shaped by our past, and from it we can shape our future. The leadership that begins this endless process is Serving the Past.

Correspondence sets the standard for authenticity. Facts link to statements directly. The world is objective, demanding our attention and inquiry. The past is potentially knowable as evidence is accumulated, tested, and interpreted. Furthermore, we are totally in charge of what we do with that history. The past is knowable, and knowledge about it is transferable. We seek ways to match what is happening outside us to what is occurring in our thinking. Leadership as Serving the Past invites—and at times cajoles and confronts—us to face and acknowledge the hard facts of our group's own past, hold on to what is worth preserving, and own up to the rest.

The metaphor *life is a gift* reminds us that all gifts, good and bad, become part of us. What is a gift to me may be a throwaway to you. Yet implicit in the metaphor is a gift's unique focused importance. It may be as wonderful as the gift of a child or as terrible as the gift of suffering. In either case, it affects a particular organization or person and becomes part of the impact of the past to the present.

Developmentally, Serving the Past comes before all else. For now, leadership energy is focused on building a secure base. If this base is shaky, the other zones will shake as well. The core competencies of stewardship include the knowledge of relevant history, a clarity about core values, skills for remembering and celebrating, a willingness to face hard truths, and the ability to preserve the sacred past.

ZONE 1 DEFINITIONS

Leadership: Serving the Past
Authenticity criterion: Correspondence
Metaphor: Life is a gift
Core ethical principle: Focused personal and communal history, or sacred history
Polarity: Stability/change, with an emphasis on stability

STIRRINGS

As we assess the past and its importance for the present and the future, reflections and arguments surface. Some are our own; some we hear from others. The following is typical of the general reflections you might have or hear about the importance of the past in our lives:

> No one's history is blemish free. Mine certainly is not. I understand that leadership grounds itself in the past and is not to be limited by it. I agree that stewardship moves communities and organizations forward, knowing that whatever the future holds, there is security and stability, even comfort, in the best of the past.

> I know that in my life there are times when deep inner struggles surface, revealing unresolved issues of my past that demand attention. I've seen that same drama in the workplace as well. I am also aware that along with my struggles I have been given gifts that I did not earn and deeply appreciate. I have a gift for speaking. I've always had it. And, as I age, I also see a life pattern that developed from my gift that provides a historical map for my future action.

> Recently a consultant helped us identify the historical gifts of our organization. We had some great memories and events to celebrate. They actually are a pattern in our everyday work with customers. We have always prided ourselves on listening. It is one of our gifts.

There are also developmental stirrings. They may be negative, trying to hold us in the past, or positive, helping us launch ourselves from the present moment into the next. You may hear or think things like these.

Negative Stirrings

> I've had it with change. If we have one more change initiative, I'm going to throw up—or quit. I learned yesterday that another merger was in the offing. I like my job, the people I work with, and really enjoy the culture around here. I don't want to lose any of it.

> Someone told me the other day that I was preoccupied with stability and resisted any change. She said I was trapped by the past. She also pointed out that I was holding on to all the wrong things—job definitions, vacation schedules, and budget. I know what I want. I want some comfort and security. I'm a department head, for heaven's sake!

I know we have some organizational troubles. We have a structure that is dysfunctional. My job is fine, but we do have difficulties getting products out on time. I know what is going to happen. My boss will hire a consultant to restructure us—again. I heard talk in the hallway of a total redesign. I am very suspicious about any alternative. Better we stick with the known than venture forth into craziness. The last time we had a merger, we inherited six people we had fired the previous year! Now what do we do with them? No one wants to discuss it, yet we all know the pain the avoidance is causing.

We have long-standing secrets around here. We all know what they are. No one wants to admit and deal with them. In fact, we are in effect sworn to secrecy by the implied message that if we approach this part of the forbidden territory on the map, we'll be in grave political danger. Our jobs could be at stake.

Positive Stirrings

I've spent considerable time reflecting about our organization and my professional and personal part in it. My worry about change is only that we will lose our core values and our deep sense of who we are. I want to preserve that. I love the celebrations we have around here. And people don't try to cover up the tough parts of our history either.

I have had very negative reactions to the change mania sweeping through this place. However, the more I ponder my resistance, the more aware I am of wanting to get unstuck from the past. I want to be able to carry the best of this organization into the future and deal with whatever we have to as the market and government regulations shift on us. I believe in change if it is grounded in a stable, affirming past. I also know that the more solid we are, the more we can deal with anything, even events in the past we thought were old history. I am truly a steward around here. I will carry the best of our past into the future and I will take the risks to confront any aspect of our past and, without shame or blame, help us face it.

My negative stirrings were, and continue to be, a gift. Without them I would have no incentive to deepen my thinking and move into stewardship. If we adapt to the negatives they control our lives and ground us in a world impervious to our being and becoming. If addressed adeptly, they position us for action. The negatives become positives. What limits us launches us. What traps us frees us. Now, this is exciting!

Positive stirrings reflect a sense of the world and of ourselves so that action is possible, so that we can make a difference, given our talents, potential, prospects, and invitations. Stability is not a preoccupation. Rather it is that sense of inner security that allows us to risk going into the next room to live. It is also that sense that the world is sufficiently friendly, or at least sufficiently fixable, to support our engagement with it.

Developmentally, Leadership in Zone 1 is the basis for the many other rooms we have yet to encounter and explore, many zones to visit on the map. When we are young and just setting out, we all bring with us the *curse of naiveté* about the world and ourselves. Some philosophers say we already have everything we need. The problem is that it is only as we mature and revisit our past, as outer or inner events call us to action, that we realize how much we did have available to us but never claimed. At the outset we understand very little of what is available, and if we claim too much we run the risk of acting out of arrogance.

Serving the Past is never completed. The past pervades our present and future, setting the context for our actions and how we interpret the world. Our cultural heritage restricts what we see and deepens what we see. Our inherited legacy of events and meaning, what others and nature have given us as a gift—wanted or not—prepares us for the next zone. None of us is totally trapped in the past; none of us has totally preserved and owned the truth of the past.

And so, as we begin our trajectory into the future and live in subsequent zones, facing more and more chaos in the world, stability is our foundation. It is not easy to serve the past. As we move from zone to zone we will see how leadership has to own all of the history without denial. The stirrings push us to turn denial into truth and naiveté into knowledge and wisdom. We are continually, often profoundly, challenged to assess and reassess what is worth packing and what is best left at home. The potential for chaos confronts steadfastness and stability as we lead in the present and toward the future, never forgetting our rootedness in the past.

We are now ready to serve the past as we couple it with skill building. A door has opened and we are entering the next room, taking the next path.

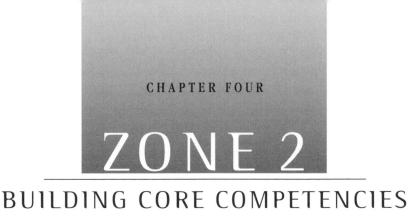

CHAPTER FOUR

ZONE 2

BUILDING CORE COMPETENCIES

EXCEL AT YOUR SKILLS; IGNORE THE FRILLS.

It was Sunday night. I was sitting on a plane next to a man of about sixty who seemed agitated or preoccupied—drinking his beer, frowning, moving his hands a lot, and shifting frequently in his seat. I noticed he was wearing a large ring. So I asked, "Are you in sports?" It turned out to be a perfect question. I got a great introduction to the world of expert task mastery, or targeted competency. He was a line judge for the National Football League, and one of the best in the league.

Bill (not his real name) had just completed his work in a Minnesota Vikings football game, and he was indeed restless. On Tuesday he would receive a call from the official organization of referees evaluating that Sunday's performance. Video cameras had recorded every call made during the game, so the facts would be objective and on tape. He wondered if perhaps he had made one error, although so far that year his record had been perfect. A lot was riding on the calls—his professional status, reputation, even future assignments in division championship games, including the Super Bowl. He and the professional association of judges were in clear agreement on the goal in his work— no mistakes. And there was certainty of outcome—the objective facts were known and could be used in feedback to improve his perfor-mance. At this moment, Bill's world was knowable and fixable.

He shared with me what happens in the three-hour preparatory meet-ing as the seven judges prepare for a Sunday game. During the first hour they review the tapes from the previous game, attending espe-cially to errors. Each judge's performance is assessed and his score recorded in an assessment book. During the second hour, one of the judges teaches a seminar to the others on some technical aspect of the game, instruction given or heard many times before. The goal is to always keep improving performance and mastery. The third hour con-centrates on preparing for the day's game—uniforms, equipment, etc.—so there are no surprises. This three-hour drill occurs before every game as experts teach experts to improve performance.

Moreover, behavior that might affect the judges' work is scrutinized. Once or twice a season, each judge must submit to urinalysis to be sure there has been no drug use. They must avoid gambling establish-ments at all times.

Bill told me that his goal was to be the best in the field, a leader who pushed the boundaries of the profession. He wanted to be the Michael Jordan of football line judges. He predicted that if the judges failed to show sufficient expertise, we would see the return of the instant replay, of the search for means to ensure objective results. He was right. A season of poor calls in 1999 triggered the reintroduction of the camera for checking calls during the game. The goal of the job after all is no mistakes.

CORE IDEAS

Leadership in Zone 2 clusters its ideas and practices around objective resources, the second feature of action on the action wheel. Leadership builds core competencies, that is, competencies targeted to a particular, knowable subject matter, because the world is know-able and fixable through scientific methods, research, and practical experience. Reality can be reduced to fundamental principles and explained by tracing causal relationships. Through independent inves-

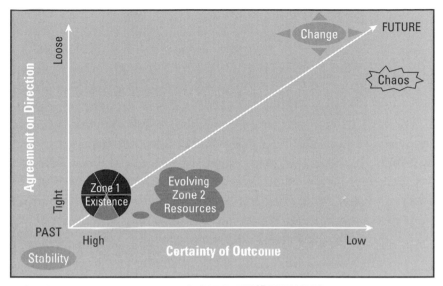

FIGURE 13 • ZONE 2: BUILDING CORE COMPETENCIES

tigation, objective reality can be comprehended. Sometimes as a result of being comprehended, it can be fixed. The polarity in this zone is potential/actual. Leadership turns the potential in the universe into actual practice. If we can understand the causes of cancer, we can eliminate it. If we can understand the genetic map, we can alter it. If we can understand cloning in sheep, we will do it with humans. It is just a matter of time. The knowable world is awaiting, even inviting, our inquiry. The more we know about how things really work, the more consistency we can establish between our resources and our actions, the wiser and more authentic we become in our actions in this zone. Tight agreement on direction and high certainty of outcome persist. Neither is quite as firm as it was when we were concentrating mostly on Serving the Past. We are moving outward on the map (see Figure 13, above). We now experience Zone 1 with much clearer and firmer boundaries. Zone 2, in contrast, is less clear because we have yet to work our way through it.

What I call targeting skill building, Stacey (1993) labels "technical rationality." It is a stage in which

> managers . . . discover how their environment and the capability of their organization are changing by gathering the facts through a continuous process of scanning, research and monitoring. They

analyse the facts using the step-by-step rules of logical reasoning to generate all the options open to achieve their objectives. They calculate the effects of carrying out each option on their objectives, choose that option which maximises their objectives, and then act to implement that option. . . . The choice is predetermined by the facts and the problem is simply one of calculation. (p. 33)

Stacey's description echoes the metaphor for this zone—*life is a machine*. The core ethical value is freedom to act, that is, freedom within the boundaries formed by analysis of the facts. The ethics and values of a leader move into this background. Entrepreneurial success takes over. For example, there is no problem equating leadership with success, even if the action is a bit underhanded. A case in point is Pete McGlade of Southwest Airlines ("Meet the Man . . . ," 2001).

[He] uses code names such as "Weasy" and "Itchy" for U.S. cities and sometimes checks into hotels under assumed names. When he meets with airport officials, he swears them to secrecy and often operates on the basis of handshakes alone.

The clandestine tactics aren't part of some government espionage operation. They've become a normal part of the workday for this Southwest Airlines executive, who holds one of the most secretive and powerful jobs in the U.S. airline industry.

Knowledge and Skills as Critical Resources

In this zone, the past ceases to dominate our attention, although we must never cease taking account of it. Now we turn to the mastery of resources—get them, distribute them, count them, justify their importance, and delight in their presence. That is the task. When the world reflects tight agreement and high certainty, this mode of leadership embodies efficiency and creates hope and comfort for both leader and led.

Authenticity is now tested by a new standard—consistency, which couples with correspondence and moves to this current phase of action. Consistency of goals and outcomes with resources and facts is paramount in this knowable and fixable zone. However, unlike the facts in Zone 1, which are about the past, the facts in this zone change. New situations continually emerge. Leadership in Zone 2 offers predictability in these new situations through knowledge, experience, and practice. New situations do not daunt leadership.

They challenge it to find new workable solutions and to implement them skillfully.

It should come as no surprise that almost all the participants who sign up for leadership seminars and training want skill development. It is no accident that the word *training* usually follows *leadership*. Leadership requires many skills. Of course, as we shall see, what counts as a skill changes dramatically as one moves from zone to zone. What is appropriate in a world that is knowable differs profoundly from what is necessary in an unknown and unknowable world. Even the category of "skill" becomes suspect as we shift to the higher-number zones. However, in this zone *skill* refers to technical rationality and to mastery of specific tasks with defined kinds of expertise. And without such skill, without targeted competency, leadership has no foundation for the reflection, skill building, and authentic action of later zones. Such skills, such expert knowledge, are among the most important resources of this zone.

Life Is a Machine

The metaphor for this zone, *life is a machine*, derives from the zone's philosophical foundation, which has a long history going back to seventeenth-century physics,

> which regarded nature as inert and (in its Cartesian form) held that things moved because of external impact, that is, because of forces acting from the outside. This is, then, a "matter and motion" view of the world, and along with it goes the idea that to understand a phenomenon you must break it up into its constituent parts and find the smallest unit, which is then seen as the cause of the larger phenomenon. The method, in short, is materialistic, reductionist, and atomistic; it is also deterministic, in that effects follow on causes in a fairly direct fashion. In addition, it is central to this method that there is an absolute distance between observer and observed. Truth is seen as unemotional, value free; the experimenter is not a factor in his or her experiment or in the equations being used to describe the situation under examination. More generally, consciousness is not regarded as a factor in understanding the world because it is seen as epiphenomenal, that is, arising out of a material base and explicable in material terms. In the postwar period and before, the behavioral school of psychology was perhaps most famous (or notorious) in arguing for this position. (Berman, 1996, p. 30)

Life as a machine profoundly informs this perspective. To the extent to which the world is knowable and directly fixable, this worldview is still totally appropriate and effective. It is when the world shifts on us and we still employ this metaphor that we will misread reality and risk grave errors of action. However, in this zone, the first umpire still reigns supreme; you can "call 'em as they are."

The metaphor also leads us to the core value for this zone, freedom to act. Life in this world is more than a set of causal relationships awaiting discovery; it is a "frictionless machine" that, by implication, should not be disturbed. Once we figure out the "laws of nature" we should let them play themselves out. Action is embodied in nature itself, and our leadership challenge is to master the laws of nature and act within them. When you hear someone say, "Do not let your emotions interfere with what is going on. Be objective; do a cost-benefit analysis," you are witnessing this metaphor at work.

Once we understand the mechanisms of any science and the laws that govern them, we can fix broken parts. Figure out the causes and take appropriate action. As Berman suggests, this mechanical view gave rise to behavioral psychology, popularized in the work of B. F. Skinner and theories like behavior modification and operant conditioning. The current research on tissue engineering thrives in this zone. Bones and cartilage can be grown in your own body to replace damaged parts. The microeconomics advocated by Adam Smith are also located in this worldview. The linear laws of supply and demand, market forces, and the invisible hand all lodge here. The belief in the power of a free market, one that operates on individual free choice, with minimal governmental intervention, still informs and guides much of economic theory worldwide. To be free in this view is to be free to live the laws of nature. Hence a free market embodies the laws of economics and we violate them at our peril. However, if we understand them and act within them, we can shape the world in conformity to them.

Organizationally, an emphasis on technical rational approaches, specialization, piecework, and time management evidences that a mechanical, logical worldview is dominant. Effectiveness is not on the radar screen; efficiency is paramount. The belief is that by focusing on each part the whole will take care of itself. The "invisible hand" is at work.

The shift to machine imagery to describe the world had a tremendous impact, one we still live with today. Aristotle distinguished four causes of action—formal, material, efficient, and final—declaring that each was central to understanding what was really going on. If you want to understand what a flag is, for example, you need to answer four questions: What is it? A flag is a symbol (a formal definition). Of what is it made? Cloth (materials). By what agent was it made? The skilled craftsperson (efficient maker). And for what end was it made? National pride (the final cause). All four questions had to be answered to grasp any situation fully.

The Enlightenment, the eighteenth-century turn to rationalism, concentrated on two of the four causes: material and efficient. Final causes are not subject to science in the sense that science has not been able to figure out the reason or significance of nature nor explain where it is heading. Nevertheless, although it is not sufficient as an explanation, it is necessarily sufficient. Advances in physics and chemistry as well as biology and the social sciences have catapulted human knowledge into hitherto unmapped spaces. A new knowledge base and new details about our world open the possibility of brilliant breakthroughs of knowledge and imaginative corrective actions. Zone 2 is a foundation worthy of serious respect because it seeks to answer questions hitherto unasked and unexamined. (For an in-depth review of the scientific perspective, see Wilson, 1998.)

APPLICATION

In Zone 2, *leader* equals *leadership*. This means that when a practitioner masters his or her subject matter and becomes a "leading expert," he or she acquires the skills necessary to deliver a superior product or service and thus lead the organization to achieve success. Hence in this zone we look for skills matched to prescribed subject matters. The line judge I met had appropriate skills.

When my son Steven asked me to spend a weekend helping him build a big deck on the back of his house, saying, "We can get a book and figure it out," I hedged, "Well, let's get together and think this through." Then I went off to conduct a retreat and seminar where I had the good fortune to meet Jeff Martin, a plant supervisor who in his off-time was a carpenter. I quizzed him intently about his skills and experience. Being satisfied, to say nothing of desperate, I hired him on the spot. We built the deck—eighty feet long and a twenty-foot wraparound—for $10,000. It was beautiful, and Steven's home increased in value by $30,000. The appraiser had never seen such a huge deck on such a small house! Jeff was our leader. He guided us through the process. Together, we did it. Without Jeff we would never have known what to do, books or no books.

In this zone, Serving the Past is not the issue. Steven's and my history were not in question or problematic. What one does with history and one's gifts constitutes the challenge in this zone. That challenge is conquered with schooling, training, and practice. To become a nurse, doctor, plumber, farmer, parent, teacher, police officer, pilot, lawyer, computer expert, hairdresser, or whatever, one must learn the skills necessary to accomplish the tasks of one's profession.

Personal Skill Building

Thousands of programs across the nation and around the globe sponsor and teach leadership skills. Often the skills, such as listening, conflict management, speaking, and goal-setting/strategic planning, fit other zones. In Zone 2, the critical skills are tied directly to tasks in the workplace. Leadership focuses on the skills required to excel in the job at hand. Thus if a leader lacks certain skills to get the job done, this zone takes over. The leadership key ties skills to task accomplishment, not just skills in general for leadership in general.

For example, every professional group has its list of essential competencies and then lists of additional competencies belonging to specialties within the main specialty. Leadership skills in this zone, rooted in the mechanical metaphor, are often referred to as "hard" or "soft." Hard describes technical content; soft refers to managing people. Disciplines are also often categorized as hard and soft, depending on whether their content is primarily targeted to material or social sciences. Chemistry and physics are seen as hard sciences, sociology and anthropology as soft. Economics wants to be hard but is often viewed as soft. Zone 2 emphasizes "hard" skills. As we shall see, "soft" skills flourish in the next zone.

Excel at your skills; ignore the frills is the motto in this zone. A person in this zone may know that other parts of the organization are functioning well or poorly. He or she is preoccupied with personal expertise and his or her own piece of the organizational enterprise. The goal is to be competent, to be the best one can be, so that one might be upwardly mobile and eventually become *the leadership* of the organization. The challenge is to turn one's potential capacity into actual delivery.

Organizational Skill Building

What do organizations look like in this zone? In the 1940s and 1950s many organizations worked in Zone 2 and considered it sufficient. Now we can see more clearly that organizations need an immensely broader focus. Looking briefly at the practices of the 1940s and 1950s can show us both some of the zone's contributions and some of the difficulties that led to the discovery that it was inadequate by itself.

The key to efficiency, it was believed at the time, was specialized, functional separation. Experts were housed with their own kindred in order to maximize accumulated, tightly focused knowledge and skills. Founded on principles made famous by Henry Ford, the U.S. auto industry was a classic case in point. The design group created the initial car concept. Once developed and portrayed in a clay model, the specifications were handed off to the engineering group. After months of review, the plans were returned to the design group with serious questions about the practicality and workability of the concept. After months of negotiating, the agreed-on plan was handed off to marketing and advertising for their expert review. This process of handing off to different groups of experts continued until final approval was given at the top and assembly line production equipment was designed, manufactured, and set in motion. Then the workers labored to assemble the parts into a car. Each laborer was challenged to be competent in a particular part of the assembly process, with no say about how the work or work processes could be improved. Technical improvements came from the "real" experts. How long do you think it took to move a car from concept to customer? It took anywhere from six to seven years.

Companies focused on numbers that allowed them to compare workers' performances, compare managers' performances, manage production and delivery more and more efficiently, run multiple product lines with their own markets, analyze tasks in terms of time and motion, and so on. Art Kleiner (1996), drawing on the medievalist Jeffrey Burton, saw this emphasis on numbers as a kind of *magic*: that is, as "a system of practice, uncanny to those who don't understand it, that attempts to manage, instead of simply accepting, the forces that shape human life" (p. 8). Indeed, "the everyday rituals of financial analysis and control used in large corporations were so effective at managing life on a large scale, and so impenetrable to outsiders, that in any other age the wielders of the numbers would have been known as sorcerers or priests" (p. 9).

Kleiner thinks the most important component in the magic was the concept of *return on investment*. Donaldson Brown, working closely with Alfred Sloan, the brilliant and practical CEO of General Motors, "hit upon a way of analyzing any business action according to the rate of return on the money invested in it" (p. 10). With this formula in hand, parts of an organization could remain separate yet still held together by financial accounting. "By applying a little numerical sophistication, managers could treat human effort, capital, and knowledge as commodities and see how those commodities would decrease or increase over time—on the scale of a community, a continent, or a civilization" (p. 11). Finance and accounting knowledge and skills remain important for leadership in this zone.

Today companies must focus on many additional forms of leadership. There are at least four ways in which Zone 2 is still critical. First, Zone 2 leadership works in a relatively stable environment with tight agreement on direction and high certainty of outcome. An operating room, for example, is a classic arena for expert task mastery. And thank goodness for it. Accounting firms, law firms, and banks are frequently organized by specialties of expertise—healthcare law or a special loan portfolio, for example. This specialization focus becomes problematic only when the world shifts. I worked with a 150-person law firm that contains fourteen separate law practices under one roof. For years this division approach worked exceedingly well. Now people are experiencing stirrings. They are wondering: Is the attention to each part sufficient to build the whole? Is the world of customers shifting so that the technical expertise model, while essential, is not enough?

Second, without leadership that builds the skills, the other zones cannot deliver any product or service. Experts are needed to construct the technical base for others to build upon. Having an idea is not the same as making it work in the real world.

Third, clarity of task and skill in a clearly defined bureaucracy that is stable and trustworthy can build character in the workforce. Richard Sennett (1998) worries that the new workplace with its emphasis on reinventing and reengineering is eroding the center of character of many workers. Traditional meaning is being lost in a relativism of opportunities and options. Comparing the stories of two workers, father and son, Sennett observed that although the son was much better off financially than the father, he seemed adrift in a work environment that lacked consistency.

And fourth, getting results is still often the ultimate criterion for success. Get the numbers and you get promotions. Such preoccupation with results does not necessarily attend to character, either. Ethical integrity is not the center of attention in this zone. In this zone, leadership can be both ethical and unethical: the real issue is results. That is the final arbiter of value.

Never discount technical competency. In this zone, skills are targeted to specific tasks and occupations. Leadership basically means stretching the skills of whatever your focus is. The search for causal connections in the universe is already revealing exciting information. I am hoping the physicists succeed in understanding and explaining the laws of nature. Let us hope medical researchers discover the causes of cancer and other killers. I want them to succeed, like those who figured out the cause of polio.

Successful executives build skills in the organization. In this zone, one can figure out the numbers and do whatever it takes to win. Be objective and dispassionate, and do not link to employees personally since you may have to fire them. Keep your distance to enable critical thought and hard decisions. Business growth has priority, competitive reality sets the context, and ecological issues are secondary to building the firm and dominating the industry. Leadership is about being the best, the first, the winner in whatever forum you are in. Do not let feelings interfere with your judgments. Be rational, efficient, and do your cost-benefit analysis. Match skills to the way the world works.

In the 1940s and 1950s, people skills, or "soft" skills as referred to in this zone, were not considered core competencies. At best, they were add-ons to the real work in plants and offices. However, the list of the skills that count as elements of competencies continues to expand. Today, for example, Valspar, a paint manufacturer, is seeking a total review of core competencies, triggered by the CEO's observation that workers were talking while he was giving speeches. He found out that they were translating his speech for people in the workforce who did not understand English. In an information-based society, more than technical skills is required. The CEO ostensibly acted to test core compentencies to check their adequacy and importance. The realization that personal and social skills are important is just down the street. Building Core Competencies expands its content over time.

Hiring and Retaining Competent People

This zone loves hard numbers that lead to expected results. The Gallup organization surveyed 80,000 managers to figure out what the world's greatest managers do differently to succeed. From the interviews, records, and reports from employees, Buckingham and Coffman identified twelve questions that measure the core elements needed to attract, focus, and keep the most productive employees. Their research revealed that most employees leave their jobs because of poor supervision or lack of promotion, not pay, unless the company as a whole underpays dramatically.

Here are the questions (Buckingham and Coffman, 1999, p. 28):

- Do I know what is expected of me at work?

- Do I have the materials and equipment I need to do my work right?

- At work, do I have the opportunity to do what I do best every day?

- In the last seven days, have I received recognition or praise for doing good work?

- Does my supervisor, or someone at work, seem to care about me as a person?

- Is there someone at work who encourages my development?

- At work, do my opinions seem to count?

- Does the mission/purpose of my company make me feel my job is important?

- Are my coworkers committed to doing quality work?

- Do I have a best friend at work?

- In the last six months, has someone at work talked to me about my progress?

- This last year, have I had opportunity at work to learn and grow?

After extensive interviews and assessment, the authors captured the essence of their research and reflections in four themes (Buckingham and Coffman, 1999, p. 67):

- When selecting someone, they select for talent . . . not simply experience, intelligence, or determination.

- When setting expectations, they define the right outcomes . . . not the right steps.

- When motivating someone, they focus on strengths . . . not on weaknesses.

- When developing someone, they help him find the right fit . . . not simply the next rung on the ladder.

Talent roots in part in Zone 1; we have natural gifts we bring to the table. Leadership identifies and releases these talents by matching them to jobs. This is an important study, a brick for this zone, worthy of reading and reflection.

ZONE IDENTIFICATION AND
LEADERSHIP QUESTIONS

To assess whether you have an actual or potential set of targeted competency issues in your organization or for yourself now or in the future, answer these questions:

1. How sturdy is my organization or community in this zone?

    • Do we have:

      the right people?

      in the right jobs?

      doing the right tasks?

      at the right time?

      living the core values?

      with the right talents, skills, and information?

      for the right pay and perks?

      getting the job done consistently, efficiently, and reliably?

      managed by the right managers who focus on talent, outcomes, strengths, and fit?

    • Is the financial plan on track according to plan and projections? What are the real numbers?

    • What are the general core competencies and talents that ensure we can deliver products or services reliably and meet appropriate standards?

    • What are the specialized core competencies that provide us market uniqueness and advantage?

    • Are there skill mastery training programs for both workers and managers?

```
10 |  |  |  |  |  |  |  |  |  |  0  |  |  |  |  |  |  |  |  | 10
Very Sturdy                                              Shaky
```

2. Where is my organization or community currently focusing its leadership attention?

    • Are other zones getting more attention than this one?

    • Is this the zone that needs direct attention?

```
10 |  |  |  |  |  |  |  |  |  | 0 |  |  |  |  |  |  |  |  | 10
Excellent Fit                                              Misfit
```

3. Am I prepared to build core competencies?

   • Am I:

      the right person?

      in the right job?

      doing the right tasks?

      at the right time?

      living the core values?

      with the right talents, skills, and information?

      for the right pay and perks?

      getting the job done consistently, efficiently, and reliably?

      managed by the right managers who focus on talent, outcomes, strengths, and fit?

   • What are my skill-acquisition challenges?

   • Do I understand the economics of the business?

   • Am I ready to be promoted/elected/assigned to the next task?

```
10 |  |  |  |  |  |  |  |  |  | 0 |  |  |  |  |  |  |  |  | 10
Ready to Exhibit Leadership                    Not Prepared at All
```

ZONE SUMMARY

Zone 2 is all about efficiency. The world is knowable through science and fixable by talented and competent practitioners. Leadership applies specific skills to tough issues and presses for breakthroughs.

The sign of success is consistency. How do we know that we know how the world works? We know when the tests and experiments that we conduct consistently reproduce the same results. Goals and social significance are epiphenomenal to the real work at hand. Master the facts and causal principles, the material and efficient causes of action. Values and missions are not the subject matter except as they affect what is really going on. Science cannot recommend values other than the freedom of inquiry that follows the rigorous rules of scientific inquiry.

In business, economics is the guiding science. We master the numbers by knowing how the world of economics operates. The theory of supply and demand, and all that follows from it, captures reality. Not to understand it and possess the skills to implement it threatens success. Competition is the name of the game.

In this zone, leadership needs the technical skills of the particular discipline or subject matter being mastered, finance and accounting knowledge and skills, skills to assess the consistency of service or product quality, and project management skills.

The guiding metaphor—*life is a machine*—matches a world that is knowable and fixable. A fix-it mentality rules Zone 2. If something is broken, take it apart and repair it, whether the malfunction is in the body, the psyche, the economy, or the culture. The core value is freedom of choice within the rules of the subject matter. Just as an object (such as a marble) can fall freely, so too can people, organizations, and nation-states be free as long as they obey natural laws germane to their action arena. One can break all the rules if the rules do not match deep research into what really works.

The polarity implicit in this zone moves us between potential and actual. Both human beings and the physical universe possess great potential. New things are being understood and created all the time. They are brought into actuality by the skills—both mental and physical—that translate theory into practice. People have long dreamed of going to the moon. The breakthroughs in physics by Newton and many others gave us the means to do it. Leadership linked to science turns ignorance into productive action. Authenticity in this zone is the consistent application of disciplined thinking to address, understand, and, where possible, solve seemingly insurmountable puzzles.

ZONE 2 DEFINITIONS

Leadership: Building Core Competencies
Authenticity criterion: Consistency
Metaphor: Life is a machine
Core ethical principle: Freedom to act
Polarity: Potential/actual

STIRRINGS

In the 1950s and 1960s, we in the United States witnessed the questioning of the dominance of a mechanistic worldview. What had been justified for its wonder-works as an industrial-revolution driver began to be doubted. Stirrings were intensifying. They eventually gave rise to organizational development, worker participation, the social movements of the 1970s, and a fundamental shift in metaphor and practice that responded to the new science and opened ecological sensibility. It also set the new platform for the "re-" age of the 1980s and 1990s—reinventing, restructuring, reengineering.

Organizationally, the tide turned when preoccupation with the numbers and the isolated mechanical functioning of the organization was seen as creating difficulties. Then effectiveness became the judge of efficiency. Consistency was not enough to match the organization with the world. A sense of coherence, a different experience, was what people longed for. Parts functioning alone were dysfunctional; connectedness was emerging as the new map for authentic action. Positive stirrings began to surface, and technical rationality was under siege.

Negative Stirrings

I am sick and tired of arrogance. We have too many experts, all isolated in their own narrow areas of expertise, or silos, not talking to each other. We are great at getting the product made. We are terrible at helping each other do even better. Walls are too high here. Mistrust fills the room, too. Different groups have their own language, styles, and beliefs. No wonder no one talks to anyone outside his or her narrow discipline.

I remember when John went to Alice for help on a project. Alice said she didn't have time to discuss it. She had no interest in helping John. John was offended and got very angry. Alice didn't even realize that John's project had impact on Alice's work. She was too self-centered to pay attention.

The other thing I realized was that the whole organization was rigged for a silo mentality. Pay, performance, productivity were all linked to one's department or function. There is no sense of connection. Everyone wants to be free to do their own work with their own tools and skills. What a mess! We are in the same organization and deny it every day at work. Two departments are even in separate buildings with different legal mandates and directions. Yet, we are in one organization. Does that really mean anything? Does the whole add any value to the parts? Or have we misspelled "whole"? We act like the "whole" is a "hole"!

I saw two leadership books the other day. One was titled *The 9 Natural Laws of Leadership*. The other was *The Leadership Machine*. What a mechanical view. I thought we were in 2001, not 1901.

Positive Stirrings

I agree, we are disconnected. We are great at consistent delivery of services and terrible at coordinating our actions for the benefit of all of us and, even more importantly, for the benefit of the customer. I met with a customer yesterday who loves our capacity for problem solving. Yet he couldn't stand our push to control everything and just get the work done. The customer was essentially ignored—not listened to, affirmed, or appreciated.

We are ready for a change. The customers are leaving us or, at least, are frustrated with us. There is a push in the market to be customer friendly. We can improve our people skills. They are not soft; they are hard. Hard to learn and hard to do, given our history. Maybe we need some new hiring standards so we can relate better with each other. Our systems separate us. Not only do we need integrative systems, we must figure out how such systems work so we can design and build them. I have worked in an organization that faced our problem. The leadership of the firm took on the issue and it worked. Now the people who represent different functions actually meet and talk to each other in a safe environment. I was in one meeting where the executive group came together and coached each other. What a delight!

I'm not alone in this. I talk to many workers who are weary of the isolation and are eager to connect. They are tired of being blamed for problems when the real problem is system dysfunction. Not only that, we need some restructuring. I worry that our infrastructure is poorly designed. If we are going to connect, we will need some fresh rules of engagement. Maybe a personnel manual would be effective. Since I am a new executive, I now see the next leadership challenge. We have to design systems for effective organizational work. The customer will be very central. So will our attention to employees.

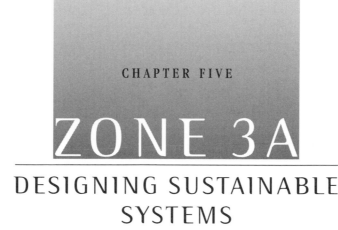

CHAPTER FIVE

ZONE 3A

DESIGNING SUSTAINABLE SYSTEMS

Leadership in Zone 3 concerns systems thinking; it concentrates on structure. The metaphor now shifts from mechanical to organic. Life is no longer seen as a machine; it is now a body. The ideas in this zone fall into two subsets. Zone 3a, discussed in this chapter, focuses on the form or skeleton of the body. It introduces the concept of systems thinking that emerged in the 1950s. Much of organizational development leadership resides in this zone. Discussed in Chapter Six, Zone 3b stretches the systems model and attends to the dynamic parts or living systems of the body. The proponents of some of the newer disciplines in science build their houses in this territory. Concerns about identity, glue, membership, and stakeholders emerge.

CONNECT THE DOTS; DOWNPLAY THE SPOTS.

I wondered what was going to happen. I had never been to anything like this before. As I was driving along the highway it was difficult for me to imagine what it would be like to be with strangers for two weeks. I remember thinking that I would commit to being totally honest with the group and myself, naively thinking at the time that this would be relatively easy. I clearly recall experiencing feelings of anxiety and trepidation, and also excitement. The date: May 1967. The event: sensitivity training. The place: Bethel, Maine. Among other things, it was to be a lesson in connections, of individuals developing systems and becoming a body.

Our group gathered, and we sat on chairs in a circle. No one spoke. Then, after what seemed like an eternity, one woman commented that her husband had been through this process and we should begin by introducing ourselves and saying what we do. Three-fourths of the group worked in corporations. I was last. When it was my turn I said, "I'm Bob Terry and I work for the elimination of white racism."

There was a pause, then someone said, "I think we should discuss what racism is and get a better handle on what Bob does."

I said, "I don't want to do that. I did not come here to discuss racism or what I do."

Another pause. Then the woman who had initiated the discussion reported that her husband thought it was a good idea to sit on the floor for more intimate conversation. Everyone quickly stood up, moved chairs, and began finding a spot to sit on the floor.

I said, "I don't want to sit on the floor. It hurts my back and I need back support from a chair."

A pause. Already I had challenged the group twice by being honest.

So far we had no idea who our facilitator was. Although he was present, we did not know it. We fumbled along with no agenda or leader, trying to figure out what all this nondirection was about. Finally, our facilitator identified himself. Part of the point of the process was not to be led by others. Rather, it was to engage in the process. The group did lead itself in many ways. The facilitator helped from time to time. Over the two weeks we bonded. We intersected with each other's lives and revealed much about our own. In part because of the facilitator and in part in spite of him, we emerged as a group that waded into tough issues. One participant's revelations so scared us, we didn't know what to say or how to react. We were so honest that during the second week people from other groups came to watch us connect.

Essentially we organized ourselves and had a profound interpersonal experience. At the end we were all stunned at how far we had come in two weeks. We were no longer strangers. We had truly touched each other's souls. We never learned much about the facilitator, how he was selected, and what criteria were used. However, it made no difference.

CORE IDEAS

As the world shifts and becomes less certain in outcome, and more complex in terms of agreement on direction, the machine metaphor that is relevant for the Zone 2 world appears less relevant for the new situation. The stirrings of Zone 2 surface in Zone 3a with Designing Sustainable Systems and organizational development strategies. Figure 14, on the next page, places this zone on the map. Again, the current zone is fuzzy, while those we have just been through are much more clear in the light of experience.

A new metaphor emerges that challenges the material, technical, rational model. Life no longer looks like a machine; it is a body, a living organism. Historically speaking, many organizations found themselves undergoing this shift in their primary view of leadership in the 1950s and 1960s.

In Zone 3a, efficiency is no longer the prime benchmark. Effectiveness takes over as the standard of measurement. The magic of numbers is no longer the sole guide for corporate success. Leadership is system design. It builds systems that both get results and create relatively safe havens from the threats of newly perceived chaos. Stacey (1993) categorizes responses like these, responses to less certainty and agreement, as *bounded rationality*: "With all facts rarely known and interpreters of those facts rarely totally objective and dispassionate, we need another way. . . . [H]uman beings invented bureaucratic processes to short cut the time and energy required to make decisions" (p. 34).

Leadership builds these bureaucratic processes, orderly delivery systems that regularize the diversity of personal goals and experiences through rules, processes, and procedures. Connectedness becomes the measure of authenticity. Justice, in the form of fairness, replaces freedom to act as the core ethical principle. In Zone 3a, all the parts must be treated seriously and balanced in relation to their contribution to the whole. Here a solid infrastructure is pivotal.

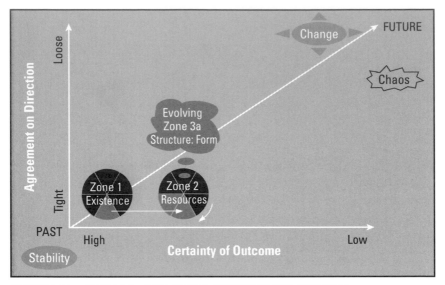

FIGURE 14 • ZONE 3A: DESIGNING SUSTAINABLE SYSTEMS

A new polarity manifests itself in this zone. No longer is the focus on stability/change of Zone 1 or potential/actual of Zone 2. Now the two dimensions are form/dynamic. Zone 3a highlights *form*, the skeleton of the body, while 3b will emphasize *dynamic*, the vitality of a living system. Lurking behind the everyday work in this zone is the commitment to create and manage systems that functionally integrate silos into healthy connections and to connect internal systems to external systems like customers and clients.

Before we examine systems more closely and explore Zone 3a, it will be helpful to look at leadership in this zone as it becomes positional leadership, and consider the work in organizational development that fueled the original emphasis on systems as they surfaced as critical to organizational life.

The Boss

In the 1950s and 1960s very little was known about the leadership of corporations. Stirrings of dissatisfaction were quietly shared among colleagues, and that dissatisfaction was not studied or assessed in terms of leadership. The perspective that leadership is positional was paramount and poorly understood. Then, in the late 1960s, Michael

Maccoby, a Harvard-educated American psychologist influenced by Eric Fromm and Ivan Illich, two advocates of a deep and expansive concept of the self in society and critics of the perceived corporate devastation of local culture, studied corporate positional leaders—corporate "winners." The revelations were astonishing.

Maccoby (1976) distinguished four types of leaders:

- *The craftsman.* This leader's focus is on the work ethic and task accomplishment. Some craftsmen are democratic; others, owing to their narrow focus and perfectionist tendencies, are authoritarian and ill equipped to lead a complex organization.

- *The jungle fighter.* This leader's focus is on power. Jungle fighters are either lions who conquer by empire building or foxes who win by stealth and politicking.

- *The company man.* This leader's focus is on belonging to a protective company. At best this leader is a people person; at worst, fearful and submissive.

- *The gamesman.* This leader's focus is on challenge, competitive activity, and winning. Life is a game to be played with delight, seriousness, and strategy. There is great pleasure in controlling the play.

The gamesman, Maccoby concluded, was best fitted to leading the organizational response to a changing world. Competition was intensifying, innovation was becoming more necessary to sustain a lead, the work of interdependent teams was becoming more important than task accomplishment by separate functions, and fast-moving flexibility was becoming essential for creating and leading a responsive system. Maccoby summarized the character and style of the gamesman this way:

> The modern gamesman is best defined as a person who loves change and wants to influence its course. He likes to take calculated risks and is fascinated by technique and new methods. He sees a developing project, human relations, and his own career in terms of options and possibilities, as if they were a game. His character is a collection of new paradoxes understood in terms of its adaptation to the organization requirements. He is cooperative but competitive; detached and playful but compulsively driven to succeed; a

team player but a would-be superstar; a team leader but often a rebel against bureaucratic hierarchy; fair and unprejudiced but contemptuous of weakness; tough and dominating but not destructive. Unlike other business types, he is energized to compete not because he wants to build an empire, not for riches, but rather for fame, glory, the exhilaration of running his team and of gaining victories. His main goal is to be known as a winner, and his deepest fear is to be labeled a loser. (p. 100)

In Zone 2, *leader* equals *leadership.* In Zone 3a, the leading executive, as head of the body, while often still the focus of attention, is not the key equation with *leader.* Leadership shifts to Designing Sustainable Systems in which executives and bosses can have oversight of and ultimate responsibility for designing and implementing effective systems.

Leadership now creates and shapes systems as stable platforms for action. Without solid formal structures, any dynamic interaction of the parts of the organization could quickly lead to chaos. At least that is the fear in this zone. Leadership concerns the boss not as an individual. Rather, it is his or her role of system designer and, as I discuss later, feedback receiver.

The gamesman is at work in a world of less certainty of outcome and less shared direction. Leading the whole, not a part, is key. It is not any particular spot that needs attention; connecting the dots in a system design is the order of the day.

Organizational Development

While positional leadership was becoming gamesmanship, the underground corporate reformers of the 1940s and 1950s were also quickly emerging. *Connect the dots; downplay the spots* was again the necessary motto if organizations were to reinforce rational task accomplishment *and* deal with the full person in a complex system. Consistency was insufficient as a criterion of authentic action. It was now being replaced with connectedness. The organizational parts had to work together, and it was the role of leadership to connect the parts. Systems thinking is still central today, although its roots go back to the work of Kurt Lewin in the late 1930s and 1940s. "Kurt Lewin was never a businessman, and yet the distinctions and methods he taught (and the institute he inspired, the National Training

Laboratory) have influenced thousands of organizations years after his death. Nearly every sincere effort to improve organizations from within can be traced back to him, often through a thicket of tangled, hidden influences" (Kleiner, 1996, p. 30). Organizational development (OD) researchers moved into organizations and sought to learn their realities from within. This was a new adventure. Out of this form of participatory research flowed the National Training Laboratory (sensitivity training), force field analysis (examination of the multiple influences on behavior), and the idea that leadership manifested itself in three basic types: autocratic, laissez-faire, and democratic. Challenging the individualism of American culture, these researchers and many other reformers learned that the structure of a group determines the character of its members as much as the members shape group values (Kleiner, p. 32).

T-Groups, or sensitivity-training sessions, thrived as participants learned that a safe and welcoming setting could release marvelous human potential. Group-process facilitation quickly surfaced as a desired skill. The most skilled facilitators became OD consultants. As the movement gained momentum, all kinds of team-building seminars were conducted nationwide. With OD thriving as practitioners conducted organizational surveys and sought ways for the parts of organizations to come together, intellectual foundations for practice were also being constructed. Talcott Parsons, then head of the sociology department at Harvard, produced massive texts on systems thinking. John Kenneth Galbraith argued for institutional economics. Family-system therapy entered the scene and challenged the traditional focus on the individual.

A massive metaphorical transformation was upon us. People in the 1940s and 1950s began saying that life is a body, not a machine. It is inappropriate for the parts of anything to act freely, and not to recognize the deep connection to the whole. Human beings are not rational calculators; they are centers of feeling and "family" linkage, all related in one system.

Defining a System

What, then, is a system? Draper Kauffman (1980) authored the best introduction to systems thinking of which I am aware. Systems thinking is, as we have seen, distinguished from the approach that breaks reality into analyzable parts (which, carried to the extreme, results in reductionism). For example,

> The difference . . . between the molecules in a mouse and those in a test tube full of chemicals is *organization*. The molecules in a mouse are organized in a precise and complex way, while those in the test tube are just sloshed together. Most scientists, in the 19th and early 20th centuries, realized that it was important to understand how the pieces fit together, at least in their own field, but they were still mostly concerned about the "parts" rather than about the "pattern." (Kauffman, 1980, p. 1)

A system, then, is a "collection of parts which interact with each other to function as a whole" (Kauffman, 1980, p. 1). It is not a heap of "stuff." Rather, it is the behavior that results from the whole shaping the parts. In the case of systems, the whole is greater than the sum of its parts. Moreover, adding parts to or subtracting parts from this whole does not necessarily change the whole. If you add or take away milk from a pail, the amount of milk has been changed, not the nature of the milk. Add a cow and you do not get a larger cow; divide a cow in half and you do not get two smaller cows. "You may end up with a lot of hamburger, but the essential nature of 'cow'—a living system capable, among other things, of turning grass into milk—would be lost," writes Kauffman (p. 2).

Moreover, any system can be a subsystem of a larger system since all systems are connected, although each has its own organizing center. A buffalo leads the herd; the herd follows wherever the lead buffalo takes it. If we are studying the dynamics of the herd, the herd becomes the system and the lead buffalo and followers become subsystems.

Peter Senge's work is housed mainly in Zones 3a and 3b. His book *The Fifth Discipline* is rife with systems examples and instruction. His bricks are excellent building blocks for the zone map of leadership, helping us see the kind of productive system the whole organization can be. Perhaps his most enduring contribution to organizational self-understanding in this zone is his concept of the *learning organization*. The term is now commonplace in organizational vocabulary. The organic metaphor is pivotal in this image of the organization as a system designed for internal growth. Senge writes,

At its heart, the traditional view of leadership is based on assumptions of people's powerlessness, their lack of personal vision and inability to master the forces of change, deficits which can be remedied only by a few great leaders.

The new view of leadership in learning organizations centers on subtler and more important tasks. In a learning organization, leaders are designers, stewards, and teachers. They are responsible for *building organizations* where people continually expand their capabilities to understand complexity, clarify vision, and improve shared mental models—that is, they are responsible for learning. (p. 340)

Then he invites us to consider an organization as an ocean liner. The leadership role on this liner goes beyond captain, navigator, helmsman, and engineer. There is another leadership role that is often neglected, "the *designer* of the ship":

No one has a more sweeping influence than the designer. What good does it do the captain to say, "Turn starboard thirty degrees," when the designer has built a rudder that will turn only to port, or which takes six hours to turn to starboard? It's fruitless to be the leader in an organization that is poorly designed. Isn't it interesting that so few managers think of the ship's designer when they think of the leader's role?

Although *"leader as designer"* is neglected today, it touches a chord that goes back thousands of years. To paraphrase Lao-tzu, the bad leader is he who the people despise. The good leader is he who the people praise. The great leader is he who the people say, "We did it ourselves." (p. 341)

System Stability

Leadership in this zone focuses more on orderly system function and less on system dynamics. That is why the fact that the design of the system platform, or skeleton, can often hold the key to change often goes unnoticed in this zone. Senge makes an analogy with a ship's "trim tab." This device is a small "rudder on the rudder" that, when turned, allows the bigger rudder to be turned much more easily and thus allows a ship to be turned more easily. Who knows about the trim tab? Hardly anyone. It is not obvious. This lack of obviousness is also true in system change. Cause and effect may be far apart and not easily connected in people's thought and action (pp. 64–65).

Many perspectives are required to grasp the larger picture in Zone 3a. The second umpire knows about this.

When asked to think of a trim-tab example, a nurse told me this story: She had been raised in a home of construction builders. She was a master carpenter and could have built a deck or a house. Recently she had received a grant to construct a mobile dentistry office so that dental services could be delivered to poor neighborhoods. In the refurbishing of the truck that would carry the dental office, she noticed the three male carpenters were making decisions that conflicted with what she wanted. She talked to them, outlining her goals and requirements. They ignored her advice and continued doing what they wanted. The nurse faced a choice—challenge the men, confronting them about their male chauvinism, or figure out another way to get her goals accomplished. She knew she would not work with these three carpenters again and time was getting short to complete the task. She developed a trim-tab strategy. She talked to the dentist who would be working in the portable dental clinic. He knew nothing about carpentry; nevertheless, she gave him her list of goals and walked him through the significance of them. His job was to talk to the carpenters as if the list were his. He did. The carpenters said they appreciated his advice and they had not heard these suggestions before. They did just what the nurse wanted.

Some people do not like this story. The behavior is manipulative, crafty, and inauthentic. The woman refuses to punish the chauvinistic men. She had a systems choice—take on the resistance directly or maneuver it. Obviously she chose the latter.

In this zone, ethics is not paramount. The authenticity standard is connectedness, confirmed by her action. She understood the system connections, and this was authentic in this zone. Within a different zone, her actions might have been questionable. Not from here.

Systems thinking 1960s-style stressed the natural stabilizing of the parts into a workable and sustainable whole. Systems have a propensity for equilibrium, and system design in this zone tends to capitalize on it. The mechanism by which this equilibrium is maintained is known as a *negative feedback loop*. Kauffman (1980) explains it through an analogy with riding a bike.

> To ride a bike properly, you need information about where the bicycle is and which way it is tilting, information you get from your eyes, your muscles, and the balance tubes in your ears. Without a

continuous flow of this information, you would find it difficult—if not impossible—to ride the bicycle at all. . . .

In other words, your brain tells your muscles what to do, your muscles push against the bicycle, and the bicycle responds by moving. The "input" is the information you had which caused you to decide to use your muscles the way you did, and the "output" of the system is the motion of the bicycle and yourself. But now, after you start the system moving, there's a new situation and a new position for the bicycle, which provides new information for your brain to work with. . . .

[The] information about the *output* of the system is *fed back* around to the input side of the system. Information that is used this way is called *"feedback,"* and any system . . . is called a "feedback loop."

Can you see now how this feedback provides stability in a system that would otherwise be unstable? Your brain receives information about where the bicycle is and compares that with where the bicycle *should* be. If there is a difference between the two for any reason—whether it's because you made a slight error or because the environment has changed—your brain tells your muscles what you did and the "output" of the action is eliminated, thus bringing the system back on course. Because this kind of system acts to cancel out or "negate" any changes in the system, it is called a negative feedback loop. This idea of negative feedback seems simple but it is extremely important for understanding the systems in our environment. (p. 5)

Negative, of course, does not infer criticism or evaluation of the feedback. The term is used, as Kauffman says, simply to describe a process that nullifies changes or disturbances in a system. In Zone 3a, system stability takes precedence over dynamic, over progressive movement, and form commands more attention than process. In Zone 3b, a positive feedback loop will become more important as leadership aims for creativity and system change to respond to increasing complexity in the world.

APPLICATION

What does Designing Sustainable Systems look like in practice, especially if we omit for the moment Senge's vision of the learning organization? Stacey (1993) summarizes the stage this way:

As managers act together, they develop rules of action and standard operating procedures in order to cut down on the need to make decisions afresh each time. Precedents are established and subsequent decisions are taken without having to repeat the search process anew. Decisions and actions come to be outputs of standard patterns of behavior. For example, next year's budget is often determined largely by updating this year's spending. (p. 34)

In Zone 3a, leadership uses roles and rules to reduce the anxiety and challenges that arise from uncertainty of outcome and agreement. Think of the comfort that comes from job definitions, personnel manuals, and organization charts, from knowing your job responsibilities and how they connect with the work of others. System designers avoid rigid functional silos and narrow foci of work and discipline because they limit the flexibility and adaptability of a system and thus its ability to respond quickly to secure market share. They look at both the system formed by the organization as a whole and all the subsystems that must function well to benefit the whole. Dysfunctionality, things behaving in ways that we do not expect them to, angers and threatens us and upsets our plans wherever it occurs in our personal lives, our organizations, and our societies. It is then comforting to have means of working toward agreement and certainty in a potentially chaotic world.

In this zone, consultants are often hired to enhance organizational functionality. Leadership ensures that organizational units conduct regular needs assessments. Worker surveys supply feedback about the successes and difficulties encountered in building and leading effective systems. Executives and middle-level managers build teams to enhance organizational performance. During the 1960s, executives who attended sensitivity training introduced to the workforce the ideas and practices they learned. People skills have now been added to technical skills to enhance performance in the competitive game. Whatever is needed to be effective and to win is introduced, usually from the top down.

The goal is to win; the means are negotiable. Power is handled through deliberate small-step decision-making processes directed and orchestrated from the top. A diversity of interests and voices are heard. However, if no consensus emerges at lower levels, decisions roll up to the boss. He or she makes the final judgment call. Veto power is never surrendered.

In the following sections, I discuss in more detail a selection of the things leadership concerns itself with in Zone 3a: developing a model of systems thinking, the teaching of systems thinking, instituting a quality program, reorganizing and conducting mergers, building teams, and carrying out effective hiring.

A Workable Organizational Model of Systems Thinking

Leadership needs a system for systems thinking. Consider, for example, the comprehensive model Bruce Gibb has constructed. Gibb is an organizational psychologist who has assisted the Ford Motor Company in creating and constructing new manufacturing plants around the world. I will return to his work in greater depth in Zones 3b and 4. For now, let us examine his model, from which leadership could quickly develop a checklist to assess the health of any organization's operations. This model divides the organization into eight subsystems (Gibb, 1997, pp. 5–10), as shown in Figure 15.

1. *Culture, climate, and relationships subsystem.* This is the fundamental intellectual and value framework of the organization: its beliefs, values, language, and a definition of what it does and how it works. Culture includes styles of behavior, speech, and dress, the actual and desired attitudes of personnel and departments, the social and emotional climate, and rituals and celebrations. Culture sets the meaning context for all the rest of the subsystems.

2. *Direction subsystem.* This system focuses on the organizational mission, formal and informal charter, and customers, and on what it commits itself to deliver. This subsystem also includes the strategic vision, goals, and issues of alignment.

3. *Work structure and process subsystem.* This organizational function includes all the processes that take resources and turn them into products and services for customers. Issues of efficiency and quality demand attention here.

4. *Management and leadership subsystem.* This subsystem addresses the ideal and actual structure and operation of the authority roles and responsibilities. This is not the information system. It does not concern organizational data but rather the communication and decision-making processes.

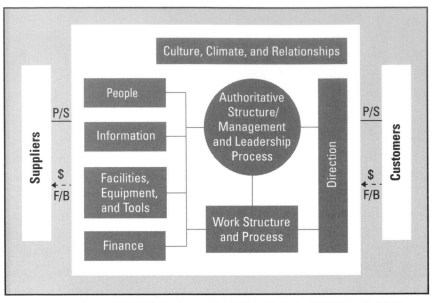

FIGURE 15 • SUBSYSTEMS IN AN ORGANIZATIONAL SYSTEMS MODEL
Note: P/S stands for product or service; F/B stands for feedback.
Source: Gibb, 1997, p. 8. Reprinted with permission.

5. *People subsystem.* This refers to the people and teams who run the system as well as quasi members such as on-site government regulators, customer representatives, and union officials.

6. *Information subsystem.* This covers all the data, documents, and pieces of information vital to the operation of the organization. The range of data includes blueprints, role definitions, surveys, and so on.

7. *Facilities and equipment subsystem.* This subsystem inventories all the physical assets of the organization, from roads and buildings to production and office equipment and even personnel uniforms.

8. *Financial subsystem.* This subsystem incorporates the processes for acquiring, storing, accounting for, and disbursing financial instruments, currency, checks, stocks, and so on.

The organization as a subsystem lives between the suppliers and the customers, interacting regularly.

Gibb also understands and appreciates the profundity of the shift in metaphor from machine to body to describe how things really are.

He captures the idea clearly in the following contrast of the two views:

From Machine Thinking	To Systems Thinking
Control	Commitment
Narrowly defined jobs	Internal customer-supplier contacts
Functional specialties	Multifunctional teams
Employees expendable	People are creative resources
External control of people	Autonomy and self-control
Information based on "need to know"	Information available to all
Control people and costs.	**Control processes and products.**

The value of Gibb's model is its functional clarity. Essential functions are identified and their importance and interaction are clearly specified.

Teaching Systems Thinking

In this zone, leadership teaches systems thinking across the organization. One teaching exercise I use in seminars to make the systems point is to ask participants to identify all the systems that have to work well for them to get from the meeting room to their home. One Department of Health employee began with the body's many systems and moved out from there. In the two minutes allotted for the exercise, her group came up with thirty or so systems. I tell participants the real count is in the billions when, for example, one considers each bolt in the car they will be riding in. The exercise makes the point: complex systems with many subsystems function all around us without our being aware of them—until one falters.

No tight, technical, rational approach can work in a multiple-system organization or world. There are too many players in the game. The situations are too complex. At best, we can try to regularize behaviors to get the desired results. Having a procedures manual is only a small part of the system.

The Six-Sigma Quality Program

One of my clients failed to deliver a product of reliable quality to its customer. The CEO was convinced that to stay competitive, a quality program had to be installed and routinized. Productivity was ruled by inefficiency; waste and errors were too great. This company's experience illustrates some pluses and minuses that Zone 3a (and 3b) leadership may have to deal with in working with quality programs, a major focus in this zone.

The organization chose the Six-Sigma quality program, "an integrated process improvement system that rests on known statistical tools. . . . As a metric, Six-Sigma refers to 3.4 defects per million opportunities for a product or process to fail. Most U.S. business processes perform at 2 or 3 Sigma" (Buckman, 1999, p. D5). The goal is to reach Six-Sigma. For many managers, it is frightening to enter this realm of precision. Yet market share may be at stake.

The formal leadership rested in the CEO and a designated manager who handled the training and implementation. Measurement criteria were created, trainers trained, programs implemented. The organization made great headway and achieved Baldridge National Quality Award status. However, one unintended result was a drop in creativity and a false sense of managerial effectiveness. Three of the heroes of the process were later terminated for ineffective organizational leadership.

This suggests some of the complexity issues leadership will face in implementing thoroughgoing quality programs. Programs like Six-Sigma that focus on systems click into being when there is system breakdown or lack of efficiency. In some ways they touch back to Zone 2, with its competency-training components. However, they are systems approaches to eliminating errors. Workers are not seen as the problem in these programs; it is the system that is not functioning properly. Some see Six-Sigma as revolutionary, slashing trillions of dollars from corporate inefficiency. Larry Bossidy, CEO of Allied Signal, and Jack Welch, chairman of General Electric, are both avid believers in its positive impact on profitability. "Nobody gets promoted to an executive position at GE without Six-Sigma training," and supposedly it will save the company billions by the time Welch retires. It is supposed to have been the key factor in Allied Signal's discovery of "a way to clean dirt, oil and stains from old carpet so that 100 million pounds will be recycled back into new rugs rather than dumped into landfills. . . . [This is] more than an environmental success. It will keep the company from having to build an $85 million plant to fill increasing demand for caperolactan used to make nylon, a total savings of $30–$50 million a year" (Jones, 1999, p. 2B). It is no accident that the new CEO of 3M, coming from GE, is installing Six-Sigma in 3M today.

Others see Six-Sigma as destroying creativity and as keeping frontline workers too busy collecting information to get their jobs done. It is expensive to implement and requires a rigorous approach to enforcement. It requires strong executive sponsors. It is not a cure-all. Motorola, the corporate founder of Six-Sigma, stumbled as the world shifted in unpredictable ways. The process does not predict external events. It is internally focused. Some think it is a marketing ploy to publicize quality commitment to the customers. The best numbers can be made public and other numbers kept private. In the latter case it might be difficult to make an empirical case for further investment.

If you are considering a major investment of time, capital, and worker energy in a quality program, check with practitioners who have used it, both those who experience success with it and those who have experienced failure. Work to ensure that the philosophy of quality becomes as important throughout the company as the implementation of techniques. (I discuss the quality movement in general in Zone 3b.)

Reorganizing and Conducting Mergers

Reorganizing is often a Zone 3a activity. In such an endeavor, make sure the infrastructure appropriately defines roles and responsibilities and provides the proper core value foundation to permit the reorganized system to prosper. Also make sure reorganization is not a code word for concentrating power at the top. Decisiveness in reorganizing is critical, but as a means, not an end.

Mergers often stimulate a Zone 3a reaction as leadership restructures systems to ensure a smooth transition, making sure everyone knows their new roles and responsibilities in the new organization. Reengineering too sometimes dwells in this zone. Some advocates for this intervention think reengineering focuses too much on formal aspects of systems and not enough on the dynamic, process aspects. In either case, what is important for Zone 3a leadership is to ensure that there is a healthy skeleton, solid yet flexible, that can become the basis upon which to build the other zones.

Team Building

Team building also ventures forth in Zone 3a, blossoming into full flower in 3b. The Tuckman team development model is useful in this zone. It identifies four stages of team development: forming, storming, norming, and performing. *Forming* establishes base-level expectations and looks for initial common ground. Members are dependent on each other. *Storming* signals power issues, including reactions to positional leadership, and members are independent and counterdependent. In *norming*, members agree about roles and processes for decision making. Negotiation and consensus are practiced. Finally, *performing* focuses on accomplishing effective results. Collaboration is key. Members are interdependent. I will say more on teams later.

The many seminars that teach coaching and team-building skills can be leadership tools in Zones 2, 3a, and 3b. Sometimes they touch empowerment issues in Zone 4. Rarely do they leave the systems zones, however. It is their home, their foundation for competency development.

Hiring

Hiring methods that select peak-performing employees are often a focus in this zone. In a peer forum of CEOs it was noted that Peter Drucker had said that "one-third of all hiring decisions are outright failures"; Verifications, Inc., reported that 30 percent of resumes are fraudulent; Merck, Inc., revealed that a bad hire costs 75 percent of his or her annual salary while a bad hire costs you 150 percent of an executive's salary; and a study by Stanford and Columbia Universities has discovered that 81 percent of employees are misplaced (see also Buckingham and Coffman, 1999).

System problems are serious. Firing employees in these numbers will not solve the underlying problem. The hiring and placement system needs review and reorganization. Posing a lengthy set of questions to candidates can ensure a better match of person to job. Even better, devise a way for them to simulate the job so you can make a better judgment of potential performance than is possible from only an interview.

Leadership Development

Zone 2 focused on talent and fit. *First, Break All the Rules* (Buckingham and Coffman, 1999) has become a pivotal player in the organizational world. When one's attention shifts from technical skills targeted to task, to a world better understood as a complex system, new questions arise. Some are very provocative and upsetting to people enamored of Zone 2 reality.

One can hire the right person for a particular job; not focus on promotion, passion, and intellectual curiosity; and ensure that little organizational leadership is developed. Early successes do not guarantee effective leadership action. The trouble begins with success. It can do one in. So argue Lombardo and Eichinger, based on research done by The Center for Creative Leadership. In their forthcoming book *The Leadership Machine* (p. 43), they identify eight strengths typically connected to leader success:

1. Bright, driver, ambitious, high standards, tough on laggards

2. Independent, likes to do it alone

3. Extremely loyal to organization, a team player

4. Controlling, results-oriented, single-minded, really nails down technical detail

5. Personable, relies on relationships to get things done

6. Creative, conceptually strong, ball of fire, finger in many pies

7. Has a single, notable characteristic such as tons of energy, raw talent, or a long-term mentor

8. Contentious, likes to argue, takes strong stands, usually

What are your strengths or those of a boss? The authors argue that, over time, these very strengths usually turn into derailment actions that undermine leadership action. Early strengths may become later weaknesses. For example, suppose you select strength number one. The downside over time is arrogance, betrayal of trust and ethics, lack of ambition, and lack of composure. Or suppose you pick number three—loyal team player. Over time, people with this early strength usually overmanage, cannot be counted on when times are tough, staff ineffectively, and end up not building a team (Lombardo and Eichinger, forthcoming, p. 44).

This report is just to give you a flavor of life in this zone in contrast to Zone 2. What happens over time as systems change? Strengths become weaknesses. Experiences are too narrow. People do not know how to learn anything new. Transitions reinforce old styles of coping with change and anxiety (Lombardo and Eichinger, forthcoming, p. 46).

Hence the restlessness with hiring for talent, etc, in *First, Break All the Rules*. Their approach, while great for technical selections, can undermine leadership development. The typical strategies can derail what is needed and desired without anyone having a clue it is happening until it is too late.

Have you and your organization done the following for leadership development of young people?

1. We assign our best and highest-potential people to our best-performing units.

2. We promote almost entirely from within.

3. We promote broadness in our starting-career people through an intensive job rotation program.

4. We focus on real work.

5. We don't punish people for mistakes.

6. We develop people fast.

7. We insure development through real time performance feedback.

8. We mentor the best with the best.

9. We develop the expertise of our people.

10. We reward performance with promotion.

11. We develop collegial spirit in our young people.

12. We accentuate the positive. (Lombardo and Eichinger, forthcoming, pp. 47–49)

I have experienced them all, thinking it was the way to go. No longer. Each approach can have the opposite impact and sidetrack leadership of key positional, professional players. Over time, numbers seven and twelve have declined in negativity. The others have endured for decades. Leadership development is no quick fix. It really requires a move to Zone 3b where the soft skills become hard and the hard are finally realized to be soft. Even though the mechanical metaphor of *The Leadership Machine* would tie more closely to Zone 2, the content of the book centers on Zones 3a and 3b. Titles are often misleading; sometimes they are revealing. The subtitle is informative: *Architecture to Develop Leaders for Any Future.* Is the blueprint expansive enough to embrace the three worlds of the umpires? Or is it descriptive of an expansive room without realizing another room awaits exploration? The book provokes thinking, and testing taken-for-granted assumptions. It actually has a database and leadership development strategies. It is worth a read.

Systems and Leadership Decision Making

There are hundreds of examples of structural systems and their advantages and problems. By and large, one is unaware of a system until it fails to work or someone tries to change it. Systems are almost invisible except to those who are looking for them. The Constitution of the United States, Robert's Rules of Order, office-space layout, computer-system integration, planning sequences, stages of development, zones, maps, laws, and penalties illustrate a few examples. Think of your own list—it's easy and instructive.

Leadership is frequently command and control in Zone 3a. Often the toughest decisions about mergers, reorganization, and other fundamental structural changes rest on one desk—the boss's. As we shall witness later, it is possible to handle some restructuring of work processes from a participatory base. However, if leaders understand leadership only from Zone 3a, participation does not occur to them as an option. Or, if participation has been advocated and built on a shaky foundation of roles and responsibilities, it will flounder and an executive decision may be justified. There are certainly times when command and control is the appropriate approach to leadership. Leadership wisdom is to know when and how. But wisdom like that is only possible if all the zones are understood so a leader can see the large picture and decide wisely.

Simulations

Systems thinking is difficult to master. Two simulations are great aids. A simulation differs from a role-play in that you are not expected to be or play someone or some role other than yourself. Situations are structured for you to cope with. Just be yourself and deal with whatever happens.

Friday Nite at the ER depicts a hospital scene, including surgery, critical care, emergency room, and a step-down space for patients on the way out (step-down refers to a transition place for patients before they return home). Seated at a table, four people play, each responsible for one of the rooms and all that goes on in it. Within a twenty-four-hour time frame, each hour being a minute, life unfolds and the systems and your decisions are tested. Emergencies, staff illnesses, layoffs, and other unanticipated events occur. When I played, we had a facilitator, ten tables of four cards to trigger actions, spaces for patients, and other devices to replicate a hospital environment.

Yes, there is paperwork, and the quality of care and costs are measured. The game takes about two hours, is very provocative, and challenges systems thinking. What rules can be broken or sidestepped and what will be the consequences? Rooms are limited in number, as are staff members. What do you do when the number of people waiting for service in the emergency room doubles? There are procedures to follow that slow down the service. However, breaking rules may have unintended impact on other aspects of the hospital. It is a good game. (For more information, contact Breakthrough Learning, 17800 Woodland Avenue, Morgan Hill, CA 95037; 408-779-0701.)

The Beer Game, first developed in the 1960s at the Sloan School of Management of the Massachusetts Institute of Technology, offers similar insights with a very different context and set of processes. It is described well in *The Fifth Discipline* (Senge, 1990, pp. 27–54). This simulation stresses the role of structure in defining and shaping behavior, and how thinking about oneself rather than of system interconnectedness can sidetrack wise action (p. 40).

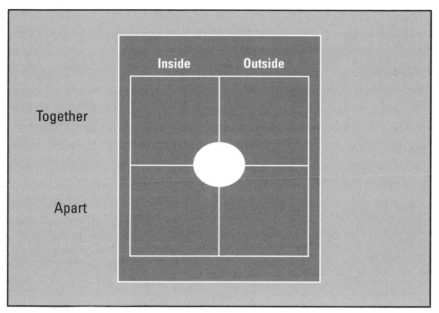

FIGURE 16 • THE CONNECTION BOX

The Connection Box: An Exercise

All kinds of forces both separate and unify people in organizations. The forces may come from inside or outside the organization, executive group, department, team, or task force. How can all of these forces be identified and sorted, and strategies crafted around them? I use The Connection Box (see Figure 16). It arranges two variable sets—apart/together and inside/outside—on the window, and asks participants to fill in the four boxes.

In the center of the box is a circle. Write in the circle what organizational unit is being analyzed and assessed. Is it a particular team, a group of department heads, a department, or even the organization as a whole? If the number of participants exceeds six, put them at round tables, six to eight per table, and fill in the boxes. Then, when the task is completed, each table reports out its findings. Then ask each table group which quadrant got the greatest number of comments. Track which quadrant received the most votes. That voting offers a quick scan of what quadrant is most problematic for the unit under review.

Based on this organized activity, the unit can begin to craft strategies for body repair and healing. If the issues point to other zones, then leadership action will shift. For example, if the participants believe a force pulling them apart internally is that executives don't listen to worker issues, then the leadership focus shifts to Zone 4, Creating Ownership. If participants think the rapidity of change overwhelms product development, then leadership shifts to Zone 5b, Setting Direction. If, however, the greatest number of issues center on silos, breakdown of connection, etc., then Designing Sustainable Systems is the leadership challenge.

ZONE IDENTIFICATION AND LEADERSHIP QUESTIONS

Use the following three questions to assess your Zone 3a issues.

1. How sturdy is my organization or community in this zone?

   - Are there clear and appropriate rules, regulations, and procedures that set the outer boundaries for effective action?

   - Do training systems introduce these operating methods and boundaries to employees on a regular basis?

   - Are role definitions clear and presented so that employees see and experience the relational connections in their and others' work?

   - How important are teams in the working group?

   - Do the teams link to each other?

   - Is the overall organizational chart clear and understood by everyone?

   - Is the system as a whole healthy, vibrant, and functional?

   - Does the work flow smoothly from function to function?

   - Do the positional leaders understand their role and function as system designers? Are they taught systems thinking?

   - Is the whole of the organization understood to be greater than the sum of the parts?

- When was the last reorganization? Did it work well? What were the problems?

- Overall, is the system effective in delivering products and services?

```
10 |  |  |  |  |  |  |  |  |  |  0  |  |  |  |  |  |  |  |  |  | 10
Very Sturdy                                              Shaky
```

2. Where is my organization or community currently focusing its leadership attention?

- If the system is the problem, is it getting proper attention?

- Are training and skill enhancements mistakenly attempting to address system issues by means of Zone 2 competency work?

- Has the positional leadership focused on vision, values, and mission; worker participation; or even creativity seminars when in fact it is the fundamental infrastructure that is in danger of collapse?

```
10 |  |  |  |  |  |  |  |  |  |  0  |  |  |  |  |  |  |  |  |  | 10
Excellent Fit                                            Misfit
```

3. Am I prepared to design a sustainable system?

- Do I know systems thinking?

- How nimble am I in identifying the trim tabs?

- Do I understand teamwork and appropriate processes?

- Do I understand and can I construct infrastructure?

- Can I construct and conduct needs assessment surveys?

- How good are my organizational development skills?

```
10 |  |  |  |  |  |  |  |  |  |  0  |  |  |  |  |  |  |  |  |  | 10
Ready to Exhibit Leadership               Not Prepared at All
```

ZONE SUMMARY

Initially Zone 3a focuses on system design, the formal side of structure. Employing the *life is a body* metaphor, it attends to the organizational skeleton, seeking to build the proper infrastructure to support and sustain the next zones. Often this zone is ignored in leadership studies because leadership is thought to dwell elsewhere and this preoccupation with structure is viewed as management. Conversely, this zone sometimes receives disproportionate attention as a means of avoiding issues from other zones. Reorganizing while ignoring problems with power is a typical error.

Leadership must embrace Zone 3a as part of its essence or the organization or community group will falter. That oft-heard phrase "We need more leadership around here" often means we need positional leadership to address formal structural issues.

Consistency, the Zone 2 criterion for authenticity, fails to rally Zone 3a to authentic action. Connectedness is more critical here. The whole is greater than the sum of the parts, and the whole is judged by its multiple dependencies. Elitism and arrogance are not tolerated in this zone. They may burst forth in Zone 2 as individuals seek to lead their field of practice. Here, though, fairness takes over. All the parts are important. Equal inclusion of functions jumps forth as the ethical standard. To undermine one part of the system undermines the whole system. All parts of the body are worthy of attention; to ignore one may weaken the whole body. Organizations have different internal functions—some are hands, some feet, some brains, and some eyes and ears—and together create the whole body, which wonderfully supersedes each of the parts as each part is treasured and respected.

In the polarity of form/dynamic, the focus of Zone 3a attends to form—the skeleton of the body. With a solid, sturdy structure as a foundation, the dynamic of a living system will thrive. Without effective infrastructure, the body will collapse and destroy any platform for effective vitality.

The competencies particularly important here are the abilities to perform systems thinking; carry out system design and assessment; create persona; create personnel manuals to connect people fairly; and set the foundation for cross-functional teams and organizational feedback in surveys.

Leadership in this zone tends to work behind the scenes, designing the work processes, standards, and bureaucratic forms that make delivery of products and services reliable and credible. The work is that of designers and architects. Without healthy, functional systems in place, the best of talent and skill is stymied. Skills without structured processes to direct and sustain their flow go nowhere. Leadership crafts those sustainable system processes.

ZONE 3A DEFINITIONS

Leadership: Designing Sustainable Systems
Authenticity criterion: Connectedness
Metaphor: Life is a body
Core ethical principle: Justice as fairness (equal inclusion)
Polarity: Form/dynamic, with emphasis on form

STIRRINGS

As "make the system work at all costs" becomes the leadership mantra, as there are more manuals, more detailed job definitions, better communications, stronger teams, and better assessments of the climate, the desire for stability and system predictability can trap the organization in the past. Hope for Zone 2 realities can lock a Zone 3a system into a false sense of reality. Systems designed to embrace ambiguity end up denying complexity. When it is wrongly believed that all problems are fixable by establishing more rules and regulations, systems start to become dysfunctional and self-destructive.

This is not a new phenomenon. In a seminar someone passed this quote by Gaius Petronius Arbiter (first century A.D.) to me: "We trained hard," he reported, "but it seemed that every time we were beginning to form into teams, we would be reorganized. I was to learn later in life that we tend to meet any new situation by reorganizing. And what a wonderful method it can be for creating the illusion of progress while producing confusion, inefficiency, and demoralization."

The boss as gamesman struggles as well. In his research on leaders, Maccoby found one detail so disturbing that he did not include it in his book. The insight cut across all companies studied and all managerial types. According to Kleiner (1996), "Maccoby's team had asked managers to name the historical figure they most admired. The answers, almost without exception, fit into a very short list: Abraham Lincoln, John Kennedy, Robert Kennedy, Martin Luther King Jr. It was an odd list—why would predominantly white managers select King?—and it took a while to notice one thing those heroes had in common. They had all been assassinated" (p. 24).

Did these system crafters feel betrayed in some profound way? Was the game all there was to life? Did they have no heroes who survived? Did they ever think it might be possible for them to transform their systems and direct them toward additional goals? Or would it mean death? Although not reporting all his findings, Maccoby did ponder whether leaders had crafted systems and trapped themselves in them (Maccoby, 1976, p. 235).

While Maccoby pioneered in leadership studies years ago, spotting the stirrings, there is a new, forceful pattern emerging today that is even more dramatic. An economic-based cultural shift is fast approaching that triggers Zone 3b big time. The shift is captured in Jeremy Rifkin's most recent book, *The Age of Access* (2000). He, more than any other author I know, understands and states clearly the move from Zone 2 to 3, especially 3b.

The ideas of private property, markets, and freedom are transforming into hypercapitalism in which one pays for experience with lifelong contracts. In Zone 2, one would buy an air conditioner. In Zone 3b, one signs a long-term lease for the experience of pure cool air. Buy or lease a car?

I am experiencing this shift as I contemplate buying a house. I was raised on the model of mortgage: eventually own a house by paying down the fifteen- or thirty-year fixed- or variable-rate mortgage. Now I am building a long-term relationship with a financial planner to refinance the house every five years or so and take the appreciated cash value out of the house and invest it for retirement—and own the house. What a change in mental models for me, locked in a Zone 2 mind-set. Do I want to invest in the property or my economic growth and retirement experience?

Rifkin hears the stirrings as the world shifts from a mechanical to an organic sensibility. He goes even farther in the zone model without realizing it. As Zone 3b becomes ever more present, the stirrings in Zone 4 surface. Lifetime contracts for experience surface issues of voice. Are we losing our power to systems that contract our total life experience? More on this when we get there.

Negative Stirrings

Listen to these voices:

> Something is wrong here. We may all be connected, yet I don't feel I belong to this organization. I experience alienation and I'm not sure why. The place is fairly formal and rules are multiplying like crazy. It seems like every day the managers come up with a new regulation. People skills are not very good here either. I get nervous when I see people being treated like things or functions. What disrespect for their lives.

> When I come to work, I want to experience a feeling of welcome. I want to be Norm at the Cheers bar. I also want a sense of shared values that we live every day. Sometimes values are discussed; they are not practiced regularly as far as I can tell. No one is held accountable for value trespass. Productivity is the only goal.

> My boss talks to us and claims we are all family. If so, we are certainly dysfunctional. That family image is funny. Last week John got laid off. Is that like firing an uncle? I feel like an orphan most of the time.

> I like my job; it's the organization as a whole—and especially my department heads—that bothers me. I still think of myself as an employee, not a member. I don't have the experience of coupling my sense of myself with the identity of the organization. Who are we, really? Our leadership, especially my boss, who used to be great, is getting worse.

Positive Stirrings

> I was in a meeting the other day that was amazing. For the first time in years I felt I was a treasured employee. I actually felt like a member of this organization. What a delight! Respect filled the room. We talked, listened, problem solved. No blaming, shaming, scapegoating. It was amazing. I tasted a new possibility here. The other thing that happened was the deep sense that we knew who we were as a team and what we were about. We shifted our goals but our

identity was firm. It didn't change. I wonder if our whole organization could live its identity every day? I don't think mission statements do it. I wonder what an identity discussion would yield? Where we are headed is different from who we are. In our meeting we came together. We were on the same page even as we changed our priorities for a new assignment and set of tasks.

What else impressed me were the wonderful interpersonal skills used in the meeting. It was truly impressive to experience great listening, sharing, and addressing sometimes contentious issues. The best was brought out of us. What made the meeting even more wonderful was the fact that two of our customers are on the team with us. I now think we all can improve our people skills. Isn't there some book titled *Emotional Intelligence*? I'm not sure what that is. I think I experienced it in the meeting. Everyone left feeling very satisfied.

I also met a former executive who shifted to another company. He blew my mind by telling me he was engaged in a "group-building" process. It differed from team building and fit his new executives' work with each other. He had to leave before I could press him about this new event. I think our organization has a lot to learn and the energy is in place to move forward. I'm ready.

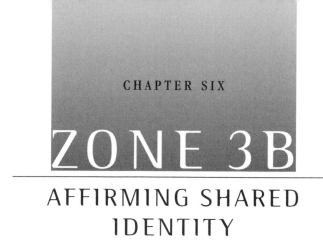

CHAPTER SIX

ZONE 3B

AFFIRMING SHARED IDENTITY

JOIN THE TEAM; DON'T SEPARATE AND SCREAM.

After the merger (a Zone 3a activity) of four South African banks, I was invited to hold a series of retreats for the new corporation's executive group. Critical issues confronted them as they sought strategies to make the merger work. They needed to become a team, yet power battles and turf struggles dominated their life together. The CEO, a very strong and decisive figure, puzzled over how to unite the group, how to guide their inclusion in the work of the organization.

I was told by the Human Resources staff that the team had never worked with an outside consultant and was a bit nervous about the upcoming event. I pondered how to begin the first retreat. Sensing the participants' anxiety about being involved in something that was too "touchy-feely" I decided on an opening strategy. We were sitting around on the porch of a very beautiful lodge in a game preserve.

I said, "I understand some of you feel a little anxious about this event, my being a stranger to you all. So I thought you might want to know what we are going to do to begin the retreat. Here is my plan. We will all take our clothes off, go in the hot tub, hold hands, and sing 'Kum Ba Yah.'"

I figured that if they laughed, we would have a great time; if they got quiet and serious, we were in deep trouble. They fell out laughing. We bonded immediately, and the event turned out to be the best, most rewarding, and most consequential executive retreat I have ever facilitated. We covered the Myers-Briggs Type Indicator *instrument, leadership choices, core values, and metaphors. We laughed together, we learned together, and the team emerged having made decisions that are still in place years later.*

At that first retreat, the senior team struggled to create a mission and value statement for the bank. All team members had been interviewed beforehand by a Human Resources person to identify their central values and beliefs. The plan was for Human Resources to mesh these values into one statement; however, the value priorities were so diverse that this effort was going nowhere. Instead of uniting the team, beliefs separated them. So, at that first executive meeting, I introduced them to the material in Collins and Porras's Built to Last *(discussed in Chapter Three) and outlined a method to identify core values: Figure out your real mission and then ask what values are essential to sustain that business. The team struggled but eventually completed the task.*

At the third retreat, the team reviewed its work and began to bring closure to the task. The core business issues turned out to be risk management and problem solving. The values were clear and straightforward —integrity, honesty, and responsibility. When the task was completed, the CEO reviewed the product and then looked directly at me. He had a reputation for asking hard, direct questions. To deal with him, one had to be well prepared, direct, and to the point. I liked him a lot and trusted his fairness and good judgment, but I had never experienced "the look." I did now.

Then he asked the pivotal question: "What competitive advantage do we get from doing this work? Any bank is in the same business and thus would have the same core values."

I looked him directly in the eye and responded, "Absolutely none, unless you live the values in your toes."

"Good point," he replied, and the meeting moved on.

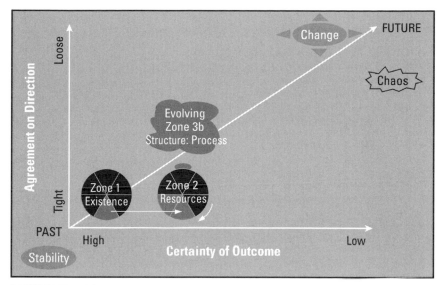

FIGURE 17 • ZONE 3B: AFFIRMING SHARED IDENTITY

CORE IDEAS

Leadership in Zone 3b builds on 3a; systems thinking continues and shifts focus (Figure 17 locates Zone 3b on the map). Now the organic metaphor highlights the body as a living system. It is not just composed of organically interrelated parts. It is also dynamic, vibrant. In the work between the poles of form and dynamic, dynamic is emphasized. Sustainable systems are not enough. Now affirming and growing the identity becomes the authentic action for leadership. Executives find themselves more removed from everyday operations. As they exhibit leadership, they seek to figure out what is happening in their organization and figure out ways to guide the whole organization. Their efforts are based on a shared belief that all employees must be included, must be considered valued members of a worthy, value-driven community. They commit to building a vibrant identity for the organization.

Reality is increasingly viewed and constructed from many angles. The second umpire was right. We all tend to view the world from where we sit. We are all umpires, calling 'em from our own unique vantage point. Leadership in this zone recognizes this reality and acts accordingly. In Zone 3b the world is less predictable, and it is more difficult to shape alignment around direction and values. Inside organizations, reality is partially knowable and fixable. In practice terms, this means it is treated as understandable and partially fixable. Leadership becomes more complex, requiring much more sophistication, system insight, dynamic communication, and interactive processes.

Organizational structures continue to develop, moving from what Harvard professor Nitin Nohria (1996) calls M-Forms to N-Forms. M-Forms are multidivisional organizations; N-Forms are networks (pp. 4ff.). The "living" part of the living system stretches the system's formal aspects. Many traditional large industrial companies experienced this change in the 1970s. They were characterized by massive scale and scope and many semiautonomous operating divisions; centralized control from a corporate headquarters that had large staffs, especially in finance; a complex budgeting process; and governance by professional managers. Just think of General Motors from the early 1920s to the 1970s.

During the 1970s the world altered. No longer was the past a sure predictor of the future. Market shifts stunned companies and executives searched for new strategies to cope with perceived impending chaos. *Change* flared up as the code word for success; stability was cast aside as anticompetitive. Firms refocused, giving up on breadth and scope. They specialized. They tried to figure out their core business, created partnerships, downsized, looked outward toward customers, focused on system processes, and shifted from managerial capitalism to investor capitalism. Power at the top became vulnerable as a split occurred between those running the organization and those investing in it (Nohria, 1996, p. 8).

Among the driving forces for inclusivity have been the civil rights movement and new equal employment opportunity laws and affirmative action policies and plans; the women's movement, which has changed the demographics of the workforce and brought forward feminist philosophies that stress systems thinking and inclusion; the technological revolution that has made computers ubiquitous and information a new and different kind of resource; globalization of the marketplace and the concurrent growth of the image of the world as a global village; the decline in union membership and political clout; and the rise of ideological and political conservatism. Finally, something was needed to substitute for the promise of lifetime employment that the traditional companies had once offered and had now abandoned. IBM's decision to abandon its strongly held and widely famed policy of job security was seen by many as marking the enormous scale of this particular change. With economic security gone along with job security, employees were thrust toward the fears and anxieties of chaos. A covenant had been broken. Workers were on their own, with no guaranteed organizational support and nothing to inspire any loyalty to their companies.

Infrastructure and restructuring are thus not the main concerns of leadership in this zone, as they were in Zone 3a. Connectedness is great. Now that sense of system connection seems inadequate to glue the organization together. Is there any meaningful center to which organizational members can belong? Authenticity in this zone requires coherence, a coming together for significant concerted collective action.

The core ethical principle of Zone 3a is justice as fairness. In Zone 3b all the parts deserve equally serious attention, and leadership highlights certain parts for special action. Justice is proportionally constructive. Fairness still obtains; however, leadership worries more about who is left out and is concerned with ensuring that all members buy into the mission, values, and vision of the organization. Now the concern is that all the players build a creative set of linkages and together construct a long-term viable system. Justice does not simply divvy up the parts equitably; it creates new systems that are flexible and resonate deeply with the organizational members' emerging bonds and affiliations. It is proportional to what is required for healthy growth and sustainability.

Trust building becomes the mantra. Join the team; don't separate and scream. Leadership spreads further down in the organization. Team leadership emerges as the new challenge. Executives still play a crucial role; however, in addition to anxiety containment, as described for Zone 3a, that role is now focused on setting and maintaining the core principles, central for organizational identity, and guaranteeing that the organization is positioned for any eventuality.

No longer is leadership understood as constructing and maintaining the skeleton of an organization. That was the task of organizational development. Now the leadership challenge focuses on building a dynamic living system on that skeleton. Hence, leadership affirms shared identity.

Top Leadership Recast

With new infrastructure in place, the head of the body, the leader of the system, the chief executive officer looks out on the workforce and ponders: "How do I lead such a diverse crowd so that we can accomplish our goals, and so that they feel like they belong to the organization? I am not in their face every day. I do not have direct knowledge and control over what happens. Yet I want to provide guidance and direction. And I want the workforce motivated to excel. What am I supposed to do to get everybody to buy in to who we are and where we are going?"

Enter Zone 3b leadership rooted in value work. Thomas Neff, James Citrin, and Paul Brown grasp this shift in leadership well in their book *Lessons from the Top* (1999). As headhunters, they are astutely aware of the shift in organizational realities that requires new competencies from executive leaders. Gone are command-and-control approaches. What they found among corporate stars were six winning strategies (p. 176):

1. Live with integrity; lead by example. "Integrity builds the trust in senior management that is . . . critical for high-performing organizations."

2. Develop a winning strategy or "Big Idea." "A successful leader must go to the company's roots and build on the things the organization truly does best."

3. Build a great management team. Great leaders hired managers "whose skills and experiences complemented their own, but whose passion, attitudes and values were one and the same."

4. Inspire employees to greatness. "Communicate continuously, listen carefully, genuinely tolerate failure as a learning experience."

5. Create a flexible, responsive organization. "The best leaders have redesigned their organizations to make sure decisions can be made fast."

6. Use reinforcing management systems. "Compensation . . . must be consistent with and reinforce the values and strategy of the organization."

Let us now turn to the context for leadership in this zone.

Chaos and Complexity Theory

A shifting world opens a new leadership challenge. Now the second umpire gets excited. Life is more complex, more lively, less predictable and orderly. On the surface, events happen that appear to be chaotic. On reflection, it is possible to discern order in chaos and identify patterns of adaptive behavior. However, the calm of earlier zones is less present here. Also the possibilities for change are more real.

Two code terms capture much of this zone—chaos and complexity. Both are rooted in "new science." This new approach goes beyond the mechanical model of Zone 2 and is more vibrant than Zone 3a. Now life presents itself as a different system, one in which dynamic builds on form and living systems grow on the skeleton and Newtonian laws of science. As this zone unfolds, you will be introduced to the basics of chaos and complexity thinking. Later, in Zone 7b, an in-depth assessment will also be offered.

Margaret Wheatley, one of the pioneers who first linked leadership to the new science, masters this zone. Peter Senge, too, is very much at home here, as are Fritjof Capra and most ecologists. Their conceptual bricks add greatly to the leadership edifice we are building here. Each thinker adds depth to the map of reality.

Margaret Wheatley's writing captures much of the essence of Zone 3b. First, she sees coherence as the standard of truth.

> Systems become healthier as they open to include greater variety. . . . A healthy system uses its freedom to explore its identity. It is free to look outward, to bring in others, to contemplate new information. . . . If we seek our own effectiveness, we cannot help but embrace more and more of those who are connected to us in ways we refuse to see. . . . Open and inquiring, such systems become wiser about themselves. They become more aware of their interdependencies. They no longer seek their security behind the stout walls of exclusion. They learn that by reaching out, they become stronger. Their support comes not from unnatural boundaries but from the inherent strength of wholeness. . . .

Often our fear stops us from encouraging such openness to new connections. We become afraid that we will lose all capacity if we open our organization to new and different members, or if we reveal anything to those we have labeled as competitors. But these are just more futile attempts to hold the world still, to stop its cohering motions. In fear, we stop the energy available to us—the energy that wants to create affiliations, systems, efficacy. . . .

"There is only the dance," wrote T. S. Eliot. There is only the dance of coherence, and it is the only dance which brings us joy. (Wheatley and Kellner-Rogers, 1996, pp. 101–103)

Second, Wheatley sees the existence of chaos, and it is apparent rather than real (a distinction explored in the Introduction). She deeply believes that order is implicit in chaos. I am not sure whether her view is new science or old theology. Her belief not only affirms that there is order in chaos. It suggests that emerging order is a source of comfort and hope:

This is a strange world, and it promises to get stranger. Niels Bohr, who engaged with Heisenberg in those long, nighttime conversations that ended in despair, once said that great innovations, when they appear, seem muddled and strange. They are only half understood by their discoverer and remain a mystery to everyone else. But if an idea does not appear bizarre, he counseled, there is not hope for it (in Wilber, 1985, 20). So we must live with the strange and the bizarre, even as we climb stairs that we want to bring us to a clearer vantage point. Every step requires that we stay comfortable with uncertainty, and confident of confusion's role. After all is said and done, we will have to muddle our way through. But in the midst of muddle—and I hope I remember this—we can walk with a sure step. For these stairs we climb only take us deeper and deeper into a universe of inherent order. (Wheatley, 1996, p. 151)

Zone 3b also functions on this premise that order will emerge from chaos, given that leadership affirms shared identity. At the same time, I find in this paragraph an apparent leap from science to spirit, from fact to faith. Is the leap justified? Is Wheatley saying, at the most profound level, Trust the system? Our systems, as I have pointed out, have produced profound evil as well as good. Human beings have contributed gloriously to the globe and to each other. We have wreaked havoc on them as well. In what, then, do we ground our hope? In what do we have faith? Are we seeking *order* in the chaos we perceive, or *meaning* in that chaos? We will return to these questions in later chapters. But, as the world becomes less knowable and fixable, they begin to be heard in this zone even as it strives toward order.

Any perceived order will set the outer boundaries of dynamic interaction. It will establish a pattern. Pattern recognition is pivotal to living systems thinking. "To understand a pattern," writes Fritjof Capra (1996), "we must map a configuration of relationships. In other words, structure involves quantities, while pattern involves qualities" (p. 81). Systems are properties of patterns. Capra continues, "What is destroyed when a living organism is dissected is its pattern. The components are still there, but the configuration of relationships among them—the pattern—is destroyed, thus the organism dies" (p. 81).

When pattern is applied to living systems, the key word is *networks*. Life is a set of "intricate patterns of intertwined webs, networks nesting within larger networks" (p. 82). Networks are non-linear; they go in many directions. Closely linked to networks is the concept of feedback loops. In Zone 3a, negative feedback loops identify changes in equilibrium and negate them. In Zone 3b, positive feedback loops offer possibilities for new creative options. In the extreme, negative feedback cultivates a rigid status quo; positive feedback trips us into chaos. Creativity and effectiveness emerge at the boundary between rigid order and disorder.

In terms of action, the extremes are adapting to the world and its chaos on the one hand, and making the world adapt to us on the other. In the first instance we are participating in what Capra calls *deep ecology*, and we view the world "not as a collection of isolated objects, but as a network of phenomena that are fundamentally interconnected and interdependent. Deep ecology recognizes the intrinsic value of all living beings and views humans as just one particular strand in the web of life." Moreover, "when the concept of the human spirit is understood as the mode of consciousness in which the individual feels a sense of belonging, of connectedness, to the cosmos as a whole, it becomes clear that ecological awareness is spiritual in its deepest essence" (1996, p. 7). Capra clearly identifies with Christian mystics, Buddhists, and the worldview underlying much of Native American tradition. He worries that human beings who claim to separate themselves from nature will destroy it. Superiority will take over and we will think we are masters of the universe. It is this kind of thinking that allows men to justify their domination of women and leads one racial group to try to dominate others. In a universe that is a web of life, this kind of elitism is misplaced; only equality works.

Most organizational and leadership literature about this zone draws on complexity theory rather than chaos theory because it offers new foundational thinking. The concept of the "complex adaptive system" is at the core of complexity thinking:

> A complex adaptive system consists of a number of agents interacting with each other according to schemas, that is, rules of behavior, that require them to inspect each other's behavior and adjust their own in the light of the behavior of others. In other words, complex adaptive systems learn and evolve, and they usually interact with other complex adaptive systems. They survive because they learn or evolve in an adaptive way: they compute information in order to extract regularities, building them into schemas that are continually changed in the light of experience. (Stacey, 1996, p. 28).

A common example involves a boss and employees. The boss has a history of command and control. Over time, the employees adapt to that behavior by withdrawal, low morale, rumor creation, and sabotage. When the boss learns of such behavior, she or he sets new policies, fires the people who are considered the main enemies, and criticizes the rest. The remaining employees self-organize, recruit colleagues, and ponder the possibility of a union.

This adaptive model roots in nature. Nature is adaptive. The question that arises is, Are human beings totally reducible to complex adaptive systems? Can human beings consider themselves apart from, and even superior to, nature? If they do, are the consequences terrible? Let's press further.

If we are totally consumed by adaptation, power belongs to the world rather than to us (either as individuals, teams, or organizations). To adapt is to fit into a situation as defined by the boundaries and requirements of the situation itself. Does it make sense to always adapt? Do we have a choice?

Yet the flip side of adaptation is also problematic. If we do not adapt to the world, we assume the world will adapt to us. Through control, domination, and overt as well as covert power we seek to make the world adapt to our direction. Heroism, social movements, planned change, wars, exploitation, and genocide are all efforts to get the world to act as people wish. In this way power issues jump back and forth between controlling vs. being controlled. In this zone, complex adaptive systems work. In the next zone, new issues will be raised.

Guy Benveniste (1994) contemplates the dilemmas of adaptive organizations. "Given the turbulent environment, the organization has two major options," he writes. "The organization can run outward: it can adapt, it can learn, it can be responsive and even incite changes in the environment. Or, in contrast, the organization can turn inward: it can manipulate and control its clients or the public. . . . In an uncertain environment, organizations adapt by controlling their environment" (p. 239).

Both sides of the polarity—adapt to the world and make the world adapt—assert truths. If we go exclusively for the first, we sell out to the world; if we go exclusively for the second, we separate ourselves in arrogance and abuse the rest of creation. This debate over action will only intensify down the road. We may find that chaos calls forth wonderful creativity. Yet it may also result in evil. There are reasons why human beings want to avoid chaos, and why we search desperately for some common ground of hope.

Self-Organizing in Living Systems

The order that leadership in this zone strives for is not rigid formal order. It is a dynamic order of the living system, a complex and creative order.

In the late 1940s, Eric Trist discovered in his work with miners in the UK that in a particular setting where old rules and authority of position didn't quite apply, the miners themselves figured out safe and effective ways to mine coal. For Trist and others, this kind of finding triggered a transformation of thought:

> Trist and his closest colleagues—particularly the Australian researcher Fred Emery—adopted several terms for their work: "Industrial democracy," "open systems," and "sociotechnical systems." They believed that corporations were analogous to eco-systems, subject to the same sorts of interrelationships that governed prosperity and survival in the wild. As business environments became

more turbulent, top-down hierarchies would cease to be effective, just as they were ineffective amid the disorder of nature. . . . Living systems coped with turbulence by *generating their own order* from the bottom up. A living creature can take its shape even from a damaged fetus or ovum, without any external control. In fact, attempts to control a living creature's growth too harshly would make it wither and die. Why shouldn't the same be true for organizations? (Kleiner, 1996, p. 65)

Such discoveries of self-organizing, of learning ability within the organization, spawned both OD and complexity theory. Now more precise research is showing us how, through feedback loops and networks of information, living systems such as the teams that are important in this zone can and do self-organize. Moreover, how they self-organize can be mapped by nonlinear equations. For example, Marcial Losada (1998) has mapped the complex dynamic of high-performance work teams, looking at three performance indicators: profitability, customer satisfaction, and team assessments by superiors, peers, and subordinates. Teams were also measured by their degree of connectivity. Looking at sixty teams (fifteen high-performance, twenty-six medium, and nineteen low), he found that

high performance teams were characterized by an atmosphere of buoyancy that lasted during the whole meeting. By showing appreciation and encouragement to other members in the team, they created emotional spaces that were expansive and opened possibilities for action and creativity. They were also fun to watch and there was rarely a dull moment during their meetings. In addition, they accomplished their tasks with ease and grace.

In stark contrast, low performance teams struggled with their tasks, operated in very restrictive emotional spaces created by lack of mutual support and enthusiasm, often in an atmosphere charged with distrust and cynicism. The medium performance teams operated in emotional spaces that were not as restrictive as the low performance teams, but not nearly as expansive as the high performance teams. They were able to finish their tasks as planned, but not with the novelty and creativity characteristic of high performance teams. (p. 3)

Three polarities were measured to track connectivity: inquiry/advocacy, other/self, and positivity/negativity. High performance results when teams equally balance questioning and asserting positions and equally focus on others and themselves. High-performance teams tilt more toward the positive—creating and sustaining affirmative emotional space for others and themselves. When mapped statistically, high-performance team patterns cluster in a format of relatively even distribution across the variables. Low-performance patterning clusters narrowly in restrictive pockets.

What makes Losada's research pioneering is its minute-by-minute behavioral observations demonstrating the connection between productivity and behavior in work-related team activities. In literature that addresses leadership in this zone, there is much emphasis on people skills. This research underscores the significance and absolute necessity of people skills that foster connectivity and inclusivity in the everyday functioning of organizations.

Leadership, then, provides guidance for self-organizing or learning, a direction for it to take. To fulfill the vision of a learning organization, says Senge (1990), five learning disciplines are necessary: "Crucial design work for leaders of learning organizations concerns integrating vision, values, and purpose, systems thinking, and mental models." It's the synergy of the five disciplines that makes the difference. Preoccupation with one or another can lead to leadership fads and leaders as "vision junkies." Where should one begin? Senge reports that leaders with whom he has worked "agree that the first leadership design task concerns developing vision, values, and purpose or mission" (p. 343).

This is an extremely rich zone. Many organizational intervention strategies rest here. Bricks abound. Let us look at some of them now, beginning with mission and values.

APPLICATION

Most of the existing leadership literature concentrates on Zones 3a and 3b. Although increasingly more consideration is being paid to the next set of zones, the massive attention paid to this zone deserves our close attention. As we sort out the major organizational themes of leadership in this zone, remember that positional leadership here struggles with what is the best way to get everybody included and connected.

Mission and Values Statements

Out comes the wallet-size laminated card. Both sides are covered with statements and bullet-pointed lists of items. It is the mission, vision, and values card. Millions of dollars have been spent to shrink crucial content onto the tiny card. Why, and to accomplish what purpose? Are mission statements really about direction, or are they more about identity? Let us begin with a more traditional view of mission, then press its boundaries.

Stephen Covey (cited in Abrahams, 1995, p. 1) believes that "mission statement work is the single most important work, because the decisions made there affect all other decisions." Typically, mission and value statements, and even vision, act as the anchor point or glue for organizations in this zone. Abrahams (1995) captures this essence: "Corporations as entities and people as individuals share certain characteristics. Over time, they develop personalities that shape their philosophies and motivate their actions. And without a purpose or a mission, both a person and a company will flounder. Shaping the identity of a corporation really begins with defining its mission. Its reason for being. Its purpose, focus, goal" (p. 33). Noted executive advisor Warren Hoffman labels this identity the DNA of organizations (personal conversation, 2000). Statements of mission, vision, and values set the outer boundaries of acceptable behavior, concentrate attention on inner direction, and provide the reason for showing up in the morning.

Let me begin our mission statement investigation with an example. One of the most comprehensive formal mission statements that actually directs a company has been in place since that company's founding in 1949. Here is Medtronic's mission statement:

- To contribute to human welfare by application of biomedical engineering in the research, design, manufacture, and sale of instruments or appliances that alleviate pain, restore health, and extend life.

- To direct our growth in the areas of biomedical engineering where we display maximum strength and ability; to gather people and facilities that tend to augment these areas; to continuously build on these areas through education and knowledge assimilation; to avoid participation in areas where we cannot make unique and worthy contributions.

- To strive without reserve for the greatest possible reliability and quality in our products; to be the unsurpassed standard of comparison and to be recognized as a company of dedication, honesty, integrity, and service.

- To make a fair profit on current operations to meet our obligations, sustain our growth, and reach our goals.

- To recognize the personal worth of employees by providing an employment framework that allows personal satisfaction in work accomplished, security, advancement opportunity, and means to share in the company's success.

- To maintain good citizenship as a company. (Medtronic, 1998, p. 20)

To label this statement comprehensive might be an understatement. Yet it works. Those who work in and with the company overwhelmingly agree that their mission, although probably too wordy, is authentic. It takes its members into the future as a united and committed group.

In contrast to Medtronic's statement, which addresses mission, vision, and values, some statements are just slogans that offer neither identity nor direction. They try to capture some sense of a place for marketing purposes, such as Lexus automobile ads that use journey imagery. While great for selling, these statements reveal little about the company itself.

There are many views of what a mission statement should and should not contain (should they address vision, for example) and how long it should be. In my earlier work, out of frustration, I reduced my own thinking on this subject to a structural word count. I suggested mission statements be no longer than seven words. What a futile search for a fix-it strategy! Today, as I reflect on leadership and organizational life, I know that mission, along with vision, is critical and that what may be the most bothersome thing about the way mission statements are often constructed is not their length or how much they cover or do not cover. It is their shallowness and glibness.

Is there a way we can conceptualize mission that will drive us toward depth and seriousness? Bruce Gibb distinguishes eight conceptual options used by practitioners:

- *Mission as inspiration.* Excitement, energy, and creativity supposedly result from these kinds of statements. "We make exciting seats for automobiles that delight our customers." Gibb wonders if this is mission or manipulation.

- *Mission as vision.* This equation is common. Vision, as Block (1987) argues, concentrates on creating a desired future, mission on articulating what the business really is. Today is mission; tomorrow is vision.

- *Mission as slogan.* Kubota, a challenger in Caterpillar's market, describes its mission as "Encircle Caterpillar." Caribou Coffee ends its ads with "Life is short, stay awake for it." So, too, does the mission become slogan for Ernst & Young: "From thought to finish."

- *Mission as task.* This kind of mission talk totally informs military thinking. Even the old TV program *Mission: Impossible* conforms to this understanding of mission as task, as illustrated by the famous words, "Your mission, should you choose to accept it . . ." Here mission is measurable, results-oriented, and doable. It is unique and time-specific.

- *Mission as calling or sending.* Religious groups see mission this way. When one is called or sent to serve, that is one's mission in life. James Hillman (1996) in *The Soul's Code* taps this perspective and expands it to secular settings. Human beings are given gifts, a calling, a vocation. Terms like *discipleship* and *faithfulness* reflect this view as well. For some, being sent is an even more powerful image than being called. *Sent* implies a divinely inspired destination for the journey.

- *Mission as purpose.* In my authenticity action wheel, mission is distinguished from meaning or deep purpose. For many, however, the terms *mission* and *purpose* are interchangeable. When mission is purpose it answers the question of why you do what you do. Why does your company make, say, microwave popcorn?

The answer describes two things—what you want your customers to experience and what you hope to get in return. Perhaps you want your customers to enjoy easily and quickly prepared snacks and you want to get a good return on investment for the firm and the shareholders. Yet each answer triggers another question— why? The questioning game can continue ad infinitum.

- *Mission as confusion.* Gibb describes the essence of this view of mission (e-mail to the author, May 1999):

> This is a catch-all category in which the term is used inconsistently or as a catch-all for many things. When the mission is to achieve the vision of the organization, it is confusing; if the mission is a task, then what is the vision if not the task to be achieved? If the mission is the plan of action to achieve the task, then how is it different from a plan? Why use a dollar word when a five cent word will suffice—a plan. Is this just creating a new set of words to keep management confused and consultants in business?

> The other version of the catch-all is the mission statements that say what the organization produces, the formal values the organization believes in, the principles they follow in operating, how they want to treat their customers, and the kitchen sink. They tend to be paragraphs long and often more amusing than informative.

From Gibb's vantage point, Medtronic's mission statement would meet the benchmark of confusion. It contains too much. The first bullet defines the business, the second focuses on vision, the third stresses values, the fourth is a goal, the fifth expresses principles, and the last is about values and goals. The content is spectacular and clear; it just puts too much content into one category. When I talk to Medtronic folks, the mission is usually reduced to "restoring people to health."

From Mission Statement to Identity Affirmation

Perhaps part of the confusion about mission statements is that their real essence is missed and mistaken. I continue to believe that mission work is really about direction and the future. That is how mission is defined on the wheel. However, mission statements are not really about direction; rather they are definitions of identity. They affirm and clarify not where the organization, function, department, group, or team is headed, but what it is. The only time a mission statement connects to the future is during the first year. In the second year, the direction becomes the identity that is lived every day.

One can try to live the mission if it is future oriented. Traditional mission statements usually begin with words like "will," "strive," "are committed to," and other concepts indicating intent. I suggest replacing such words with notions like "are" and "do." If one tries, one can fail without disastrous results. To sabotage one's identity is betrayal causing serious consequences.

I am not engaging in linguistic games. Mission statements in most organizations are throwaways with little everyday reference. At Medtronic, the mission statement really functions as an identity claim. Every day, everyone at Medtronic actually alleviates pain, restores health, and extends life. This is not a future goal; it is an identity that is lived constantly. Bill George, the soon-to-retire CEO, affirms that identity every time he speaks. It is part of his being. It is who he is. He practices leadership as Identity Grow.

To conclude, I have proposed that mission focuses more on the future, identity more on the present. To solidify the point, picture a map in your mind. Suppose you want to go to Maine to view moose. What makes it possible to accomplish that goal? You have to know where you currently are. You have no way of getting to Maine if you are lost. Direction and a plan presuppose knowing your present location as an anchor point.

Without knowing who we are—personally, professionally, and organizationally—what we project for the future is a waste of time and energy. With a solid identity—with this zone firmly secure—not only can we project future visions, but we also can anticipate what the future holds for us. It is no accident that futuring lives in a zone farther out toward chaos. Ideally, the map image makes this distinction between mission and identity very clear.

Identity Construction

If you were shopping in the Yellow Pages for a potential source for a product or service, what would you like to know? The following four central features might be helpful:

1. What type the organization is (e.g., supplier, producer, provider, designer, manufacturer, builder, creator; or just the name of the organization).

2. Who the customers are (actual or potential: clients, patients, consumers, users).

3. The products, services, information, output, or energy the organization provides.

4. The standards the organization is committed to achieving in providing these outputs (personal attentive presence, one-day turnaround, guaranteed reliability or full money back, etc.; these usually specify cost, quality, timing, quantity, and service standards).

Here is how identity affirmation sounds when it has all four of these components. The company and the statement are hypothetical, but the process is transferable to any organization: *Flashy Foto provides state-of-the-art chemical and digital development and photo finishing for professional and amateur photographers at competitive prices, on time, and at professional standards of quality.*

- "Flashy Foto . . ." (This is component number one, the name of the institution.)

- "provides . . . chemical and digital development and photo finishing" (This is component number three, products and services.)

- "state-of-the-art . . . competitive prices, on time, and at professional standards of quality" (These are the standards referred to in component four.)

- "professional and amateur photographers" (These are the actual and potential customers from component two.)

Each department within Flashy Foto can now craft an identity affirmation for itself that aligns with the overall identity of Flashy Foto. This process can even be carried over to individual job descriptions. Gibb constructed this mission for the customer service department: "The customer service department takes and delivers customers' orders, provides consultation services, maintains contact with customers as necessary while their projects are in process, and resolves customer problems in person and on the telephone with respect, courtesy, and efficiency" (Bruce Gibb, e-mail to the author, May 1999). And here is the job definition for a supervisor in the photo-processing department: "The processing supervisor provides the processing team with direction, information, coaching, and support; represents the processing team in production meetings; and coordinates with other production supervisors to plan development projects and programs consistent with the values, guiding principles, goals, and objectives of Flashy Foto" (Bruce Gibb, e-mail to the author, May 1999).

This kind of identity affirmation offers immediate clarity and a foundation for action.

The process for developing this kind of four-factor identity affirmation is relatively easy and can be done in two hours. There are five steps (Bruce Gibb, e-mail to the author, May 1999):

1. Make sure everyone knows the four components of the mission statement.

2. On a flip chart, list under each of the four components the group's ideas about what should be included.

3. Evaluate the items listed and select the ones with which everybody agrees.

4. Create a statement including the selected items.

5. Review and polish the statement to get the pizzazz in it you want.

Identity statements define the essence of the organization to which one belongs. At their best they offer a critical brick for Zone 3b. They tell you who you are but not where you are going. They differ dramatically from the vision work I will describe in Zone 5a.

What should blossom from identity in this zone is the identification of core values. If they have not been clarified in Zone 1, they must be made clear here. Now leadership becomes more aware and intentional as it figures out the organization's value center. Values linked to the business or community set the foundation of identity.

Core Values

The acknowledgment of the importance of values in the workplace is not new. The worker-priest movement in France in the 1940s and 1950s and the industrial mission movement in the United Kingdom following World War II are examples of earlier efforts committed to connecting values to the workplace. I was privileged to have participated in part of that movement in the United States in the late 1960s when I worked at the Detroit Industrial Mission, a religiously ecumenical organization committed to connecting faith and work. Values were central to our enterprise. Businesses were mystified, put off, intrigued, amused, or even offended that the mission would advocate values as central to the workplace and leadership (then thought of mostly as positional). I began work on July 1, 1967. On July 23 the city was consumed by riots and flames. Business leaders later admitted to us how out of touch they were with urban life, and many committed themselves and their resources to creating a new Detroit. We also made headway working inside corporations such as Chrysler and General Motors.

Corporate responsibility was the expression used then, not *core values*. Corporate responsibility is a much broader notion, examining shared cultural or religious values linked to everyday living. That work continues today, through, for example, an organization named Seeing Things Whole led by Richard Broholm, a colleague from my Detroit Industrial Mission days (Seeing Things Whole, 423 Oxbow Road, Shelburne Falls, MA 01370, 413-625-2685, STWhole@aol.com).

However, now there is a growing preoccupation with the concept of core values as defined in 1994 by Collins and Porras in *Built to Last*. As I described earlier, the authors wanted to figure out what made great organizations great for the long term. All the companies, including such corporations as 3M, Procter & Gamble, and Philip Morris, were begun before 1950 and were premier in their industry and widely admired by knowledgeable businesspeople; all had made a powerful and lasting imprint on society; and all had been through multiple generations of chief executives and multiple product or service cycles.

The great companies did not have to have a great idea to begin. Nor did they require great and charismatic visionary leaders. They did not focus primarily on bottom-line profit, yet made more money than companies that did. They found stability in a world of change, yet tried Big Hairy Audacious Goals. They were not good places for all workers, did not always use strategic planning, and tended to promote from within. They focused more on continuous improvement than on beating the competition, embraced polarities, and knew that vision statements did not create greatness. Instead, living the company's core values in the toes was the key to long-term success.

It was around this discovery of core values that Collins and Porras centered their analysis. As I mentioned earlier, a core value differs from a shared value. A core value is a value of the organization as a business or nonprofit or community. A shared value is a value held in common by stakeholders, primarily employees. In order to determine the core values, leadership first has to clarify the nature of the business or the mission—the core business, excluding vision, structure, and, obviously, values. For example, Disney is in the family entertainment business, Philip Morris is in tobacco, 3M is in inventing solutions to a particular range of technical problems. The core values are the values necessary to sustain that business. Some people call them business values.

In the tobacco industry, what would one core value be? Not honesty. Not health. *Choice* is one core value. "The right to personal freedom of choice is worth defending." For 3M, a core value is innovation; for Boeing, product safety and quality; and for Disney, no cynicism allowed. These values are so central that to violate them is to destroy the business. Values like these are not an add-on to business. They are the life-giving heart of the organization.

Core values, however, are not universal; they may not be meaningful to everyone. That is why some companies are not good places to work. If my personal values conflict with company values, I am not a satisfied worker. Core values might also conflict with serving the customer.

For example, when would a company tell a customer to shove off? If a customer's requests or actions violate the company's core values, he or she is not a valued customer. The mantra of the quality movement in the early days requires a bit of modification: Do not just seek to meet or exceed customers' expectations; rather, seek to delight the customer *without losing your soul*. What is "soul" in an organization? Core values. If you work for a bank and a customer wants fraud, you do not delight him or her by saying, "No problem. We have a small fraud package, a medium fraud package, and a really large fraud package."

The most critical finding for leadership in *Built to Last* is that incarnating core values in the organization—living them every day, in the toes—is the secret to organizational durability and greatness. Authenticity is key. The CEO of the South African bank, as I described in the story at the beginning of this chapter, understood that authenticity is a competitive advantage.

In order to live one's core values, some practical steps are necessary. Some organizations assert values without defining them. It is assumed, for example, that everyone knows what *respect* and *honesty* mean. Not so. People bring their own interpretation to such terms. It may be necessary, as some organizations are now beginning to do, to define the terms and clearly describe behaviors that arise from their values.

Values may sometimes be seen to conflict, leading to employee cynicism and disillusionment. If you are in the human resources business, two core values are honesty and confidentiality. Which takes precedence when, and under what circumstances? In a company that is a client of mine, an older man nearing retirement fouled up—not for the first time—a long-term customer connection. The employee's peer group knew what had happened, and also knew that customer service was a primary core value. The group thought their colleague should be fired. The boss talked to the employee, discussed the issues honestly, and did not fire him. Why? Another core value was fairness, and the boss felt that to fire a person so close to retirement was unfair. Values can clash. Value education, including exploration of conflicts among values, must accompany value definition and affirmation if more serious problems are to be avoided.

Finally, values face alignment. Companies typically devote very little time to this part of values work, but 80 to 90 percent of the time they spend working on values should be focused on achieving alignment (Collins, 1996, p. 24). What does alignment look like? The values are posted everywhere (although when they are lived deeply this is less important). They are talked about and understood; they are linked to job requirements and performance appraisal, hiring and firing, and team assessments; and they are an essential part of celebrations.

In Zone 3b, values pulsate throughout the body. They are more than the heart; they are the lifeblood of the organization. Be they core or shared, they are the glue, the bonding, the identity of the place. They give the organization the courage to move into a less-known world. They are its strength, something I witnessed in an Innovation Associates seminar conduced by Peter Senge in the early

1980s. Peter invited a participant to come forward. As I remember, the person was female and slight of build. She was asked if she was left- or right-handed. Going to her strong side, Peter asked her to extend her right arm. He placed his right hand under her hand, and his left hand gently on her bicep, and asked her to resist as he tried to bend her arm. As he pushed up with his right hand and held his left hand steady, he easily bent her arm. Then he invited all of us to do the same, this time with someone our own size. Some arms were hard to bend. Most of us could do it.

Then he returned to the woman and said, "Now, imagine you have a steel rod an inch thick running down the center of your arm. Concentrate on the rod and let me know when you are ready." She nodded, and using the same procedure as before, he tried to bend her arm. This time he could not bend it. We were not convinced until we tried it too. Behold, it worked for us as well.

Steel rod is a wonderful metaphor for the identity of an organization. With identity in place, believed and lived, an organization is a mighty force, a solid player in the world of potential chaos. Leadership affirms the shared identity, making it authentic.

ZONE LEADERSHIP ACTIVITIES

There are many other leadership activities important to this zone: strategic planning, maintaining quality, reinventing, reengineering, and realigning—and, of course, activities specific to including organizational members in the work of the organization—attending to all stakeholders, building self-directed teams, and groups, coaching and mentoring, fostering emotional intelligence, and seeking new ways to be inclusive.

Strategic Planning

The work of organizational development often stresses long-range planning, with laundry lists of improvements to enhance organizational performance. Strategic planning, an approach that challenged OD in the eighties, saw OD as too participatory, too process-focused, and lacking attention to organizational direction and priorities.

Strategic planning rejects the long-range-list approach. Instead, it seeks to identify two or three critical issues that have to be addressed if the organization is to move forward. Strategic planning is a leadership focus in this zone.

Maintaining Quality, Reinventing, Reengineering, and Realigning

Quality circles, small groups of workers and managers gathering to solve problems, popped up in the late '70s. They were precursors of the full-blown quality movement that was about to blast into U.S. organizational life. Notice the image: a circle, not a hierarchy.

The 1980s rolled out. *Quality* became the key word. W. Edwards Deming's star shone brightly as U.S. businesses, beaten badly by the Japanese, embraced the quality movement that had powered Japan's success. *Quality* became the code word for an enduring legacy—customer focus and customer service. Sadly, what was proposed as a fundamental change in organizational philosophy, a top-led effort to transform the whole mode of doing business, often became little more than a set of organizational procedures and techniques. What was touted to be a new worldview, a move toward creativity, innovation, and transformation, instead was rapidly reduced to a rigid process directed by a quality manager.

Today, *quality* means customer focus and service and reliable production of goods and services. It still pervades organizational mental maps, but it has become a floor rather than a ceiling, a necessity to remain competitive rather than a competitive advantage. As I move through organizations today, quality is often dismissed as an organizing focus. "Been there, done that" reflects the mood. Personally, I am a believer in TQM. My worry is that it has been reduced to a fix-it mentality rather than explored as a philosophy of organizational leadership. This situation defines a challenge for leadership in Zone 3a if employees are to be included in ensuring and improving quality rather than just learning a set quality drill.

The "re" age also struck in the '80s. Reinventing, reengineering, realigning—all had their advocates and were tested in practice as ways to improve systems thinking. And, according to a growing number of studies, each produced mixed results (see Hamel and Prahalad, 1994).

Reengineering, reinventing, and realigning live in this zone. Leadership should attend, however, to what Michael Hammer (1997), the inventor of the concept, says in his latest book, *Beyond Reengineering*: "Since I first coined that term in the late 1980s, I have consistently used the same definition for it: Reengineering is the radical redesign of business processes for dramatic improvement" (p. xii).

It is not, in other words, the radical, start-over mentality that is the critical aspect of the definition, although that concept often is what triggers managerial excitement. For Hammer:

> The key word in the definition of reengineering is "process": a complete end-to-end set of activities that together create value for a customer. The Industrial Revolution had turned its back on processes, deconstructing them into specialized tasks and then focusing on improving the performance of these tasks. Tasks—and the organizations based on them—formed the basic building blocks of twentieth-century corporations. The persistent problems companies faced in the late twentieth century, however, could not be addressed by means of task improvement. Their problems were process problems, and in order to solve them companies had to make processes the center of their attention. In taking this momentous step, corporate leaders were doing more than solving a set of vexing performance problems. They were bringing down the curtain on close to two hundred years of industrial history. . . . Process-centered organizations demand the complete reinvention of the systems and disciplines of management. (pp. xii–xiii)

Attending to All Stakeholders

Introduced in the 1970s, the idea of stakeholder in contrast to stockholder endures today and ensures Affirming Shared Identity. Bruce Gibb is right to include stakeholder analysis (in his terms, analysis of the "people subsystem," as described in Chapter Five) as part of any system analysis. Picture the organization as a tent with a tall center pole. The pole supports the tent cover and is held in place by ropes staked to the ground, surrounding the outside of the tent. Similarly, stakeholders, surrounding the organization, provide the political tension that keeps the pole centered and upright. Take away or weaken attention to any one stake, and the whole tent becomes shaky and unstable.

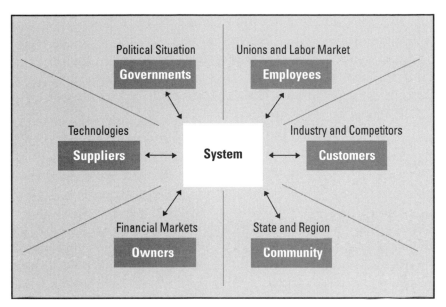

FIGURE 18 • SYSTEM AND SUPRASYSTEM STAKEHOLDERS
Source: Bruce Gibb, 1985, unpublished materials. Reprinted with permission.

Typically stakeholders include customers, employees, owners (stockholders), communities, suppliers, governments, and other entities involved in some way with a particular organization (see Figure 18, above). Stakeholders have diverse missions and values, yet each often thinks its mission and values are the most critical for the firm's success. Nevertheless, leadership must attend to all stakeholders, or the tent falls to the ground.

The South African banking organization I referred to earlier worked this through. The executives identified the business the bank was in, the company's core values, and its stakeholders and their interests. For example, employees wanted opportunities for growth and development, and valued participation and being heard. Communities wanted resources and valued bank involvement in community issues. Stockholders wanted sound long-term return on their investment and valued wise business choices. The executives figured out that their job was to lead and manage these stakeholders without letting one group dominate the direction of the bank. Executives live at the center of contradictory stakeholder forces. They guide, they include, they weigh and balance these complex forces. And they reject any stakeholder who claims to represent the firm's total fundamental interests. When an accounting firm was invited to the bank, a rather young consultant with that firm argued for focusing mainly on stockholders' interests. The executives rejected him out of hand. They wanted their tent to be strong.

Robert Kaplan and David Norton's Balanced Scorecard approach (1996) reflects this inclusive stakeholder perspective. Linking shareholders, customers, internal management processes, and innovation/ growth replaces one bottom line with four.

To test inclusion and identify guidance issues, executives or designated teams should assess the firm's performance with each of its stakeholder groups. For example, a team or working group can identify the stakeholders, identify the goals that each stakeholder group has for the firm as a whole, and then assess how well the firm is balancing these goals by grading (A through F) the effectiveness of the firm in meeting each stakeholder's interests. The patterns become apparent quickly. Depending on the results, further research and actions may be required.

Building Self-Directed Teams and Groups

Teams flower in Zone 3b, including self-directed work teams. These teams differ from self-organizing teams, which are natural adaptive responses to current organizational realities. Self-directed work teams are created by executives and thus can be canceled.

What makes teams work? Barry Heerman advocates "spirited teams." He identifies six phases of spirited team development (1998, pp. 9–10). Each exemplifies leadership growing and nuturing the identity.

- Initiating: Foster relationships that affirm a sense of belonging.

- Visioning: Invite team members to share their individual visions for team performance.

- Claiming: Watch for begrudging compliance, and engage members in committing to roles.

- Celebrating: Acknowledge the work of team members.

- Letting go: Embrace the dark side.

- Service: The will to serve is seeking expression in the hearts of all team members.

I have found the most difficult of these phases is the fifth. Letting go is not easy for some people. Conflict avoidance only confounds the problems. As Heerman rightly observes, "Team members sometimes believe that feelings of anger, disappointment, sadness or damaged relationships with team members can be reasoned away or ignored. They can't. I have learned that letting go, backing off, helps create a safer place for real issues to be addressed" (p. 11).

Teams vs. Groups

Wisely understood, teams are not fix-it strategies. They are a philosophy of identity in action. Driving them from the top does not always work. Confusing teams and groups triggers mischief as well.

Teams: What is a team? Think, for example, of a hospital operating team, a basketball team, a military combat team, or a project team. Do not think of golf, which is individual competition, unless one plays for the Ryder Cup where U.S. players and European players compete as a team.

What constitutes a team? A team shares focused goals within a specified time frame (which can change depending on circumstances), and all members work together to accomplish them. Teams are relatively small. To refer to a company as a team seeks to reinforce inclusion; however, it distorts what teams actually do.

Groups: What is a group? A group shares broad goals with no specified time frame, and does not have to work together to accomplish them. Executives usually operate in groups, not teams. They have broad strategic goals, usually focused on their own department or division, with no sharp time frame, and do not work together regularly to make them happen. Their primary responsibility is to the success of their own department. An executive gathering shares information and coordinates activities.

To send a group off for team building is inauthentic. Very little changes. Why? They are a group. What, then, is group building?

I recommend this group-building process only under the following conditions: There must be trust, respect, and no underground politics for it to work without terrible consequences. I have done it many times. At other times, I have refrained from recommending it.

I learned the hard way when a group lied to me. After the event, the CEO fired half the group. Be wary of this process.

Be sure to have a facilitator to set the tone and move the process along, building a safe environment as it unfolds. The members discuss the process prior to the event with the facilitator. This is crucial for buy-in. Once the process has been clarified, the group will decide to proceed or not to proceed.

If the group chooses to proceed, the process can begin. Each member is given a sheet listing the following statements:

- This is what I like about how you are doing your job:

- These are areas for growth and improvement:

- I need the following from you so I can do my job better:

- This is what I can offer so you can do your job better:

The members fill out the sheets ahead of time and give them to the person receiving the feedback.

The exercise begins with feedback to the highest-ranking person in the room. She or he is the center of attention. All the group members share their comments. I usually go around question by question, although sometimes I have one person respond to all four statements at the same time. The recipient of the comments can make only two kinds of responses—questions for clarification and requests for examples. The recipient is invited to take notes. When completed, the receiver is asked to summarize what she or he heard to make sure the message was received accurately.

Everyone gets a turn to receive. For ten to twelve people, it takes about two seven-hour days. Do not rush or give short shrift to the last persons due to lack of time. An outside facilitator is required. Do not have a person in the group try to facilitate, as it will constitute a conflict of interest. Remember, do not try this if the group members fear each other. Trust must be in place for trust to bloom more fully.

Of the many benefits, one continues to strike me as very powerful. Most performance reviews are conducted in private. No one else knows what is discussed. In this process, everyone hears. The impact magnifies. It is not a 360-degree feedback process. It is a 180-degree process. If one member gets feedback from a boss, it may or may not be taken seriously. I have talked to many executives who receive negative feedback and dismiss it by saying, "Consider the source! What does he know about what I do?" In this group feedback process, a pattern often emerges. It is no longer "consider the source"; it is "consider the sources." When many people make similar observations, it is more difficult to dismiss the comments.

If you are a member or facilitator, give close attention to answers to question 2. Watch for the following: If person A says to person B that his work could be improved with more follow-through, check what kind of feedback person A receives. It is often the same. One wonders if A is talking about B or really projecting A onto B. At the end, if this pattern emerges, it is worth some serious and playful reflection. In this zone, distinguish teams and groups. Build both when appropriate.

Coaching and Mentoring

Coaching and mentoring are both very popular today. When properly understood and used in the right context, each enhances leadership. However, as with the words *team* and *group,* the difference between them is blurred because these terms are often used interchangeably and at the wrong time. As I have reviewed many books on both subjects, I suggest the following distinction:

Coaching: One coaches for success. A hospital operating team is struggling to be more effective in its work. A baseball player wants to improve in the sport. Hire a coach to assist you or your team to become more successful in whatever activity needs improvement. Coaches bring skills and smarts to the table. Sometimes they are experts, sometimes consultants, and other times process wizards. One of the best texts on coaching, *Co-Active Coaching* by Laura Whitworth, Henry Kimsey-House, and Phil Sandahl (1998), centers on the client and outlines processes to release her or his gifts and insights for success in work and life. Another useful text links coaching to the MBTI personality inventory. Entitled *Introduction to Type®
and Coaching*, it offers useful advice for determining the personality preferences of the coach's client (Hirsh and Kise, 2000). It is very clear. Coaching is hands-on, concrete, and task-oriented.

Mentoring: One mentors for significance and satisfaction. A hospital operating team is struggling to decide whether it wants to remain in the health profession. A baseball player questions whether baseball is a sport worthy of commitment. Find a mentor to help you wrestle with who you are and what is important to you. Mentors bring wisdom to the table, a depth of understanding, and years of experience. It is hard to hire a mentor because the relationship is built over time, based on trust. Mentoring explores in depth the realities and the profound struggles of life. It is less focused on problem solving than coaching is. It should come as no surprise that some mentoring books ground their thinking in spirituality, even religion. One example is *Connecting* by Paul Stanley and J. Robert Clinton (1992).

Coaching focuses on mission accomplishment, mentoring on meaning discovery and creation. While both fit into this zone, coaching roots here totally while mentoring begins in this zone and adds its real value in Zones 6 and 7.

Teams and groups can utilize both coaches and mentors. However, coaches are a better match for teams, mentors for groups. Remember, teams have clear goals and have to work together to accomplish them within a specified time frame. Coaching enhances team success. Mentoring fits better with groups, as group members share their wisdom with each other and build quality, trust-based relationships over time.

It is not uncommon to know successful people who find no meaning, significance, or satisfaction in their lives. Conversely, it is possible to find deep meaning every day even in the face of unwanted pain, intense struggle, and failure to accomplish important goals.

Improving batting skills when baseball itself is the problem is inauthentic. Likewise, exploring the meaning of baseball when one wants to field better is also inauthentic. It is the proper match that releases authenticity.

Fostering Emotional Intelligence

American Express has launched a training program to teach workers how to master their emotions of anger, rejection, and other difficult aspects of their lives. According to American Express, the investment of $5 million to develop the first program of its kind has yielded dramatic results. Sales jumped 18 percent in three regions where financial advisors received the training, in contrast to a control group that did not receive the training (Barshay, 1999).

And as Daniel Goleman (1995) shows, research continues to link employee performance to the bottom line. Goleman has coined the term *emotional intelligence* to describe a quality that strongly influences that performance. These are the five components of emotional intelligence at work:

- Self-awareness—a deep sense of one's own moods, feelings, and emotions as they affect others

- Self-regulation—self-control of one's own disruptive emotions and ability to pause, to think before acting

- Motivation—passion that transcends money or position, pursuit of goals with commitment and persistence

- Empathy—ability to understand others' situations and feelings and the skills to react and treat them accordingly

- Social skill—ability to work relationships and build networks, find common ground, and build mutuality of support and understanding

Each aspect of emotional intelligence involves a set of "hallmark" competencies. Self-awareness, for example, involves self-confidence, realistic self-assessment, and self-deprecating sense of humor. Self-regulation implies trustworthiness and integrity, comfort with ambiguity, and openness to change. In many ways, Goleman turns the soft side of leadership into hard data for business prosperity.

Leadership understands these five components in this zone just as it knows financial numbers and system thinking in Zones 2 and 3a (see Goleman, 1995, 1998a, 1998b). The question, however, remains: Is emotional intelligence the sine qua non of leadership, as the *Harvard Business Review* implies in titling an article by Goleman "What Makes a Leader?" (1998a)? It is a foundation that is necessary. Is it sufficient?

The next zones will build on this and other foundations from Zone 3b, challenging leadership to go beyond Zone 3b competencies as the world shifts again and again. The third umpire waits to call a few balls and strikes. The fourth umpire has not even come to the party yet.

Selling Beyond Demographics and Contracts

As the world shifts, selling strategies shift. The old, Zone 2 model focused on demographics and cutting the deal. Now, *The New Strategic Selling* (Heiman and Sanchez, 1998) practices a new approach that links traditional selling habits with organization savvy and value coherence. This approach challenges the mechanical model, replacing it with a need to understand the dynamics of the organization you are seeking and to know when to say no to a potential customer. Some customers are not worth the effort or income.

Insights into Personal, Interpersonal, and Organizational Realities

Noted executive advisor Warren Hoffman pushes linguistic boundaries. Word use often opens windows into what is really going on and/or reveals interpersonal competencies in another way. Here are a few clues that do not necessarily show up in ordinary discussions, and that reveal a lot about both the speaker and listener. Each clue is organized around a word that, when used frequently, tells a great deal about the user.

- **Why**—This word is fine for scientific inquiry. Knowing what is really going on supports the "why" question. However, it is not good when asked of a person to describe her/his behavior. "Why did you do this?" creates defensiveness and questions motive. Instead ask "What was going on?" The "why" question often implies suspicion and disguises anger.

- **Should**—This word produces guilt and a please-me mentality. Instead say *could* or *must*, which imply that the listener has choices. *Should* carries a moralistic tone that separates rather connects in the conversation.

- **Try**—This word is often a code for avoidance and denial. "I am trying to meet the time line" usually means "I am not going to." Mission statements often imply the word *try*. Just do it.

- **Can't**—This word often means *won't*. The oft-heard comment "I can't make the meeting" usually implies "I do not want to go there." If *can't* connects to a particularly important competency or skill, it may be appropriate. For example, "I can't perform surgery" fits if the person is an engineer.

- **But**—What a way to wipe out what you just said. "I like how you accomplish tasks, but your speaking style needs improvement." Bye-bye praise; enter criticism. Put in the word *and*. Leave *but* out altogether with no *and*. Either works. An either-or mentality, while often fitting in Zone 2, does not fit in Zone 3. It separates rather than connects. "Well, I will *try* to do it, *but* I don't think I can!" *But* also destroys polarity thinking: "I love the way you are a strong individual, but you are not a good team player." Maybe teams require both strong individuals and connectedness at the same time. More on this later.

New ideas for improving organizational life are rife in this zone. Every now and then, one that is new, novel, and relatively quiet emerges and deserves attention. In the 1990s, with massive mergers and buyouts, workers once again viewed themselves as pawns in a chess game over which they had no control. To counter this trend, one small company challenged the prevailing pattern. Benchmark Computer Learning's two owners, Phil Hinderaker and Scott Schwefel, embarked on a program untried elsewhere. They set up a Growth Sharing Program that had three goals:

- Fairness—To recognize that employee efforts will be a key factor in Benchmark growth

- Incentive—To provide greater incentive for Benchmark employees and give them a stake in the success of Benchmark

- Teamwork—To get everyone working toward the same goal and to foster a culture of "we" rather than "us" and "them"

The immediate result of this initiative was a buyout offer of $4.4 million. It was rejected, but the amount set the standard for the growth-sharing program. If the company were ever sold, the employees would share in the profits. The money to be distributed would come from the difference between the sale price and the $4.4 million baseline offer.

The amount each member of Benchmark will receive depends on assigned points. The more points, the greater the share. The points are assigned as members meet certain criteria determined in part by the owners and in part by management and the workers themselves. As the guiding document states: "Each employee's level of participation will be determined under a point system. Points will be awarded initially based primarily on value of individual contribution to the growth and success of the company. Management may, in its sole discretion, issue additional points for various achievements from time to time" (p. 1).

Through interviews and personal reflection, Hinderaker and Schwefel each identified criteria for management. Then they merged their ideas into six management assessment categories: results, lives the values, a bar raiser, a strategic thinker and a leader, customer oriented, a team player. Management was given the same assignment and, with input from the workers, identified a similar list for the workers. Points were assigned. Fifty percent of the points goes to management, 50 percent to the workers. Ten percent of each pool will be withheld for assignment to later additions to the membership. Everyone gets a percent number and it stays with the person until the business is sold. If the 10 percent is unused, it returns to the pool. If a person is terminated for cause, she or he loses all rights. If a person leaves six months before closing, she or he gets 50 percent of the point value. There is also a six-month waiting period before points are assigned to a new employee. Managers decide about workers; Hinderaker and Schwefel decide about managers.

When Hinderaker presented this idea in its early stages of development at his peer-executive tech group, his colleagues generally panned the idea. After reflection, some of the other owners are currently giving it serious consideration for their organizations. I thought it a worthy idea. It is also a perfect leadership fit to Zone 3b.

Other new ideas flood this zone. Corporate programs that attend to family needs are appearing more often. Eddie Bauer seeks to keep the workplace personal by keeping its headquarters café open late so overworked employees can take home prepared meals. The company also offers a "balance day off" each year to ease the juggling of work and home (see Hammonds, 1996).

NationsBank offers a work and family program to build loyalty and trust. Its philosophy reverses the TQM sequence. Instead of beginning with the external customer and working back, this organization focuses heavily on its associates (members). It is assumed that if they are well cared for, the external customers will be well cared for.

Nick Martinski (1998) identifies "Twenty-Five Ways to Retain Your Best Employees." All of his recommendations fit Zone 3b. A few examples reflect the tone: Make new employees feel welcome; manage with your heart, not your head; know your employees as people; educate your employees; have fun; pass out a "blooper" award; and practice what you preach.

Finally, *Positive Leadership* is one of the best journals I have found to help executives connect leadership to organizational life. It is value-centered and dwells most of the time in Zone 3b. It offers hands-on suggestions for leadership in everyday situations, excellent quotes, and the most current thinking on critical organizational issues.

This zone opens vast arrays of indentity development. Let us step back a moment and reflect on all that is happening in this zone. Major shifts have challenged old ways of doing business. Dramatic new ways of doing business fill books, journals, and seminars, achieving various levels of success when put into practice. Even though results have been mixed in terms of effectiveness, great strides have been taken.

The world indeed is shifting from an exclusive mechanical Zone 2 reality to an organic sensibility, necessitating a very different understanding of leadership. Hence the critical shift from Building Core Competencies to Designing Sustainable Systems and Affirming Shared Identity. Another way to frame the move and put Senge's contribution in context is the following:

In Zone 2 the fundamental dynamic in education and research was from theory to practice. Experts know more than students; they pour out the knowledge into the students' heads and the student pays for the product—an education often defined by a degree. Faculty are trained with technical skills and information; they pass it on and do the research. In contrast, in Zone 3, especially 3b, the order reverses. It is not theory to practice. Rather, it is experience and then reflect. Reflective practice is the dominant mode of learning. Hence, a learning organization. Faculty now become perpetual learners, engaging fellow and sister learners in the ongoing process of inquiry. This change is monumental. While lip service about learning organizations is everywhere, the practice often reverts to the old model. Experts are still hired to teach in seminars, which in the business are often called part of the Learning University. It is no accident that I have designed each zone to kick off with a story, then move to core ideas, then application.

Nitin Nohria (1996) concludes his study of M-Form shifting to N-Form organizations by stating his belief that organizations have in fact changed dramatically. In my terms, we are now witnesses to leadership in a world of great vitality and vibrancy.

The widespread business interest in emotional intelligence, whose home is solidly located in Zone 3b, is easily justified. The links between people skills, productivity, and profitability are evident. Guiding people to authentic membership in organizational life delivers on the promise that people inclusion equals business success.

The science of the Enlightenment still prospers in this zone. Yes, the world is more complex. Perhaps the new sciences are really new. There is even a new discipline evolving—psychoeconomics. What a connection between Zone 2 and Zone 3. Nevertheless, the search for scientifically based research, formal evaluations, and a fix-it mentality has not ceased. Knowledge and skills still matter a great deal. They are just a different kind of knowledge and a new set of skills. Moreover, multiple perspectives from multiple stakeholders now inform and transform research and acquired wisdom. The world is at least understandable, if not as knowable as it was in Newtonian physics. In the earlier zones the pressure is always to return to the safer, more predictable modes. In this zone, new questions about performance evaluation, rewards systems, the nature of competition and cooperation, and especially governance confront our best thinking. As Nohria says, "The N-form requires an entirely different set of managerial skills [than the M-form], and the adjustment for many will not be easy" (p. 52).

While Stacey does not discuss all of the material presented here, his framework accounts for it. He is an advocate of complexity theory. Stacey captures much of this zone well (See Stacey, 1996, pp. 35–36; Quinn, 1980):

- Effective managers do not manage strategically in a piecemeal manner. They have a clear view of what they are trying to achieve, where they are trying to take the business. The destination is thus intended.

- But the route to that destination, the strategy itself, is not intended from the start in any comprehensive way. Effective managers know that the environment they have to operate in is uncertain and ambiguous. They therefore sustain flexibility by holding open the method of reaching the goal.

- The strategy itself then emerges from the interaction between different groupings of people in the organization, different groupings with different amounts of power, different requirements for the access to information, different time spans and parochial interest. Senior managers orchestrate these different pressures. The top is always reassessing, integrating, and organizing.

- The strategy emerges or evolves in small incremental, opportunistic steps. But such evolution is not piecemeal or haphazard because of the agreed purpose and the role of top management in reassessing what is happening. It is this that provides the logic in the incremental action.

- The results are an organization that is feeling its way to known goals, opportunistically learning as it goes.

Again, in this zone *leadership as headship* is tested and challenged. Decision making spreads out. Members of the organization are included in the organization as full members, are placed on self-directed teams, and feel and experience the spirit of the organization. These facts push key decision makers to examine their own power and reflect again on the amount of influence they really have over everyday operations.

Nevertheless, when all is said and done, leadership still fundamentally rests at the top in this zone. Positional leadership sets the identity. Workers are invited to belong. Affirming Shared Identity encourages all employees to buy into the team; don't separate and scream. Now that teams are contrasted with groups, the rhyming slogan might also read: "Build the group; that's the new scoop."

One final example of leadership reflects the shift from Zone 2 to Zone 3b. I was struck by the title—*The 9 Natural Laws of Leadership*. It seemed so locked into Zone 2, like *The Leadership Machine*. However, probing the content shows the linkage between the zones and the shift from one to another. The author of this book, Warren Blank, a colleague I met in government counseling, lives in Zone 3b big time. He knows classical physics and is on the quantum side, similar to Bruce Gibb and others. His nine laws capture much of what has preceded this report of his work:

1. A leader has willing follower-allies.

2. "Leadership" is a field of interaction—a relationship between leaders and follower-allies.

3. Leadership occurs as an event.

4. Leaders use influence beyond formal authority.

5. Leaders operate outside the boundaries of organizationally defined procedures.

6. Leadership involves risk and uncertainty.

7. Not everyone will follow a leader's initiative.

8. Consciousness—information processing capacity—creates leadership. (Blank, 1995, p. 10)

He is making choices like you were invited to do in Chapter Two. It is clear which side he is on.

ZONE IDENTIFICATION AND LEADERSHIP QUESTIONS

There are so many issues in this zone it is sometimes difficult to know just which ones are most deserving of leadership. The following questions will walk you through the assessment:

1. How sturdy is my organization or community in this zone?

- Do the members of the organization feel that they are part of the organization?

- Are processes in place so organizational members can and do buy in to the executives' mission and value statements?

- Are individuals valued as members of teams, not just seen as cogs in the mechanics of production?

- Are there "practice fields" for people to try out new procedures and relationships in safe places before going out into the rough-and-tumble real world?

- Have the executives participated in a strategic planning process?

- Are there symbols and logos that identify the essence of the place?

- Has the organization tried reengineering processes? If so, who drove the process? Were the outcomes for the process identified, and did they occur as anticipated?

- Are employees encouraged to buy in to the identity?

- Has the quality movement been introduced to the organization? Driven by whom? What were the stated desired results? What was the actual outcome?

- Are groups distinguished from teams?

- Are there any self-directed teams at work? Who created them? Have any ever been taken out of existence? Under what conditions?

- Are discussions of complexity and chaos theory floating around the organization? Who is pushing these ideas and why?

```
10 |  |  |  |  |  |  |  |  |  |  0  |  |  |  |  |  |  |  |  |  10
Very Sturdy                                              Shaky
```

2. Where is my organization or community currently focusing its leadership attention?

- Is this zone the center of attention?

- Is this platform shaky but leadership attention is focused elsewhere?

```
10 |  |  |  |  |  |  |  |  |  |  0  |  |  |  |  |  |  |  |  |  10
Excellent Fit                                                Misfit
```

3. Am I prepared to affirm shared identity?

- Do I feel that I am a full member of the organization?

- Are my people skills finely honed?

- Do I understand the strengths and weaknesses of the interventions tried in this zone?

- Do I know, believe, and live the organization's identity?

- Are the stakeholders real to me, and do I understand their differing missions and values? Do I see how to guide the organization so that it honors all stakeholders without favoring any one of them?

- Do I see any value to complexity theory?

- Am I prepared to be a team leader, group leader, and participant?

```
10 |  |  |  |  |  |  |  |  |  |  0  |  |  |  |  |  |  |  |  |  10
Ready to Exhibit Leadership                    Not Prepared at All
```

ZONE SUMMARY

To use the organic metaphor so fertile in this zone: Life blossoms here. What is required is vibrancy, a dynamic that brings life to a system rooted in a shared identity. Employees become members of the club, members of the group and team. Numbers alone do not capture the vitality of the human spirit. Connected systems do not offer a sense of belonging and possibility. Identity sets the foundation.

Coherence judges authenticity. Organizationally, know who you are, what you value, and why you are here. Come together, cohere, be members.

The competencies in this zone include the full array of emotional intelligence competencies (Goleman, 1995, pp. 26–27), including personal competencies (self-awareness, self-regulation, motivation) and social competencies (empathy and social skills), team-building skills, ethical awareness, a sense of core and shared values, and executive strategic thinking and planning skills.

Fairness sets the outer boundaries of authentic action. However, special parts of the system receive special attention as issues arise. One standard does not fit all. Proportional fairness is built on equality. New processes often have to be constructed if the system is to flourish. The arthritic body can be healed if the new processes reflect the core principles and are lively and engaging. Reengineering is more process than form, more dynamic than regularized in this zone.

Science still works. The world is understandable. It just requires everyone who is an umpire to call 'em the way they see 'em. However, all umpires are not equal. Some are senior umpires, who have the functional responsibility to make the final call. That is their leadership challenge. They are more genteel than their counterparts in the earlier zones. Nevertheless, their job requires leadership—Affirming Shared Identity.

ZONE 3B DEFINITIONS

Leadership: Affirming Shared Identity
Authenticity criterion: Coherence
Metaphor: Life is a body/living system
Core ethical principle: Justice is proportionally constructive
Polarity: Form/dynamic, with emphasis on dynamic

STIRRINGS

The stirring in this zone is about being heard, being listened to, being taken seriously. Less experienced organizational members may have something to offer to the more experienced. If there has been down-sizing, morale is likely to be low and the company is likely not to be reaching its goals for the downsizing (Sennett, 1998, p. 50). Efforts to motivate employees may have had the opposite effect. Consider pay for performance. Suppose you can double your pay if you sign up. You sign. Then you quickly figure out that what the new plan rewards is the opposite of what you believe your job to be:

> For instance, you're a customer service representative, answering the phone all day long, and you figure that part of good customer service is listening to customers' complaints and fixing them. A big hunk of your paycheck, however, will now depend on how many extra services you sell on each call, and how quickly you get rid of one caller and go on to the next. Furthermore, if you fail to meet your monthly sales goal, your pay is docked. If you do meet it, you'll get the bonus—but next month, you'll find your quota has been raised. (Ganzel, 1998, p. 35)

So, how might you feel? Do you have a deep sense of belonging, of inclusion? Probably not. Is good customer service contrary to cost containment and overall profitability? And who should work out the answer—workers or management or both? Get ready for Zone 4.

Negative Stirrings

When you start hearing comments like these, the stirring is well underway.

> The executives were the ones who announced the values at a big rally where they made them public. Now, I see these values plas-tered everywhere. I'm not sure I believe they are for real. I certainly had no say in their creation.

> I think I'll just do my work. It's a good organization. I'm just not excited about working here. I have no deep passion for what I am expected to do. And I wonder, if I speak up, will I be punished like some of my friends have been? The rhetoric around here is to express your opinions. When you do, you get nailed for not being a good team player. It comes out in your performance review. I have a good boss, but some of them are abusive. You are better advised to be careful. Don't risk much and just do what is minimally expected of you, is my advice.

> One executive, I've been told, thinks we need skill training. Would that make us happier campers? I want to be listened to, to have a

voice. The boss needs training—listening skills. I'm just not sure it's possible here. Skills are not our issues; we need to be listened to and taken seriously. I may be called a member. I still think I'm an employee.

My deepest fear links to all this merger talk. We just merged and went through a reorganization. I sense the reorganization and rhetoric about integrated systems is really power talk. Bye-bye independence and creativity. Hello team conformity. While they claim to share power, the fact seems to be there is more power at the top.

Negative stirrings manifest themselves in cynicism. Empowerment talk remains talk. There is no real shared power. Self-directed teams are created by bosses and can be easily disassembled by the same bosses. Inauthenticity pervades the place. When workers are asked to buy into values, it is hard to trust that the label "core values" is not a cover for "executive values."

Positive Stirrings

Such cynicism can be the stimulus for positive stirrings. We would not be cynical about matters that didn't matter. This feedback can be a positive stimulus for creativity and change.

I want more. I want to be heard. My goal is not to be CEO. I have insights. I have learned a lot working with colleagues about how this place really operates. Upper management could benefit from my insights. My boss listens well. I have made a difference. Sometime I think I am leading him. I love it. I don't challenge the core values. They define what we do and believe. I just want to participate more fully by contributing to our future. No boss can know enough. My view can add insights he does not have.

The positive stirrings reflect a deeply held belief that organizational members have significant insights to offer and want to offer them. The world is inviting the organization to listen and speak and, together with its members, build the next platform for authentic action.

Buy-in can be transformed into ownership. Fear can be replaced with creative participation. At its best, Zone 3b constructs a platform of inclusive processes. Positive stirrings show that members feel connected to an organization that knows who and what it is. Identity boundaries are firm. Values are clear, real, and lived personally and organizationally. The organization is now poised for the next dramatic shift.

It is not enough to include, to assimilate, to belong. Members, including all stakeholders, want voice, not necessarily to challenge the outer boundaries of the system—its identity. Rather, they want to contribute boldly to its implementation. The question before us is, Are the positional leaders prepared to share power? Is the fear that members will scream rather than join the team? Or will they turn their screams into voices and commitments into action? Leadership shifts again. Creating Ownership awaits.

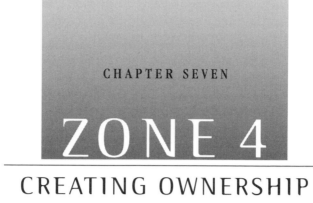

CHAPTER SEVEN

ZONE 4

CREATING OWNERSHIP

GET DOWN FROM THE TOWER; SHARE THE POWER.

Ralph Stayer, CEO of Johnsonville Sausage, discovered the practice of political engagement when he wanted "employees who would fly like geese." What he had was "a company that wallowed like a herd of buffalo." Deeply aware that his successful company faced uncertainty in the market, he became conscious of a frightening vulnerability. Accustomed to the top-down, fix-it leadership mode, he searched for a recipe book. It then dawned on him that his management style of respectful command and control was the problem. He said to himself, "Thank God I was the problem so I could be the solution." Next he needed a vision—a flock of geese with shared leadership. The buffalo had to fly. So he turned to empowerment. "If I wanted to improve results, I had to increase their involvement in the business." So what did he do? Abdicate. " 'From now on,' I announced to my management team, 'you're all responsible for making your own decisions'" (Stayer, 1990, pp. 2–4).

Stayer figured out that what he was called to do as a positional leader in these circumstances was to politically guide engagement. Results still mattered. However, they were no longer to be tightly orchestrated by him. He had to figure out what to let go of and what to hold on to. Power was the central issue, participation and owner-ship the central behaviors and beliefs. He could share power because of his deep sense that his workforce was competent, committed, and confident. In this thinking, he learned some things (1990, p. 10):

- People want to be great. If they aren't, it's because management won't let them be.

- Performance begins with each individual's expectations. Influ-ence what people expect, and you influence how people perform.

- Expectations are driven partly by goals, vision, symbols, and semantics and partly by the context in which people work, that is, by such things as compensation systems, production practices, and decision-making structures.

- The actions of managers shape expectations.

- Learning is a process, not a goal. Each new insight creates a new layer of potential insights.

- The organization's results reflect me and my performance. If I want to change the results, I have to change myself first. This is particularly true for me, the owner and CEO, but it is equally true for every employee.

He took very seriously his perception that he was the problem. He also found that "as I gained one insight and mastered one situa-tion, another situation arose that required new insight and more learning. As I approached one goal, a new, more important, but more distant goal always began to take shape" (p. 10). He made his use of power the focus of change even though it was the hardest thing to change. The company flourished, in terms of both explosive energy and profitability.

CORE IDEAS

Power is the center of our attention in Zone 4; leadership is Creating Ownership. My definition of power is simple and straightforward: *Power is making and keeping decisions over time.* Thus power can be

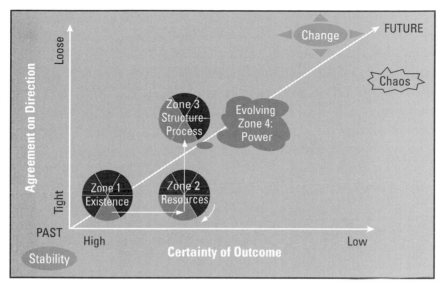

FIGURE 19 • ZONE 4: CREATING OWNERSHIP

individual or collective, actual or potential, and inwardly or out-wardly focused. Once power is perceived as real, is believed to exist, it can exert great impact even if it is not overtly exercised. The decisions made may focus on self-determination as well as on influencing others. They must occur over time to be perceived as real power and not a one-shot lucky event. There is pattern and persistence in power (see also *Authentic Leadership*, chapter 9, pp. 194ff.).

The zone leadership model (Figure 19, above) illustrates that Zone 4 is a world that is less knowable and fixable than the world in Zone 3b. Agreement on direction and certainty of outcome have decreased again. The wavy lines are expanding as we move from zone to zone. It gets more frightening and more exciting as the world changes. Two broad leadership strategies for political engagement emerge in this world. As uncertainty of outcome raises problems, positional leadership shares power in the hope that collective wisdom and action will prevail over them. When there is little agreement on direction, power is taken from positional leadership and action arises out of the mobilization of the newly empowered. Zone 4 political engagement is committed to whole-system deployment and affirms great faith in "the people." Hence, leadership is Creating Ownership.

Buy-in and belonging, while critical for long-term organizational vibrancy, are now inadequate by themselves. Ownership and participation emerge as hallmarks of Zone 4. That is, leadership politically engages others. The second umpire loves this political zone because life is really the way you see it. Perspective is all we have here. The challenge is to ensure that all relevant perspectives are heard and all critical issues are addressed. The authenticity standard shifts again. Correspondence, consistency, connectedness, and coherence now are supplemented by codetermination, which becomes the main standard. Shared power infuses leadership as it dialogues with multiple voices. The struggle is to discover what codetermination and shared power look like in practice.

A new metaphor informs this zone. Life is no longer best viewed as a living system. Now life is a conflict between ups and downs. Embedded in this metaphor is another polarity. Form/dynamic is replaced by conceal/reveal. Those with less power, the *downs,* possess a great deal of knowledge. Their wisdom is often blocked, discounted, or dismissed by *ups,* either by use of personal force or by means of organizational processes. The leadership challenge in this zone is to create conditions where concealed wisdom reveals itself via voice.

As I mentioned briefly in Zone 3b, Jeremy Rifkin worries that the new hypercapitalism, where everyone is networked for life to gain new experiences, will trigger voice issues. If we end up paying for access to delightful and sustainable processes, we will eventually feel trapped without much power. Downness will rise; voices will protest. It is no accident that Zone 4 follows Zone 3b. It is not the number sequence; it is the dynamic of losing voice.

Relevant Views of Power

In the late 1980s and early 1990s, when I was writing *Authentic Leadership*, little attention was given to issues of power in leadership. Senge, for example, discusses powerlessness briefly in *The Fifth Discipline.* In his view, power seems to be structurally or system constrained (Zone 3a) and shaped by identity (Zone 3b). Thus it is more important to talk about fixing the system than about power in its own right. In the literature in general, power seems to be an enigma, ever present in life and leadership yet rarely acknowledged.

And until recently there has been almost no discussion of courage, except in the military literature. Now courage is emerging more frequently as a leadership characteristic, perhaps because as the world gets more unpredictable in outcome and we are less certain in agreement, courage seems more necessary.

Power, too, is being discussed somewhat more openly by some writers; perhaps as pressures for power sharing and empowerment grow, understanding power seems more important. One of the more insightful and provocative books, *Eyewitness to Power* (2000), offers wisdom to be treasured. Author David Gergen, presidential advisor and staff member from Nixon to Clinton, directly links power to leadership. For Gergen, power is grounded in character. Nixon and Clinton had serious character problems. Carter, grounded in great character, had other problems. Another major player in this zone is Peter Block. His view of stewardship (1993) directly assaults positional leadership. For Block, stewardship does not preserve and remember the past as defined in Zone 1. Rather, it focuses on taking responsibility for one's own life. In this view, positional, command-and-control leadership is distinct from the self-governance and self-empowerment of stewardship. The top of an organization cannot empower a workforce. It can set up a context. People empower themselves. This suggests that a challenge of positional leadership in this zone is to create the circumstances in which this self-empowerment can occur—a different focus than Gergen's to be sure.

In *Leading Without Power* (1997), Max De Pree also invites us to empower ourselves and direct our commitments and passions toward service to others. He captures how energy flows into action. He writes, for example: "What qualities give an organization vitality? Vital organizations exude health and energy and enthusiasm. Like vital people, they are full of hope and anticipation for things to come. Confident of their own place in time and space, they respect their history without being ruled by it. They look at their own PR and only half believe it" (p. 99). Essential qualities for leading without power are truth, access, discipline, accountability, nourishment for persons, authenticity, justice, respect, hope, workable unity, tolerance, simplicity, beauty and taste, and fidelity to a mission (pp. 99–113).

Some positional leaders may encourage empowerment throughout an organization; others, however, may abuse the power they have. Power has more than one side. Abraham Zaleznik and

Konosuke Mastsushita (1993) offer in-depth examinations of abuses of power by positional leaders and explore the impact of psychological and organizational forces on those who head organizations.

Power calls forth many different reactions. Authoritarianism, which may seem like abuse of power to people accustomed to Western individualism, may be viewed differently by others, as Sterling Seagrave (1995) found in his study of the Chinese and their use of power to control their destinies. "Most Asians are extremely poor and terrified of violence," observes Seagrave. "Desperate people will back anyone who claims to have a solution. Asian regimes use the craving for prosperity to build a consensus for authoritarian rule" (p. 307). In this instance collective consciousness outweighs individual assertion.

The most outrageous book on power, Eric Broder's *The Below-the-Belt Manager* (1998), captures the essence of power abuse in contemporary organizations. The subtitle reveals the *Dilbert*-like quality of the content—*This Book Shows You How to Make Your Employees Sick with Fear in as Little as 30 Seconds!* The examples are very funny; the message is serious. The potential to abuse others through the exercise of power exists in all of us. If you believe you are not capable of abusing another person this way, you either have not lived long enough or have not examined your thoughts and actions closely enough. For instance, do you spout the rhetoric of teams yet reserve a secret doubt about their viability? Broder brings this doubt to the surface in the form of a how-to lesson for the below-the-belt manager:

> Many management gurus insist that employees should be "included" as part of a "team." This, they tell us, will make them happier and, thus, more productive. . . . The next thing you know, that punk fresh out of college who's been with the organization eight months begins to think he's on your level and wants you to "open" your books and give everyone the chance to take a gander at them. . . . The minute any of your managers even breathes a word about "teams," you have to transform, like magic, this manager into an ex-manager and, ultimately, ex-employee. Because if you don't, he'll form a team, all right—he'll team up with other managers to make sure your ass is out on the street and his is sitting behind your desk, smoking your Cubans and drinking your Cutty. (pp. 44–45)

One particular kind of power abuse occurs all too often. I call it *dual persona*. Some people label it "passive/aggressive" or "bipolar."

These terms describe the positional leader who acts one way in public and another in private. At meetings, large events, or in the media, the person's behavior seems gentle, caring, thoughtful, and mature, but in private meetings in the office with a handful of subordinates, the behavior changes dramatically. Yelling, swearing, rage, and psychological abuse and humiliation of people blast from the "gentle" leader. I am never sure what triggers these outbursts. Is it insecurity, perceived threat, or just plain immaturity? Employees often see no response other than quiet coping, withdrawal, underground sabotage, or leaving the job.

Some positional leaders take the opposite tack; they are abusive in public and nice in private. They might rant at the media in public, for example, over some issue, but it is just a public show, not deeply felt. I have found Broder's book a safe tool to use to gently confront dual persona power problems. I invite executives to read it and find themselves in it. Its humor sometimes opens the door for more thoughtful reflection on contrasting public and private behavior.

Then there are less obvious modes of abuse of power. For example, executives often fail to let teams know when their role is advisory rather than decisional. If these teams then make decisions that run counter to the executives' wishes, those decisions are discounted, ignored, or outright repudiated. Team-member morale suffers, and the executives blame the teams for not understanding rather than blaming themselves for not addressing the issue of power directly.

When employees are encouraged to offer suggestions for organizational improvement but few suggestions show up, again the employees are blamed, this time for not participating. The problem I have seen in these situations is that leaders give no feedback on the ideas. People must see the value of their contributions in order to keep contributing. Giving people the opportunity to drop ideas into a black hole does not empower them. Creative ideas are everywhere. The challenge is to reveal this concealed wisdom.

Zone 4 is all about power, about voice. Developmentally, it lives between those preoccupied with expertise, who are crafting and leading healthy systems, and those who are worried that the world is ever more unknown and unknowable. The bridge between the two is built on widespread participation. When leadership is political engagement it no longer lives exclusively at the top of organizations; it begins to move around. Stakeholders—especially employees, customers, and communities—want voice. They know a lot and they are wise. In the earlier zones they are rarely asked for their wisdom by those at the top. In Zone 4, this changes. We are moving beyond Affirming Shared Identity because with agreement on direction and certainty of outcome becoming more problematic, leadership now is fully engaged in multiple-perspective thinking. Ann Howard's research (1995) reveals this shift, showing that the traditional roles of executives—controller, commander, judge, ruler, and guard—mostly become dysfunctional in a rapidly changing environment. Of the five old roles, only commander was still valued by employees because they believed leaders ought to enforce compliance with rules. The most important new roles that emerged in the study were empowering roles. Modeling trustworthiness, characterized by "consistency in words and actions," was identified as the most important role. Leadership of this sort created more satisfaction in the leaders themselves and in the workers, and positively affected the spirit of the organization.

Howard identifies eleven expressions of the new form of leadership: delegator, visionary, change agent, inspirer, model of trust, supporter, champion, coach, team builder, facilitator, and partner. Through these roles, leadership discovers the way, lights the way, encourages the way, enables the way, and smooths the way.

As I mentioned earlier, in this zone the world invites us to shift from *buy-in* to *ownership*. This is a huge jump. In buy-in, someone else is in charge and I am asked to agree and come along. In ownership, I codetermine the outcome with others. The kind of leadership that supports this, the leadership Howard describes as delegating, championing, partnering, and so on, is not for the weak of heart. It often requires courage. To really believe in participation is to have great confidence that citizens, customers, constituents, and colleagues can come together, dialogue, and collectively decide on important matters affecting all of them.

Encouraging this kind of courageous leadership is the growing research base directly linking participation (like emotional intelligence) to organizational prosperity. Organizational researcher Daniel Denison (1997) finds that a participative culture produces this prosperity for a number of reasons. It encourages worker ownership and pride. Coordination is maximized as individuals seek both their own and collective interests. Work habits are more fully developed and, finally, groups can solve more complex problems than individuals.

The Metaphorical Shift

Because power is so seldom addressed in the leadership literature, a guiding metaphor for this zone is less obvious than the metaphors for the earlier zones. However, it is there. Life is not a body or a living system; it is not a machine; it is not a gift. Life is a conflict between ups and downs. Those who see this zone through this metaphor are always downs themselves, advocates for downs, or people who are aware of the ignorance that comes from being "dumb ups." Here is the parable that I used to explain ups and downs in *Authentic Leadership* (pp. 194–96).

The Parable of Ups Versus Downs

What makes an up an up and a down a down? An up can do more to a down than a down can do to an up. That's what keeps an up up and a down down. Ups tend to talk to each other and study the downs, asking the downs what's up, or what's coming down, for that matter.

The downs spend a lot of time taking the ups out to lunch and dinner to explain their downness. The ups listen attentively, often amazed about the lives of downs. They contrast one down's experience with another down's experience. At times they don't worry too much about what the downs are up to because the ups know that the downs never seem to get it together. If they did, the ups would have to shape up.

After a while, the downs weary of talking to the ups. They think, "If I have to explain my downness one more time to an up, I'll throw up." So downs form networks and form support groups. This makes some ups nervous, for ups know three ups standing together is a board meeting; three downs, pre-revolutionary activity.

In order to cope with this rising up of downness, some ups hire downs, dress them up, and send them down to see what the downs are up to. These downs are often called personnel or affirmative action officers. This creates a serious problem for the down who is dressed up. That down doesn't know whether he or she is up or down and that's why downs in the middle often burn up.

Sometimes ups, to smarten up, ask downs to come into a program created by ups to explain and justify their downness. The ups call this "human relations training." Of course, ups never have to explain their upness; that's why they're ups.

There's good news and bad news in this parable. The good news is that there is no such thing as a perfect up or a perfect down. If people were perfect ups, they wouldn't be able to stand up, they would be so heavily burdened with downness.

The bad news is that when ups are up, it often makes them stupid. I call this *dumb-upness*. Dumb-upness occurs because ups don't have to pay attention to downs the way downs have to pay attention to ups. The only time ups worry about downs is when downs get uppity, at which time they are put down by the ups. The ups' perception is that downs are overly sensitive; they have an attitude problem. It is never understood that the ups are "underly sensitive" and have an attitude problem.

I used to think that when downs became ups they would carry over their insight from their downness to their upness. Not so.

Smart down, dumb up! One can be smart one minute, dumb the next.

Block's work is a classic expression of the ups-versus-downs metaphor. Positional leadership is upness, and usually dumb-upness. So, get down from the tower; share the power. If truth is concealed, figure out how to reveal it. Great wisdom lives with the downs. What does it take to release these deep truths so that authentic action can flourish? This is also the metaphor of social movements, million-man marches, protests, rebellions, and affirmations of self-worth in spite of put-downs and abuse.

Many advocates for stakeholder participation draw heavily on Zone 3b living-systems thinking. Yet I find that the ups-versus-downs metaphor often lurks behind these publicly professed living-systems theories. An example: Bruce Gibb, as we have seen, is a strong advocate of systems thinking. Yet the driver behind his work is to give the worker voice. He is an advocate for downs. When he and I were working together for a law firm that was searching for common direction and glue to hold it together, we proposed a large-scale intervention for organizational members. Some of the lawyers wanted only senior partners to attend. Secretaries did not deserve a voice. Bruce was deeply upset. This was not a systems problem. It was a power and participation issue.

Another friend, Jim LaRue, is a noted advocate for *green housing*, living spaces that sustain both human beings and nature. Listening to him, it would not be difficult to believe the organic metaphor was foundational for his life. In our ongoing discussions, however, Jim revealed that his deepest call to action was to serve "the least of these," the downs. In part, that commitment was rooted in his own sense of being a down.

This is not to say that the organic metaphor is not a Zone 3b foundation for Zone 4. Zone 4 builds upon it and is not reducible to it. The organic metaphor limits our view of certain human actions and thus is not adequate for this and the following zones. How well does the living systems metaphor address profound power conflicts? Systems thinking stresses connectedness and coherence, rarely conflict. In Zone 4, conflict surfaces repeatedly. The body metaphor of Zone 3 does not lend itself to depicting conflict. Would we imagine the heart in conflict with the lungs, for example?

Each zone adds value not present in the ones before it. The value of this zone is its explicit attention to power in all its forms—destructive as well as constructive—and to the conflicts surrounding power, the ups versus the downs.

The task of leadership in Zone 4 is Creating Ownership. The task is to figure out how to turn destructive power into participatory codetermination by ensuring that the downs are heard.

APPLICATION

Creating Ownership takes different forms at different organizational levels. Let's look at three broad levels, top, middle, and bottom, and what each can do to become engaged.

Creating Ownership by the Top

The president of Luther Seminary called me after an executive meeting with selected faculty and staff. He was getting impatient with the progress of a fundamental initiative at the seminary. Those at the meeting could feel him pushing hard and using his power. A couple of faculty offered feedback to him, suggesting they needed more ownership of the process. In other words, they asked him to back off a bit. In terms of Ralph Stayer's metaphor of turning buffalo into geese, they had said "Fly with us rather than be a buffalo." So I told him Stayer's story. It hit home. The next day I received an e-mail from him. "Have you ever eaten at Perkins Restaurant?" he asked. "I did last night. Guess what I ordered? Buffalo wings!" What a wonderfully playful way to embrace a serious point.

Stayer's story offers a number of specific examples of political engagement. The way he handled one very consequential decision where agreement and certainty were problematic is especially noteworthy. A larger company offered to expand its contract with Johnsonville Foods. The opportunity was growth and profit; the threat was great stress on the current system and pressure on the employees to go beyond their normal workload and responsibilities. In the past, decisions like these were made at the top, by the strategic leadership team. In the company's new way of being, the top involved everyone.

As Stayer describes the process, "We asked the teams in each area to discuss these questions [of opportunity and threat] among themselves and develop a list of pros and cons. Since the group as a whole was too large to work together effectively, each team chose one member to report its finding to a plantwide representative body to develop a plantwide answer" (p. 10). Within days the teams had collectively decided both to take on the challenge and to raise production standards to ensure the increased business would not depart after the company's investment of time, people, and money.

Another challenge for leadership in this zone is the 360-degree performance review. Do not just do top-down reviews. Get input from subordinates, peers, and your boss. I have seen the results devastate a buffalo who thought he was a goose. I have also witnessed great growth when the peer review affirms much of a person's self-perception and also opens arenas for growth. For effectiveness, make sure the performance instrument is tailored to your organizational realities. Are all the zones covered in the leadership section? Are the zones covered in depth where the organizational leadership challenges are for the future?

In this zone senior executives learn that they can never talk off the record. Every word uttered carries political significance. A recently promoted one-star general once told me of his first visit to a base in his new capacity. While walking through an assembly hall, he made an offhand comment about the lack of light in the meeting space. A year later, he returned to the base. Now the room was filled with new lights and even some windows. He had not requested the change; however, no comments from ups go unnoticed.

To find safe spaces for discussion, many executives, especially CEOs, join peer groups. Meeting monthly or so, these groups offer opportunities for sharing and peer coaching. As the longevity of membership increases, authenticity increases proportionately.

When ups try to lead other ups, another set of leadership issues involving power surfaces. When equals try to influence each other, suspicion quickly emerges. What is the real agenda of the one asserting herself or himself? Up versus down hovers around apparent equality. Caterpillar and the UAW have fought for years over contractual deals. Each claims to be an equal partner in the negotiations, yet each fears the other is the real up and it is the down.

A common reason mergers often flounder, fail, or do not proceed at all is unresolved power issues. The planned $70 billion merger between the two drug giants SmithKline Beecham and Glaxo Wellcome floundered over control, "including who would be the chief executive of the merged company and how many SmithKline officials would be on the combined company's board" (Langreth and Lipin, 1998). The Daimler-Chrysler merger, thought to be a partnership, turned into a power takeover by Daimler. Of course, mergers work. My hypothesis is that those that work best are those that attend to power issues most directly. And when there is an overlap of shared values and strategic direction, success is even more assured.

Creating Ownership by the Middle

Block (1987) states the dilemma of middle management well: "The process of organizational politics as we know it works against people taking responsibility. We empower ourselves by discovering a positive way of being political. The line between positive and negative politics is a tightrope we have to walk. We must be powerful advocates for our units in a way that does not alienate those around and above us" (p. xiii).

The tightrope image reflects the issues in Zone 4 political engagement. Do we adapt and maintain the system or expand our horizons and strive for greatness? Do we maintain caution and control risk, or do we live courageously, at the edge of comfort? Do we live dependently or affirm our own independence? (Block, 1987, p. 11). Block's answer always favors political astuteness and adept choice.

Some negative political activities that Block (1987, pp. 50–51) identifies are:

- Saying what we don't mean—deceiving and sidetracking

- God is my ally—name dropping and power plays

- Understating the downside—distorting the full picture

- Communicating devices—using techniques to get one's way

- Padding—asking for more than we expect

- Language that masks reality—seeking approaches to tough issues without being honest

What do all these negative acts have in common? Inauthenticity. Very few people in organizations and communities abuse power outright. The abuse is disguised, experienced more as manipulation than oppression. At times this can make power issues more difficult to address.

As political engagement grows in an organization, the middle in a sense comes to include almost everyone. As Block comments (1987, pp. 63–64):

- Even people at the top are in the middle. There is no absolute authority in an organization. We can talk as if the boss is in control, but it is more a wish than a reality.

- Change from the top down happens at the will and whim of those below. As managers we state our intentions and give direction, but many of the most critical choices are made by the people below us.

- The power of a boss is asymmetrical. It is easier to use authority to tighten up, shrink, and make an organization more cautious than it is to use power to open up, expand, and make an organization more courageous. There is a readiness of people in low-power positions to believe the worst. If it is fear that we want to instill in our subordinates, they are quite ready to respond.

Block's descriptions parallel my experience in organizations. It is easy to stimulate fear among the workers; below-the-belt managing is all too common. In contrast, it is difficult to share responsibility and trust and thus create positive politics, especially if there is a history of abuse and mistrust. Block proposes work along the lines of the identity discussions presented in Zone 3b. He also reaches into Zone 5a, Setting Direction, and suggests using the power of metaphor and symbol and of creativity to empower oneself and one's organizational unit. Authenticity must be present throughout. To work, empowerment must be true and real, in oneself and in the world.

Robert Kelley (1992) also offers useful bricks for followers, for those in the middle in Zone 4. What do you do if you think an order is wrong or you want to make a positive contribution in a situation that is stagnant? Kelley outlines ten steps to a courageous conscience (pp. 184–98):

- Be proactive.

- Gather your facts.

- Before taking a stand, seek wise counsel.

- Build your fortitude.

- Work within the system.

- Frame your position so it will be heard.

- Educate others on how your view serves their best interests.

- Take collective action.

- If you meet leader resistance, seek higher authority.

- Have the financial and emotional cushions to exercise alternatives.

As authors discuss the middle and the bottom, the followers, courage becomes a bigger issue. Block at least mentions the word; Kelley develops it. And Chaleff (1995) devotes a whole volume to it.

Creating Owernship by the Bottom

When power abuse is obvious, rampant, and outright oppressive, it results in social movements and revolutions. Vaclav Havel's pioneering analysis of the political power of the powerless confronts the myth of top-down control as a complete monopoly in Czechoslovakia and other Eastern European communist states. In *The Power of the Powerless* (1985), he states a compelling case for political empowerment and, in language akin to Block's and Chaleff's, centers power in the self. Individually we can take charge of much of our life; collectively we can shape our destiny.

Barbara Kellerman (1986) addresses the follower issue from a positional view. Leaders meet individual or collective follower needs, thus allowing followers to follow by offering them some benefit. Of course, the benefit could be avoiding the pain of not following.

In the corporate world, the union movement is the most obvious example of a movement in response to power at the top. Of course, there are many other movements that influence corporate life daily— civil rights, feminist, and ecological. I have written on other movements elsewhere (see Terry, 1975), so I will comment briefly on current union and management issues here.

The concern about globalization centers in this zone. The little people believe their voice is being ignored by international corporations and governments. Globalization is a code word for "ups." Historically, union–management relations embody the classic ups-versus-downs metaphor. Management and owners were the up enemy, clearly oppressive; unions were the down liberators, clearly resisting. Over the years this embattled conflict has been institutionalized, with rules and regulations for negotiation. Contracts became commonplace once the right to show up at the table to bargain was won. Are labor rights continually challenged? Of course they are. There are still threats to union legitimacy. Political countermovements bash labor; labor bashes back. The struggle goes on. This is familiar territory, and union leaders and members know the drill: organize, organize, organize.

What is more difficult for both sides is another trend. Unions are often challenged and invited to build partnerships with management, the former enemy. Today, this is a formidable leadership challenge. On what grounds can they come together? Can partnership coexist with contract negotiations? In some public arenas, totally new forms of negotiation are emerging that seek to reduce rancor and suspicion and replace them with honest, direct dialogue. Building on the pioneering ideas in Fisher and Price's *Getting to Yes* (1983), some government agencies and unions spend hours identifying their real interests for authentic discussion and resolution. I know of considerable numbers of such efforts that resulted in fair and civil participatory conclusions. *Power over* becomes *power with*.

We are also gaining a deeper understanding of a particular reason negative, politically loaded feedback should be avoided—it becomes self-fulfilling prophecy. Have you ever been in a situation where everyone knew what was going on except the positional leader, yet no one said anything, and mutual mistrust, suspicion, and blame persisted? Instead of addressing the issues of power abuse, everyone silently colluded to continue it. Gibb offers a model of the way these self-fulfilling negative-belief spirals work. Just follow the numbers in Figure 20 on the next page.

Inauthenticity lurks everywhere under these conditions. Someone has to break the cycle. Often it requires third-party intervention. Everyone must own responsibility for continuing the political avoidance. Most likely, the initiative will come from below. The boss is so isolated that she or he will not address the issue head on. It is frightening to lead from the bottom. If bosses are buffaloes it takes courage for the downs to act. There is no guaranteed outcome.

Parker J. Palmer (1992) observes that movements begin when a repressed need awakens and key players act courageously with internal energy to move forward without regard to constraining boundaries. The movement self-organizes and recasts the traditional rules of engagement. Parker describes these four stages of the unfolding of movements (pp. 10–17):

- Isolated people choose authenticity.

- These people discover each other and connect for mutual support.

- Empowered by their collective energy, they learn to translate private dilemmas into public issues.

- New reward systems emerge to sustain the movement's vision.

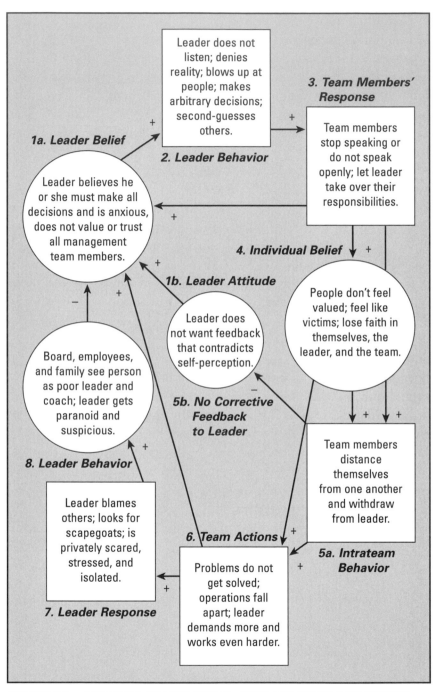

FIGURE 20 • NEGATIVE BELIEF SPIRAL: SELF-FULFILLING PROPHECY
Source: Adapted from Gibb, 1997.

An incongruity, avoidance, escape, or denial grabs the spirit. The experience of inauthenticity inspires the human spirit to make another stride toward what is true and real. Denial exits and a fresh embrace of authenticity takes over. The new feels more real than the old.

Large-Scale Participatory Interventions

What can be done to engage workers and managers authentically? If the buffalo positional leaders want the geese to fly, they have to fly as well. And to get shared power in motion, participatory engagement methods are critical. Instead of always seeking expert advice, invite those who live with the issues every day to address and solve them using large-scale participatory methods.

How does one engage a whole system for rapid and enduring change? The most comprehensive overview of the full array of such participatory interventions is Bunker and Alban's *Large Group Interventions: Engaging the Whole System for Rapid Change* (1997). Such interventions are needed because "the truth is that we live in uncertain times. No formula exists for global success. If a right answer exists, it is unknown. . . . Although management clearly has the leadership role in taking action, in today's complex work environment they seldom have all the answers. Figuring out what is going on and what we ought to do is not the same kind of task that it was in a more predictable world" (p. 7). Bunker and Alban do such an excellent job summarizing and contrasting the different approaches (which include The Search Conference, Future Search, Real Time Strategic Change, The Institute of Cultural Affairs Planning Process, The Conference Model, Fast Cycle Full Participation Work Design, Real Time Work Design, Simu-Real, Work-Out, and Open Space Technology) that I will not attempt to duplicate their work. (See also Anderson and Bryson, 1998.) What unites all of the methods is authentic participation by significant numbers of people in an organization or community. And each mode of engagement accomplishes a different outcome, depending on the situation requiring participation. Some are more top-guided, some clearly bottom-up.

Robert Jacobs's *Real Time Strategic Change* (1997) describes one of the participatory models. Jacobs illustrates in detail the philosophy and methods created by the people (including Bruce Gibb) who developed the first large-scale interventions, which were designed to increase worker participation at Ford in the early 1980s. The plan involved bringing the whole organization—hundreds, even one to two thousand people at a time—into the same room for three days, and, using small-group methodologies, taking them through a rigorously disciplined process so that together they could codetermine their future.

Gibb calls these large-scale conferences camp meetings. Everyday work is still accomplished via the hierarchy. Periodically, however, people need to come out of the narrow confines of ordinary work life and in effect go to camp. They need to meet with others for authentic dialogue and shared decision making. Then they return to their regular work with fresh energy, commitments to new activities, and a deep connection with colleagues.

Gibb contrasts the two arenas of work as shown in Figure 21.

What happens at the camp meetings? The methods have been drawn from small-group research. For one thousand people, for instance, the room is arranged with one hundred round tables, ten chairs per table. Each table is a microcosm of the organization and through a variety of table activities and shared roomwide events, the groups address and decide what is really going on and what they might do about it.

In Jacobs's *Real Time Strategic Change,* a formula works behind the scenes: $D \times V \times F > R$. That is, the meeting focuses on Dissatisfaction with the current situation (D), Vision for the future (V), and First steps (F; first steps means someone can actually make something happen). If there is agreement on D, clarity of V, and workable F, Resistance (R) disappears. If the converse is true, resistance goes underground, bosses become buffaloes, and participation happens in rhetoric only. Note that the formula uses multiplication signs, not addition signs. All three parts of the formula must receive high votes if resistance is to fade away. So, on a scale of 1 to 10, how dissatisfied are you? Oh, very: 10! How clear are you about where we are headed? Oh, very clear: 10! Are you clear about what to do next? Not a clue: 0. Do the math: $10 \times 10 \times 0 = 0 > R$. No first steps known (no change) equals total resistance.

The three-day event is organized around this formula, each day attending to one of the three—D, V, and F. (You can also use this for-

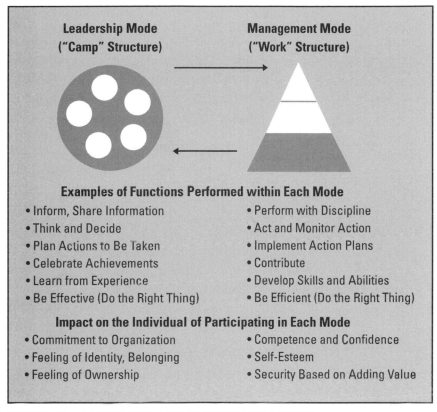

**Leadership Mode
("Camp" Structure)**

**Management Mode
("Work" Structure)**

Examples of Functions Performed within Each Mode

• Inform, Share Information	• Perform with Discipline
• Think and Decide	• Act and Monitor Action
• Plan Actions to Be Taken	• Implement Action Plans
• Celebrate Achievements	• Contribute
• Learn from Experience	• Develop Skills and Abilities
• Be Effective (Do the Right Thing)	• Be Efficient (Do the Right Thing)

Impact on the Individual of Participating in Each Mode

• Commitment to Organization	• Competence and Confidence
• Feeling of Identity, Belonging	• Self-Esteem
• Feeling of Ownership	• Security Based on Adding Value

FIGURE 21 • LEADERSHIP AND MANAGEMENT MODES
Source: Gibb, 1997, p. 9. Reprinted with permission.

mula any time you have to pitch a change: make sure all three parts are equally and persuasively argued and agreed upon. Or use the formula as your own internal sorting device. If you are resisting change, why? Is it lacking D, V, and/or F?)

Camp meetings raise anxieties in executives. Gibb has identified seventeen of these fears and worries about large-scale participatory events. Although the list is long, it is very instructive if we want buffaloes to fly. It can serve as an internal buffalo check (adapted from Gibb, 1997, unpublished, used by permission).

1. Self-presentation: some executives do not think that they are charismatic or can present themselves to people positively or speak effectively. Better to remain unknown and able to exercise power from mystery. However, honesty is real charisma and the king has

to be seen at least once a year. (There is a 20 percent increase in employee satisfaction where they have seen the executives.)

2. Temperament or personality of leaders: introverted leaders who need time to think about situations, decisions, or issues before deciding fear that they will be pressed into deciding too rapidly, without time for due consideration.

3. Management/leadership style: an authoritarian or totalitarian personality may find this type of process inimical to his or her style of leadership/management. The person may feel this type of process would be a show of weakness and indicate loss of power.

4. Role conflict: the executive sees his or her role to be one of making strategy and maintaining strategic relationships for the organization; the role of middle management is developmental and operational. By holding a leadership conference (camp meeting), the executive may be taking away the responsibility and accountability of middle management. The executive could become distracted from what she or he is really supposed to be doing.

5. Loss of power: if everyone is involved, the range of options or choices available to the executive could be limited or circumscribed.

6. Loss of control: some executives selectively give information to subordinates while ensuring that they themselves are the only ones who have the whole picture; the whole picture will become clear and this will undermine the ability of the executive to use information as a source of power and control.

7. Blame: especially if the organization is in trouble, executives could be publicly accused, blamed, held responsible, and embarrassed, and as a result could feel a sense of guilt and failure. If this word gets out, stockholders and boards of directors will call for their resignation.

8. Chaos or, at worst, a riot: the fear that having a large group together will be unmanageable; nothing can be accomplished with such a large group of people. If there is a lot of dissatisfaction with the organization and how it is being led or managed,

the executive's worst fear is that there will be a riot and his or her personal safety would be threatened by mob rule.

9. Employees are not trustworthy: the executives fear that they could be asked questions about aspects of strategy or tactics, or will have to justify decisions or resource allocations which they will feel obligated or pressured to answer and that the information revealed will be given to competitors or the media.

10. Unfulfillable promises: in a meeting, promises that cannot be fulfilled could be made to avoid conflict and controversy; this will lower employees' confidence and trust in the organization.

11. Employee domination: the executives are responsible to all the stakeholders of the organization and they fear that the self-interest of employees will take precedence over what is good for the whole organization and the rest of its stakeholders. The meeting will turn into a conflict of groups advocating for their self-interest, a massive labor negotiation.

12. Ideological: organizations are not democracies. Democracies are too slow. They cannot make people do things; they are messy ways of getting things done; they have no bottom line to achieve.

13. Fraternization: military model of not being close to people because you may have to send them into battle to be killed and you can't allow feelings of closeness to keep you from doing the right thing or to lead you to show favoritism.

14. An experiment: this approach is an experiment, a theory in search of a test.

15. Fad, flash in the pan: these types of processes are fads that run their course; we need to stick with what we know and how we do things. "A camp meeting like this would be a one-time event and usually nothing changes afterwards. Habits and traditions run too deep and are too hard to change."

16. Waste of time and resources: this is a "touchy-feely" activity that will have no impact on the bottom line and will both take additional resources and lower productivity during the time of the conference; the costs will exceed the benefits.

17. Excessive inclusion: camp meetings will include people more, build more sense of commitment, caring, ownership, and identity. Employees already spend a third of their lives at work. They could begin to have more loyalty to the organization than to their families, churches, etc. Organizations already want people's labor and ideas; to structure situations in which they also give their hearts and souls is too much. Work organizations should only partially include people. It is just a job; their real lives need to be elsewhere.

When should you use large-scale intervention?

- When workers have been left out of critical decisions, know it, and are stirring

- When the bosses want to fly

- When resources and commitments are in place to follow up the three-day event

- When it is carefully planned

- When the organization wants a burst of authenticity and co-determination

- When frequent meetings of small groups separately have produced very little

- When middle managers are wondering what their jobs really are

- When functional silos dominate the workplace

- When you want the whole and the parts of the organization to connect and be affirmed—a systems-based approach

- When you have confidence of covert agreements in the workforce that could benefit the whole place, not just individual self-interest

- When you want empowerment and ownership to be lived

- When you believe all truths have merit and all deserve to be listened to

- When you have confidence in the value of peer pressure

- When you know that external and internal forces need to be addressed

- When clear and important issues require the organization's attention

These large-scale participatory processes are not value neutral. For them to work, planning teams must address the values that undergird the whole system. These values that ought to be in place include stakeholder balance, member importance, participation, equality and diversity, openness, availability of information, respectful treatment, no hidden agenda, responsibility, no retaliation or retribution, follow-up commitment, and performance measurement in tasks and relationships.

Executives do not give up veto power in this process. However, they know if they use it often, the geese become grounded and will refuse to fly in public again. They will fly at night, however, to secret locations for private self-organized meetings.

Here is some further advice and some warnings:

- Have a clear, important purpose.

- Be sincere; no ulterior motives.

- Consider all stakeholders.

- Be frank and open.

- Prepare well.

- Be realistic; do not expect this to be a panacea.

- Find a partner.

- Integrate current processes.

- Follow up; follow through.

These events are not a quick fix. Camp meetings could be held at least once a year, preferably twice. Regular meetings breed authenticity. What was not addressed at the last meeting can now surface, and commitments made at previous meetings but not enacted can be reviewed and evaluated.

Finally, authenticity must live in these events.

Underlying [these methods must be] . . . a bone-deep belief in participation—a fundamental conviction that when people have the important information about a system and are allowed to become collaboratively and fully engaged with others around these issues, they become highly motivated to take responsibility for change and improvement. . . .

People know when they are being manipulated. Many organizations have a history of management's using the newest theory of organizational development design to railroad employees into what management thinks is best, without ever consulting the employees. This is why employees often come to these events, at least at the start, with what we consider a "healthy" degree of distrust. If the decision makers do not share in the value of participation, fear loss of control, or are unwilling to trust in the goodwill latent in their people, these methods should not be employed. (Bunker and Alban, 1997, p. 217)

The long-term impact of these types of participatory events on the organization and its stakeholder members has not been thoroughly researched. Bunker and Alban are currently gathering data to assess the consequences, and plan to publish a volume soon. However, when Gibb was hired by Ford Motor Company to join recently promoted or hired plant managers who were to launch an overseas plant, he used regular camp meetings. Once the top group was selected and assembled, its members went to a camp meeting. When the next level of the new organization was hired, these people joined the top group at another camp meeting. The process continued until, finally, the whole organization had participated in the meetings. Once the whole place was up and running, camp meetings were held twice a year. The results have been so astonishing that camp meetings, or "off sites" as they are now called, have been used for startups in Mexico, Spain, Portugal, Hungary, Thailand, and India. Ongoing meetings are held twice a year: first to plan performance, development, and review, and, at the half-year, to review performance and modify plans as appropriate.

Offering and Claiming Voice

Leadership has many options for fostering ownership. Here are a few especially noteworthy examples.

Some organizations have sought to institutionalize voice by creating forums and councils for codetermination. 3M has implemented this process with great care and commitment. It has built and supported a technician forum and councils so that its five thousand technicians can have a voice and make a difference. Membership in the Tech Forum is limited to regular full-time and part-time 3M employees who have signed a 3M employee agreement and have received written approval from a director. The Tech Forum consists of four parts: the governing board, which acts as the administrative arm; the senate, which acts as a voice between members and the greater senate, a larger business representative group; chapters, which are organized by major disciplines of focus; and committees, which perform various administrative and community outreach duties (3M, 1999).

Technicians are selected or volunteer to serve a two-year term on the senate. It meets once a month, and consists of about eighty people. They select their own officers, set up their own processes, and surface their own issues. The positional leadership of the forum takes the concerns the members identify to the appropriate part of 3M, and, if necessary, someone from that part of 3M attends the next forum meeting to help address and collectively solve the issue or problem.

The forum assembles the working chapters to address twenty-nine topics such as adhesives and adhesion, business intelligence, computers, and intellectual property. Any tech who signs up can come to the topical sessions; this helps ensure that the sessions cut across the silos of expertise. Fourteen committees oversee, plan, and administer many Tech Forum activities. For example, the Academic Relations committee encourages young people to get involved in technical fields. The forum meets monthly for three hours on company time. It has the complete blessings of the top.

Paralleling the forums are councils made up of representatives who manage technicians. They act similarly as they give a voice to a different level within the organization. Now there is some energy to encourage collaboration among the forum and council members for even more collective decision making.

Bill Gross, founder and chairman of Idealab, an incubator for Internet start-ups, believes deeply that employee ownership, when real, magnifies economic returns. He distinguished three forms of equity ownership: no equity—salary is the only stake in the company; token equity—there is some stake, but salary still dominates the economic rewards; significant equity—the potential equity dominates salary, owning at least 1 percent of the company. The implications of these different forms of ownership for infrastructure and other Zone 3a and 3b realities are profound. Gross observes that "once people are fed and sheltered, the rest is basically about fulfilling their fantasies. And equity is a wonderful tool for harnessing the power of fantasy because it involves a story. There's a protagonist (the company) and an antagonist (the competition); a struggle; and a victor and a hero. Equity means drama. Annuity, by contrast, is boring because you already know the ending. It's a dull story" (Gross, 1998, p. 4). Boyett and Conn (1991) support this belief. From their research they conclude that companies that combined employee stock option plans (ESOPs) and involvement grew faster than similar companies that did not (p. 139).

Having the Courage to Speak

No matter what structures and systems are put in place, participation is what makes them work. For the work to be serious often requires courageous speaking. Without the courage to speak up, to challenge the current mindset or cultural assumptions, the forum, council, team, or whole organization can engage in "group-think." Voice is central.

One way to educate people about this hazard is to use the video *The Abilene Paradox* (based on Jerry Harvey's book *The Abilene Paradox: The Mismanagement of Agreement*, 1974). It captures beautifully how lack of courage results in families, organizations, and even couples ending up where no one wanted to go. It centers on a family of four who agree to have dinner in Abilene, Texas, a drive of fifty-three miles in a car with no air conditioning in 100-degree heat, and come back furious with each other. No one really wants to go. Each is pleasing the others. Does the family ever resolve its conflict? No. Why? The family members were not in conflict; they were in agreement, and working on conflict when agreement is the issue is irrational.

The story captures the danger of unreflective adaptation. Each member of the family adapts to the other in a pleasing but false manner. Group-think takes over and the strength of the individual is lost. One should not take the "I" out of team. As noted earlier, there's a tee-shirt around that claims "There is no *I* in team." But teams need strong I's with great courage. Abilene trips await the loss of the I in teams.

Where does courage come from? As a minimum, it requires choice. Later, I shall explore other dimensions of courage. For now, let us attend to a platform for choice. I created the idea of an exit card, not necessarily to leave one's job; rather, to take charge of one's life. Over the years I have developed and used the notion of the exit card (see Figure 22, on the next page) as a stimulus for courageous action and identification of personal core values. Some people call the card a power card, a courage card, or a choice card.

The card must be filled out authentically. You are being asked to make a choice of what you could be doing that meets your real lifestyle necessities. We are not talking about the vacation you would like to take. The three conditions under which you would use the exit card should focus on real actions that are intolerable to you: a certain kind of abuse, dramatic loss of power, gross dishonesty? You have to figure this out for yourself.

I recommend that you fill out this card, review it every six months, and update it as needed. And here is the beauty of the exit card. You do not have to leave your present job. You can fill one out and love your job. What the exit card does is to give you courage in that job. Without it, you have not made a choice about your real options and attitudes; you are trapped and ready for victimhood. If you have made no choice you have no power, and with no power you cannot act authentically and adeptly. You adapt rather than become adept. You inappropriately conform rather than create your own future.

All employees, including bosses, can fill out a card. Bosses can introduce the idea to employees. However, with all the downsizing taking place today, I advise caution. Create a comfortable context in which to discuss the idea.

Using a Power-Based Simulation

One particular simulation exercise exposes the heart of this zone. It is called *Star Power*. Because power is so difficult to address in

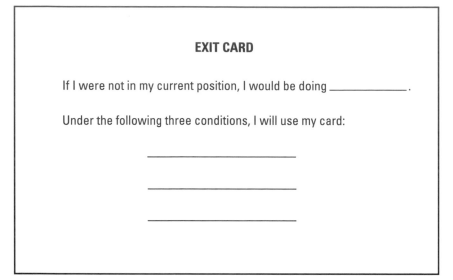

FIGURE 22 • EXIT CARD

organizations and many team- and group-building exercises avoid it or give it only marginal attention, I suggest employing this simulation or a similar activity if Zone 4 requires leadership. The brief description that follows suggests the focus of such activities.

Remember from Zone 3a that simulations differ from role-plays. In the latter, participants are asked to behave like someone in a particular position, e.g., play the position of a doctor or mother. In a simulation, you are to be yourself and respond to constructed situations. In role-plays, participants always have an excuse if the game disappoints the players. In a simulation, there is no excuse. You are making decisions based on your own experience and reading of the situation. Of course, simulations are limited, just like metaphors, in that no one structured experience can duplicate life's rich variety and complex relationships. Each simulation has a point to make and should be selected and used accordingly. These two address power issues: the first more generally, the second in an explicit business context.

Star Power, created by Gary Shirts in the late 1960s, continues to work as an educational experience to address power as long-term decision making and keeping. You may already have heard of it or played it. The simulation works best with twenty to fifty people.

(When the numbers are larger, people do not participate well.) The room is arranged with chairs in a circle. Each participant is asked to contribute one dollar to play. Poker chips in five different colors are mixed in bags. Different chips are assigned different values. Each member takes five chips to use for trading. The rules for trading (for example, trading chips one for one; no talking prior to handshake between potential traders) are explained. The different values of the chips are posted. After a certain number of rounds, the three players with the most points will win the game and divide up the money.

Trading, for the first two rounds, lasts about three minutes. The scores are posted and are then used to divide the large group into three subgroups—squares, circles, and triangles. The highest five or six scorers are the squares, the next ten or so are the circles, and the rest are triangles. Note the hierarchy: the downs are more numerous than the ups.

After the second round, the squares are given the authority to make rules for the next round. They can announce them at the beginning of the next round or at the end, making them retroactive. Circles and triangles can communicate to the squares only by written memo. The squares may or may not take the memos seriously. The only rule the squares cannot make is to end the game or set up conditions that would end it, like creating some means to divide up the money.

Almost without exception, the squares announce rules that are totally self-serving. Sometimes the rules are minor, almost inconsequential, and sometimes they are outright oppressive. In any case, after a couple of rounds in which the squares are the decision makers, the triangles rebel (usually alone, but sometimes in partnership with the circles), confiscating the prize money, which is sitting near them on a chair or table—thereby ending the game. The squares have no idea what is going on and usually do not even know the money has been taken. They think they are still in charge. They really have only formal positional power, no enforcement power, and thus are helpless. And they have set up the conditions for their own overthrow.

The debriefing begins with the reflections of the triangles on what it was like to be a triangle. Attention then turns to circles, who usually talk about not really wanting to link with triangles and yet not being able to make it into squareness. Finally, the squares talk, usually admitting that their goal was to stay in power, no matter what. As the discussion unfolds, all the players learn that the bags of chips were rigged from the outset by putting the more valued chips in one bag, and that what constitutes real power is often what circles and triangles give away. They go passive or follow rules the squares can change at will. Certainly squares had no enforcement power. They only had what was given by the other two groups, who, when they decided to take it back, had all the power they needed. The whole process takes about two and a half to three hours to complete, including the follow-up discussion.

After I use this simulation, I tell about one group that did not follow the pattern. It was composed of Catholic nuns. After the squares were given the decision-making power, the square sisters met for three minutes, then turned to the rest of the members and announced that they wanted two representatives from the triangles and two from the circles to meet with two of them in the center of the room. The six would make decisions that would benefit all. The game was over. The potential buffaloes shared power and all became geese.

The question the participants are left with in this simulations is: Can these power issues be addressed from within the bureaucracy? Or is a camp meeting required? The simulation drives home the point of how difficult it is to come together as equals and sort out issues when up-and-down realities overwhelm the possibility of side-by-side possibilities and time and results are constant pressures.

ZONE IDENTIFICATION AND
LEADERSHIP QUESTIONS

How well is your organization addressing Zone 4 issues? Check out these questions to assess leadership as political engagement.

1. How sturdy is my organization or community in this zone?

   • How important is worker (member) participation in this organization or community?

- Are there safe and respected processes in place for voices to be heard?

- Is ownership viewed as an alternative to buy-in?

- Do executives explain to the employees the difference between advisory and decision-making teams?

- Have any large-scale participatory events been held? If so, why were they held, and who ran them?

- Were the executives authentic listeners and responders who fully participated in the event?

- Has there been follow-up to the large-scale event? Have the promises made at the event been kept—by the top, the middle, and the bottom?

- How is discipline handled? Do peers have any say?

- Are there forums for voice so people in the organization can talk to each other, learn from each other, and make a difference? Are the forums run by their own members and supported by the top? Does the top respond quickly to voices of the middles and bottoms?

- Is feedback and performance evaluation top-down or 360-degree?

- Is the union, if there is one, taken seriously, involved in critical decision making, and listened to by management?

- Has top management abdicated its responsibilities and sold out to unions? Do the unions run the organization?

- Does the union take responsibility for disciplining unproductive members and those who do not live the core values?

- Is collaboration a viable alternative to labor–management negotiations?

- Is there more than one bottom line?

10 | | | | | | | | | | | 0 | | | | | | | | | | 10
Very Sturdy   Shaky

2. Where is my organization or community currently focusing its leadership attention?

  • If this is the zone needing attention, is it being attended to?

  • If not, where is the organization or community directing its energy?

```
10  |  |  |  |  |  |  |  |  |  |  0  |  |  |  |  |  |  |  |  |  | 10
Excellent Fit                                                    Misfit
```

3. Am I prepared to create ownership?

  • Do I have the core competencies to lead in this zone?

  • Is my exit card in place?

  • Am I willing to exhibit courage?

  • Do I have negotiation and conflict-resolution skills?

  • Am I ready to participate and lead in a large-scale participation event?

  • What am I doing to empower myself?

  • Have I done a buffalo-versus-goose assessment of my leadership engagement?

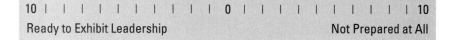

```
10  |  |  |  |  |  |  |  |  |  |  0  |  |  |  |  |  |  |  |  |  | 10
Ready to Exhibit Leadership                          Not Prepared at All
```

ZONE SUMMARY

Leadership focuses on power. It requires attention from the top, middle, and bottom. The metaphor that life is ups versus downs couples with the polarity of conceal/reveal to open a set of leadership challenges often ignored or sidestepped in the literature. The authenticity standard now emphasizes codetermination, where shared power challenges the old method of command and control. Buffaloes seek to transform themselves into geese and to share leadership. The downs, with exit cards in hand, must empower themselves by making informed choices. Position does not equal leadership. Leadership moves around. It has the potential to spread from top to bottom. Leadership is Creating Ownership.

The most important core competencies now include conflict management and negotiation skills (including the ability to listen), letting go of and taking on tasks (buffalo self-assessment and participatory tasks and events), and assuming ownership of one's own actions (personal empowerment and the exit card).

Leadership in this zone faces empowerment issues authentically. No games and false messages. Power boundaries are clear. People know what they can decide on their own, what they share, and what they retain for themselves only. Dual personas are not tolerated. There is no fear of repercussions from telling the truth as one sees it. The second umpire rejoices in this zone. All we have are multiple perspectives, and they must engage each other. We all call 'em as we see 'em. So we must come to the round table for serious conversation. Vibrant participation sets the ethical guide.

ZONE 4 DEFINITIONS

Leadership: Creating Ownership
Authenticity criterion: Codetermination
Metaphor: Life is ups versus downs
Core ethical principle: Participation
Polarity: Conceal/reveal

STIRRINGS

The stirrings reflect that the world in this zone can be overwhelming. It can be daunting. It can be scary. And yet into that world we thrust ourselves, to set direction and shape the world. What is the point of having power without direction? Leadership is more than power *over*. It needs to shift from power over to power *with*. It is vision.

It is knowing where we are going and being committed to getting there in partnership. Setting Direction from a participatory base redefines the leadership challenge.

Negative Stirrings

Negative stirrings might sound like this:

> I know I have voice. I'm just not sure of what I want to say. I want to shape my life, and I can shape it, but I have no clue as to what direction I want to take. I'm scared. I'm not sure I have the courage or capacity to create a sense of direction for others or myself. And even if I did, who would follow? Maybe I'm a better follower than leader. Leadership involves exposure, risk, living the values, authenticity. I'm not ready; I'm not confident I can take the next step. I'll respond with my voice; I won't lead with vision.

If negative feelings get too strong, vision talk will create the fear of a retreat to buffalo land. Participation and disagreement will be sacrificed for the sake of common direction. One more time there will be the call for buy-in. Ownership will be faked and cynicism will return. Under these circumstances, a large-scale intervention is un-likely to deliver. Instead, people may say:

> Although we were all excited, very little happened. Our unit took some actions and our boss's boss criticized us. We are now afraid to act on the vision we thought we all agreed to. Instead of moving out into the world boldly, we seem to be retreating.

> We enjoy the dialogue with colleagues. Then we differ and go our separate ways. I respect their points of view—we are connected. We just don't seem to be able to come together. *Vision* may really be a code word for idle dreaming. Maybe it is just an occasion to talk, to have voice. Maybe that is all we really need. If we talk thought-fully, maybe we will find common ground for action. I'm not too hopeful.

The pessimism about participation intensifies; the futility of vision blocks collective movement.

Positive Stirrings

The positive voices sound like this:

I'm ready to move forward. I have a clue of what kind of visionary I am. However, I am more excited to join with others to shape a future for all of us. We are too stuck in process. All this group stuff wears me down. It doesn't seem to offer direction. I want direction and I'm ready to help create it. I want to be a player in our organization's future. I want our community to figure out where it is going and focus our plans around a shared vision. I'm ready.

Hamel and Prahalad (1994) capture the essence of the shift from Zone 4 to Zone 5a.

> There is not one future but hundreds. There is no law that says most companies must be followers. Getting to the future first is not just about outrunning competitors bent on reaching the same prize. It is also about having one's own view of what the prize is. There can be as many prizes as runners; imagination is the only limiting factor. Renoir, Picasso, Calder, Seurat, and Chagall were enormously successful artists, but each had an original and distinctive style. In no way did the success of one preordain the failure of another. Yet each artist spawned a host of imitators. In business, as in art, what distinguishes leaders from laggards, and greatness from mediocrity, is the ability to uniquely imagine what could be. (p. 27)

People with optimistic stirrings have glimmers of glorious possibilities. The world does respond to such vision, and social movements are rooted in participation. When only one person has the vision, it requires buy-in by others. When many people converge—when collectively they discern, create, and embrace a shared vision, a shared direction, a shared sense of a preferred future—leadership is ready to move into a new zone. Creating Ownership is not enough for people who long to shape what is in front of them. When leadership engages us all to create and live into that preferred future, the zone of Setting Direction calls us.

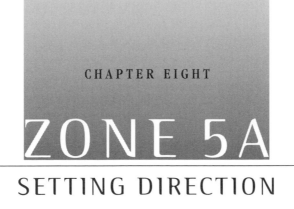

CHAPTER EIGHT

ZONE 5A

SETTING DIRECTION

Action in Zone 5 focuses on the future. The metaphor shifts to an image of life as a journey. Like Zone 3, this zone is divided into two subsections due to the amount of material in the field and a critical distinction between ends and means. Zone 5a, Setting Direction, concentrates on the end point of the journey, the destination; Zone 5b, Anticipating Change, attends to the trip, on the means to get there. Leadership in Zone 5a determines the ends—the destination, vision, strategic intent, or preferred future. Leadership in Zone 5b thinks more about means, and what might happen in the future that could dramatically affect where the organization is going or even destroy its potential. In thinking about Setting Direction in Zone 5a, we project an image or a picture that will guide action. In thinking about Anticipating Change in Zone 5b, we map the future, moving toward more informed, thoughtful, and creative expectations.

SHARE DIRECTION; AVOID DEFLECTION.

A community in the Midwest is determining its own destiny very self-consciously. This story began when the mayor, deputy mayor, elected council, and city manager were planning their annual retreat to set strategic priorities. The recently elected mayor, young and somewhat inexperienced but very energetic, had been asked to review the video

Back from the Brink, *which describes towns that have taken charge of their futures.*

The mayor's imagination soared. He tried to get the city manager to view the video. After some resistance, the city manager watched it and became intrigued. The mayor and the city manager then encouraged the city council to watch it. The retreat agenda was planned; futuring took over; and, as a result, the town engaged in a yearlong process involving hundreds of citizens.

During the first public meeting in the process, some history of the town was shared. A futurist presented trends and patterns emerging in other communities. The town organized six task forces: citizens self-selected to address the future in areas such as lifestyle and lifestyle choices, lifelong learning, community services, government and inter-governmental cooperation, and economic vitality. The challenge for members in each group was to construct a shared vision in their topic area that could be melded with the ideas of other task forces, and then for the task forces together to commit to shaping the town's future. Their work was presented to the community as a whole and then handed off to a professional planning firm for operational implemen-tation strategies.

While the firm's plan looked good on paper it contained recommenda-tions that had not surfaced in the six visioning task forces. A new meet-ing was proposed to take out what the citizens had not put in. The process took a year, which some chairs of the citizen committees also thought was too long. Energy began to fade. Nevertheless, in spite of these hurdles, the members who participated felt the work worthwhile.

The process has offered the promise of a community taking charge of its own destiny. In this town, leadership equals Setting Direction. Community members owned the shared direction. It worked, as it has in hundreds of communities.

CORE IDEAS

Life is no longer ups versus downs or even a living system; as we move outward on the map and toward the future the metaphor that

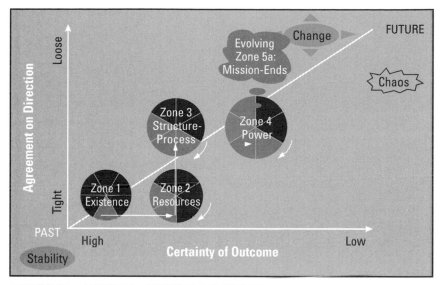

FIGURE 23 • ZONE 5A: SETTING DIRECTION

has the most meaning is that life is a journey (Figure 23). In Zone 5a, the world invites us to shape the future. The polarity with which leadership must deal is ends/means, and in this zone we focus on the destination (the ends) more than the trip (the means). We also commit to ensuring that the future we shape actually comes to be. Zone 4 valued participation to ensure all voices were heard. Now, having given people permission to speak, is it possible to have the voices come together, to blend and harmonize in concerted collective action? Convergence sets the standard for authenticity in this zone. What does this standard mean? Convergence invites and judges the extent to which stakeholders and/or other players come together—converge—around a shared direction, goal, or vision. "Caring as sharing" sets the ethical boundary. To venture on a journey, one must care about the others on the trip. Without sharing we fail to join a common direction.

In this zone and this world, with loose agreement on direction and low certainty of outcome, fix-it strategies are no longer an option. Yet we are not helpless. Great human energy can be focused and released toward building a shared future. Chaos hovers around us. Yet with participation as a foundational platform, stakeholders can now converge to invent their own desired alternative reality.

Vision Statements

Just as mission statements blossomed in the '90s, so too did vision statements—and with the same questionable impact. You have already experienced my effort to transform mission statements into identity affirmations. Now let me work with the traditional use of vision statements. Let us begin with the traditional, common approach. Then I will propose an alternative for leadership as Setting Direction.

For many customers the shopping channel QVC defines the best of the business of home shopping via television. Its vision stretches toward an exciting, desirable future: "Change the way the world shops." That vision is connected to the present and is also the clarion call for QVC. Disney does not just want to provide family entertainment; it wants to *be* entertainment. Home Depot's initial vision was a retail warehouse with "huge quantities of in-stock items, everyday low prices, and highly paid and knowledgeable workers" (Bennis and Mische, 1997, p. 6).

Many vision statements mention being the "leader," "first," "best," etc. Here is Hershey Foods Corporation's statement: "Hershey Foods Corporation's mission is to be a focused food company in North America and selected international markets and a leader in every aspect of our business. In North America, our goal is to enhance our number one position in confectionery and achieve number one positions in pasta and chocolate-related grocery products" (Abrahams, 1995, p. 306). This statement is part mission, part vision, and part strategic initiatives and goals. Words like "be number one" and "leader" may seem appropriate handmaidens. My advice is, Do not put words like these in vision statements. If you do, then number two is in charge, framing your existence. To excel, figure out what you are great at and maximize it. As Collins and Porras (1994) discovered in their research into the successful habits of visionary companies, the enduring and prospering firms did not focus primarily on beating the competition. They focused on bettering themselves:

> Success and beating competitors comes to the visionary companies not so much as the end goal, but as a residual *result* of relentlessly asking the question "How can we improve ourselves to do better tomorrow than we did today?" And they have asked this question day in and day out—as a disciplined way of life—in some cases for

over 150 years. No matter how much they achieve—no matter how far in front of their competitors they pull—they never think they've done "good enough." (p. 10)

Leadership does not prosper by imitation. Focusing on others' rather than one's own organization eliminates leadership as future shape. When leadership is preoccupied with the competition it quietly turns into risk management and adaptive responses to others. Wise, adept choices cease to exist.

Vision Pictures

Vision statements can offer some guidance to organizations. However, my experience is that they inspire little energy. *Full* vision work, futuring, constructs a comprehensive picture of the preferred future, turning the glimpse of insight of the statement into a full-blown image of that future. Clarifying the target of the futuring activity first directs leadership attention and action. Are you building a future for your organization, a particular market, a department, a product, or a service? In other words, what are you visioning about? Without focus, there is no vision. What is it that Setting Direction is trying to shape? Vision pictures excite the imagination and stimulate action.

Since most vision work concentrates on the organization, let us focus there. Suppose you are on a task force to construct a vision for your organization. What would the content include? Here is where focusing on constructing a vision statement can slow comprehensive work or even block it. Coming up with a vision statement is not the goal; the goal is portraying a vision picture. What would that picture look like?

A good place to start might be with the eight subsystems in Gibb's (1997) model, which I discussed in Zone 3a. A comprehensive organizational vision will address the future desired for all the eight subsystems:

- Cultural subsystem

- Direction subsystem

- Process subsystem

- Political subsystem

- People subsystem

- Information subsystem

- Facilities and equipment subsystem

- Financial subsystem

Together the eight subsystems constitute the organization as a whole system; customers to be served, the physical environment, and a larger suprasystem surround the organization. This suprasystem is composed of the same eight subsystems operating at the next level of inclusion. Any system, like a department, can be broken down into smaller subsystems which themselves are a sort of subsystem.

Once one figures out what is going on in each of the subsystems in the present, the subsystems can be cast into their preferred future state. Some subsystems may be targeted to change more than others. It is important to remember that the organization is an integrated system and if one subsystem changes, all other systems will be affected. Similarly, if customers or other features of the external environment change, the internal effects can be dramatic. When a merger is part of the desired future, all eight subsystems are directly affected, too. Each part has to merge if the whole is to merge smoothly.

A comprehensive picture articulates the vision of the whole organization. On one side of a piece of paper write "Current System"; on the other, "Preferred System." Then articulate how to get from one side of the paper to the other. Vision statements seldom do this. They are often slogans more than vision pictures. In the application section of this chapter, I suggest ways to construct vision pictures. Suffice it here to point out that vision work seeks to create a map that the whole organization can use to see its destination: this is how we are today, this is where we envision being in the future, and this is the plan to get there. For example, a company that has produced one product line changes its focus to a cluster of products. It then tries out the system implications, drawing on the earlier zones.

Strategic Intent

Strategic planning almost eliminated organizational development in the 1970s. While both still exist, today it is strategic planning that is under siege in some quarters. Mintzberg blasted it in *The Rise and*

Fall of Strategic Planning (1994). Like others before him, he is contemptuous of the zones behind him. He lives either here or in Zone 5b, perhaps even in Zone 6, where life is art. For him strategic planning presupposes more order and predictability than is possible. Putting form over dynamic destroys the creative process and promises a false comfort through planning. Thus strategic planning is an oxymoron, "The Grand Fallacy":

> Because analysis is not synthesis, strategic planning is not strategy formation. Analysis may precede and support synthesis, by defining the parts that can be combined into wholes. Analysis may follow and elaborate synthesis, by decomposing and formalizing its consequences. But analysis cannot substitute for synthesis. No amount of elaboration will ever enable formal procedures to forecast disconti nuities, to inform managers who are detached from their operations, to create novel strategies. (p. 321)

Somewhat similarly, Collins and Porras (1994) found in their study that highly successful companies did not make their best moves by strategic planning, even when the planning was brilliant and complex. Instead they experimented, using trial and error, opportunism, and often accident. "What looks *in retrospect* like brilliant foresight and preplanning was often the result of: 'Let's just try a lot of stuff and keep what works'" (p. 8).

Of course, Mintzberg's book angered many strategic planners, who believed he did not understand or really appreciate the field. There is a route through this battle. One of the best guides I have found to address the strategic and political aspects of planning is *Making Strategy: The Journey of Strategic Management* by Colin Eden and Fran Ackermann (1998). These two authors understand well the connection between Zones 3b, 4, and 5a. They say that the parts of the system must cohere, be energized, and aim toward a shared goal. However, the process is amazingly dynamic; rather than being planned in any formal sense, it *emerges*. All organizations operate as emergent processes. Some are explicit about it; others just let it happen. In either case, it is possible for leadership to understand and identify the emergent *strategic intent* and then have impact upon it.

Strategic intent may be a more useful term than *strategic planning* for leadership to use in this zone. Strategic intent focuses the organizational stakeholders' energy and understanding of shared direction.

Strategic planning attends too much to formal processes of intervention and thus produces questionable results. Eden and Ackermann convincingly argue that organizational capabilities coupled with resilience, grounded in solid identity, set the foundation out of which strategic intent emerges (p. 13). Without some implicit sense of shared direction, the organization fumbles and stumbles. With clear and convincing strategic intent, the organization can prosper. For example, a company sets three critical agendas—write scenarios about the technology trends in the market; realign manufacturing for more effective response to market shifts; and test whether the right people are in the right jobs. These are commitments for action. Is it certain that they will occur? Not necessarily.

One further value of the term *strategic intent* is that intent is generally recognized as something that does not always translate into predicted results. Like Zone 5 itself, intentionality lives in a world that offers little surety of outcome and slim agreement on direction. Any dramatic shift in this uncertain world can change the proposed implementation and, more important, the fundamental adequacy of any intent.

Strategic planning in Zone 3b is executive driven. Workers are expected to buy in. In Zone 4 leadership offers shared power—some participation in strategic planning. For strategic intent to work in Zone 5, it must be lived every day by large numbers of people in the organization. While buy-in might work in the short term, it is ownership of strategic intent that creates the energy for emergent strategic thinking and action.

In Zone 5a, the organization needs geese who share leadership and give followership for the sake of a common destination. However, it is also in this zone that a limitation in the metaphor of buffaloes and geese is revealed. Human beings, unlike geese, are not programmed to fly toward a set destination. We have to collectively figure out where we want to go and then agree to make the trip. The answer is not in our gene pool; it is in our minds, hearts, and histories as we seek to discern our destination.

Authenticity requires convergence among organizational members, and this act of coming together is predicated upon the ethical principle of caring as sharing. In caring, people attend to each other. Even if they do not agree on all matters, they can still share a common vision, a strategic intent, and an organizational mission.

Diversity is real and present in this zone. So, too, is unity. Through participation, diversity finds common ground. Together, members of an organization share a joint adventure. Leadership in this zone sets direction.

APPLICATION

Through conversations with participants in leadership programs, I have learned that most people choose vision over framing as a leadership tool. That does not surprise me. We have been programmed from childhood to fix, to solve, or to cure even before we know what is wrong. I am surprised, though, by something else. Most participants believe that visions are easy to imagine and create. It is almost as if a vision comes to one in a dream and is implemented the next day. This view trivializes the seriousness of the leadership challenge to set direction. Even if one is an intuitive thinker (NT in *Myers-Briggs Type Indicator* [MBTI] language) and, moreover, is labeled a visionary leader, that does not guarantee authentic vision. Having a big futuristic thought is not enough. Although it is a good platform, it is not a guarantee of depth or delivery. One's MBTI type is no predicator of wisdom. NT types may be shallow when it comes to vision, whereas other types may be deep. These other types will have earned the vision; often NTs think it is an entitlement or a gift.

Futurists face the same dilemma. They are great, even spectacular, at their job, which is articulating alternative futures. They study trends and patterns and love to share the results with interested groups. Sharing a new insight does not constitute leadership, however. It is a resource for leadership, not leadership itself.

The futurist I mentioned earlier did a marvelous job in the town's futuring kickoff conference. As he shared urban trends and ideas that other cities are addressing, his voice quickened, his spirit soared, and he engaged the audience. His challenge was to offer new ideas to consider, not construct a vision for the town. That was to be the responsibility of the citizens and of the professional planning company that developed the implementation strategies.

Even a futurist in a position of power cannot always implement a vision. Harlan Cleveland, himself a world-renowned futurist, exhibited Zone 5a leadership when he was dean of the Humphrey

Institute of Public Affairs at the University of Minnesota. Part of his vision for the school was that it should become a place where practitioners and scholars could unite in public-policy discussions. He was more interested in deep reflection on practice than in theory leading to practice. In keeping with his vision and commitment, he challenged the faculty's worldview by questioning the institute's current beliefs. Traditional status and standings were tested as the academics and practitioners were invited to share as equals in the policy research. His vision achieved only modest success, however. Most faculty did not buy in to his vision, despite the fact that it clearly came from deeply held beliefs and passions.

Participatory Futuring

For vision to engage folks, they must have some voice in shaping it. What strategies are available to link futuring, especially picture creation, with participation?

Two kindred theories pioneered participatory visioning. Future Search is one; preferred futuring is the other. Let me sketch the theory and then detail procedures and processes.

The historical roots of these modes of participatory futuring are the same as the roots of large-scale interventions and organizational development discussed earlier. It is clear that the thinking of the 1950s and 1960s still inspires creative engagement, even in the twenty-first century. More specifically, these two approaches were triggered by the increased recognition that problem solving or gap analysis did not work well.

Both problem solving and gap analysis are very popular today. Why don't they work? Basically, both concentrate too much on the past. Instead of creating a new future, both look backward as the starting point. Gap analysis is particularly limiting. Here is the rhetoric: What is the problem? Where do we want to head? What is blocking us from getting there? Let's get rid of the gap and move forward.

Why does this not work? Because going back into the gap triggers all the old baggage, killing any excitement and delight about the future. Problem solving has the same result. Lawrence Lippitt (1998, p. 5) contrasts problem solving with preferred futuring:

Problem Solving	Preferred Futuring
List problems	Review how we got here
Prioritize problems	List what is working and not working
Determine strategic starting point	Determine the future you want
Plan actions to solve problems	Plan actions to achieve preferred future

The results of the two processes are different as well.

Problem Solving	Preferred Futuring
A list of problems	A sense of heritage
Key problem identification	A realistic assessment
A solution	An exciting destination
Action plans to achieve a solution	Action plans to create future of choice

Rather than simply rejecting gap analysis and problem solving as insufficient compared to futuring, perhaps it would make sense to label these two processes as *management activity* and futuring as *leadership*. Are there conditions that warrant both problem solving and futuring? I think so.

The underlying principles are similar for both future search and preferred futuring. Make sure the critical stakeholders are in the process. Keep the big picture in front of the group before considering specific local action. Build a preferred future, look for common ground, and self-organize to take action and own one's responsibility for the action.

The basic approach and process design are parallel as well. Develop activities to claim the past, articulate trends and patterns in the present, move to a constructed future, look for common ground, and then engage in action planning. Build and maintain momentum toward the future.

This participatory futuring approach often frightens positional leaders. What if the vision the group envisions is stupid, narrowly constructed, ideologically based, or not in agreement with the leader's? Command and control should be long gone in this set of events. In this zone, leadership is not a person or a position. It is a process of engagement that requires trust in the commitment of the participants and their good will. When futuring in an organization, no executive buffaloes are allowed. If they are present, the process will fail. Collective futuring requires character and caring in order for convergence to occur.

What else makes participatory futuring processes work? There are at least three realities that must be in place: two implicit, the other explicit. In large measure, I believe what make these processes work are implicit shared values that define the boundaries of acceptable behavior for futuring. So far I have found that the best identification of the necessary shared organizational values is given in the extensive research by the Lebow Company. The research, begun in 1972, studied 2.4 million employees in the United States and encompassed thirty-two Standard Industrial Code (SIC) areas. In addition, 14.6 million supplemental surveys from employees in forty countries around the world were included. The research found eight values that appear to be important to employees in all cultures (Lebow Company, 1995, p. 3):

- Honesty—individual and organizational

- Truthfulness—individual and management

- Trust

- Openness to new ideas

- Encouragement to take risk

- Giving credit

- Putting the interest of others first

- Mentoring—individual and management

Futuring methods embody these values. Participants live and share these values. They do not do so because they have to, because of external control and imposed standards. The values come with the process, are inherent in it when it is authentic, as they do in whole-system interventions. These values are more inclusive than core values, those that are tied to the business. These values are linked to the people who collectively exhibit leadership. Participants can share direction and avoid deflection from that direction because their collective values are solid and connected. These shared values set the platform for sharing a future.

The second implicit reality that must be in place is that participants must have confidence in the information shared in the futuring sessions. There is always the danger that some players in the process will exhibit arrogance. Among those who have the formal task of presenting trends to the rest of the participants, this arrogance may result in casting trends as facts. Belief and possibility may be presented as certain knowledge. Humility leaves the zone and hubris takes over.

In addition to the shared values and the confidence in information that participants must have, a third critical condition must be met and must be made explicit. The stakeholders must have compelling reasons to connect and interact. If they do not understand the importance of the task, the process will lack commitment and will falter.

Personally, I have great confidence in the futuring approach in most circumstances. What worries me are the hidden buffaloes who can sabotage this work. In large-scale interventions, positional leaders retain veto power. In a truly participative approach, veto power evaporates. Authenticity of the process is paramount if it is to succeed. Hidden agendas destroy the credibility of the events.

Futuring Processes

Typically, *Preferred Futuring* and *Future Search* are two-to-three-day events. They may involve twenty to one hundred people, with sixty to eighty participants is common. The numbers can be greater, like a camp meeting. However, sometimes it is good to narrow the participation a bit, then hand off results to a large camp meeting for review and ownership.

Preferred Futuring

In Preferred Futuring, broad participation is crucial. However, there is often a sponsoring leadership group, usually made up of senior executives, that blesses and supports the process. Both top management and all other participants must come to see the value of the process and to believe that, collectively, members of the organization or community can effectively shape their own future.

In both Preferred Futuring and Future Search, a planning design team is chosen. Sometimes a nominating committee selects the planning group; sometimes people volunteer. The key is to use methods congruent with the ideals of the process itself.

This team operates on the belief that people will do the best with whatever they bring to the action table. The most critical task facing the team is to target the real issue that can bring the group together for the event. Success is heavily dependent on addressing an issue that is serious to the critical stakeholders. So the team rehearses the whole event prior to its actual implementation. Decisions are made about who should attend, why the event is to be held, and what processes are to be followed. Consultants facilitate the actual event, while participants make it happen. All have voices that are heard.

Resistance is always a worry at the beginning of a futuring process. Lippitt (1998) recommends inviting the preferred-futuring planning group to identify the different images that discourage and encourage futuring. These discouraging images might include thoughts like these: "Face reality, get your head out of the clouds, God has the plan, why stick your neck out." The encouraging images might sound like this: "Go for it, today's truth is tomorrow's limit, you have to have a dream to have a dream come true" (p. 118). The planning group may also make an effort to acknowledge irrational beliefs that bind rather than release us. Lippitt borrows from rational/ emotive therapist Albert Ellis to produce a list of such beliefs. Here is a small sampling (p. 119):

- I am the person I am because I have always been this way and I always will be; there is nothing I can do about it.

- There is something wrong with people who commit misdeeds toward me, and they need to be shown that they are wrong.

- I must prove myself thoroughly competent, adequate, and achieving at all times in all situations.

The planning design team also collects data on the organization, and they and other stakeholders set the purpose of the event, create a plan for the event, and set up processes to evaluate the results. The same steps are taken during the event itself as the assembled members interact with the groundwork already done by the planning team. If the design team informed them well, Zone 4 reality would take over. The planning is preparation, not the delivering of a final answer.

In communities, the steps differ somewhat and are akin to what is happening in the Midwestern town dicussed previously. In a community the events are likely to be more spread out over time and to involve more task forces. Lippitt (1998, pp.132–40) outlines the steps:

- Phase 1: The Future Sampler Meeting, at which key community leaders decide whether Preferred Futuring is something they want to do.

- Phase 2: The Start-up Conference, which is attended by block and neighborhood leaders. The Start-up Conference spreads the Preferred Futuring process to the next level within the community.

- Phase 3: Multiple Preferred Futuring sessions held throughout the community.

- Phase 4: The Preferred Futures Scenarios Conference, which can be attended by anyone in the community. At this conference the information from the communitywide futuring sessions is used to agree on the strategic priorities, that is, Action Goals, Action Steps, and Responsibilities.

The process begins with the few and moves to the many. It ends with reviews of success and celebrations along the way. And thus the future is shaped.

Future Search

Future Search is somewhat different, and a quick review of this approach can complete the picture of possible approaches. After the planning group has completed its work, the event begins with a focus. "This is what we are here to address," announces the planning team. Then the process begins.

A timeline with evenly spaced dates is spread across the wall. Participants are asked to fill in the history, as they experienced it, of the topic of the futuring event. In that way the group comes to own its collective memory.

Next the group identifies trends and patterns relevant to the topic. The facilitator uses a large piece of paper, six square feet or so, with the topic written in a circle in the center. The facilitator places participants' comments on the sheet on lines coming off the center circle. Suggestions that tie to an already established line are added as branches. When the activity is complete, the whole paper is filled with a weblike pattern of interconnected observations. Participants are given dot stickers and asked to place them on the five trends they think are most critical for the targeted issue. Now the participants have completed their own trend analysis, revealed in the clustering of the dots.

The third major step is the futuring process itself. The past and present now quicken the work to create the new future. Members are asked to think into the future. They must imagine a scenario in which all of them have left the organization or the community and then have been invited back five years in the future. They are excited at what they see. In their minds they are asked to talk to organizational or town members, see the sights, and get totally reacquainted with their former home or workplace. Then, after mental touring, they are invited to describe *in the past tense* what they experienced. The requirement to speak in the past tense gives a certain palpable reality to what they envision. In saying, for example, "I *saw* four new buildings and *was told* the firm now employs 2,100 people," participants are forced to be concrete.

Agreements on what is seen are captured on flip-chart paper, and differences are also recorded. Then action plans are created for issues where there is agreement, and future work is planned where there are disagreements deemed worthy of shared investigation.

The group members do not have to be in total alignment before significant action can occur. Once common ground is discerned, the agreements can quicken appropriate strategies and steps for collective action. Now the group shares direction and avoids deflection.

Other Futuring Tools

Earlier I noted that strategic planning has been criticized for not opening doors to the future. However, it can embody leadership if it is participatory and stresses strategic intent. One of my mentors in this field is John Bryson, known for conducting strategic planning events for government agencies and nonprofits as well as for writing some of the most comprehensive and widely used books in the field (Bryson, 1989, for example). Bryson engages in a curious hobby, given his professional work. He collects old maps. Of course, all these old maps are in some degree incorrect. He owns one that portrays California as an island. I was struck and amused by the irony of his hobby: he collects unusable maps while he works with groups to help them create their own accurate maps. To him, the match is perfect. "What is life anyway?" he asks. "It is an adventure into an unknown future."

From Bryson's perspective, if we have an accurate map we don't need strategic planning. The planning process rests on the admission that our current map is outdated, probably wrong in many ways. Even old maps have points of truth in them, though if followed exactly they would mislead us and we would get lost very quickly. Bryson collects old maps in part to remind himself that new maps are always in demand. There is no final map to end all maps. A new terrain or set of circumstances awaits our next inquiry. Not surprisingly, Bryson's most recent research focuses on mental maps. Attend to intent, he might say.

Bill Mills and his colleagues have created a very useful tool for this zone—the StarMap System Strategy Map (Mills and Associates, 1998). It is a four-sided, two-page, fold-over document. On the folded document a group or team records its core business values, team values, and organizational strategic objectives, as well as particular individual or team strategies. When it is opened, the map is apparent. Each intent is matched to appropriate action steps, challenges, and solutions. The last page lists outcomes, results, and coaching opportunities. What I like about the tool is its format. One can picture the intent and implications on one page. As new issues emerge, it is easy to trace the implications for remapping.

Futuring Caveat

Harlan Cleveland, a great believer in finding common ground, has two major concerns about futuring: first, that we won't find unity, and second, that even if we do, we will then lose it again if we ask the wrong question. He said, "The most dangerous thing to ask both countries who have just come to a negotiated agreement is why they have agreed" (conversation with the author, 1988). In zone action terms, this means go for mission and vision; don't argue about meaning. Agree on direction; worry less about why the agreement exists.

Calling 'Em as You See 'Em: You Can Make It Happen

Vision is very powerful in this world. As agreement on direction and certainty of outcome lessen, vision is the driver. Back in the mid-'80s, Wendell Willis caught a vision that illustrates this significance. Willis worked as a manager at Honeywell, participated in the Reflective Leadership Program at the Humphrey Institute of Public Affairs for two years when I was director, and was an avid tennis fan with a link to the United States Tennis Association (USTA). Tennis had been struggling with declining popularity, was perceived as a very ethnocentric organization—very white and very male—and seemed stuck in the past. In the leadership program, however, a theme had lodged itself in Wendell's being—"You can make it happen." Then it came to him. He saw a future picture in which thousands of children of diverse backgrounds could play tennis at schools and learn not only the game. They could learn lessons of life as well. There was no model for this program. He created one. Through friends, connections, and robust energy, the vision took hold. What started as an idea in the early '90s involving two hundred children has been translated into programs for eleven thousand children throughout Minnesota and North Dakota and is quickly moving to other states. Tennis tied to a developmental curriculum is now engaging all kinds of kids.

Not only are children's lives being enhanced, the USTA itself is benefiting from Wendell's pioneering work. He now heads a national multicultural committee that is affecting tennis in the United States. He has built a participatory base by engaging the association in ongoing visioning processes. The USTA board of directors now wrestles with core values and the implications of those values on diverse memberships.

In the summer of 1999, Wendell and his colleagues convened the Trent Tucker Celebrity Pro Am Tennis and Golf fundraiser to benefit the USTA Northern Section Multicultural Tennis Program and also children's hospitals and clinics. More than seven hundred people rallied to support the cause, including Chris Carter, David Dinkins, Patrick Ewing, Michael Jordan, Charles Oakley, Rep. Jim Ramstad, and Ahmad Rashad. The event raised over $400,000. The vision works: the kids benefit and the USTA is a better organization. Vision can make a great difference when lived every day.

Leadership indeed sets direction. It defines the destination for the journey with active participation of many people.

ZONE IDENTIFICATION AND
LEADERSHIP QUESTIONS

To what extent is Zone 5a central to your leadership challenge? Check out these questions. Have you been doing your visioning primarily in Zone 3b or here?

1. How sturdy is my organization or community in this zone?

   • Does my organization currently have a clear and lively sense of direction?

   • Who decided that direction?

   • Has my organization ever tried future search or preferred futuring? If so, which one, and how well did the processes work?

   • Does my organization have a vision statement in place? Does it meet the standards of this zone?

   ```
   10 |  |  |  |  |  |  |  |  |  |  0  |  |  |  |  |  |  |  |  |  | 10
   Very Sturdy                                                 Shaky
   ```

2. Where is my organization or community currently focusing its leadership attention?

   • Is this the zone where leadership should abide in the organization?

   • Is this zone getting serious attention by the tops, middles, and bottoms?

   • If not, what zone is the current organizational focus of attention?

   ```
   10 |  |  |  |  |  |  |  |  |  |  0  |  |  |  |  |  |  |  |  |  | 10
   Excellent Fit                                               Misfit
   ```

3. Am I prepared for participatory process to set direction?

   • Do I have a deep sense of my own style of futuring?

- Do I own the organizational sense of direction?

- Have I ever tried any of the futuring processes?

- Do I have the requisite knowledge and skills?

- What am I doing to prepare the organization for the future?

```
10 |  |  |  |  |  |  |  |  |  0  |  |  |  |  |  |  |  |  10
Ready to Exhibit Leadership                    Not Prepared at All
```

ZONE SUMMARY

Zone 5a is preoccupied with the future. Setting Direction is key. Figure out what the vision or strategic intent is and can be, then live into it. Then employ processes that can paint a picture of the preferred future. Include all the systems and subsystems in the picture.

The leadership competencies for this zone require knowledge of the visioning processes and collective strategic planning processes as well as the ability to inspire and to create optimism and confidence.

The authenticity standard shifts again. The previous standards continue and are supplemented with convergence. The organization comes together in a shared sense of future possibilities. To do so requires listening and caring about those who are with you. Life is a journey; in this zone we concentrate on the destination more than the trip. We can find common ground and act in concert without agreeing why we are together. Partnerships may bring different deep purposes to the table. All that is needed for leadership to express itself is alignment on shared futures.

In Setting Direction, the ends are more critical than the means, although the means are not entirely ignored. They hover, always challenging whether the ends will be realized. For intentions to be translated into credible actions, great commitment and will must be summoned. That kind of focused energy comes from participation, from ownership rather than buy-in, in the shaping and sharing of desired outcomes.

ZONE 5A DEFINITIONS

Leadership: Setting Direction
Authenticity criterion: Convergence
Metaphor: Journey with focus on destination
Core ethical principle: Caring as sharing
Polarity: Ends/means, with emphasis on ends

STIRRINGS

We may know where we are going and possess great passion for that destination. However, the world does not always cooperate with our plans. At times it seems outright stubborn—even mean or tragic. We know this from experience. All of us have gone to work certain of what we were going to accomplish that day, only to find the comfort of our plans confounded by unanticipated events. For many, the world in this zone is too close to chaos, too insecure, too threatening for them to venture forth with much vision. While professing a lively sense of direction in public, privately they may feel currents of fear rush through them, eroding their confidence. The world is unknown and surprises us daily both negatively and positively.

Negative Stirrings

> Our organization has been devoted to securing market share for years. No doubt about it, we have a great track record. But yesterday three of our major customers abandoned us without warning. We didn't see it coming. A task force has been set up to review our best customers so we can secure their loyalty. These are very scary times for us. Our jobs are at stake and our future questionable. I love the vision our company has. It is just not working and we don't know what to do.

Negative stirrings abound when the world does not cooperate with our vision, with our best efforts to shape the future. Leadership that sets direction seems inept. It does not help us position ourselves in an unknown world. We may know where we are going; we may not know where the world is flowing. We don't like this and are frightened by it.

Positive Stirrings

You are right. The world is unpredictable today. The speed of change is overwhelming. New technology pops up every day. I'm old enough to remember the '40s and '50s when change was moderate and more easily understood and anticipated. Vision is not enough. I'm glad you shifted from vision statements to vision pictures. Something else must happen as well. We have to anticipate the future. And I know that is possible. I know we can't *predict* the future, but we can look for patterns and position ourselves with scenarios that capture future possibilities.

Actually I get excited about hanging out in the future. I love watching it emerge. I heard a futurist speak the other day. She was awesome. What a grasp of trends and patterns. I came away from the seminar with two new market opportunities I had not considered. The old idea of market share seems to be shifting to possibility share. I'm going to convene a group of creative folks next week and facilitate a discussion of market opportunities for our firm. I heard a community group was doing this as well. It's very exciting. I'm eager to go there.

It's true that the road ahead has many curves and bumps. I'll drive on with careful anticipation, aware that some oncoming drivers are responsible, some are drunk. I will not allow the drunks to keep me from my destination. I'll drive with courage, confident that I can spot bumps and keep a watchful eye out for erratic drivers. Maybe the trip will be more exciting than the arrival.

Setting Direction is appropriate for leadership; it just does not go far enough. The world is increasingly unknown. That does not limit us; it challenges us to expand our understanding of leadership. It is possible to anticipate an unknown world without predicting it. The positive stirrings entice us on a journey where the destination is shifting and often unclear. The future is filled with possibilities and, yes, even disasters. It will require courage to live in a Zone 5b world. But we anticipate that if we can figure out the flow, we may be able to go. The world is inviting us to thrive without clear destinations to direct our actions. Detours await; side trips may be more interesting than the planned vacation. Work itself will finally capture our creativity. Maybe there is something more than market share by which to judge success. Leadership is changing again. It is becoming Anticipating Change.

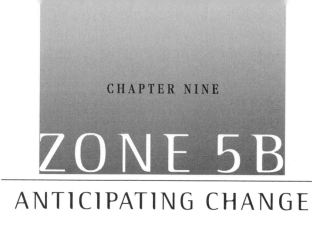

CHAPTER NINE

ZONE 5B

ANTICIPATING CHANGE

**THINK LESS WHERE WE ARE GOING;
THINK MORE WHERE THE WORLD IS FLOWING.**

As I was flipping through TV channels one night I came across a panel of business executives discussing organizational strategies, and I heard Bill Gates describing this Microsoft practice: any person in the company who has firsthand contact with an external customer writes up the essence of the meeting and e-mails the summary to a specific address. Once a month a team reads the messages, looking for patterns. Then once a quarter, Gates and his senior staff spend three days reviewing the mail. They ask only one question: "Where are we vulnerable?" Not "Where are we successful?" They are trying to anticipate the future, knowing full well that they cannot predict it.

CORE IDEAS

For leadership in Zone 5b, Anticipating Change, life remains a journey; now, however, leadership focuses on the adventure, the dynamics of the trip itself. In the ends/means polarity of this zone, the emphasis is now on means. Real chaos hovers nearby, palpable yet

243

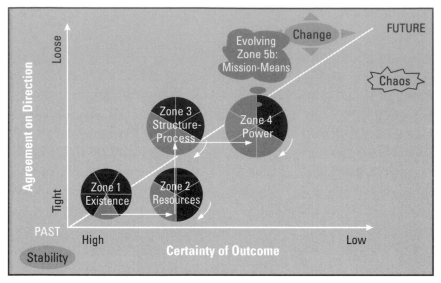

FIGURE 24 • ZONE 5B: ANTICIPATING CHANGE

not fully present (Figure 24). In this zone, strangers assemble with some still recognizable and credible commonality. Even though we know each other from earlier zones, this world creates strangers, at least for a while. Agreement on direction and outcomes wavers. I'm not sure what is really going on. All of life is a bit strange in this zone. The world is unknown, yet not totally unknowable. Emerging patterns are the reward of careful attention and listening. We are not helpless. We can anticipate aspects of the future even as we recognize we cannot predict them.

Vision falters in this zone. While central in Zone 5a, where destination was paramount, here in Zone 5b the focus shifts. Leadership is less preoccupied with shaping the future than with watching for it. Leadership directs attention outward, into external reality, looking for clues and patterns that might offer anticipatory wisdom about possible events and their significance. As the motto for this zone puts it: Think less where we are going; think more where the world is flowing. Concentrating on where we are going limits, even hinders, our recognition of what is emerging.

For many people this is a scary zone. The uncertainty of the future and our ability and capacity to address it activate the wavy line in the model (Figure 9). Chaos appears real; it feels real. Notice the wavy line continues to expand. The sense of uncertainty grows as the world becomes unknown. Nevertheless, while it is more difficult to discern agreement of direction and certainty of outcome, there is engaging work for those who seek to exhibit leadership. Authenticity sets a formidable new standard—conveyance. We are challenged to convey our attention into the future, not to create a vision picture but to question deeply what is currently going on and what might go on. Care for the future by listening to it. Caring, the guiding ethical principle in this zone, opens us to a novel and unknown world. We do not have to agree with what we sense; we do have to acknowledge and try to make sense out of it. In the earlier zones, leadership deals with change that is closed and contained, change of a kind it has seen before so that experience helps to link cause and effect. Now leadership encounters open-ended change.

Open-Ended Change

In open-ended change, as Stacey points out (as mentioned briefly in Chapter Two), there is no sure knowledge of what caused the change, why the change occurred as it did, or what the results will be. The future is open. This is both scary and promising. Visions flounder, tested procedures become problematic, and outcomes are unknown and unknowable. In the face of open-ended change, leadership requires strikingly different sets of decision-making activities and organizational interventions.

Courage, creativity, and wisdom quickly take center stage. In essentially uncharted terrain, leadership takes on extraordinary dimensions, hitherto unknown and untested. *Extraordinary* is Stacey's label; it describes living at the edge of real chaos. Stacey believes that old paradigms shatter and new ones resist codification. Sure outcomes disappear as lack of agreement on direction and long-outdated rules offer little guidance. Persuasion and conversion, requiring the contributions of advocates and champions, become central to the dialogue. Incremental change, while powerful in earlier zones, falters in this and the next zone. Sudden flashes of insight often break through after agonizing weeks of struggle and argument.

Stacey (1993) labels this mode of engagement revolutionary rather than evolutionary. He observes that:

> Paradigm changes cannot be organisationally intended. Those holding an existing paradigm do not decide in advance to find a new one. Indeed, they resist the new one when it is first noted. Consequently, new paradigms have to emerge from the confusion created by anomalies and the contradiction of the existing paradigm. Ordinary incremental management with competitive trial-and-error experiments is bound to uncover anomalies and so lead to crisis and revolution. That revolution need not, however, be on a grand scale. Any small change in an organisation that requires groups of people to change their mental models qualifies as a revolution in the sense the word is being used here. Such revolutions are probably more prevalent than we might first imagine. (p. 72)

For futurist Joel Barker (1992), who popularized the term *paradigm*, leadership takes you where you do not normally go, a view suggestive of an open-ended journey metaphor for life. The new definition of leadership proposed for the Center for Creative Leadership—"making meaning in a community of practice" (Drath and Palus, 1997)—also suggests the necessary action of leadership in this zone.

What a contrast of perspective with Zone 3b and the positional leader's preoccupation with mission statements and results. However, that prior work, the political engagement of Zone 4, and the vision work of Zone 5a build a sturdy and necessary foundation for the adventure in this zone. Knowing who you are, having voice, and knowing where you want to go is a base, a known point of comparison at least, for facing a future filled with unknowns and surprises—although it is not yet as unknowable as it will be in Zone 6.

Thus here leadership is less about vision than about scanning the horizon, looking for blips on the radar screen. It anticipates the future and the changes that often lie hidden, awaiting discovery and labeling. The difference between vision and scanning was once vividly demonstrated to me by Michael Popowits, a principal at Tracker Consulting, Inc., an experiential training firm based in Chicago. While he and I were working with some folks at 3M's Camp Wonewok, Michael offered an exercise that helped us experience the essence of Zone 5b. We were all gathered on a gently sloped hillside awaiting instructions. "Shut your eyes," he said. "When I count to three, open your eyes, and count the number of brown objects you see." On the count of three, everyone frantically looked everywhere, counting quickly as they spotted many brown objects. "Shut your eyes," said Michael. "OK, now the exercise is over. How many of you counted at least five objects?" All hands went up. "Over twenty?" Many hands went up. "You know," he said, "I'm not interested in brown. How many of you spotted anything that was red?" One hand went up. I received an enduring insight. Vision focuses our attention. The goal is clear (look for brown) and limits our sight field; scanning (look for brown and red and any other thing that might matter) expands our attention and enhances our sight field. Without scanning, we cannot be prepared for the unexpected. Signs may be very small, even insignificant, yet their presence may anticipate an important event or series of consequences. Leadership in this zone seeks to maximize scanning—looking for red even when the organization is attending to brown.

Anticipating Change is indeed a journey. Not only are we not focused on the destination; our destination often changes as our trip invites us in new directions, toward new goals and possibilities. As the world flows, we are challenged and invited to convey ourselves into that unpredictable yet anticipatable new reality.

As I argued earlier, authenticity is both inward and outward. Thus we must scan both outwardly into the world about us and inwardly into our organizations, our professions, and ourselves. We cannot fix the world into which we convey ourselves, nor does the management–worker dialogue expand our horizon enough to anticipate broadly. However, from dialogue emerges this leadership challenge.

Strategic Thinking, Framing, and Strategic Opportunity

Several theorists discuss modes of leadership thinking that are appropriate for this zone. Two internationally valued consultants, Hamel and Prahalad (1994), offer a view of leadership, a brick, that adds greatly to the leadership edifice I am constructing here. They suggest leadership should be less interested in organizational strategic thinking than in industry strategic thinking. Since the world is unknown, leadership should worry less about restructuring and reengineering and concentrate more on action in an unknown and yet-to-be-created marketplace.

For most companies, market share is the primary criterion for measuring the strength of a business's strategic position. But what is the meaning of market share in markets that barely exist? How can one maximize market share in an industry where the product or service concept is still underdefined, where customer segments have yet to solidify, and customer preferences are still poorly understood? Competition for the future is competition for *opportunity share* rather than market share. (p. 33)

If leadership assumes an anticipatory stance toward the marketplace, then serious and exciting questions arise. If an opportunity share is discerned, then current core competencies require review.

Bolman and Deal's pioneering work *Reframing Organizations* (1991) becomes especially relevant when leaders fail to anticipate a world in motion and when framing—looking at reality from multiple perspectives, as discussed in Chapter One—takes over for vision. Although framing may be used in any zone, Bolman and Deal build their brickwork primarily in Zone 5b. Journey and art metaphors are central to their thinking. I deal with these metaphors in more detail in Zone 6. For now, suffice it to say that the four frames they suggest using—structural, human resource, political, and symbolic—make more sense to folks when they have at least moved into this zone. Framing is not inherent in the earlier zones. It is triggered and thus natural in Zone 5b. Once understood, however, it has relevance in the other zones as leadership brings this insight back into those zones.

Framing, while a critical skill, receives relatively little attention in the leadership literature. Fairhurst and Sarr's *The Art of Framing* (1996) is an excellent introduction to framing in everyday life. Through hundreds of examples it demonstrates the methods and importance of the skill of framing. Moreover, not all framing is ethical. Spin control, for example, is a "believability framing tool" that distorts reality to make a desired point. For leadership, credibility is central. If you want to be credible in what you say, Fairhurst and Sarr suggest asking yourself the following questions (p. 191):

- Is what I intend to say factual?

- Is it truthful?

- Am I objective in saying it?

- Is it legitimate? On what grounds?

It is equally important to understand how others frame us. Others' negative perspectives can counter our sincerity.

Conger and Benjamin's *Building Leaders* (1999) lives in this zone as well. Because the world seems to be changing at a breath-taking pace, leaders will have to become "strategic opportunists, globally adept, capable of leading across organizational boundaries with alliance partners, keen data analysts and learning evangelists" (p. 242). Strategic opportunity is the platform for everything else. Multicultural awareness is a clear necessity, partnerships open new opportunities, and pattern recognition and learning open creative thinking.

Why Focus on Means After Focusing on Ends?

I am often asked, "Why place Anticipating Change after Setting Direction? Wouldn't the reverse order make more logical and developmental sense?" Logically it is difficult, if not impossible, to propose a trip without some sense of destination, even if the destination is insight from the trip itself. Thus leadership in Zone 5a begins with an end state in mind. Insofar as simply designating an end goes, "I want to experience the wonder of the adventure" is no different from "I want to get to Boston." Both process and end state can be goals of action. Thus Setting Direction necessitates the trip.

Once the trip is underway, Anticipating Change clicks in. The engagement with a surprising future makes sense only if one is targeting some general direction. The destination envisioned in Zone 5a sets the initial reference point for futuring. Futuring requires some kind of immediate focus. We may change our focus dramatically once some patterns are discerned. It is the focus that at least begins the process. We might not want to narrow our search to looking for brown. We could focus it on looking for color. We need to avoid both the excess restriction I described earlier and aimless looking that leads nowhere. Focus sets the context for framing; framing recasts the focus by reframing it. The third umpire loves this discussion. Even in postmodern thinking there is some doubt about the grounding of thought, and this doubt stimulates the targeted discussion of what constitutes reality. Focus guides the framing while framing transforms the issue itself. A polarity is at work.

APPLICATION

In this zone, boundaries are undefined and rules of engagement are unclear. Short-term focus is replaced with long-term perspective. Is any given event going to happen? No one knows for sure. However, with the map produced by anticipation, organizations can target their energy, and interests are more easily directed. We'll look at three methods of constructing this map—scanning outward, looking for open spaces, and scanning inward. We'll also explore the reasons leadership should resist the urge to continue to rely on perspectives and methods from earlier zones, and look at a simulation that helps people understand this zone's process of learning from failure.

Scanning Outward

Royal Dutch/Shell Group's top management understands and lives Zone 5b leadership and organizational strategy. More than any other company, Shell practices outward scanning. And it does this scanning with great discipline and huge allocation of resources. I had the privilege of working for many years with Shell, and linked with the scenario team a few times. This team had a clear mandate—help Shell anticipate the future. Since there is no cause-and-effect certainty in this zone, the goal was not to predict or project the future. Rather, it was to build two or three plausible story lines that offered different patterns of how events might unfold. At the end of a two-year process, the team presented two scenarios to senior management for strategy judgment calls. These scenarios provided pictures of alternative plausible futures.

The organizational payoffs from thoughtful scenario work are immense. When our visions falter, we know the world has altered. Scenarios offer options for wise, adept leadership choices. If you are interested in the details of scenario work, the how-to of the process, see Peter Schwartz's *The Art of the Long View: Planning for the Future in an Uncertain World* (1991). The most recent focused reflection of the process can be found in *Scenarios: Art of Strategic Conversations* by Kees Van De Haijden (1996). Some methods for both external and internal scanning are suggested in the section on scanning inward on pages 255–256.

Three very provocative futurist volumes have expanded my own horizons. *The Road to 2015* by John Petersen (1994) covers almost every conceivable issue from ideas in the new science to population, from values to health. Jeremy Rifkin's *The Biotech Century* (1998) concentrates on gene research. *Natural Capitalism* by Paul Hawken, Amory Lovins, and L. Hunter Lovins (1999) is perhaps the most dramatic. These authors propose and describe a new industrial revolution that marries capitalism and ecology, and offer a transformative understanding of a revived economy. All three books exemplify Zone 5b leadership at its best.

Surprise can confound you, even do you in as an organization. If you do not see an external event coming, it can knock your strategic plan off its supposedly secure foundation. Zone 5a can be sidetracked by a Zone 5b action.

Charles Schwab & Company is among the organizations currently revolutionizing the way stocks are traded. Stock trading can be done at home via the Internet. While challenging to the stock world, this change is not totally unanticipated. That's not all Schwab is changing, however. The company is also dumping outside travel agencies and, thanks to the Internet, making its workers' travel arrangements entirely by itself (Woodyard, 1999). Other companies are also taking this function in-house. Suppose you run or work at a travel agency? If making travel arrangements in-house becomes a corporate trend and if your organization does not live in this zone and exhibit Zone 5b leadership, it could be hit by this trend without ever having seen it coming.

Here is another example of unanticipated change.

Enron Corp. has recognized and responded to uncertainty creatively by opening three gas-fired power plants in northern Mississippi and western Tennessee that are inefficient—deliberately so. They will generate electricity at an incremental cost 50 percent to 70 percent higher than the industry's best. Most of the time, the production costs of these spanking new plants will be simply too high for them to compete.

Enron hasn't gone crazy. By building less efficient plants, it saved a bundle on construction. It can let the plants sit idle and then fire them up when prices rise. Last June 25, the price of a megawatt-hour of electricity in parts of the Midwest soared—briefly—from

$40 to an unprecedented $7,000. With such volatility, Enron executives figure they can make money from their so-called peaking plants even if they operate only a week or so per year (Coy, 1999, p. 120).

When he left Shell in 1987, Peter Schwartz wanted to create a consulting firm to help companies build anticipatory wisdom. How do you help organizations move from data to information to knowledge to understanding and then to wisdom? At the time, most OD-type consulting firms focused more on vision, strategic intent and direction, alignment, and implementation. And they were protective of their market share. Schwartz (1991) proposed an open network of corporate participants without turf boundaries. Even today, this remains a radical idea. Face-to-face as well as computer-aided meetings were held, with no expectations other than the discovery of unknown dimensions of the world and perhaps identification of patterns and connections. This adventure was not just for a network of executives. Membership was inclusive and diverse. Diversity is crucial when we are trying to build rich cultural maps and identify metaphors that will pinpoint and highlight differing aspects of an unknown reality.

Tom Peters thrives in this zone and the next as well. He plays up his image as corporate bad boy, pushing boundaries all the time. The *Pursuit of Wow!* (1994) tests limits on every page. Incrementalism is innovation's worst enemy, he claims. Revolution is now normal. Peters condemns the preoccupation with quality: "We focused on quality because we got our butts kicked by the Germans and the Japanese. The good news is, we've caught up. The bad news is, so has the rest of the world. The new mantra . . . is agility and humility, the most important qualities of a company" (Tevlin, 1998, p. D8). Leadership addresses a dramatically dynamic world. What does it do? It pays attention, opens new images of life, and rejoices in surprise. There are indeed opportunities for new, vibrant actions.

Finally, scanning means paying attention to critical issues affecting all of us. It does not mean we necessarily agree about the importance of what we see. The public-policy research organization Worldwatch, for example, continually scans environmental issues. Some people now believe that old models of our relationship to our environment no longer serve the planet well and allow us to be dangerously destructive of the environment. Others believe the environment is much less threatened by human activities. Scanning outward opens new leadership challenges every day. Nothing can be taken for granted.

Finding Opportunities to Anticipate

Among the things for which we are scanning outwardly are opportunities and open spaces for potential new markets.

The search for open spaces and opportunity shares drove Medical Innovation Partners, a venture capital group, to create The Nucleus Group, a unique Midwestern incubator for entrepreneurial research and development. Begun in the early 1990s, this creation sought to leverage new technological advances for small firms with very limited resources.

If groups could learn to share, The Nucleus Group reasoned, new inventions were just an idea away. What made this approach novel was what was shared. For example, some entrepreneurs decided to share a building to cut costs. In this project, tenants share not only receptionists and copiers but also intellectual property, lab equipment, and other resources. Four firms, each with six or eight employees, inhabit the building. To join, each president works out an agreement, using the services of intellectual property lawyers so that no one need fear ideas will be stolen or exploited. This agreement sets the foundation for trust and cooperation.

Researchers work in the same space, often crossing boundaries to help each other solve tough problems. Space also exists for products to be manufactured in simulated production processes. These practice trials help identify glitches that could thwart or undermine mass production. When a product is ready for marketing and production, the firm moves out to a plant, and a new firm moves in.

The secret is in the sharing of intellectual resources, not just physical space and equipment. For example, two of the companies sharing the space are InoMet and Diametrics. "When InoMet 'borrowed' two Diametrics scientists, the scientists worked with InoMet during their lunches or in the evenings. . . . Diametrics lost nothing and their scientists received both stock options and a consulting fee" (Vincenti, 1994, p. 42).

It was an open-space insight that set Mark Knudson, a physiologist and investor, in motion, leading him to establish HeartStent, one of the four firms currently in the partnership. While he was listening to med-tech executives pitch their companies' products, the image of clots building up in coronary arteries and blocking blood flow ignited his imagination. "It struck me, as I was listening to this, that it was a market really in pursuit of the answer. And it hadn't recently asked the question" (Manning, 1998, p. 45). With patent in hand, HeartStent is now researching the viability of a device, resembling a hollow Allen wrench, that increases blood flow. While having good success in the early test stages, the company still faces formidable barriers. Persuading doctors to alter established procedures is only one. Yet an open space has been filled, a potential new market created.

Mostly unregulated and extremely lucrative check-cashing companies thrive today. Do large financial organizations like GE Capital and Citibank spot an open space? Bob Gnaisda, cofounder of the Greenlining Institute, a San Francisco public-interest group, thinks banks are missing a $5 billion opportunity in check-cashing services alone (Branch, 1998, p. 208).

Mark Cress had wanted to be a "business guy" since he was eight. He created Success Stories, Inc., which was number 137 on the 1993 *Inc.* 500, a ranking of America's fastest-growing private companies. However, in 1993 he also set out on an eight-week, 9,000-mile trek looking for a particular kind of opportunity, an inward transformation. He did change—dramatically. At 37 he simplified his life, sold a majority stake in his company, sold his house, and went to a seminary. In 1996 he discerned and created another open space. He began Inner Active Ministries (IAM), a tax-exempt nonprofit organization that rents chaplains to businesses. IAM attends to employees' personal side—the stress and duress that result from the rapid speed of change. What most CEOs miss, or want to miss, IAM addresses. Cress believes this business could exceed $100 million a year. The demand is escalating, not declining. He is creating a market opportunity (Welles, 1997).

Of course, perceiving an open space and filling it are different things. Scanning also needs to look at things that relate to the appropriateness of the opportunity. Microsoft Corporation once sought to enter the credit card business, for example, as a middleman for credit card transactions conducted over the Internet, offering customers and sellers Internet security and easy connections. Firms did not trust Microsoft, however. It seemed too big and too self-serving. Now, little firms with more credibility in customer service and partnering have found this open space (Bank, 1999).

Scanning Inward

Conveying ourselves into the future opens the possibility of curiosity. Curiosity leads to scanning, and scanning creates many maps that may help us understand a world that does not easily yield the new insights and wisdom we so eagerly pursue. We may scan outwardly, as discussed earlier, or inwardly, within our organizations.

Harrison Owen has created an important internal participatory Future Watch process. He calls it Open Space Technology. In 1983 he was asked to plan a large conference. It took a year to make the detailed arrangements. At the conclusion of the event, everyone thought it had been great but that the best parts had been the coffee breaks. New ideas present themselves in curious ways. The response to this conference made Owen wonder if it was possible to develop a process that combined the liveliness of coffee breaks with substance. Open Space Technology was the result.

In this process, folks gather, self-assemble groups according to topics they determine, and then engage in exciting discussions. Management of the process is mostly limited to the logistics, making it easy for diverse people to come together for serious conversations on questions that have no obvious answers. Owen's *Open Space Technology: A User's Guide* (1992) walks you through the process. As he says, it can be done very easily and takes a lifetime to master. It is a good method to use when diverse people want to openly explore issues that may be complex and conflictual and that may require innovative and productive inquiry. And it can be done with large numbers of people. It should not be used when the answers are already known and the underlying objective is buy-in. Then the process is manipulative. Nor should it be used when there is a buffalo who must be in control or who wants a certain answer. Do not use it for technical problem solving, like installation of computer systems. But do use it for organizational inquiry on future prospects and opportunity share. In this zone, no one person is smart enough to link new ideas together. We have to offer our insights together so that anticipatory wisdom may emerge from all of us.

Stacey points us to the shadow side of organizational life (the stirrings) as a subject for scanning and creativity. In this hidden world, new insights are generated, new linkages forged. Instead of dampening stirrings, which will curb new knowledge, leadership's challenge is to listen and work in their midst.

Suppose you want to tap suppressed creativity. Bring the most creative people in your organization together for a day to imagine open spaces. Figure out who your open-space thinkers are and get out of their way. Find ways for members of the organization with special passions to spend time together, sharing ideas on what is happening in the field. You and others in the organization might work on developing the ability to think in terms of metaphors to enhance pattern-recognition abilities. Your organization might contract with a futurist who knows the organization's arena of action and can offer ideas about what might change and where scanning might take place.

At one television station I know of, news executives engage in both external and internal scanning. Quarterly, the team of twelve holds a two-day retreat. On day one, the team scans outside the organization; on day two team members scan for the voices in the shadow organization. Periodically, they expand these meetings to ensure all voices are being heard.

Another technique is to share new learning with others in your group. Think of how many essays and articles in any field are available to us today. Instead of reading them, people often let them pile up and then finally toss them. At one firm, however, an executive group (not a team) divides up the relevant journals by specialty. At monthly meetings, each person gets five minutes to share a key insight from the journals in her or his field of specialization or interest. Twenty minutes is then given over to connecting the dots, seeing if there is an open-space opportunity the group had previously missed. Companies can also arrange ways for people to share their learning from seminars.

The Need to Change Perspectives

Recall Zone 3a's preoccupation with restructuring and Zone 3b's excitement about reengineering? Some companies that are facing Zone 5 issues continue using these processes to manage change. However, as we saw, restructuring and reengineering had their problems even in those earlier zones. Moreover, these processes are more about "catching up than getting out in front" (Hamel and Prahalad, 1994, p. 14). What happens if a company gains the ability to produce flawless products and absolutely reliable services only to find no one wants them? While catching up is critical, it is no guarantee of long-term success.

"We come across far too many companies," write Hamel and Prahalad, "where top management's advantage-building agenda is still dominated by quality, time-to-market, and customer responsiveness. Although no one questions that such advantages are prerequisites for survival, to be still working on the advantages of the 1980s in the 1990s is hardly a testimony to management foresight" (1994, p. 15).

Reducing errors and defects in design and manufacturing, while appropriate for a more stable and predictable world, is an insufficient response to the more chaotic environment of Zone 5. The information world requires a different interpretation of quality. For example, General Motors has created and installed more than 7,800 distinct software systems worldwide, with more than 1,800 of them dedicated to financial issues (Prahalad and Krishnan, 1999). This explosion of formats inhibits communication and information flow in the GM system. Acquisitions and mergers surface the same issue. If one puts four banks together, each with its own computer system, those four systems remain separate until one system is created. Quality involves, among other things, installing the new system without disrupting customer service.

Of course, customer service itself is becoming increasingly problematic. Some organizations are not eliminating defects only in the product. Now they are focusing also on elimination of defective customers. The value of customers is now under review in some companies. Moreover, in Zone 5b a service view of quality replaces product view of quality. Ford Motor Co., for example, plans to offer customers opportunities to select their unique car directly, over the Web.

The customer base becomes more heterogeneous in this zone, making it more difficult to solidify quality specifications. Organizations must engage in more active dialogue with customers. Rapid changes in technology require reassessment of the longevity of technical platforms. For products like Microsoft Windows, the good news is their stability; the bad news, their lack of innovation. As decision making by customers becomes more robust but also more diffused, the formal, more rigid technological systems die.

Such new realities confront traditional organizational infrastructure. Highly structured organizational systems still work when the products offer simple user controls. Loose systems must kick in when user behavior becomes highly variable. Prahalad and Krishnan (1999) conclude that "as we move into the new millennium, we may take a lead from Charles Dickens and describe the competitive environment as representing the best of times and the worst of times. Turbulence creates major opportunities, but it also represents major risks for those who don't change. In such an environment, organizations must learn to react fast and make decisions in a decentralized mode. A high-quality information infrastructure lies at the heart of this capability" (p. 118).

Market share becomes opportunity share in this zone, yet many companies deny this zone's reality and hope to practice in Zones 2 and 3. Leadership stuck in more stable zones fails to understand the shifting context and the change of adept leadership choices.

Even among those executives who do recognize the need to move on to Zones 5a and 5b, there may be problems with perspective. They may want to move directly to these zones from Zone 3b, skipping Zone 4. They decide they will do the futuring. The stakeholders, especially employees and customers who have great insights, are ignored. The community is also relegated to the background. Some businesses never think of the members of the community as having valuable insights.

Executives ignore stakeholders at their own peril. Zone 4 builds the foundation to launch Zones 5a and 5b. Bill Gates certainly values stakeholder information. As the opening story for this chapter described, customer contacts at Microsoft are seen as sources of information about possible organizational vulnerability. To anticipate the future with depth and breadth, the executives need everybody's anticipatory wisdom.

Failure in this zone is not necessarily fatal. Failing in the same way repeatedly, that is, failing to develop anticipatory wisdom, is what must be avoided. Geoffrey Moore (1999), chairman of the Chasm Group, identifies four known failure modes for high-tech start-ups. The first he labels the "slow fail." It occurs when new companies turn their growth over to managers living in earlier zones. They fail to comprehend or anticipate what it is like to live in Zone 5b. The outdated strategies have some value, of course, but it is not enough for this zone, and eventually (if not rapidly) these companies fail.

The second mode of failure—the "chasm trap"—results when it is decided that a product should stand on its own. With no support from a vertical product line, the product in effect falls into a niche market that is a chasm and out of sight. "To get going, new technologies need to be incubated in confined markets where the problem set is manageable and the competition modest. This permits smaller, more vertically focused players to pitch in and do the heavy lifting, as Aldus and Adobe did around the Macintosh in desktop publishing" (Moore, p. 90).

Alternatively, forget the chasm, jump into the maelstrom. This creates a third source of failure—the "tornado jump." Don't look to niche markets, go all out for mass market. "This appears to me," Moore observes, "to have been the strategy of 3DO, as well as of Iridium and Go—an all-or-nothing bet that everything will come together at exactly the right time. In every case, an unproven hardware platform and a whole new generation of software had to roll out without a hitch, and a whole new value chain to support it had to show up—all on day one, all ready to go. This is simply a crazy level of risk, a genuine failure mode" (p. 92).

Finally, there is the "dead zone," in which high-tech products promise good but not outstanding gains and can be adopted by customers with modest but not excruciating pain. For example, "Hewlett-Packard's LX series of handheld devices, which had the dominant share in the PDA market prior to the Pilot, has languished in the dead zone—lots of applications compromised by lots of complexity. The Fire Wire serial data-transfer protocol, sponsored initially by Apple Computer and currently by Sony and Texas

Instruments, also falls into the dead zone: it offers better performance than the Universal Serial Bus standard but lacks ubiquity" (Moore, p. 94).

What is the answer? Fail quickly and explicitly, correct your course, and move ahead. Mistakes made one time are learning opportunities, mistakes made twice are real mistakes. Moore similarly distinguishes failing from losing. In this zone, failure is part of the event. Creativity can still reign; new options can open up. Losing, in contrast, means persisting in the old ways that repeatedly fail. Fail, do not lose. That is the wisdom from Moore.

Anticipating Change built on Zone 4, Creating Ownership, offers a new set of competencies not grasped by those who do not map this zone. The fear of chaos permeates the zone as leaders at all levels in organizations and communities try to figure out what is really going on and what is required for leadership. Leadership must be quick-witted and quick-footed. Old strategies, well tested in earlier zones, do not work here. For some this is the most exciting zone so far. For others, it is so scary that old answers are sought, even though they accelerate losses.

Zone 5b Test Case—What Do You Think?

Maynard and Mehrtens (1993) have painted a picture of the next revolution for business, a fourth wave (following the third wave identified by Alvin Toffler, 1991):

> The First Wave was the agricultural revolution.
>
> Second Wave is rooted in materialism and the supremacy of man. From this orientation flows a stress on competition, self-preservation, and consumption, which has led to such current problems as pollution, solid-waste disposal, crime, family violence, and international terrorism. As the Third Wave unfolds, we become more sensitive to the issues of conservation, sanctity of life, and cooperation. By the time of the Fourth Wave, integration of all dimensions of life and responsibility for the whole will have become the central foci of our society. The recognition of the identity of all living systems will give rise to new ways of relating and interacting that nourish both humans and non-humans. Each wave has a distinctive world-view, epitomized as:

Second Wave—We are separate and must compete.

Third Wave—We are connected and must cooperate.

Fourth Wave—We are one and choose to co-create. (pp. xii–xiv)

The parallels between waves and zones are clear. The second wave is Zone 2, the third wave is Zones 3a and 3b pressing toward Zone 4. And the fourth wave is linked to Zones 5b and 6. While I appreciate this framework, it raises deeper questions for me. Does it for you? For example, the authors, like many futurists, are very optimistic. Are they really mapping a scenario or are they projecting and advocating a vision? Have they really owned the living-system metaphor and let it be the road map? There are even more worrisome questions –What are the forces pushing in the opposite direction that may have merit? Is there any enduring value in the earlier waves? Are they platforms for the next waves? And what about tragedy? What are the limitations to the fourth wave?

ZONE IDENTIFICATION AND
LEADERSHIP QUESTIONS

How well is your organization preparing for a Zone 5b world? Review the following questions to assess your situation.

1. How sturdy is my organization or community in this zone?

   • Do organizational members understand that vision is not enough in this zone?

   • Is the organization aware of the difference between market share and opportunity share?

   • Does the organization send people to seminars and require them to report to other members what they have learned?

   • Is there concern about the vulnerability caused by open spaces?

   • What are the major open-space challenges facing the organization?

   • What is the organization currently doing to anticipate the future?

- Is any individual or team writing scenarios?

- Are new partnerships being formed to create opportunity-market niches?

- Are any entrepreneurial activities occurring now?

- Does the organization set up simulations to anticipate potentially serious events?

```
10 |  |  |  |  |  |  |  |  |  |  0  |  |  |  |  |  |  |  |  |  | 10
Very Sturdy                                              Shaky
```

2. Where is my organization or community currently focusing its leadership attention?

   - What zone is currently demanding or getting leadership attention?

   - Is this the place for serious work?

   - Who are the critical players who attend to this zone?

```
10 |  |  |  |  |  |  |  |  |  |  0  |  |  |  |  |  |  |  |  |  | 10
Excellent Fit                                            Misfit
```

3. Am I prepared to anticipate change?

   - Do I have the core competencies for this zone?

   - Am I an out-of-the-box thinker?

   - Do I listen to the stakeholders well?

   - Am I in touch with futurists in my field of specialization?

   - Do I share what I learn in seminars?

   - Do I get excited about opportunity-share creation? If not, why not?

- How would I respond if I were invited to a creativity session with coworkers?

- Am I worried about the totally unexpected hitting us?

```
10 |  |  |  |  |  |  |  |  |  |  0  |  |  |  |  |  |  |  |  |  | 10
Ready to Exhibit Leadership                    Not Prepared at All
```

ZONE SUMMARY

Vision still concentrates the attention of this zone. Life is a journey. However, here the focus shifts from the destination to the trip. What is exciting is the adventure of anticipating the future in an unknown world. With little agreement on direction and no certainty of outcome in this zone, the third baseball umpire is now right on target: the way you call 'em is the way they are, and they ain't nothing till you call 'em.

On this trip the core ethical principle is the necessity of caring as listening. As we travel together in this zone, it is incumbent upon us to attend to each other and be acutely aware of what is happening. Caring does not imply agreement; it does imply profound listening and intentional understanding.

The authenticity standard shifts in this zone as well. It is not enough to converge, to come together in a shared vision. Now the challenge is to move beyond vision to framing, to convey ourselves into a future that we do not understand or anticipate. As we do so, we look for patterns and possibilities so we can understand and prepare for what might happen.

In the ends/means polarity that leadership must work with in this zone, means is now the center of attention. The end suggests the appropriate means, but the means determines the end. Try to achieve a nonviolent goal through violent means. The violence will be reflected in the resistance that surfaces when the controlling forces back off.

Organizations practice leadership in this zone through such competencies as pattern recognition, framing, outward and inward scanning, scenario writing, metaphorical thinking, and the generation of new insights. Not all the members of the community or organization need to live in this zone. However, some significant part of the organization or community must take on this leadership challenge. The more the world moves toward uncertainty of outcome and lack of agreement on direction, the more unpredictable markets become, the greater the demand for Anticipating Change.

ZONE 5B DEFINITIONS

Leadership: Anticipating Change
Authenticity criterion: Conveyance
Metaphor: Journey, with focus on the trip
Core ethical principle: Caring, with emphasis on listening
Polarity: Ends/means, with emphasis on means

STIRRINGS

If we accept the challenge of this zone we can look ahead to meaning creation in Zone 6. If the anxiety in Zone 5b overwhelms us, it can throw us back to Zones 2 and 3. We shrink back to safer places, hoping that whatever might occur will not hit us. Strangers scare us. Assimilate them or eliminate them. How can we live with no agreement on direction and no certainty of outcome?

Negative Stirrings

Listen to the voices:

> This world is getting too crazy. Nothing is predictable anymore. Nothing is safe and sure. I remember the good old days when job security meant something. Now, even the promises that employers make ring hollow. Yesterday I read that Honeywell was bought out. One of my best friends who works there did not see it coming. When I talked to him, I could feel his anxiety. His wife faces a similar situation in a different firm.

All this talk about scenario writing and trying to anticipate the future just doesn't do it for me. There are so many terrible things that happen to people that don't show up on anybody's radar screen, I wonder if it's worth the effort. My company just hired a futurist to help us. What does she know? She is just guessing like the rest of us. In her initial speech to us, she was all over the place and seemed to enjoy messing with our comfort level. I asked her during the break what her advice would be if we had no clue what might happen. Know what she said? "Cope!" We are paying her to tell us that? Why don't we just forget this useless effort to try and anticipate the future? I really think the world is unknowable. We really do not know what is going to happen. Maybe she was right—cope. I'm not too excited about our current situation. The world is out of control and we are the victims, just waiting to be hit.

Anxiety is palpable. We know events occur that are on no one's radar screen. We occupy ourselves with mapping the world to reinforce our illusions of security, naively thinking we can still fix the world if we can just see it coming.

Positive Stirrings

Listen to the tenor of the conversation:

Last week one of my friends had her house destroyed by a tornado. Three neighbors were killed. She and her family survived. Not only was she stunned by the event, she was stunned by the response to it. Neighbors rallied, supported each other, and took personal responsibility for getting through the crisis. Nobody blamed anybody; they just improvised. None of them had ever faced this kind of crisis. They didn't know what to do so they did what seemed natural. The community came together. It was wonderful and startling. I was impressed and profoundly moved and changed by the event. I will never be the same.

I'm glad you survived. I have never experienced anything like that. I heard that some community people ravaged a few houses and stole personal property. Was that true? That's like a double hit. You don't see either hit coming.

Yes, that did happen. Community members rallied and policed the area themselves until the police could set up appropriate procedures. You are right, we did not anticipate the storm or the responses. We were vulnerable and took charge of our personal and community lives. I was terrified and thrilled.

Excuse me, my pager just went off. I'll be right back. [Pause.] Oh my God, one of the senior vice presidents just committed suicide at work. I've got to go. Nobody knows what to do. I don't either. We'll figure it out.

At some level we all know there is no place to retreat to. The world has surprised others who did not see it coming, and they coped. Some even benefited from terrible events. Yes, the future is frightening; it is also profoundly challenging. We are never fully prepared for what might happen, yet leadership emerges in an often inspiring and dramatic fashion. Now we are stepping into Zone 6. Leadership challenges us to create meaning in chaos. Chaos is no longer a looming threat; it is a reality. Leadership acts in its midst.

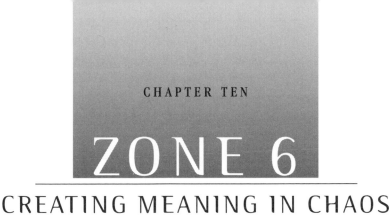

CHAPTER TEN

ZONE 6

CREATING MEANING IN CHAOS

SURPRISES APPEAR; COPE WITH THE FEAR.

The group was divided into three teams. Each team was blindfolded and then led into a separate room. Scattered about in each room were all the parts of a tent. The task: each team was to assemble its tent as quickly as possible. The first two teams, after much conversation and trial and error, accomplished the task. The third team had a retired military general among its members. Early on, the general announced loudly, "I am a retired general. I have assembled hundreds of tents. Follow my lead and we will win." He led in his own mind. No one followed, and eventually the other members of the team totally avoided him and collectively accomplished the task on their own. They moved around his "buffaloness"; they co-created their solution.

CORE IDEAS

Radar does not work for leadership in Zone 6; we are too close to chaos (Figure 25). The world does not cooperate with any of our anticipatory skills. There are no blips on the screen. We have no idea what is going to happen; then something does happen. We struggle

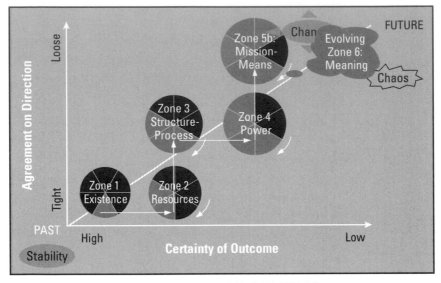

FIGURE 25 • ZONE 6: CREATING MEANING IN CHAOS

to create meaning, to make sense of what is happening when situations seem meaningless.

You think your community's vision is clear and solid—provide a safe place for people to live, love, and grow. Then a tornado wipes out the downtown area and half the homes.

Your company's vision is clear and solid—develop pharmaceuticals to enhance the physical health of children around the globe. Then a disgruntled employee breaks into one of your manufacturing plants and kills six of your staff.

Your family's vision is clear and solid—ensure a college education for all six children. Then your oldest child is diagnosed with cancer.

Your personal retirement vision is clear and solid—give back to society by volunteering to serve in the Peace Corps. Then you are in a car accident that leaves you disabled.

When you experience such unexpected and life-changing events, you have no action plan, no strategic vision, and no anticipatory map. The world has changed again. It has shifted from unknown to unknowable. You now reside very close to chaos, even in it, challenged by unanticipated events to experience the universe's devastating potential for both terror and creativity and your own powerlessness to change that universe.

Although most often terror signals our entry into Zone 6, unanticipated events can be overwhelmingly positive as well. Even events that begin with terror can, if our creative response is successful, result in some positive events. All these events still make no sense on a deeper level. In this zone, events simply happen, and we cope. Leadership creates meaning in chaos. A community discovers a valued resource its members had no idea existed, like oil or gold. A company uncovers a new idea that could change the direction and significance of its whole operation. A family inherits a large amount of money from a relative who they thought lived near poverty. You are offered an opportunity to change jobs and enter a field in which you have little or no experience.

This zone not only manifests itself in dramatic events; it also reveals itself in small everyday events. Few of us live in a place where the everyday world is entirely unknowable. We constantly encounter ordinary but still unexpected processes that Peter Vaill (1996) describes as the "permanent white water" in which we live.

Zone 6 differs dramatically from all previous zones. There is no confidence we are all going in the same direction and no certainty of outcome. The new, the unexpected, the sense that the immediate situation is almost overwhelming makes the fact that the world is unknowable very real and personal.

Our questions now focus not on the destination and the trip but on meaning, deep purpose, or raison d'être. We want to know why. Why this? Why us? What is the significance of what is happening in the world and to us? A new accountability, deeper and more pervasive, enters our consciousness, and the core ethical principle for this zone becomes *responsibility*. It is not enough to care about others; we have to assume total responsibility for our actions. And we have to live this and other values, not hold them as if they somehow existed outside our interactions. Leadership is everywhere. It moves in and about all interactions. It improvises in the present as meaning eludes immediate answers.

Authenticity sets two additional demanding standards in this zone—centeredness and co-creation. When we cope with events we have never faced before, all we have to rely on is our deep sense of our self and our relationships with others. Any hope we have that we will cope well is grounded in trust—trust in our own intuitive judgment and trust that others have good intuitive judgment also.

In this zone, life is art. This is the metaphor that can penetrate the unknowable and unimaginable aspects embodied in Zone 6 as none of the other metaphors for the other zones can. As the world is creating us, we are creating the world. We desperately make meaning. When the world surprises us again and that meaning escapes us, we do it again. And we cope.

Coping with the Unknowable

Leadership in Zone 6 creates meaning in chaos. In this zone, we are asked to act together to be the co-creators in order to face the turbulence of life. As the world alters, visions falter. In place of that vision, we can innovate with hope that meaning will emerge. We are called to confront the seeming absurdity of life, make sense of it, and act in the immediacy of the present. Zone 6 is exceedingly temporal. Hence, leadership acts in the immediacy of the present. Leadership can attend only to the now. It seeks to create meaning and discern significance of the unanticipated as it occurs in the present. In this world, meaning creation is on the one hand serious because of the profundity of the events with which we are faced, and on the other hand playful because of the creativity we must employ to address it. Nothing happens unless we are totally engaged. Seriousness and playfulness are the opposing poles in this zone that leadership must attend to when living at the edge of chaos or in chaos.

Few theorists willingly explore this zone. Ralph Stacey (1996) was the first thinker who introduced me to the idea of an unknowable world. His five insights about life in organizations summarize the central themes of his perspective on living in this unknowable world (pp. 108–109):

- "Creativity lives at the edge of disintegration." Typically, human beings escape ambiguity and anxiety by holding onto supposedly safe havens of traditional roles and responsibilities. We will even resort to covert politics and other forms of game playing to maintain the status quo and resist disintegration. However, at the edge, "we are able to contain [that is, hold on to] the anxiety provoked by complex learning. Then we are able to question the fundamental assumptions we are making about our world and engage in true dialogue, beginning an exciting journey of discovery."

- *"Paradox and creative destruction."* Life is filled with messes. There is no easy resolution to the tensions, conflicts, and forces pulling in opposite directions. Emotions, fantasies, aspirations all fill human spaces. "To remove the mess by inspiring us to follow some common vision, share the same culture, and pull together is to remove the mess that is the very raw material of creative activity."

- *"Cause-effect links disappear."* Life is far removed from certainty of outcome. Long-term outcomes are truly unknowable. Thus no one can be in control. The interactions are too complex and rich to support any process of control. And efforts to control only drive creativity underground and intensify the shadow side of the organization.

- *"Human beings create nonlinear networks."* There are public and formal modes of relating and there are covert and informal modes. The first are created by the most powerful players or else are captured by shared visions and values. The second constitute the shadow organization, created in relation to the formal modes of relating but resisting and modifying them. Shadow systems are very diverse, and have fuzzy boundaries. They discover and exploit openings in apparently closed systems.

- *"Shadow as positive feedback is necessary for creativity."* Without shadow organization, formal organizations and individuals remain stable. When they are affected by external events, they return to their previous state. That is, the external event is converted into negative feedback (as described in Chapter Five). Negative feedback dampens outcome, forcing a system to revert back to its earlier state. Positive feedback "does the opposite, feeding back information to amplify the gap between expectation and outcome." (I discuss this theme of the shadow organization in more depth in Chapter Twelve.)

As I reported earlier, some advocates of chaos theory, including Stacey, believe there is deep order in chaos. However, I believe that in this zone the question is not whether there is order in chaos. The question is, *Is there meaning in chaos?* Even if we do discern a pattern "brought about by redundancy and cooperation," by "spontaneous self-organization" that "produces emergent strategies," the question still lurks, What is the significance of the pattern? Further, suppose no pattern is apparent. Now, seemingly, there is neither order nor meaning. These realizations trigger deep anxiety, even despair, in many people. Now they feel that their world is like the world in *The Twilight Zone*, that they have been given a starring role in a Kafka novel or Sartre's *No Exit,* or that they are living through Saint John of the Cross's "dark night of the soul."

Because meaning may escape us, leadership does not discern it. Rather, it improvises immediately to address whatever is going on. The action itself creates significance to cope with whatever happens.

Choosing a Metaphor—an Art Event Itself

The third umpire thrives in Zone 6: reality ain't nothing till you call it. And as we call it, as we make meaning, we rely on our creative use of metaphor. In the postmodern world, we cannot escape from metaphorical thinking. Each metaphor informs another. Even our choices of metaphors are shaped by a deeper metaphor. So part of leadership in this zone lies in understanding the metaphorical choices we have, and, if possible, discerning the deeper metaphor informing those choices.

If we look back on the defining of other zones from our Zone 6 perspective, what is really going on is art. Each zone is mapped by a different metaphor—gift, machine, body, ups versus downs, and journey—that is, by an artistic construction. In Zone 6, leadership understands better than it does in other zones the necessity of using the creativity of multiple framing. Framing is an event of imagination, of art. Of course that observation comes from a retrospective glance. As you live in each zone, the worldview of that zone does not seem metaphorical to you. It is just the way the world really is.

The *life is art* metaphor, which makes us all co-creators, parallels many of Stacey's descriptions of the potential for creativity in life. However, Stacey never adopts that metaphor, continuing to work with the organic metaphor *life is a body/living system* and occasionally *life is a journey.* One of the choices involved in the organic metaphor is whether to see human living systems as having some qualities different from the qualities of all other natural systems or as simply part of natural systems. Stacey chooses not to collapse human living systems into natural systems. This choice suggests to me the possibility of seeing in Stacey's view an intellectual foundation for the role in human life of shadow relationships, paradox, and the art metaphor (see Stacey, 1996, pp. 108–109). Moreover, the *life is art* metaphor does not deny our connection to nature. Seeing our lives as art can affirm our intimate participation in the web of life and simultaneously assert our uniqueness in nature.

As improvisational artists in life, we all are deeply responsible for our personal and collective actions. Yet we also run to denial, attempting to escape our most destructive and hate-filled shadows. Rather than accept personal responsibility, we say that if the organization cannot set and follow a vision, it had better just give up, that anarchy will result if everyone self-organizes, that positional leaders have nothing left to do.

What skills are really needed in this zone? Do organizations really survive here? What are the examples where this has worked? Stacey (1996) has some advice:

> Instead of concerning themselves with the ends, which they cannot determine in advance, managers [leaders] are compelled to judge what it is appropriate to do entirely based on the means. The criteria for quality actions become, not ends, but ethical considerations and criteria having to do with maintaining positions, keeping options open, retaining flexibility, and revealing errors as fast as possible. The quality action is not one with a predetermined outcome, because that effectively excludes all creative actions, but the action that is morally good in itself, the action that keeps options open by allowing an organization to stay in the game and not yield to competitors, the action that allows managers to detect their errors as soon as possible. (p. 271)

Instead of not wanting surprises, which interfere with the vision, executives in this zone should want to be surprised as often as possible. This can lead them to reflect on their reflections and to think about thinking, and this action leads to creativity. Called double-loop learning, a phrase coined by Chris Argyris (1996), this mode of inquiry looks at the behind-the-scenes assumptions of thinking, attends to the voices from the shadow organization, and questions beliefs about life. Leadership opens inquiry since the old patterns trap improvisational breakthroughs.

Stacey, like Block and the advocates of participatory interventions, also believes that people who self-organize do not produce anarchy. Instead they will take on the task at hand, be mature and responsible, and may well produce creative new strategic directions (1996, p. 274).

Positional leadership still has a role, although it differs from the direction setting and motivational work of earlier zones. When the world is unknowable,

> The leaders of the legitimate system [that is, positional leaders] are simply participants in the functioning of the shadow system, albeit rather important and influential participants. They are particularly important and influential because other members of the shadow system project leadership and authority into them. The manner in which they cope with these projections has a profound effect upon the degree to which the anxieties of creative learning are contained rather than avoided.

> Leaders, then, do not determine direction when they take up their roles in the shadow system. Instead, they become important participants whose primary function has to do with the containment of anxiety. They need to be involved in the group processes of the shadow system, but from a position on the boundary, where they can understand the processes but not get sucked into them. (Stacey, 1996, p. 275).

Positional leadership lives a polarity in this zone. It calms anxiety through empathy with people's fears and anxieties. Yet it also contributes to anxiety by supporting double-loop learning, that is, by framing issues through multiple metaphors, listening, and making a space for innovation and improvisation.

However, for Stacey the real leadership in this world doesn't derive from position; it emerges spontaneously. It is not defined by role. Rather it centers in those who are perceived to make a contribution and who attract others for shared tasks. Experience-based intuition rather than concrete sequential thinking finds a friendly reception in this zone. And *play* is essential: no play, no creativity. Stacey observes that play and efficiency are enemies. Play requires loose allocation of resources; efficiency requires tight accountability. Play requires trials; efficiency wants first-time success. However, in the unknowable world there are no guarantees of success. Trust the processes and trust each other. Those are the grounds of hope.

I have spent a fair amount of time with Stacey's work because he so clearly articulates the foundation for Zones 4 through 6. For a closer understanding of the immediacy of this zone and its everyday presence in our lives, we can now turn to the work of Peter Vaill.

Ongoing Responses to Chaos

Vaill, whose earliest book was *Managing as a Performing Art: New Ideas for a World of Chaotic Change* (1989), has long understood that life is art. He understands the importance of improvisation, process, and the creation of meaning. His most recent volume, *Learning as a Way of Being: Strategies for Survival in a World of Permanent White Water* (1996), also demonstrates his depth of understanding of this zone. His notion that we live in permanent white water evokes a wonderful image of the world that hits us in the solar plexus. In this book, Vaill identifies five characteristics of permanent white water (pp. 10–13):

- Permanent white water conditions are full of surprises.

- Complex systems tend to produce novel problems.

- Permanent white water conditions feature events that are "messy" and ill structured.

- White water events are often extremely costly.

- Permanent white water conditions raise the problem of recurrence.

These five characteristics aptly describe Zone 6 life. Surprises abound, often in systems that do not predict them. Problems do not present themselves in neat, orderly packages, easily solved by one disciplined consultant or expert. As the surprises surface, they demand attention and lead to other surprising and often disturbing events and insights. The mess can be very costly, taking time away from other events also requiring attention. And, finally, there is no way to predict the next event because it too will be a surprise, a novel event.

To gain wisdom in Zone 6 requires constant learning. In this zone, learning is not optional; it is a way of being. In this zone, we are all beginners and remain so. We begin again with each novel event. However, through reflection we can become smarter beginners; we can be open to what I call adept wisdom. According to Vaill (1996, pp. 82–83), a reflective beginner is

- Conscious of the learning process itself and able to engage in a continual process of learning about learning

- Able to separate one's overall feeling of self-worth from personal deficiencies on a particular learning project

- Able to ask for help without embarrassment or apology and able to allow dependence on someone who has more knowledge or experience

- Able to see the learning process as continual experimentation rather than as a system that gives the learner only one or two chances to "get it right"

- Able to understand the peculiar communication problems that arise when a person with a lot of expertise tries to communicate with a nonexpert—how the expert often forgets that the beginner does not have the overall understanding within which particular facts and techniques can be fitted

- Able to recognize other beginners (even though they may be trying to hide their novice status) and able to support them rather than regarding them with indifference and/or falling into competition against them

- Able to maintain a sense of humor about the sometimes lamentable state of beginnerhood

- Able to know that feeling of wanting a cookbook, five easy steps, a magic bullet, anything to cut through the confusion, and able to know the temptations and the dangers of this feeling

- Able to internalize the profound truth of "one day at a time" that manifests itself as patience while living with and through a learning process that at times seems to be going nowhere

In this zone, events are novel and should be considered as such. Old baggage from external or internal history undermines creativity.

Old patterns do not work. Old recipes fail. In Zone 6, life is art. It is new; it challenges us to be novel in dealing with it.

In the revealing essay "The Unspeakable Texture of Process Wisdom," Vaill pushes the boundaries of Zone 6 thinking even farther. Process wisdom is the "feeling of moving *through* situations and problems and yet somehow acting 'wisely' in relation to them" (1998, p. 25). Vaill lists eighty phrases we use daily that highlight our rich experience of process: for example, bouncing an idea off someone, dancing with a problem, freewheeling, hitting your stride, keeping the faith, rolling with the punches, waltzing around something, working without a net, writing the book as you go (pp. 26–27). Every phrase begins with a word that ends in "ing." Thus each suggests engagement.

Organizational players, while talking process, do not often understand it. And we rarely teach it as part of leadership preparation. For Vaill, time anchors process wisdom. We teach time management, a hope from an earlier zone. In Zone 6, time management is an oxymoron. Time cannot be managed, only led through. As Vaill (1998) rightly points out, events have their own "rhythms and pacings, pauses and accelerations, beginnings and endings" (1998, p. 28). Organizational members have to be linked in time as well as space.

In addition to adopting learning as a way of being, leadership in this zone must exhibit credibility. James Kouzes and Barry Posner (1993, 1996), two authors who see credibility strongly linked to leadership and who live the art metaphor, map this zone well. In *Credibility: How Leaders Gain and Lose It, Why People Demand It* (1993), they report that followers want leaders to be excited and committed to them and to act with them. In 1993 the top four things followers wanted their leaders to be were:

- Honest   87%

- Forward-looking   71%

- Inspiring   68%

- Competent   58%

At the bottom of the authors' list of twenty characteristics were:

- Ambitious   10%

- Loyal   10%

- Self-controlled   5%

- Independent   5%   (pp. 13–21)

For Kouzes and Posner, credibility, while grounded in honesty, forward-looking, and competence, is deeply rooted in trustworthiness. Followers want leaders to be believable, to keep promises, and to act responsibly. "Credibility," write Kouzes and Posner, "is the foundation of leadership. . . . [It] is about how leaders earn the trust and confidence of their constituents. It is about what people demand of their leaders and the actions leaders must take in order to intensify their constituents' commitment to a common cause" (p. 22).

I found it revealing to contrast the top four with the bottom four. The bottom four are the flip side of the top four. If a leader is too ambitious, she or he may run over followers. If too loyal, he or she may not tell followers the truth. If too self-controlled, he or she may not offer inspiration. And if too independent, he or she may have little desire to connect with followers at all. Cynicism undermines credibility, erodes trust, and derails leadership.

Improvisation—a Deeper Look

In this zone, we feel our way along, go with the flow, try to make sense of the craziness amongst us, and live through it. We improvise. Improvising, in theater, music, or life, unites time and space. If something is out of joint or out of rhythm, the process crumbles.

"If managerial leadership is a performing art," says Vaill (1989), "it is definitely street theater, where the script, the characters, the props, and the drama are all unfolding in real time." And wisdom in this situation is not a "stock of knowledge and skills" as much as it is "sizing up situations" and "learning as you go" (p. 34). Learning as a way of being is wisdom.

Wisdom is often used to describe a fixed aspect of a person's character or mind, something that lifts one above the flow of events. Vaill and I both believe it lives amid the events, in the swirl. Words like *nimble*, *adroit*, *quick-witted*, and *streetwise*, Vaill argues, point to what he calls process wisdom. I use the word *adept* to indicate this kind of wisdom. For Vaill, process wisdom permits one to dance with change without losing one's sense of direction and purpose. This sense of direction and purpose is not the same as the vision that was important in Zone 5a; rather, it is particular. It goes from "one foot to another" (p. 36). As in improvisational jazz or theater, the music and plot unfold within the process, not outside of it. In this zone, process wisdom is not learned; it is *learning*.

Even our principles are now in process, according to Vaill; ethical principles and significance emerge over time. They are discovered in the flow, not outside of it. They are not entities or abstractions that rise separately from our creative interactions. And principles are plural. To hope for one overarching principle is naive. Life's processes are messier than that.

In earlier zones, we see implications that we live near or in chaos but we do not acknowledge them. In Zone 6, with its permanent white water, chaos increasingly registers in our everyday awareness. We live initially as strangers to each other in this zone. Are the others in agreement with my direction? Are the others going to react in a predictable manner with my engagement? We do not know because they are strangers in their thoughts and intentions. Creative interaction is our only means to find out. The world itself is unknowable.

Yet in spite of this scary world, most of us are able to participate in chaos while not being totally overtaken by it. A stranger is a paradox. A part of us knows deeply to avoid strangers at all cost to protect ourselves from potential danger. We also know deeply that every stranger is part of the human community and a potential friend. Thus we are called to reach out in faith and courage. Pull back and protect; reach out and engage—an either/or dilemma that is never solved. Do we isolate or befriend the stranger? Because our personal and collective history urges us to move in both directions—to disconnect and connect—we live in perpetual ambiguity. Action informs reflection; reflection happens amid the action.

This zone not only presents the most profound challenge to our understanding of leadership; it also provides the context for the most transformative connection with organizations, societies, and the world. And, paradoxically, it requires both wild play and profoundly serious engagement. It is the zone of creativity and novelty and it demands the intense commitment of our whole being. It is the place and space in which we exhibit leadership as Creating Meaning in Chaos.

APPLICATION

Core leadership competencies certainly shift in this zone. Understandings of framing, interpretation of symbols and culture, thinking agility, process wisdom, courage, anxiety containment, pattern recognition, temporal awareness, tactical ethics, and, of course, serious play allow one to thrive here. Each ability reinforces the others. Let's look particularly at framing, courage, and serious play as underpinnings of leadership action in this zone.

Framing

What do you think is happening in this brief story? *A man is at home. He is wearing a mask. Another man is coming who is afraid of the man in the mask.* I encountered this story in a seminar. We all wrestled with the task of making meaning out of it. People tried out different plots involving Halloween, crime, the dentist, and so on. None fit the story. Then a woman got it. The story was about baseball. That frame made sense of the facts. Welcome once again to framing.

While vacationing in Zone 5b (as I discussed in Chapter Nine), Bolman and Deal live their everyday lives in Zone 6. This is where their leadership brick fits. They are masters at framing. This zone requires multiple framing from leadership, since framing generates process wisdom. One cannot improvise with only one perspective. "To cling to a single vantage point," argue Bolman and Deal (1991), "is to imprison oneself in a frustrating, self-made, and narrow intellectual jail cell. People who understand their own frame—and who have learned to rely on more than one perspective—are better equipped to understand and manage the complex everyday world of organizations. Sometimes, indeed, they can make a significant difference in how that world responds to its challenges" (p. 14).

The four major frames Bolman and Deal distinguish—human resources, structural, political, and symbolic—can be easily linked to the zones in which each one is emphasized. HR ties to targeted competence (Zone 2); structural to design and guided system inclusion (Zones 3a and 3b); political to political engagement (Zone 4); and symbolic to meaning creation (Zone 6) and portions of Serving the Past (Zone 1). These frames pay little attention, however, to Zones 5a and 5b, and Zone 1 is only partially covered.

Nevertheless, the analysis of the frames is rich in insight and revealing in its stories. All the frames are applicable in this zone; however, I will concentrate on the symbolic frame. In the other zones, especially in 5b, Anticipating Change, multiple framing may be used. Here it is the basis of creativity and serious inquiry. Indeed, the subtitle of Bolman and Deal's *Reframing Organizations* reveals its home in this zone—*Artistry, Choice and Leadership*.

Why is symbolic-meaning creation stimulated by the twin issues of loose agreement on direction and low certainty of outcome? Bolman and Deal state the answer clearly (p. 244):

1. What is most important about any event is *not* what happened, *but what it means*.

2. Events and meanings are loosely coupled: the same events can have very different meanings for different people because of differences in the schema that they use to interpret their experience.

3. Many of the most significant events and processes in organizations are *ambiguous* or *uncertain*—it is often difficult or impossible to know what happened, why it happened, or what will happen next.

4. The greater the ambiguity and uncertainty, the harder it is to use rational approaches to analysis, problem solving, and decision making.

5. Faced with uncertainty and ambiguity, human beings create symbols to resolve confusion, increase predictability, and provide direction. (Events themselves may remain illogical, random, fluid, and meaningless, but human symbols make them seem otherwise.)

6. Many organizational events and processes are important more for what they express than for what they produce: they are secular myths, rituals, ceremonies, and sagas that help people find meaning and order in their experience.

Life is bewildering. Events that are totally unexpected happen. Good things happen to bad people; bad things happen to good people. Paradoxes tear us apart—freedom and justice, peace and armaments, accountability and forgiveness, economic expansion and sustainability. Bolman and Deal tell us, "The symbolic frame assumes that organizations are full of questions that cannot be answered, problems that cannot be solved, and events that cannot be understood or managed. Whenever that is the case, humans will create and use symbols to bring meaning out of chaos, clarity out of confusions, and predictability out of mystery" (p. 253). To lead, serious and multiple frames are essential.

If this framing is done superficially or with only self-serving motives, the meaning found will often only compound the struggle. We need to press on to deep meaning and to the most profound spiritual, even theological/God-talk, inquiries. These kinds of questions begin the stirrings that will move us to Zone 7.

Framing the Organization as Theater

You go to a theater to witness a play. Something weird and wild occurs. The constructed fiction, created by a playwright's imagination and delivered by actors on a set designed to entrap us, opens our minds, addresses our spirits, and leaves us speechless. Scientific reports rarely touch our souls; theater does. What a mystery: fantasy embodies real-world wisdom.

In this zone, we can see our organizations as theater. Organizational members create meaning to inspire, challenge, change, and touch those who come into its presence. Remember the Medtronic party from Chapter Three? It was not conducted just to help people remember the past. It was also theater to quicken the souls of current organizational members.

As players in the organizational theater, organizational members may position themselves to reveal truths or posture to conceal them. This tension between the formal or public organization and the shadow organization can be creative. When leadership understands it, it can leapfrog an organization beyond its competitors. The next breakthrough may be lurking backstage in the shadow organization, awaiting the cues that will bring it forth for a performance on the public stage.

However, very few positional leaders frame their organizations as theater—let alone street theater, as Vaill urges. And if they do, it is probably to cover up some embarrassing truth rather than rejoice in the creativity of the theater presentation itself. The quality movement is plotted but not enacted. Affirmative action is applauded but hiring practices do not change. The shadow organization is driven to greater concealment rather than being revealed by these tactics. It is no accident that we use the term *confidence artist*, or con artist, to describe those who engage in this kind of meaning making that is not what it seems. Of course, concealing is not always done for shoddy motives. Sometimes the con artist is truly a great artist. Slaves used songs and quilts to pass on information about escapes, fooling the slave owners. Military forces misinform enemies with dramatic sideshows. During World War II, the Allies constructed fake air bases to mislead the German military.

Zone 6 troubles most organizations I serve. The uncertainty of outcome and lack of agreement on direction threatens creative action. Yet where the ideas in the shadows are admitted and embraced, authenticity makes a breakthrough. Co-creation thrives. Where they are thwarted, co-creativity submerges and intensifies the members' anxiety about chaos.

I was invited to work with a teachers' association. Midway into the two-day event, we were discussing power. The association's entire image was one of participation. But one of the members said she felt betrayed—it was not a place of participation; it was one of top-down control disguised as participation. Total quiet grasped the room. No one spoke for at least two minutes. The group had a choice—explore or deny and blame. To its credit, it explored; and then it faced her truth. We had one of the most probing, revealing, and relatively nonthreatening conversations I have seen in a long time. Others rallied with their own stories, and the organization was able to find a deep wisdom in its process. Power went from below the table to on the table. The drama seared itself into the memories of the members. Denial collapsed in the light of honesty and reflection. A Zone 6 world invaded a Zone 3b conference. Unexpected questions took over the group. The group members led each other to deeper truths. Leadership was palpable in the room.

Courage

All too often the very character of existing structures is in the way of realizing Zone 6 reality. It takes a shift in metaphor to understand this zone and concomitant courage to live in it. Courage goes way beyond risk. Earlier zones give rise to risk-management seminars. They never result in courage seminars. Yet to turn chaos into creativity, to live the process wisdom, to face the anxiety of an unknowable world requires courage. In *Authentic Leadership* I spent a whole chapter wrestling with the concept and experience of courage. On reflection, I did not capture the heart of the phenomenon. I now define courage as *risk taking toward a virtuous goal with no guaranteed result.*

Criminals take risks; they do not exhibit courage. Courage embodies values and goals triggered by temporal events in the present. Many people think there is a fine line between courage and stupidity. Yet it's stepping out into the chaos that makes an act courageous. Just think of the courage manifested by people rescuing friends and neighbors in a flood. Or consider the courage of Daryl Davis, an African American boogie-woogie pianist who was so exhausted by the years of strife over racism that he decided to change the world—one Ku Klux Klan member at a time. Davis has sought out leaders of the Ku Klux Klan. He has talked with them, dined with them, even befriended some. He's become a self-appointed, if highly unorthodox, ambassador for racial healing (Thompson, 1998; Davis, 1998).

The Zone 6 motto is *Surprises appear; cope with the fear.* Courage allows one to face the fear that exists in Zone 6, embrace it, and ultimately transcend it. Fear can stifle courage or be the platform for it.

Adept living in and near chaos is critical in this zone. James Ogilvy (1995) proposes how we might find the courage to engage in "living without a goal." Go for tactical ethics rather than universal principles. Focus on the particulars of life. Be responsive in judgments rather than moralistic in commandments: "Morally vacant relativism is the dark edge of pluralism. But it is not inescapable and does not have to become the pernicious alternative to the old absolutes. There are ways to defend values that transcend the individual without depending on universal, absolute commandments covering everyone everywhere always," he observes (pp. 155–56). Chaos is real, and responding to it by searching for the deep rock of stability for all time will fail. Serving the Past is historically grounded; it is particular and predictable; it is factually based. In

Zone 6, we are far removed from that neat causality. At best, there is probability. At the most scary, there is randomness.

Rather than suggesting that we can find order in chaos, Ogilvy invites us to

> Call upon the skills of artists and poets, among whom we find the skill for dealing with *ambiguity and duplicity.* . . . The scandal of Goalessness demands that we wrestle with the question of good and evil, *but we do so in the context of the sublime.* . . . The outcome is far from definitive. In the absence of the Grand Goals provided by religion and ideology, the individual is thrown back on humbler resources like the literary critic's skill at interpreting texts where no definitive reading, no final conclusion, no perfect solution is ever reached. (p. 160)

Seriousness/Playfulness

As we have seen, polarities inform and anchor all zones. In Zone 6, where life is art and leadership creates meaning in chaos, the polarity seriousness/playfulness guides all actions. Because the two words are a bit long, with too many syllables, I have reduced the polarity to serious/play. I know that one of the words is an adjective, the other a noun. In this zone, we can mess with the language. It is "the way I calls it."

What, then, is serious/play? It parallels tragic/comedy. Play opens possibilities that are worthy of serious inquiry, and serious inquiry seeks new depths due to imaginative, playful thinking. To have only one half of the polarity bankrupts both. Play alone trivializes what it touches; seriousness alone can lead to depression and fate's control. When both sides of the polarity are affirmed and fully embraced, we get art. And we experience leadership. When meaning is in crisis, when nothing makes sense, when there is no balcony or helicopter high enough from which to discern order or patterns, all we have is improvisational action in the present. As actors, responsible for our actions, we create meaning. The haunting question always remains, Is the creation of meaning grounded in anything or is it just made up? What is behind the third umpire's calls? What is behind postmodern meaning making?

To explore what serious/play looks like in leadership, I will go to one side of the polarity, then the other. As one side is explored, the other side will be very apparent. One defines the other; they cannot be separated. So let us begin with playfulness.

Playfulness

Play opens the spirit in miraculous ways; it touches the soul and allows us to drop our defenses. Play creates free space for process wisdom to occur. Play leads us to creativity.

Tom Peters believes this. His book *The Pursuit of Wow!* (1994) catches the spirit of Zone 6. Peters is a wild guy with wild notions and reasoning. He hates rigidity and confinement. He is a boundary stretcher and a creative contributor to the business community. Because he is so far out, he is dismissed by some as lacking in substance. Nevertheless, he prods out-of-the-box thinking, which is a kind of play. Here is one example from the hundreds he offers:

> Consider these words from Phil Twyman, chief operating officer of AMP Australia, that country's biggest insurance firm: "In the past, if a new business idea came along that threatened to cannibalize one of our existing businesses, we would have stayed out of it. . . . Our view now is that if any organization is going to cannibalize AMP, it should be the son of AMP. We have discrete businesses for different market segments and we let them compete."
>
> Twyman admits he's even willing to accept the occasional confusion in the marketplace that internal competition generates. And perhaps a bit of customer confusion, too. Twyman's on the money as far as I'm concerned. Tidy times call for tidy strategic schemes. The times aren't tidy, and so our strategic schemes shouldn't be, either. I.e., disrupt yourself, stupid! (p. 186–87)

Topsy-turvy times call for topsy-turvy solutions. Peters proposes them. Note, though, that playfulness does not mean that the ideas that result won't still be scary—seriousness always haunts us.

Play often involves humor. Herb Keller, CEO of Southwest Airlines, stands out as one of the pioneer champions of humor in the workplace. Keller is usually the first to find humor in tense situations. He plays very hard so that people can be themselves, and believes that frontline employees who are treated well will pass that good treatment and the humor and fun on to customers (Rosato, 1998). Keller lives the polarity—play for serious life.

If you want to experience another play-filled organization, go to Seattle and buy fish at Pike Place Fish Market. Here employees play with the customers. When you want a fish, the employee selects one with you, then throws it across the counter at great speed to be caught by another person for wrapping and packing. Humor abounds; this play is the company's philosophy and secret to success. Many people show up just to watch and enjoy the experience. I have been one of them, many times. This philosophy has been captured in a wonderful video entitled *Fish* (Charthouse International Learning Corporation, 1998). I recommend it as a teaching tool to show how play can inspire both the customer and the worker. It also shows how serious the play can be.

To ease some executives into the competencies of Zone 6 leadership, we teach improvisational theater skills in the Advanced Leadership Program at the Carlson School of Management, University of Minnesota. For half a day, senior executives in the program play with Bob Wells, owner of the Chicken Lips Comedy Theater in Denver, Colorado.

Within two minutes, very staid and often reserved leaders are rolling with laughter as they experience Wells's improv examples. Then they do it themselves. One exercise involves storytelling. Six-person teams evolve a story. The first person begins the story with a sentence beginning with the letter A; the second continues it with a sentence beginning with the letter B, and so on until Z is reached, where the story ends. Each person has to listen intently to others' contributions to the story and build on them. *Listen without an end state in mind*—that is the critical learning. Vision does not work in Zone 6. If you think you know where the story is headed, that you have a vision of the outcome, invariably you will miss the reality of flux and mess. Improvisation is an example of living without a goal yet contributing to life through innovation.

Although rules for improvisation may sound like an oxymoron, Wells and his colleague David Johnson (1998) do offer some basic rules:

- "Yes, and . . ." is always better than "No" or "Yes, but . . ."

- Always agree. Never deny any verbal or physical reality.

- Accept what your partner does or says as you would a *gift*, not a *challenge*.

- Everything is important. Everything matters.

- Once a choice is made, there's nothing so stupid or banal that we can't respect it.

- Accept the other player's reality.

- Every decision is relevant.

- The challenge is to lose control ("mental vertigo!").

- Show; don't tell.

- Always take the *active* choice rather than the *passive* one.

- Ideas reveal more in action.

- Move action forward, not sideways or backwards.

- Don't ask questions. Instead assume something and build.

- *Surrender to the loss of control.* Give up. It's OK to be confused.

- Surprise yourself!

- *Make your partner look good, and you'll look good.*

- Be alert.

- Listen.

- Start in the middle.

- Trust your instincts.

- Be prepared for anything!

I currently use the storytelling exercise in seminars to give participants a visceral understanding of the unexpected in Zone 6. As a story emerges, I take a turn at contributing a line, one with outrageous content, such as "Jumping out the window, the couple made love as they fell to the ground!" The next person is thus handed a new reality and must improvise and create meaning. This intervention is necessary because many people who do this exercise will get a vision of a plot that is emerging and then supply lines to support it. But in real life, plots shift unexpectedly.

Remember Michael Popowits's exercise discussed in Zone 5b, the one that differentiated vision from scanning? Michael is the most creative Zone 6 outdoor-exercise facilitator I have ever met. He creates opportunities for courageous spontaneity. At the 3M camp, for example, he divided the group into teams of seven and announced that each team was going to start a fire by rubbing wood sticks together. We gathered around him as he demonstrated with a flat 1" × 6" board, a slender tapered pole about eight inches high, and a bow with string. At the base of the tapered pole, he placed some lightweight fluffy material that would easily catch fire. By wrapping the string once around the vertical pole and attaching it to both ends of the bow, he could make rapid back-and-forth movements that would and did generate enough heat to ignite a fire.

Then he asked for two volunteers from each team to accompany him to get the materials for their team activity. Off they went. What they returned with was six-foot logs, tapered at both ends; 2" × 10" boards; rope; and six-foot poles. They were also told where they could pick up axes, hammers, and fluffy material. One group started the fire in 45 minutes; the last group took three hours.

The improvisation was amazing. No one had ever faced this challenge. Some teams, after completing their task, offered to help others with advice and labor. Some of the help was welcomed, some rejected. Two people ignored the rejection and helped anyway. The event was the talk of the trip.

Personality types make a difference in this zone. If you want play, assemble people who are different. Diversity of styles quickens imagination (Leonard and Straus, 1997). If you don't have all the necessary people, try *jamming*. John Kao (1996) reports that "recruiting outsiders to 'sit in' and jam—perhaps on a just-in-time basis—on specific projects has become common in business. Like outside musicians who sit in and shake up a tired tune, these migrant virtuosos are never more essential than when in-house creativity flags. As piano player Billy Taylor says, 'A man faced with the kind of challenge you get in a sitting-in session is not so prone to imitate. He's apt to concentrate on building better and more original solos'" (p. 119).

Play may call upon the organic metaphor as well as the art metaphor for life. Leadership scholar Tom Heuerman (1999) compares the "enduring organization" to the jazz band. Jazz builds on a solid musical platform, but then takes that music to amazing and astounding new areas not experienced before. "No one is in control of the jazz band, and the music is not predictable. . . . Imagine what would happen to the creativity of the musicians and to the beauty of the music if the performers tried to dominate one another, tried to control the outcome of the improvisation, resisted change, or imposed artificial structure over the artistic possibilities. . . . Leaders of enduring organizations are artists at heart and understand intuitively the dynamics of living systems."

Without the concerns generated in Zone 5b that cause us to be looking out for opportunity share and open spaces, the urgency of Zone 6 may be discounted. However, without the play from Zone 6, Zone 5 advocates can fade away from unkept promises. Zone 6 leadership offers the creative play needed for leadership in Zones 5a and 5b.

The literature about creativity tends to express flaming optimism; the authors invite us to an exhilarating future. In *Breakpoint and Beyond* (1992), for example, Land and Jarman offer just such a window on the world. Personally, I get excited reading such works. I am indeed encouraged to be hopeful that we can make meaning in this zone. The danger, of course, is the violation of the polarity. Play is not a goal of its own. If authors treat it that way, play will end in trivia and not-real play will be in the room. Real play is important. It is serious. It permits deep inquiry.

Seriousness

Our play, our artistry, is serious. Art is not a journey. Art reveals new insights, a much more astute and demanding task than briefing and preparing for a traveler's trip. Art creates symbols that generate thought. At its best, it is provocative and insightful. Once seen, the wisdom can be handed off to others to operationalize. In this zone, art is the end in itself. Means and ends unite in the process of "learning as a way of being." Don't travel; stand still and look around to understand deeply what is going on.

We all know that art can also be used for denial and distortion. It may be escapist rather than insightful. Moreover, symbols do not speak for themselves. They require interpretation. And interpretations can be driven by many motives, not all of which are authentic.

If we live in a world of strangers and strangeness, a world of mess and bewilderment, what does seriousness entail? Playfulness is certainly necessary. It is not sufficient. Seriousness pushes art into a new standard of authenticity.

In totally new situations, there is no assurance that shared values or ethical principles are present. Yet we are called upon to act as if they exist. Since we cannot be sure they are in place, where does our courage come from? From what do we get the strength to act as if others are respectful, responsible, and willing to work together?

As in art, we are left to our own deepest integrity. As Jack Fortin, a theologian and the head of Wilder Forest, a retreat center for community development, told me: "One of the secrets of life . . . is to be centered on the inside and totally open into the world" (personal communication to the author, 1998). Deep, thoughtful *centeredness* coupled with openness to *co-creation* anchors authenticity in Zone 6.

We live as if others are centered because we know we are. Internal boundaries have replaced external constraints or contracts. We make an implicit covenant with others to be present with us, whether or not they are willing to be that way. Centeredness permits total presence in a nonthreatening way. It is being with another to face chaos together. It is not enough to find meaning in chaos—we have to live meaningfully in its midst.

Courage flows from our centeredness, the foundation for our authentic engagement. There are no institutional rules and procedures, no power brokers, no vision. There is only *being present* to act responsibly with others to address whatever demands our attention. This is the core of that created meaning in chaos.

Daryl Davis acts from this centeredness every time he meets with a Klan member. Strangers who act selflessly in a flood to save each other act from this centeredness as well. Stories abound about shared action in an emergency. No plan exists. Together, groups improvise and face harsh realities together.

Also, there is no guarantee of success. Former North Carolina governor Terry Sanford stood boldly for racial integration at a time when this was tantamount to treason in the minds of some whites. He tried to run for the presidency in 1972 and 1976 to no avail. In fact, George Wallace beat him in the 1972 North Carolina Democratic primary. Integrity does not ensure positive external results.

In this zone, leadership expresses itself as centeredness in action. The great news of such leadership action is the authenticity it expresses. The bad news is, does anyone care? We never know for sure. Judy and Kenneth Dayton, heirs of the Dayton Department Store fortunes, recently pushed the leadership envelope by deciding to cap their wealth, giving the extra income to charity. And even as they took this step, Kenneth Dayton wondered out loud whether he and his wife would "ever have the courage and fortitude and intelligence" to take the next step—reducing their wealth (Franklin, 1998, p. A1).

This action was stage seven of what they had learned were nine stages of philanthropy. Stage one gives to satisfy a request. Stage two volunteers time and money to projects. Stage three stretches the giving to as much as possible. Here a plan is required. Stage four gives as much as the IRS says is possible. Stage five becomes more creative by initiating, not just responding to projects. Stage six breaks a barrier—percentage of wealth. Seven caps wealth. Eight reduces the cap, and nine commits bequests beyond family members. This is a road map under development, discerned while on the journey. Now, the Daytons' challenge is to test the next stages, with no sure outcome. They have not been this way before and do not know the likely consequences. how will family members respond? Pioneers do not have maps; they create them as they live into an unknowable territory.

ZONE IDENTIFICATION AND
LEADERSHIP QUESTIONS

Have you ever experienced Zone 6? Assess these questions:

1. How sturdy is my organization or community in this zone?

    - Has the organization ever faced any serious Zone 6 crises—certain kinds of events it has never faced before?

    - What happened in the organization as it coped with the mess?

    - Is framing done regularly? Is the symbolic frame employed?

    - Does the idea of process wisdom make sense?

- Are people aware of it and do they address the leadership challenge of it?

- How playful is the place?

- Does courage manifest itself in organizational actions?

- Have buffaloes tried to control an improvisational situation? What happened?

```
10 |  |  |  |  |  |  |  |  |  |  0  |  |  |  |  |  |  |  |  |  | 10
Very Sturdy                                            Shaky
```

2. Where is my organization or community currently focusing its leadership attention?

   - Does this zone need attention?

   - Is the organization encouraging attention to meaning-creation as serious play?

   - What zones are getting attention?

```
10 |  |  |  |  |  |  |  |  |  |  0  |  |  |  |  |  |  |  |  |  | 10
Excellent Fit                                          Misfit
```

3. Am I prepared to create meaning in chaos?

   - Have I faced the terror of this zone?

   - What did I do? What was my improvisation?

   - Do I understand process wisdom?

   - Do I ever consider courageous action? Do I do it?

   - Am I struggling with spiritual issues? Do I have a sense of what the word *spiritual* means?

```
10 |  |  |  |  |  |  |  |  |  |  0  |  |  |  |  |  |  |  |  |  | 10
Ready to Exhibit Leadership                 Not Prepared at All
```

ZONE SUMMARY

The world shifts from unknown to unknowable. It cannot be fixed; it can only be responded to. Life in this zone is art. *Journey* is not a creative enough image to handle and interpret the ultimate novelty that repeatedly surprises us.

Vivid, life-changing events define much of Zone 6. We do not see them coming. They hit and we cope. They are on no one's anticipatory radar screen. These events are often terrible—like road-rage killings—or positive, like winning the lottery. Negative and positive results can come from both. The magnitude of the happenings forever changes some aspect of the rest of our lives.

This zone also expresses itself in the everyday experience of surprises. "Process wisdom" constantly requires our attention. We cannot anticipate events; they just pop up every day in ordinary living. In some sense we are always beginners, coping afresh with a novel set of events.

As we struggle with surprises, authenticity sets a new standard—centeredness. Figure out who you are deeply within and let that understanding provide the foundation for anything that happens. Authenticity also requires co-creation. We work together, helping each other create meaning that is both serious and playful. A core competency in this zone is improvisation. Listen, act, and hand off to others. Buffaloes are extinct here.

Caring carries into this zone, and one is challenged to take responsibility for oneself and with others. Since life is art, we are artists who co-create life with other artists. We know at a deep level that the third umpire was right. Life awaits the defining call. Art interprets the significance of reality in all its gore and beauty. Truth does not easily express itself. It is hidden, requiring the artist to probe beneath the surface to challenge all of us to avoid denial and confront the really real. Con artists are real, too. Authenticity's question is never far away—What is *really* going on? In this zone, the question often forces deep pondering because what is on the surface may have little connection to the revelations of deeper meaning.

Core competencies include framing, process wisdom, virtual leadership, humor, creativity, empathy, deep self-awareness of one's personal center, and symbolic activities. With little certainty of outcome and agreement on direction, chaos is present and palpable. Living with surprises frightens, engages, inspires, and transforms us. Leadership faces this zone's realities. It creates meaning in chaos. All we have here is the present. To live in an unknowable and unfixable world, leadership co-creates options with no plan and no guaranteed outcome.

ZONE 6 DEFINITIONS

Leadership: Creating Meaning in Chaos
Authenticity criterion: Co-creation and centeredness
Metaphor: Life is art
Core ethical principle: Responsibility
Polarity: Seriousness/playfulness

STIRRINGS

What a confusing world! Six zones, three umpires, and bricks everywhere. Does this all make sense? Now the puzzles go broader and deeper. There are three of them. First, remember the choices of Chapter Two? Where do they all fit? When does "born" match a zone, and when does "made" match? The leadership literature does not connect them. The puzzle awaits attention.

Second, a number of intellectual challenges have arisen throughout the zones. Notions like complexity and chaos theory, polarities and leadership development still need more reflection. Is it essential that leadership go there?

And third, a profound set of questions has haunted much of the earlier work. What is behind what the third umpire creates? Is the postmodern reality of meaning creation enough for hope and courage to prevail? So what, if there is nothing beyond shared solipsism? What about evil? Did we just invent the idea? Is it real? If so, what does that say about life, my life, and leadership?

Where do we go from here? We are in chaos, struggling to get to tomorrow. "White water" swirls all around us. What more could leadership mean beyond Creating Meaning in Chaos?

Negative Stirrings

Three people are talking:

> *Devyn:* I was in a seminar the other day on zones. Next week we return for Zone 7, whatever that is. I'm not sure I get the zones. The seminar began with choices about what constituted leadership. We had eight to make. The two that were the hardest for me were leadership is coercive and noncoercive vs. only noncoercive and ethical and unethical vs. only ethical. Then the presenter said all were appropriate under certain circumstances. I didn't get it. How could opposites all be applicable? It made no sense. Is it okay for me to be unethical at times and still exhibit leadership? Can I beat someone up and still lead? I fear being overwhelmed by choices and never able to lead again. I thought I knew what leadership was. Now I am totally confused.

> *Connor:* If you think that is confusing, Devyn, how about this? I did not attend that seminar. I have been dipping into the leadership literature and am stunned by the array of advocates of differing perspectives. I read one book on complexity theory. It made little sense to me. What does that perspective have to do with leadership? I also noticed ten books in the bookstore on polarities and paradoxes in leadership. That blew me away. What is the connection between paradoxical thinking and leadership? And what is a paradox anyway? I haven't a clue about polarities. What is the difference between a paradox and a polarity and does the difference matter? Who cares? I have more important things to do, really. Golf starts at 2 P.M. Got to go. See you later.

> *Spencer:* So long, Connor. Devyn, I am experiencing a deep uneasiness as I think about life. I have had a recent death in my family and the funeral haunts me every night as I go to sleep. The person who died was a baby. Run over by a drunk driver. The mother escaped. Her grief never seems to subside. What a tragedy.

> I remember growing up being taught that God was an entity who controlled life, had a plan, and was worthy of total submission. Of late I have been reading books about spirituality. I am searching for a deep sense of meaning that is not just constructed by human beings. Yet spirituality itself means so many different things to different people, I wonder about its depth. Is spirituality enough? I don't know if meditation, going deeply inward, is enough. Maybe I have to fight some cause to experience deep satisfaction.

> *Devyn:* Spencer, you may be right. I know I have a stirring in me to fight ecological destruction. And I know you are a committed anti-

racist. Are social causes the answer? I struggle every day over these questions.

Spencer: The leadership literature certainly highlights spirituality today. I read *Leading with Soul* by Bolman and Deal the other day (1995) and it intrigued me yet seemed too shallow. I want more and see nowhere to go. Tragedy is everywhere. I have no answer. I despair when it hits home. The funeral image does not go away. I feel stuck.

Leadership choices, intellectual puzzles, and faith crises face us whether or not we acknowledge them. Negative stirrings trap us. They also push us to new depths as we garner the courage to go there.

Positive Stirrings

Here is a different conversation among three people:

Jean: I have been thinking a lot about leadership lately. I'm convinced that leadership shifts as the context shifts. What is not clear is when to do what. I'm excited to figure that out. I do not want to be all things to all people. I do want to make sure everything is done that needs attention. I know I am a leader. I have been for years. What I am eager to figure out is how to deepen my wisdom to make the right choices in the right setting. I've seen too many people screw up by making wrong choices. I have made some inappropriate choices. I want to be wiser. I'm ready for leadership insights and development. I can hardly wait to figure out if leadership is always ethical. Someone raised the Hitler question recently in a seminar. People were all over the place. I want to know.

Steven: That Hitler question often comes up, Helene, and it intrigues me as well. What puzzles me is the big picture. I heard someone the other day talk about a zone presentation. Supposedly there is a seventh zone that is huge. I like big-picture thinking. A map of all of leadership would be great. Some notions intrigue me. Chaos, complexity, paradox, development, and one I love because it scares me—shadow. I'm ready to explore these ideas for depth and breadth.

Rose: You all are amazing. I just dropped by for a casual chat and I am challenged by all of your observations. I like your energy too. I have had a couple of very serious events happen in my life this year. Both of them have quickened my spirit. As you know, I am a skeptic on matters of faith and religion. Yet something is stirring in my world, pushing me deeper into life's most provocative questions. I want to go as far as I can into troubling, yet uplifting inquiries. What is evil? What is God? What does either have to do with leadership? My sense is that no one in the field of leadership studies goes there. Spiritual talk is common these days. Theology is not. Religious talk makes me nervous. The U.S. election in 2000 certainly blurred spirituality, religion, and theology. I want to sort them out and see what I really trust. I want to experience some foundation that transcends postmodern make-it-up reality. I don't think life is art. I don't know what it is and I want to find out. I'm ready.

Enter leadership that serves the promise of authenticity. Welcome to Zone 7.

PART THREE

THE PROMISE OF AUTHENTICITY

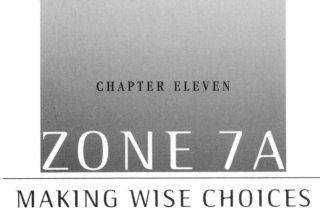

CHAPTER ELEVEN

ZONE 7A

MAKING WISE CHOICES

Zone 7, Serving the Promise, focuses on fulfillment, the seventh dimension of action. Remember the action wheel in Figure 1? (See page 4.) Fulfillment surrounds all the other aspects of action. It differs from the other zones in that it encompasses them all and still is unique in itself. This is the "get it all together" zone, looking out over the whole map, locating more uncharted territories. Zone 7 targets three inclusive expressions of leadership: Making Wise Choices (Zone 7a), Probing Deeper (Zone 7b), and Living the Promise (Zone 7c).

Obviously, the concept "promise" dominates this zone. A promise declares that one will or will not do something. It also points to future success, excellence, and/or satisfaction. A promise is an assurance pledge, an anchor point for action, that which is worthy of trust and commitment. As these three zone subsets unfold, promise will take on great importance. It will be fulfilling.

Before entering this zone, which will briefly reference all of the earlier zones, you might want to do a quick review of Zones 1 through 6. Reread the summaries and list the zone leadership match in the spaces below:

Zone 1_____

Zone 2_____

Zone 3a_____

Zone 3b_____

Zone 4_____

Zone 5a_____

Zone 5b_____

Zone 6_____

Zone 7a requires knowing all the zones, matching leadership to what is really going on.

CATCH THE STIRRING; IT IS NOT ALWAYS PURRING.

An administrative department in a state government had just completed a large-scale intervention. Energy soared. How often does one experience a standing ovation for a commissioner? It happened. And it happened at the end of a three-day session that had begun with deep cynicism. I had suggested the intervention. Now the question was, what next? Would the agreed-upon initiatives and commitments be implemented?

At best, the follow-through was spotty. I was somewhat out of the loop. Cynicism returned, this time with more gusto. I got a call to attend an executive meeting. Some time earlier I had shared my new thinking on the zones with the executives. They had been intrigued and challenged, especially by Zones 5 and 6. At this meeting, called about four months after the large-scale event, I was introduced to two leadership trainers from the department. The trainers and I were asked to assemble a weeklong leadership program for supervisors and middle managers, focusing on people skills such as feedback, conflict management, and situational leadership. I was asked to kick off the course with the zone ideas and conclude it with a story of authenticity development. The trainers would perform the skills training in the middle.

The course was "strongly recommended" to people in the department, just short of "required." The first audience was to be senior executives, so that they would know what was going on; then the course would be opened to all in the department, in groups of fifteen to twenty. Initially, I thought the course was a good idea. However, it soon became obvious that something was not working. Energy was low, attendance dropped, and the other trainers and I did not look forward to the events. Evaluations were average, yet no one offered much reflection on the course. They just went through it.

Near the end of the series, I had lunch with a woman from 3M who introduced me to the ideas behind the 3M Tech Forum (Chapter Seven). That conversation gave me an idea about this course. Instead of concluding the current session with a story of authenticity development, I told the group I just wanted to talk about what was going on in these sessions. As the participants began, somewhat reluctantly, to express their dissatisfaction, my insight grew more vivid. Finally, I shared with the group what I thought might be going on.

I had not used my own zone framework to figure out what was happening. The discussion with the participants made it clear. The issue facing the seminar members was not lack of skills; it was lack of voice. The organization had a Zone 4 issue and was trying to use a Zone 2 solution. Competency was not the overwhelming concern. What people wanted was to be heard and to relate across the organizational silos. The choice of the design for this course had been neither wise nor adept. It had made assumptions. It had not considered the reality. Leadership was not in the room. We had made unwise, nonadept choices. The seminars ended after the first round. The real issue was sidestepped.

CORE IDEAS

Much of leadership concentrates on choices. Here is the promise: Make the right choices and leadership works; make the wrong ones and disaster awaits. Wisdom distinguishes between making the fit proper and improper. A leadership skill lives here as well—adeptness. Wisdom guides the choices; adeptness makes them work. The choices focus one's attention on what is really going on. And the promise is delivered.

As leadership makes wise choices, it must meet two authenticity standards—congruence and comprehensiveness. Leadership in this zone knows both when to act and how to engage, which requires congruence with what is really going on. At the same time, leadership must see the whole picture in order to bring both knowledge and skills to the proper zone. This requires comprehensiveness. To achieve congruence and comprehensiveness, leadership operates in another polarity—one/many. Attend to all the choices from the vantage point of a deep and abiding sense of leadership that cuts across all of them. A metaphor informs Zone 7 as well: *life is a polarity*. As we shall see later, polarity will shift to paradox. That occurs in a later zone.

Remember, leadership embodies one profound skill—adeptness. In order to understand life and leadership in this zone more deeply, let us begin with an exploration of adeptness and then move to wisdom. The last section will identify matches that fit and work.

Adeptness

Adeptness did not become an important concept in my wrestling with leadership until I read Stacey and other complexity theorists. They love and live with the idea of complex adaptive systems. The concept "adapt" penetrates their thinking and framing of issues, hence it also frames concepts of leadership. To adapt means to adjust to new or different conditions. Animals adapt to ecological changes. Those that adapt well sustain themselves. Those that do not, disappear or struggle to endure.

While it is appropriate in Zone 3b, I do not think the concept "adapt" is adequate for a more comprehensive understanding of life and leadership. In an adapt mind-set, the world is too much in charge and one yields too quickly to worldly realities. Leadership requires adeptness that lives at the intersection of personal, professional, and worldly realities.

To be adept is to be highly skilled. Wisdom plus choices inform and guide adeptness. To exhibit leadership one has to know what to do when. Choices demand adeptness, even if it means adapting in Zone 3b. In other words, adapt skills are a subset of adept skills, not the reverse. Wisdom knows when adept action should adapt. It also knows when it should not. Adept is a more inclusive skill than adapt, and meets the authenticity criteria of Zone 7a.

At the time the term *adeptness* came to me, the Whitbread Round the World Race was taking place. The more I understood the race, the more *adeptness* captured my mind. Think of nine yachts sailing in weather conditions so unpredictable they can change in seconds. Extremely competent teams, both on the boats and on shore, work adeptly, and each competes fiercely yet fairly within the rules of the contest. Do the teams adapt to the weather? Yes and no. Do they dominate the weather? Yes and no.

Teams bring historically grounded experience together with on-site reflection and action to work *with* the wind and water. In sailing, neither the weather nor the sailor is in total charge. As in life, there are disasters. Some are triggered by nature, some by human error, and some by outright cruelty. However, in most sailing events, it is adeptness that makes the positive difference.

For a year or even longer before a sailing race, each team pre-pares. Creativity abounds. New strategies are implemented. New boats and endless enthusiasm and commitment are essential. Anxiety, moments of doubt, despair, and questioning are also present. Boat design, strategy, infrastructure, team selection, funding, and corpo-rate support preoccupy each organization. There is often political debate, particularly in the early stages of preparation and planning. Should we enter the race? Is it worth it? Team members do not always agree, and the costs and benefits are assessed.

There is no doubt, as the kickoff event nears, that the race will be both exhilarating and strenuous. Long hours, unpredictable weather, great expenditures of will and commitment, rapid judgment calls, and positional and shared leadership will all be in play. The team that has created, constructed, and sustained the most efficient boat; has the most effective organizational system; has the most trust-worthy, knowledgeable, and skilled members; and makes the wisest leadership choices will most likely win. Yet, there are no guarantees. It will also take faith, hope, wisdom, and courage to engage the chal-lenge. Adeptness is at stake.

I have been a sailor for more than a decade. I am not adept in very difficult conditions, although hopefully I am adept enough to avoid them. I remember vividly, in my early days of learning to sail, the frustration of oversteering. Too hard to the right, too hard to the left, never just right for an easy flow of energy. Finally, I caught it. What a deep sense of satisfaction flooded my being. I was getting it. I was a sailor. I know the sheer delight of sailing, of finding the match between the strength and direction of the wind, the sail that creates the forward pull, and the keel that keeps the boat upright and keeps it from sliding across the top of the water. Looking up and seeing the full extension of the sails, feeling wind brush against my skin, and standing upright behind the wheel as the boat slips through the water—that is the joy of sailing. Adeptness is not just a theory for me. It involves both the experience of fear—the anxiety of sailing—and the overwhelming glory of living in and with the wind.

What does this sailing imagery teach us about leadership? It suggests, in part, that leadership intrinsically involves making adept choices. Leadership involves listening to the world's stirrings, seeking to understand them, and acting authentically in anticipation and response. When we are adept we live at the intersection of polarities. We can go both inside and outside, we can be centered and boundless, historically rooted and open to others, stable yet changeable, firm yet flexible, and unified yet diverse.

When we are adept we acknowledge that one set of truth criteria or one person cannot define the world. No one frame can fully grasp divergent, paradoxical realities. As the world changes it invites, even demands, us to see it on its own terms. When we are adept, we can shift lenses to get a complete picture of what is really going on.

Of course, being crafty, sneaky, or underhanded could also be an example of adeptness. On the surface, adept action does not guarantee ethical action. Yet, on deeper reflection, if we know what is really going on in the outer world and the inner self and then act accordingly, we are being authentic. And what is authentic, what is true and real, embodies ethical principles. That is why each zone is informed by a core ethical principle for leadership. In leadership, authenticity informs adeptness while adeptness embodies authenticity.

Conger and Benjamin (*Building Leaders*, 1999) explore the concept of "adept" and identify what will be required of leaders in the future. Their term *globally adept* describes "workplace savvy" about contexts that are demographically, culturally, and gender diverse (pp. 245–53).

To be adept requires a vast array of competencies. No one person embodies all of them, so it is critical to know which ones we have and then to surround ourselves with those who have complementary abilities. If you are a positional leader, do not try to be all things to all people. Just ensure all things are being addressed. It is also important to remember that the competencies do not necessarily reside in a person or even a group of persons. Many are processes in which we participate, and by participating we exhibit leadership. The competencies have been mentioned throughout the discussions of the zones. Here is a list of the most important commitments and abilities that require development and/or action:

Zone 1: Serving the Past

- Historical sensibility and knowledge

- Core-value identification

- Willingness to face hard truths from the past

- Commitment to preserve the best by means of celebration, orientation seminars, speeches, and other Past Share events

Zone 2: Building Core Competencies

- Mastering of technical skills of the discipline or subject matter needed

- Finance and accounting knowledge and skills

- Assessment of consistency of service or product quality

- Project management

- Supervisory excellence

Zone 3a: Designing Sustainable Systems

- Systems thinking

- System design

- Team participation

- Awareness and need for needs-assessment surveys

- Willingness to break out of silos and share wisdom across boundaries

Zone 3b: Affirming Shared Identity

- Commitment to develop the full array of emotional intelligence competencies including:

  - Personal competencies—self-awareness, self-regulation, motivation

  - Social competencies—empathy and social skills

- Team-building and group participation

- Ethical awareness and sense of core and shared values

- Executive strategic thinking and planning

- Knowledge of the critical importance of identity affirmations

Zone 4: Creating Ownership

- Conflict negotiation skills

- Personal empowerment with Exit Card

- Buffalo self-assessment—know what decisions to keep, what to share, and what to release

- Commitment to participatory actions and events

Zone 5a: Setting Direction

- Commitment to participatory visioning processes with appropriate foundations and planning skills

- Awareness of necessity of clarifying the destination

- Confidence to move forward

- Collective strategic planning process skills

Zone 5b: Anticipating Change

- Pattern recognition

- Scenario writing

- Scanning

- Framing

- Metaphorical thinking

- New insight generation
- Commitment to authenticity thinking

Zone 6: Creating Meaning in Chaos

- Process wisdom
- Courage that moves beyond risk-taking
- Framing
- Pattern recognition and serious writing
- A profound understanding of serious/play

Zone 7: Serving the Promise of Authenticity

- Deep self-awareness
- Faith in the promise of hope
- Wisdom
- Adeptness
- Learning agility and inquiry
- Listening to the stirrings
- Mapping complex issues
- Polarity and paradoxical thinking and living
- A commitment to face spirituality, even theology, without getting trapped by exclusionary religious boundaries

When one is first facing all these competencies, it is easy to be overwhelmed. Yet as experiences accumulate, wisdom informs and adeptness directs authentic action. To put it another way, "inauthentic adeptness" is an oxymoron. Adeptness requires an understanding of reality and a sense of oneself. To misread either will produce a living lie, intentional or not. Jesse Ventura, the governor of Minnesota, struggles with this dilemma. He claims authenticity, and walks off a cliff from time to time. He does not understand the importance of the role of governor. His *Playboy* interview, while appropriate if he had still been a radio commentator, made him appear out of control (see Ventura, 1999). Then he blamed the media for his choices.

Wisdom

Making choices requires wisdom. Most leadership-training programs stress skill development. Very few focus on wisdom. In part, this reluctance may stem from a worry that wisdom means a fixed idea of truth and knowledge etched in concrete (see Chappell, 1993, p. 86). However, wisdom resists saying, "I have truth, you do not. I will instruct you." Rather, wisdom continually emerges out of our interactions with others and our experience of complex events. Complexity is not just in the world; it is also within us. Wisdom cannot be arrogant. It is humble. Part of being wise is the deep recognition that there is much we do not know, and that even what we do think we know is always worthy of being tested.

I hope that over the years we have come to realize that using skills apart from thoughtful knowledge and reflection can create and perpetuate terrible situations. Acquired skills do not guarantee insights into what is really going on. If you want to check this out, just recall how little you knew about life in your youth as you were bundling skills for your career. Talk to professionals, be they lawyers, doctors, or clergy, and ask them how prepared they were for their field as they left school. Technical knowledge was only one part of what they needed to know to deal with the contingencies of their practice.

Zone 7a offers a unique and special wisdom challenge for leadership. Unlike the other zones, which focus on particular worlds, this zone encompasses all the worlds we have discussed, and challenges us to make the right call in a specific context while never forgetting the larger context. That is, it requires us to assess the authenticity of our actions by both comprehensiveness and congruence.

What is missing in leadership education in both schools and organizations is the understanding that comprehensiveness must be coupled with congruency. Too many people advocate "the truth" of only one or two zones. These are parochial arguments. Without a comprehensive perspective, we are out of touch with all our options and thus limited in our choices. We're not choosing from all the bricks we have at hand. We're failing to grasp the depth and breadth of the world, our relationship to it, and the profound requirements of leadership. Wisdom lives at the intersection of the whole/part polarity. While knowing and attending to the big picture, leadership also connects to the particular situation for authentic action.

When we are wise we listen—paying attention to the stirrings. All too often, signals are missed; thus the action taken is inappropriate. Sages see more deeply, hear more clearly, and feel more profoundly than the rest of us. Yet as we mature, we, too, can become sages. Often what is clear to one person is totally missed by another. What is missing is a frame, a larger context for interpretation. The zones map the stirrings for sage-like listening. Attending to inauthenticities also opens the possibilities for leadership. Acting to address the stirrings that arise because of leadership inauthenticity is leadership at its most insightful and creative.

To figure out what is really going on, it is critical to know the following:

- The history of the situation

- The knowledge and skills required

- The systems in question

- The stakeholders involved

- The direction and anticipation of the future

- The significance of what is at stake

Choices

By the time we understand and experience Zone 7, we know in our being that life is a series of polarities. Thus many of our choices are what wisdom tells us are equally true and viable options. As I reported earlier, the polarity informing Zone 7a is one/many, and it cuts across all zones. Leadership decisions confront this polarity daily. Leadership is always facing many choices and having to make a decision.

We all make choices. Some are ethically reflective and wise, some spontaneous, some political, some practical, and some instinctual or habitual. These types of choices certainly express themselves in leadership. In the story at the beginning of this chapter, we saw choices being considered and made. Throughout the zone analysis, I have offered many stories that illustrate the necessity of matching context with the right choice of leadership action. Hiring the carpenter to lead my son and me through the process of building his deck in Zone 2 and understanding and living in process wisdom in Zone 6 demonstrate the vast differences of context we encounter, and hence the different types of leadership we may be choosing to enact. Congruence is the key. By finding the fit, leadership makes wise choices.

We need to know what we are choosing leadership to be in each situation. Here's a simple example. Suppose Al's boss, Sue, identifies Al as having great leadership potential, and she tells him so. He is excited and pleased that she noticed. Also suppose she defines leadership as engagement and he defines it as results, and neither knows the choice the other has made. As a matter of fact, Al's boss does not even know there are choices to be made. So Sue praises Al for his leadership and Al says to himself, "Sue has finally realized that I can really get things done. My future here looks great." Sue is saying to herself, "Al is a great manager; I will coach him on leadership. He runs over too many people in pursuit of results and engages no one's spirit."

Now, reverse the order. Sue believes in results and Al in engagement. Now Al is thrilled that Sue recognizes his quality of engagement, his ability to motivate and inspire people. Sue is thinking, "I wonder what Al does all day. He has great leadership potential— if only he would complete a project on time. He seems to walk the halls singing 'Kum Ba Yah.' I'll be his coach and maybe suggest he take a course in leadership that stresses results."

Are Sue and Al on the same page? No, not at all. Yet they are both talking about leadership. Do conversations like this ever occur? All too often. People are making choices about what leadership means without being aware that they are doing so.

I want to return to a comprehensive overview of choices from another angle. In Chapter One, you had the opportunity to define your view of leadership by choosing among eight pairs of options. Leadership is

- Born or made

- Individual or relational

- Positional or everywhere

- Results or engagement/intent

- Coercive/noncoercive or only noncoercive

- Vision or framing

- Ethical/unethical or only ethical

- Secular or spiritual

Now, after rigorous inquiry and reflection, and an introduction to the zone map, we can locate each choice by the zone in which it fits, affirming the relevance and importance of all the views of leadership. As we do this, reviewing your own choices from Chapter One will give you deeper insight into your preferences of leadership choices and thus what zones you may be most comfortable leading in. For example, if you chose results over engagement, you like the earlier zones more than the later. On reflection, you may shift your preference as well. Leadership requires adeptness. Know your preference. Do not always act on it.

APPLICATION

Before we start the analysis that begins this section, please review your choices from Chapter One. Also pay attention to the strength of your conviction and the opinion you gave about whether making the choice was easy or hard. With this information in front of you, you will be better able to assess your own perspective.

Analysis of Choices

Born or Made

In the 1950s and '60s, the dominant theory of leadership was that leadership is born. Labeled *trait theory*, it referred to those characteristics an individual brings to leadership such as charisma, vision, and decisiveness. The newest is Collins's paradox: humility and fierce resolve. We might call this particular theory *born exclusive* because it says some individuals are born with the traits and some are not.

Whether the traits are totally or mostly inherited, they constitute part of the package that we bring to leadership. *Trait*, in contrast to *type*, refers to predicted behavior. One strategy that goes with this theory is to study great leaders of the past and tease out characteristics that may predict leadership capability in others. Born exclusive lodges in Zone 1. Why? Born is part of the past. Life is a gift, traits are gifts, and some traits are better than others. Leadership identification by trait lodges in a history-based zone—Serving the Past.

Leadership that is made resides heavily in Zone 2, Building Core Competencies. Leadership is learned in schools, from practice, and through reflection on all kinds of experiences. Skill mastery is key. As appropriate skills are demonstrated, and with some good fortune, one moves up through the organization, hoping to become the leading expert and boss. In many ways, this Zone 2 perspective still operates with gusto in universities, religious organizations, law and medical firms, and other technical organizations. What does it take to become a dean; a pastor, priest, or rabbi; or manager of a law firm? All too often the answer is just technical mastery of the discipline in question.

Zones 3a, Designing Sustainable Systems, through 4, Creating Ownership, are transitional. Leadership in Zone 3 combines technical mastery and systems management skills. And there is little doubt that the importance of sterling past performance is still primary for promotion. However, leadership in this zone also begins to take advantage of the diverse gifts of many players. With teams and relationships so important in Zone 3, the early stages of a *born inclusive* perspective are taking hold alongside learned leadership. This is the perspective that people are born with different sets of traits and that each set, not just one predefined set, has some value for leadership. One can hardly go to a team-building seminar without having one's personality profile tested, reported upon, and discussed. "Know who you are, know your colleagues, and draw on one another's strengths" is the mantra of team building from the born inclusive perspective. It is here we see the use of the *Myers-Briggs Type Indicator* assessment and many other instruments that systematically identify and reveal differences, a process that can be good and necessary.

In Zone 4, although the buffalo is beginning to fly like a goose, veto power still lives. Attention to diversity of styles increases as more people get into the action. As leadership roles loosen and shared leadership surfaces, inclusive natural gifts deservedly receive heightened recognition. Because the ups-versus-downs metaphor is so dominant in this zone, what is often missed is the implied message in the metaphor that what it takes to succeed is to imitate the ups— the positional, learned leadership.

In Zones 5a, Setting Direction, 5b, Anticipating Change, and 6, Creating Meaning in Chaos, the born inclusive view takes over without reserve. Diversity of leadership styles is no longer optional; it is essential. As "power with" replaces "power over," diverse players are necessary as members of the organization come together to scan the horizon for future possibilities. All who come to the arena are valued because of their variety of perspectives.

A number of leadership theorists dislike the whole debate about born versus made. Kenwyn Smith, a professor at the Wharton School, University of Pennsylvania, believes the debate is nonsense and serves only to reinforce the heroic individualism so destructive and dominant in organizations today. (He surfaced the issue in the Advanced Leadership Program at the Carlson School of Management to young aspiring executives.) Yet the issue is tenacious, perhaps because the born-or-made debate is grounded in the nature/nurture polarity. Polarities never go away.

From a zone perspective, my worry is that a person might conclude, perhaps from personality testing, that she or he is a natural in a particular zone and must live only there. When that happens, leadership evaporates. This zone requires abandoning your preference for one leadership action when the situation requires you to use a different action. Do not use your preference to justify single-zone dwelling. Leadership moves among zones. It does not dwell only in one place.

Some people are seeking a third space in this nature-or-nurture, born-or-made debate. They are concentrating on character. Covey (1992), Jacobs (1997), and others think character unites born and made leadership and still maintains the focus on the soul of the leader. I expect we will see more talk of "talent" as well, as in *Now, Discover Your Strengths* (Buckingham and Coffman, 2001), the newest book by the authors of *First, Break All the Rules* (1999). And that thought carries us to the next choice.

Individual or Relational (Team)

As leadership moves from Zone 1 to Zone 6, leadership choices shift from individual to relational. When I ask people to vote on this one, they consistently say leadership is individual—by about two to one. However, relational leadership becomes useful during Zone 3 and becomes central in Zone 4 and beyond as focusing on parts yields to focusing on connections.

Team mania scares some people from the relational view. Many people think teams are out of control, failing as often as succeeding. If relational and team are connected, they cast their vote for individual. Although relational leadership leads to teams, teams do not necessarily imply a full relational perspective. A team leader is still an individual, the focus of leadership.

The reason Zones 3a and 3b are transitional rests in the perception of boss. For many people, a boss is an individual person with a name, characteristics, etc. For others, however, being the boss is a role responsibility defined by its place in the system. There is no such entity as a boss apart from being a boss of something. The relational view kicks in.

This debate never seems to end. Why? Because individual versus relational is another polarity. If human beings are both individual selves and parts of the larger whole, it is easy to see how our focus can shift from one side to the other.

Positional or Everywhere

While positional leadership is pivotal in Zone 3, it decreases in importance as leadership deals more and more with chaos. Ninety to 95 percent of the people in my seminars vote that leadership exists everywhere. Only one group tended to shift dramatically in a different direction: When I worked with a group of elected officials, their vote was 50/50.

In the field of leadership studies, hardly anyone explicitly advocates a positional view of leadership anymore, yet what I am struck with is the extent to which writers on leadership only study, talk to, or report on positional-leadership perspectives. Many of the established gurus in the field, like Warren Bennis and Burt Nanus, seem preoccupied with leadership as headship. Nanus's *Visionary Lead-*

ership (1992) sounds as though it would describe at least Zone 5. Yet look inside. Who has the vision? Positional heads are the primary players. Coaching is for executives. So while we praise and laud shared leadership rhetorically, we anchor ourselves to trust in headship.

Positional leadership thrives in Zones 1 through 3a. Zones 3b and 4 are transitional. Zones 5 and 6 require a *leadership is everywhere* model. One of the great dangers in leadership is to misread this zone analysis. Too many buffaloes try to soften their history of domination in Zones 1 and 2 as they lead in 3b and 4. Then they try to lead with authority in Zones 5 and 6. It does not work. The world rejects positional actions in those zones. It invites participation.

Results or Engagement

Of all the leadership choices, perhaps this one between results and engagement is the easiest to position in a zone. Result orientations for leadership flourish in Zones 2 and 3, and spark the move to Zones 4 and 5. Engagement resides in Zones 5b and 6. Zone 5a, Setting Direction, creates a desired worldly outcome. While results-oriented, the vision is often framed so broadly and vaguely that much wiggle room is included.

In my seminars, the vote is always overwhelmingly that leadership gets results. Only a few buy the argument that leadership engages, and when a goal surfaces, the goal is turned over to a management team to implement. The business culture is so powerfully focused on results that any effort to stray from that dogma is quickly sacked. However, leadership can get results only when the outcomes are clear, measurable, and seen as important and doable by the implementers. In Zones 5b and 6, there are no specific goals. Some would argue that scanning is a result in itself. This is partially true. However, to see scanning only as a result misses the essence of the zone. Shell Oil did not set out to predict the future and marshal resources and talent to shape a desired future. It did not know the future. At best, it might spot a signal that could alert it to possible events. In Zone 6, accomplishment is not planned. Co-creation, improvisation, and intuition do not marry easily with the rigor and force of Zones 2 through 4. Only by engaging others, listening, and building on what they say and do can one lead in Zone 6.

Coercive/Noncoercive or Only Noncoercive

Leadership that is only noncoercive begins in Zone 4 and takes charge in Zones 5a through 6. Leadership that is partly coercive and partly noncoercive lives in Zones 1, 2, and 3a. Zone 3b is the transitional zone as the organization's core and shared values are emphasized and inclusion is stressed. About two-thirds of the people in my seminars vote that leadership is only noncoercive. They accept the argument that bosses select employees, followers select leaders.

When the buffalo begins to fly or even disappears, so, too, does coercion. Shared leadership does not condone or reward force of will. Veto power, while still present in Zone 4, especially during large-scale intervention, is not the heavy-handed force that often occurs in Zones 2 and 3, where experts expect compliance. It is a backup strategy, hopefully never needed and actually rarely used. Power becomes much more diffuse as one moves through the zones.

Is coercion ever central to leadership? Yes, and it must be constrained by ethical boundaries. Remember the example of the police officer who had to arrest her own troops for abuse of power? As I reported, the St. Paul police force to whom I told this story did not like it. Yet they admitted it is believable and does happen. It takes great courage to intervene coercively with peers. You do it when it is right. When power is abused, the perpetrators must be stopped. Those in my seminars who believe that leadership is noncoercive argue that the arrest *managed* the problem. Those who believe that leadership is coercive/noncoercive see courage as central to leadership and hence see the arrest as more than management. My own reading of this tough issue is that most leadership activity in Zones 2 and 3 admits both ethical and unethical uses of power. Thus Hitler's tyranny does not mean that he was not a leader. When ethical standards plus courage enter the scene, leadership looks different in Zones 3a and 3b. Positional leaders often have to make a series of calls for a purpose they believe virtuous: to go to war, to cut the size of the workforce, to acquire or sell a new business. All require courage if ethically directed. In such cases, leadership expresses itself authentically. If, on the other hand, positional leaders use a military campaign to take the heat off when citizens are angry about the nation's economic health or politicians' personal embarrassments, or if they cut the workforce for quick personal profit, that is not leadership. That is exploitation and egocentric behavior. It is inauthentic.

Power in Zones 5 and 6 is only noncoercive. In each, "power-with," not "power-over," models is central. Just as leadership is shared, so, too, is power. Coercion of any sort flies counter to the reality in these zones. It is only in the atmosphere of mutual inquiry and respect that the leadership activities of scanning and meaning-creation occur.

Vision or Framing

As pointed out in the zone analysis, vision surfaces in Zone 3b, where it may be part of an executive-driven vision statement, and erupts full tilt in Zone 5a. Leadership as vision is replaced completely by leadership as framing in Zones 5b and 6. In the leadership literature, *vision* has been the marquee term. In the voting in my seminars, also, vision almost always wins, although of late it seems to be losing ground.

However, Bolman and Deal (1991) and others (including Fairhurst and Sarr, 1996, and myself) add leadership as framing to the literature. In a generally participative, shapeable world (Zones 3b, 4, and 5), visioning finds its most comfortable home. Zone 5b worries about the future. Its scenarios are in part visions. Because there are many of them, they function more as frames than as a unified organizational vision. In Zone 6, in an unknown and unknowable world, vision is not a viable option. Framing makes more sense.

Using only one metaphor or frame will kill creativity and grossly limit new perceptions. As I have argued elsewhere in this book, every metaphor both reveals and conceals reality. Only multiple lenses provide a broad view.

Ethical/Unethical or Only Ethical

Ethical considerations are not pivotal for leadership in Zones 1 through 3, although core values are often grounded in the past. Remember that a core value does not have to be ethical. In an unethical business, the values tied to the business may be core to that business and yet not meet a reflective and expansive definition of ethical. In Zone 3b, leadership revisits core values. If they did not exist at the founding of the organization, they are discerned and verbalized as part of guided system inclusion.

The transition occurs in Zone 4 and leadership as only ethical emerges full bloom in Zones 5 and 6. Burns (1978) was the first to argue that leadership was inherently ethical. Prior to Burns, all leadership educators, though perhaps advocating ethical leadership, knew that leadership could be both ethical and unethical. Hitler was the test question. Did he exhibit leadership? Or, phrased another way, can you be a leader who does not exhibit leadership?

Ethical considerations tend to be excluded when the dominant metaphor is *life is a machine.* They are extraneous to the subject matter at hand. Just as emotions are not appropriate variables in a cost-benefit analysis, so ethics does not even enter the inquiry. Ethical reflection by leadership is considered to block serious and hard inquiry into leadership action. In the early zones, basic ethical considerations are implicitly addressed by the high level of agreement on direction and certainty of outcome. Ethical reflection resides outside the narrow parameters of the technical-rational approach.

When the metaphor that *life is a body* is dominant, there is a similar constraint on ethical reflection. Leadership can be both functional and dysfunctional, just as a body can. So ethical reflection is possible yet not essential to functional or systems leadership. Ethical action is instead a by-product of adaptive interactive behavior within the system.

For practical reasons, the linking of values and ethics to the heart of leadership becomes more apparent in Zone 4. If power is to be shared to enhance the business, and the current positional system is to be changed, then engaging in up-down relationships takes on ethical importance. All the players have to set, and conform to, new shared principles of honesty and participation.

Leadership in Zones 5a, 5b, and 6 transfers ethics from outside to inside the unit of analysis. As the external constraints of systems and collective actions decline in importance, internal ethical reflection and action increases. By the time we engage in serious play in Zone 6, all we have is internal integrity. There are no outside boundaries, only inside centeredness. If there is little agreement and little certainty, what is left? Our internal principles bump up against those of others who may have very different ones. In Zone 6, there are no sure rules for engagement and there is a question whether any universal ethical construct is even possible, given the wide diversity of perspectives.

As we all know, even if we can discern a universal ethic, which I think we can (see Terry, 1993, pp. 144–48), there is no guarantee that ethical behavior will burst forth and abound. And even if we are ethical, that does not guarantee external victory or success in war, community, or family life. However, in Zone 6 leadership is rooted solely in credibility, since here followers select their leaders; leaders no longer select their followers. Credibility arises from authenticity and thus from the ethical principles that inform and guide authenticity.

Secular or Spiritual

When I ask people whether leadership is ethical/unethical or only ethical, most people vote for ethical/unethical. However, when I ask whether leadership is secular or spiritual, most, usually about 80 percent, vote for spiritual.

Somehow debate on this issue resonates with many people, although it creates discomfort for others. When I presented this idea to executives in Europe, they appeared dumbfounded. One woman and two men in Amsterdam were reluctant to discuss the issue in public; then, during a break, they raised serious reservations about the concepts connected with the term *spiritual*. While they had voted that leadership is spiritual because I had connected that view to the creation of meaning, they were very concerned that *spiritual* might be a code word for a particular religious tradition. Each had been raised as a fundamentalist, had broken from that tradition, and was now deeply secular. They worried lest spiritual concepts open a channel for traditional religious beliefs to pour into organizational life and leadership definitions.

Yet leadership as only ethical is not enough for Zones 6 and 7. In these zones, leadership now embraces the most disturbing and troubling issues of fear, hope, courage, and faith. It is no wonder so little leadership literature dwells in these zones and tackles these issues. When entered upon, the discussions are filled with paradoxes and shadows, and they raise provocative questions about our planet and the human species.

Nevertheless, an intriguing phenomenon is occurring in the leadership literature. Of late, many leadership writers are concluding their books with a chapter on spirituality, even when the primary topic of the text seems quite far removed from spiritual matters. Maybe more and more thinkers in the field are hearing stirrings.

I even wonder if the popularity of *Dilbert* is not a signal of spiritual unrest. Could increased interest in spirituality be a response to the vast cynicism in today's organizations, triggered in part by many workers' feelings of betrayal and by the insecurity caused by reengineering, reinventing, reorganizing, merging, and aquiring? Are we in a meaning crisis? Is chaos too close? Are more and more people in touch with the deep stirrings of unease, aware of the false securities in the other zones? Is this unsettling the reason that Wheatley (1996) finds comfort in order? For myself, my spiritual anxiety roots in my deep belief that chaos in our human world is not apparent; it is real. Our long-term well-being is not found in nature. Rather, it requires a radical faith that confronts the chaos inside each of us as well as in our world. (We will investigate this further in Chapter Thirteen.)

Summary of Leadership Choices by Zone

Location	Transition	Location
Born exclusive: Zone 1	Zones 3–4	Made: Zone 2
Born inclusive: Zones 5 & 6		
Individual: Zones 1 & 2	Zones 3a & 3b	Relational: Zones 4–6
Positional: Zones 1–3a	Zones 3b & 4	Everywhere: Zones 5–6
Results: Zones 1–4	Zone 5	Engagement: Zones 5b & 6
Coercive/noncoercive: Zones 1–3	Zone 3b & 4	Only noncoercive: Zones 5–6
Vision: Zones 1–5	Zone 5	Framing: Zones 5b & 6
Ethical/unethical: Zones 1–3	Zones 3b & 4	Only ethical: Zones 5–6
Secular: Zones 1–3	Zones 3b–5	Spiritual: Zones 5b–7

Reflections on Leadership Choices

Now that you have reviewed your personal choices and matched them with the zones, where do you go from here? You can probably see that you have already worked on the choices that you found hard. That is why I believe you should now work on the easy ones. It is the easy ones that may now be the real teacher.

Leadership stretches our comfort zone. If the choice was very easy, there is probably an issue on the side you didn't choose that needs your thoughtful attention. Our preferences in leadership choices often tell us a lot about ourselves and very little about the world. As we place those choices in zones, we have to begin paying attention to the things in the real world.

We are lured to the zone that fulfills our sense of leadership. If all the zones are leadership, don't we need competence in all of them? My advice is this: Know the overall map. Know your own comfort spaces and preferences and then go to a not-so-comfortable place. Live in the leadership zones you like the least. Master those skills. Encounter and embrace all the zones, including the ones that take you closer to human chaos. Become adept. Make the wise choices. It requires thought agility. There are no quick fixes for leadership development. Grow into the full richness of leadership as Serving the Promise. (See Figure 26 below.)

Another Set of Choices: New Realities—New Choices

So far the zones have been portrayed and framed as equidistant from their nearest neighbors and as moving evenly outward along both outside boundaries. What if, however, this parallel structure were not the case? Could we find ourselves in a situation that puts us way out on outcome and close in on direction (Figure 27) or the reverse (Figure 28)? What, for example, would leadership action in Zone 5a be if there were little agreement on direction and high certainty of outcome?

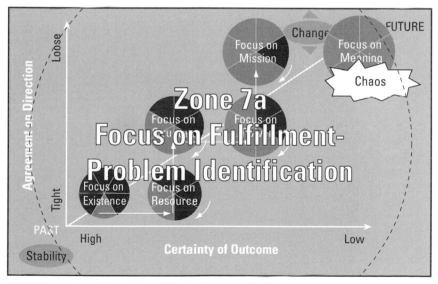

FIGURE 26 • ZONE 7A: MAKING WISE CHOICES

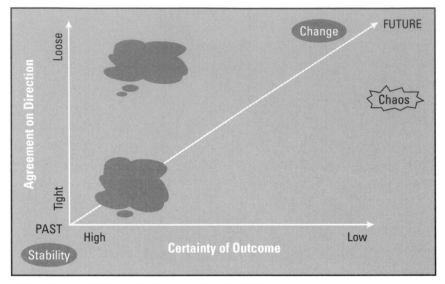

FIGURE 27 • NEW REALITIES, NEW CHOICES I

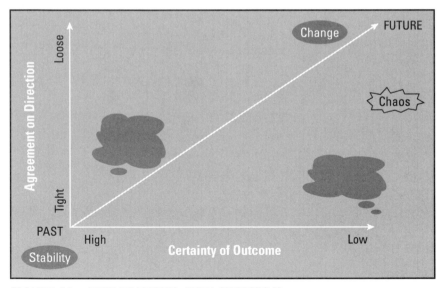

FIGURE 28 • NEW REALITIES, NEW CHOICES II

Two medical experts differ on the diagnosis for a patient and agree on their commitment to the patient's health. There is tight agreement on direction—the patient's well-being—and low certainty of outcome—no guarantee of what will happen when a particular decision is made. In this situation, the patient or the primary care doctor must make an intuitive judgment in order to select one diagnosis over another. I lodge this example here because the vacillation of certainty of outcome and shared direction reflect the two sides of the zone. First, one is Zone 2, the other is not. Then, the reverse takes over.

Consider an example where leadership sets direction. In a military conflict, all military forces agree that winning is the goal. There is tight agreement on direction. The outcome, however, is exceedingly uncertain. Officers thus end up making intuitive judgments daily as they maneuver to win. The reverse situation exists when two battle strategies conflict. Each has clearly defined and expected outcomes. There is, however, no agreement on which to choose. The advocates for the two strategies must make a political compromise.

Another way to look at the choice between political and intuitive judgments is to determine whether an inside decision or an outside decision is required. If you are in one group that advocates one goal and another group advocates another goal and the groups must make one choice between them, then it is agreement outside your group that is missing, and a political settlement that is required. If you are in a group where there is agreement on the goal, the outcomes are uncertain, and no other group is involved, then you are making an inside decision and it will be an intuitive one. That is, an inside focus requires an intuitive judgment and an outside focus requires a political judgment.

Yet another factor to consider is whether the consequences are short- or long-term. Political judgments tend to be made when consequences are short-term. Intuitive judgments tend to be made when they are long-term.

Serving the Promise of authenticity can be complex. It is essential to provide a thorough answer to the essential question of what is really going on.

Leadership Versus Management

Occasionally in this book, I have suggested that some actions are management rather than leadership. Are these two terms really distinguishable, are they simply interchangeable, or is there a third way of looking at them? Kotter (1990), for example, distinguishes management from leadership and devotes a whole book to that topic.

His model looks like this:

	Management	Leadership
Creating an agenda	Planning and Budgeting—establishing detailed steps and timetables for achieving needed results, and then allocating the resources necessary to make that happen.	Establishing direction—developing a vision of the future, often the distant future, and strategies for producing the changes needed to achieve that vision.
Developing a human network for achieving the agenda	Organizing and Staffing—establishing some structure for accomplishing plan requirements, staffing that structure with individuals, delegating responsibility and authority for carrying out the plan, providing policies and procedures to help guide people, and creating methods or systems to monitor implementation.	Aligning people—communicating the direction by words and deeds to all those whose cooperation may be needed so as to influence the creation of teams and coalitions that understand the vision and strategies, and accept their validity.
Execution	Controlling and Problem Solving—monitoring results versus plan in some detail, identifying deviations, and then planning and organizing to solve these problems.	Motivating and Inspiring—energizing people to overcome major political, bureaucratic, and resource barriers to change by satisfying very basic, but often unfulfilled, human needs.
Outcomes	Produces a degree of predictability and order, and has the potential to consistently produce key results expected by various stakeholders (e.g., for customers, always being on time; for stockholders, being on budget).	Produces change, often to a dramatic degree, and has the potential to produce extremely useful change (e.g., new products that customers want, new approaches to labor relations that help make a firm more competitive).

Whetten and Cameron (1998) collapse leadership and management together. "Leadership," they report, "has been equated with dynamism, vibrancy, and charisma; management with hierarchy, equilibrium, and control" (p. 14). In today's world, they contend, leaders need good management savvy and managers must be good leaders. In the choices you were invited to make in Chapter One, I often either affirmed or blurred the distinction between leadership and management. Clearly, it is possible both to distinguish leadership and management and to understand them as interchangeable. However, is something else going on that permits both alternatives to be true?

Many authors housed in a particular zone acknowledge and often criticize anyone living in an earlier zone, one with a world of greater agreement and certainty. Although other authors are not familiar with my zone frame, they engage in brick throwing, not building. Let me illustrate the brick throwing. Stacey (1993) distinguishes "ordinary management" (Zone 2) from "extraordinary management" (Zones 3 through 6). While acknowledging the early zones, he is using them primarily to clarify the new value of complexity and chaos theory for organizational analysis and action. Block (1987, 1993) limits leadership to a positional definition (Zones 3a and 3b) when advocating empowerment of the downs (Zone 4). Experts do not even show up in his discussion. Hammer (1997), an advocate of system process reengineering (Zone 3b), rejects restructuring (Zone 3a). Hamel and Prahalad (1994) bash reengineering, restructuring, mission statements, etc., as the two of them push for futuring and creating opportunity share (Zones 5b and 6). Vaill (1996) is similarly suspicious of earlier zones as he looks back from Zone 6.

Conversely, all of these and other theorists affirm their preferred zone(s) with great passion. Even if they do not call what happens in their zone leadership, they imply that the thinking and action generated in their zone are what add significant value to organizational, even community, life.

However, working on the leadership zones has led me to an alternative way to view leadership and management. *Whatever zone you are currently in, leadership resides in the zones in front of you, and management resides in the zones behind you* (see Figure 29). Thus any given behavior can be either leadership or management, depending on which zone you are currently residing in. Remember the example I gave of building a deck with my son? Our roots were fine. He called me because I was his father. The past was alive and well. However, we confronted a Zone 2 Building Core Competencies problem. We had no competence to fix the fixable situation we faced. I sought a leader—Jeff, the carpenter—who provided the leadership to build the deck. He led, we followed, and together we constructed

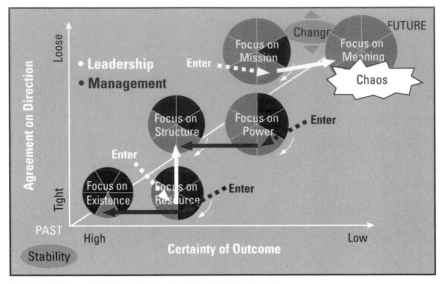

FIGURE 29 • LEADERSHIP AND MANAGEMENT

a beautiful addition to my son's house. Vision advocates would argue that my son's dream of a deck was the real leadership. However, that wasn't the focus of attention. Vision was not the problem; we needed technical leadership. That was the focus for authentic action.

Suppose, however, Jeff, my son, and I and now experience a Zone 6 crisis. Jeff transforms into a technical expert who may or may not engage in Creating Meaning in Chaos by responding to the fire, flood, or whatever disaster is upon us. If such a crisis hits the deck-building project, he might lead or he might become a buffalo. In a Zone 6 reality, Jeff is no longer our building rescuer exhibiting leadership as in Zone 2. Instead we are all Creating Meaning in Chaos actors as we co-create adept responses to our difficult and novel situation.

Leadership moves toward or within chaos; management moves toward certainty and agreement. Without management, leadership has no floor or foundation for action; without leadership, management has no impetus to open new territories. Authors err, in my judgment, by critiquing zones behind them as they advocate a particular zone that embodies their passion. Even vision can become management (although it always appears on lists of leadership abilities). If the world calls for leadership as Anticipating Change (Zone 5b) for constructing and writing scenarios, leadership then hands the insights from this process off to Setting Direction (Zone 5a) for implementation. One then manages the preferred futuring process in Zone 5a. In effect, leadership and management are distinguishable and not distinguishable at the same time. Leading and managing in all the zones is absolutely necessary for viable, long-term personal, professional organizational, community, and global life.

ZONE IDENTIFICATION AND
LEADERSHIP QUESTIONS

How prepared is your organization for Zone 7a realities? Check out these questions:

1. How sturdy is my organization or community in this zone?

   • Is the word *leadership* used in my organization? What does it mean? What choices are being made?

   • How well positioned is my organization or department to offer leadership in each zone as prompted?

   • Does wisdom ever come up in our leadership discussions?

   • What core competencies are best represented in my organization and which ones need work?

```
10 |  |  |  |  |  |  |  |  |  |  0 |  |  |  |  |  |  |  |  |  | 10
Very Sturdy                                                Shaky
```

2. Where is my organization or community currently focusing its leadership attention?

   • How good is the match between stirrings and action?

   • Are there people who can see the big picture and still make informed, focused choices on particular issues?

   • How would I grade the authenticity and inauthenticity of the organization?

```
10 |  |  |  |  |  |  |  |  |  | 0 |  |  |  |  |  |  |  |  | 10
Excellent Fit                                          Misfit
```

3. Am I prepared to make wise choices?

    - What zones do I believe I know best and have experienced the most?

    - What zones make little sense to me?

    - Is there a pattern to the leadership choices I made in Chapter One? How does it tell me about what zones I am most committed to?

    - What steps can I take to enhance my competence in the choices I rejected?

    - What do I think of the leadership-versus-management discussion? Does it help me understand what is behind the distinctions?

    - Could I now read a book on leadership and figure out the choices being made by the author?

    - Can I define leadership for myself?

    - Have I been tested for my personality preferences? Does my preference match the leadership choices I made in Chapter One?

```
10 |  |  |  |  |  |  |  |  |  | 0 |  |  |  |  |  |  |  |  | 10
Ready to Exhibit Leadership                    Not Prepared at All
```

ZONE SUMMARY

Zone 7a reflects on practice, bringing theory to the table. Making Wise Choices never loses the big picture. Authenticity in this zone, and in all the zones, combines congruence and comprehensiveness. Many polarities inform this zone and become a unified lens through which to view life. Leadership continually demands maintaining an overview and taking particular actions; it demands attention to the polarity between *one* and *many*. The eight choices of leadership types can be mapped by zones. Part of wisdom is getting this match right. Do not try to be a buffalo in Zone 6, though being a buffalo is often very useful in Zone 2.

Leadership and management differ depending on what zone one views life from at the moment. Actions taken in the current action zone are leadership; actions taken in the earlier zones are management. Both leadership and management are needed at all times. Thus the zone model does not exclude particular views of leadership or management, as many advocates of particular theories do. It affirms all of them as platforms, necessary for support and future travels.

Leadership as Making Wise Choices embodies the principles of authenticity every day as it matches choices. It serves the promise of authenticity. Getting it right and not mismatching is the authenticity challenge; stirrings can alert us to misjudgments such as throwing skills at a problem that requires participatory action or building a participatory base when there is no clear infrastructure or shared values. Listening for the stirrings never ends. No one person can hear and interpret all that is going on. Listening is a group commitment and a team activity. *Catch the stirring; it is not always purring.*

ZONE 7A DEFINITIONS

Leadership: Making Wise Choices
Authenticity criteria: Congruence and comprehensiveness
Metaphor: Life is a polarity
Core ethical principle: Authenticity
Polarity: One/many

STIRRINGS

As they experience all the zones, people find that puzzles and questions seem ever present. They may ask, for example, Is this complex zone framework really helping us diagnose situations and figure out what leadership means in differing contexts? Because an organization is also complex and has many things going on, all the zones are always present—so how do we know which most deserves our attention? Can zones really be both sequential and simultaneous? Maybe some parts of the world are not fixable. Then what do we do? Is this zone scheme really developmental? Would it make more sense to think of it as a map in which you can go in any direction you choose? Why not jump all over the place? Can't we travel to any destination we choose?

People have both negative and positive reactions to such questions, which is apparent in the organizational stirrings.

Negative Stirrings

Listen to some of these reflections:

> I'm not sure I can or even want to explore all of the questions I'm thinking of and hearing. I'm a hands-on kind of person. This is too abstract. What is the payoff of such analysis? I want some research, some science. I liked the first umpire who dealt with the real world, not all this postmodern multiple-perspective vagueness.

> I thought the first umpire was naive. I identified with the second guy, who stressed the importance of view and perspective. I like inclusion and dialogue, but I worry that some comprehensive picture will be adopted as the alleged ultimate truth and that we will dismiss important differences of views.

> I resonated with the third umpire, who constructs reality by perspective. My worry is that we will stop there. I'm a postmodern kind of person, yet a part of me longs for the good old days of objectivity, of facts and firm ethics grounded in some sense of ultimate reality. I love theory. I just worry that it will just be more postmodern reconstruction with no firm foundation. Is there really any ground to stand on?

The heaviness of the questions and the sheer number of them may burden the mind and bewilder the spirit.

Positive Stirrings

Alternatively, you may hear these stirrings:

These questions are not discouraging. They are questions that deserve our attention, that are worthy of thoughtful and serious inquiry. We need to probe more of these intellectually challenging puzzles directly. Otherwise our leadership practice will be reduced to technique; it will not rest on a foundation of rich, informing ideas. The deeper we go, the wiser we can become, and the wiser and more adept our choices will be. I think that we need frames to understand what is really going on. The more we know about what is really going on, the more insightful and enduring our leadership will become. I agree it looks like a puzzle, but I believe we can assemble this puzzle, even for parts of reality that are unknowable and unfixable.

When we see that Making Wise Choices serves the promise of authentic practice, we want to answer the questions raised by our experiences so we can enhance authenticity. The stirrings quicken a new leadership action: Probing Deeper.

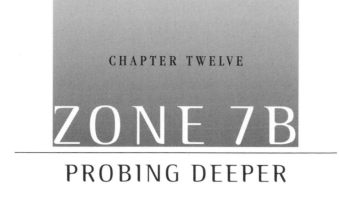

CHAPTER TWELVE

ZONE 7B

PROBING DEEPER

ACCEPT THE PUZZLE; AVOID THE MUZZLE.

Gordon MacKenzie's thirty-year career was spent with Hallmark Cards. As he describes in his book Orbiting the Giant Hairball *(1996, pp. 142–52), he spent three of his last few years with the company as "leader" of a dozen independence-minded creative geniuses in Hallmark's Humor Workshop. Then his boss invited him to shift jobs, to go from outside the established business structure to inside it. What the new job would be was unclear. The boss talked about MacKenzie's being a "burr in his saddle." Was this to be the job of institutionalized devil's advocate? Not a career choice MacKenzie craved. So what would the job entail, he asked his boss at one point.*

"I was thinking of something like 'aide-de-camp,'" the boss responded.

Nervousness and anxiety spread through MacKenzie's body—"I hate that! It sounds militaristic and servile."

"Well, you come up with something," the boss replied.

Nothing came to mind immediately. But while he was jogging one day, a single word popped into his head—paradox! "This is what

I want to be. This is who I am.” Racing home to check the dictionary, he found the following definitions: “1: a statement or proposition that seems absurd, intellectually self-opposing, or contrary to common belief, yet may be true. 2: a statement that is false because it contradicts itself. 3: an experience or thing that seems self-contradictory. 4: a person who exhibits contradictory or inconsistent behavior.”

The boss had no idea what MacKenzie had discovered. “Paradox,” said MacKenzie.

“Could we put a modifier on it?” asked the boss, who loved words and images.

“Like what?”

“Something like ‘Office of the Paradox.’ ”

Too institutional, argued MacKenzie.

“What about ‘Creative Paradox?’ ” They were working in the Creative Division. MacKenzie bought the title. Management, without a soul knowing what it meant— including MacKenzie—approved the title.

MacKenzie was well aware that Hallmark Cards’ public persona was creativity. Share ideas, bring the insights, was the mantra. Yet management was nervous that creativity might get out of hand. Management intellect, writes MacKenzie, “worships the predictability of the status quo and is, thus, adverse to new ideas.” It was not uncommon for new ideas to get squashed in the midst of the rhetoric of praise for creativity. Frustration among the idea-mongers was palpable.

A woman whose ideas had been squelched complained to a friend who suggested she discuss it with the Creative Paradox guy, since he didn’t have anything to do anyway. She did, and Gordon praised her idea. She returned to her own boss, citing the affirmation from the Office of Creative Paradox. The leverage was sufficient; the idea was adopted and made money. The rush to confer with MacKenzie took off. He never bashed a single idea.

He went from nonentity to power figure, without external clout. It was all in reputation. No one really knew where he stood in the Hallmark hierarchy. People started guessing he was powerful and acted accordingly. As he commented: "A number of people assumed I had more power than I actually had. (In fact, I had none at all.) But as soon as they assumed I had a certain amount of power: I had it" (p. 148).

He redesigned his office as a corporate version of Merlin's den, darkening the daylight and replacing the electric lighting with candles. A sculpture entitled "Angel Chair" hung from the ceiling at a 45-degree angle directly above his drawing board chair. Perhaps visitors would conclude he had just slipped down from heaven to share his insights. He changed his voice to appear frail, genteel, and wise. He affirmed his visitors' ideas, and they left feeling encouraged. It was a wonderful job, lasting three years and completing his career at Hallmark. What a paradox—no job description and a title without meaning, yet a job that provided, he said, the most "enriching, fruitful, productive, joy-filled years of my entire career" (p. 150).

CORE IDEAS AND APPLICATION

In Zone 7b, everything is up for grabs. Everything is problematic. Everything is scary. In Zone 7a, we could figure out what was going on and act to address it, even if the events in Zone 6 were unmappable and unknowable. Can we put together a complete map for this zone? In the zone map (Figure 30) on the next page, the wavy line for this zone extends to all the previous zones.

In this zone much looks like a puzzle awaiting assembly. Leadership takes the form of Probing Deeper. It offers the confidence to explore the puzzles, open to what will be discovered and learned. Puzzles not only persist but seem to intensify in today's rapidity of change and chaos. Yet the inquiring mind does not give up. Truth seeking never ends. Maps may be suspect, overall theories lacking, but the stimulus to redraw and reconfigure the map persists and intensifies. Clearly, brick making or research in the literature is rapidly expanding, even when the brick maker or theorist has no building or theory in sight or on site.

The stirrings in Zone 6 tell us that the issues for leadership, and thus for leadership studies, are indeed rich, and deserving of our

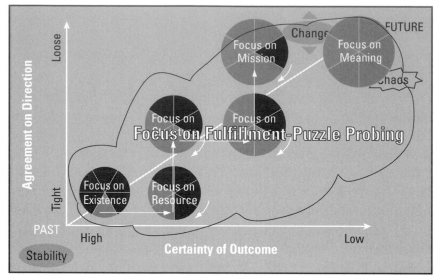

FIGURE 30 · ZONE 7B: PROBING DEEPER

most thoughtful reflection. I have selected four topics or themes to explore that offer some of the most perplexing leadership puzzles:

- The significance of chaos and complexity theory for organizations and leadership

- The meaning of polarity and paradox, and the relationship between these concepts

- The uses of the concept of shadow (especially in organizations)

- The foundations for a developmental theory of leadership

I chose these topics for three reasons. First, because each is emerging as an important issue in the literature. Second, because of their application to and utility in organizational life. And third, because they have the potential to lead us to even deeper inquiry and truth seeking. Moreover, the ways in which they figure in the discussions of individual zones are important in understanding those zones individually as well as collectively.

When leadership is Probing Deeper, the metaphor is *life is a paradoxical puzzle.* The authenticity criterion becomes configuration. We must find an authentic pattern or assembly for things.

For many people, this zone deepens confusion. Not everyone likes theory and broad mapping considerations. Yet, as a truth seeker, if I have a brick, it is only useful if it helps build a building. If I have a view of leadership, it is only fully understood if placed in a comprehensive map. If I have intellectual puzzles, they are only assembled if addressed directly. The parts, while treasures, implicitly connect to a whole. That is *whole,* not *hole.*

If we want to avoid throwing bricks at each other, we must not only understand the bricks. We must grasp how the bricks connect to each other. One can consider each of the four ideas in this zone as bricks—complexity and chaos theory, polarities and paradoxes, shadow, and development. While each claims to be a building or large map, the questions here are: What is each? How do they connect to each other? If we can see the whole puzzle, not just the parts, we will have made great progress in leadership wisdom.

The discussion format changes slightly in this chapter. Since the discussion of each of the four topics addresses both theory and practice, I combine the core ideas and application sections in each topic discussion.

Chaos and Complexity Theory

In many ways, my thinking about zones and maps finds its origin in chaos and complexity theory from the natural sciences and in the thinking of other writers in the field of leadership and organizational studies about that theory. Ralph Stacey's work opened the possibility for me to expand my earlier action-wheel analysis into a developmental framework. Margaret Wheatley's work challenged me to address similarities and differences between natural and human systems, questions of real and apparent chaos, the nature of adapting versus making adept choices, and whether order is a necessary and sufficient foundation for human belonging and ultimate meaning. Thus it is with admiration for, and with the support of, her work and the work of others in this orientation that I attempt to assess the value of these natural-science models for leadership and organizational life.

Two more authors are excellent guides into chaos and complexity theory. Glenda Eoyang's *Coping with Chaos* (1997) identifies core ideas and applies them to real cases. A more comprehensive volume, *Life at the Edge of Chaos* by Mark Youngblood (1997), explores a full array of issues and implications of the new science worldview for leadership and organizational realities—although, as Eoyang says, "The world in which we travel is not only uncharted; it is unchartable. Like a shifting sand dune, it evolves from moment to moment in surprising and unpredictable ways" (p. 5). It is apparent that chaos and complexity thinkers are master mappers. Science is still in the map business. The map just looks different from earlier Newtonian maps and thereby suggests different forms of engagement with a different kind of world.

If you want to read about the actual history of the science of chaos, I recommend *Chaos: Making a New Science*, by James Gleick (1987). For complexity theory, turn to M. Mitchell Waldrop's *Complexity: The Emerging Science at the Edge of Order and Chaos* (1992).

What, then, are the core concepts that kick in when reality shifts from a mappable Newtonian-physics world to an unchartable quantum-physics world? The most common term is one we have already explored—*complex adaptive systems* (Chapter Six). Let me repeat Stacey's compact definition here:

> A complex adaptive system consists of a number of agents interacting with each other according to schemas, that is, rules of behavior, that require them to inspect each other's behavior and adjust their own in the light of the behavior of others. In other words, complex adaptive systems learn and evolve, and they usually interact with other complex adaptive systems. They survive because they learn or evolve in an adaptive way: they compute information in order to extract regularities, building them into schemas that are continually changed in the light of experience. (Stacey, 1996, p. 28)

Such systems seem to make up the large map of a complex world. There are other terms, however, that also inform the new perspective: butterfly effects, boundaries, transforming feedback, fractals, attractors, self-organizing, coupling, and emergence. Let's look briefly at each.

Butterfly effects. All of us have most likely experienced the following situation: A person in a meeting makes an offhand comment. The consequences are immense. One wonders how such a little trigger could evoke such a huge response. This is the butterfly effect. Positive effects can be encouraged; negative ones discouraged.

Boundaries. We explored boundaries in Zone 3a with the introduction of systems thinking. Without boundaries, there is no possibility of perception. Go into a cave, have the lights shut off, and you can perceive nothing. Once boundaries of light and dark are re-moved, nothing can be seen.

Transforming feedback. In complex systems, information flows back and forth between sender and receiver. As we saw earlier, this feedback can be negative or positive. Organizational development and early systems thinking stressed negative feedback, which re-turned the system to equilibrium. Complexity theory stresses positive feedback, which opens the possibilities for new emergent realities and leads toward transformation.

Fractals. Youngblood (1997) tells us that "Benoit Mandelbrot, one of the framers of 'chaos theory,' coined the term *fractal* to describe patterns in nature that repeat themselves at different levels of magnification or complexity. . . . You can see fractals in the pat-terns of clouds, rivers, leaves, broccoli, and snowflakes. The fractal pattern is self-similar in that it is always recognizable, but never the same" (p. 49). And Stacey (1996) takes the idea into organizations, saying that fractal "refers to behavior that 'fractures' so as to produce self-similar copies of itself. It is found in the phase transition between the stable and unstable zones of operation of a system and is a form of bounded instability" (p. 288).

In the zone map, each zone is a fractal. The structured format of the fractal is the action wheel. All seven aspects of action are im-plicit in each zone.

Attractors. Apparent randomness takes on order when one steps far enough back from the details to discern a pattern. These patterns are labeled *attractors*. Remember the research that identified patterns in high-, medium-, and low-performance teams (Chapter Six)? The researcher was tracking attractors and using the pattern to frame pos-sible consulting interventions that would encourage greater team effectiveness. Eoyang (1997) outlines three attractors—point, peri-odic, and strange. In a point attractor, all activities of a system move toward a single point. That point could be obedience to a law or company policy, for example. Shared vision is a point attractor. Periodic attractors are regular behaviors that occur at regular time intervals, be they timed traffic lights, regular elections, or seasons of the year. Strange attractors appear to be random, but when placed in a larger context the behaviors take on a discernible pattern. The team research demonstrated locating random attractors.

Self-organizing. When complex adaptive systems become sufficiently disorderly and disorganized, they reorder themselves. By understanding this phenomenon, managers and leaders can recognize, encourage, and support self-organizing. Stacey sees self-organizing as the source of organizational creativity if it is not dampened and controlled. Of course, self-organizing cannot be controlled. Such efforts only drive creativity underground. Self-organizing teams, as described in Chapter Six, are different from self-directed teams. A self-directed team is created and terminated by an external authority; a self-organizing team is created and terminated by its members.

Coupling. Coupling links systems to each other. It can be tight or loose, excluding or including parts of each system. Systems can also be uncoupled, having no connection. Tight coupling is often found between equal parts that have strong power relationships with each other, such as labor and management. Loose coupling gives influence to many more parties and exhibits an easier flow of power when power has less to do with control and pressure and more to do with influence. Uncoupled systems go their own ways. Eoyang recommends loose coupling as the most effective type of organizational connection (p. 190).

Emergence. As systems interact, new realities blossom forth. They emerge and create new realities amid old systems. Efforts to control the emergence serve only to reduce it. "The intricate properties of complex systems emerge at the edge of chaos. Such systems self-organize—no kind of technique (control) can put them together. They have an unanalyzable, holistic dynamic of their own," writes Danah Zohar in *ReWiring the Corporate Brain* (1997).

With these concepts in front of us to help us delineate, what are the strengths and weaknesses of chaos and complexity theory for leadership and organizational life? While both are crucial, complexity seems more relevant to everyday organizational life than chaos. Since chaos is apparent, complexity takes over. I believe that most leadership and organizational theorists who apply these theories apply them to leadership in Zone 3b—Affirming Shared Identity. As I noted in Chapter Six, this is the zone where the sense that the world contains chaos and complexity begins to impinge more strongly on leadership action. So even though the ideas of chaos and complexity are important to later zones as well, the discussion here about the limits to the theory focuses on theorists who live in Zone 3b.

I spent a day at the Complexity Consortium with complexity advocates, learning from them and sharing the zone model. I was struck by attitudes toward three topics: vision, ethics, and evil.

In a conversation with Glenda Eoyang, I mentioned vision statements. Her response was that "vision statements themselves are a waste of time. They do not direct the company into the future. They can be useful when they create conditions for ongoing conversations and dialogue." On reflection, I decided this view made sense for leadership in Zone 3b, not in Zone 5.

I believe she was essentially saying beware of vision when it functions as a point attractor. Too much focus on one vision can reduce creativity and suppress strange attractors. Point attractors are most effective when a short-term project requires a small team to accomplish it with limited resources, when a fairly homogeneous group takes on a task, or when "the organization has clarity around the focus and mixed messages are few and far between" (Eoyang, 1997, p. 113). In contrast, periodic attractors offer stability, reinforced by rituals, celebrations, and shared understanding of repeated actions. Strange attractors trigger creativity in diverse workforces because the boundaries for new ideas remain open. "The key to success is to be sure your organization incorporates multiple attractors and to ensure the attractors harmonize with each other according to the shifting needs of the corporation, its employees and customers. . . . Each [attractor] serves its purpose, and all work together to form a dynamic and adaptive pattern of macroscopic behavior" (Eoyang, p. 117).

The organic metaphor is alive and well in most applications of chaos and complexity theory to leadership. Affirming shared identity is the critical understanding of leadership when this metaphor is present. Command-and-control leadership fails to address the deeper desires of member belonging. Viewed from Zone 3b, shared vision not only offers direction; more important, it secures meaningful connections. According to Youngblood (1997):

> A shared vision should carry a sense of destiny, of hopes and dreams, of the organization's unique place in the world. People are inspired by participating in something important, something from

which they can derive personal meaning and satisfaction. Chester Barnard, past CEO of New Jersey Bell, captured this thought perfectly: *People want to be bound to some cause bigger than they, commanding, yet worthy of them, summoning them to significance in living.* (p. 139)

Authentic membership results from internalization of the big picture of the organization. External authority ceases to work well as shared internal belonging takes over. As we saw in Chapter Six, reflecting on the business you are in, the organization's core values, and living these values in your toes is pivotal for identity. It is no wonder then that Wheatley links spirituality to chaos and complexity theory. Finding one's place in the universe, discerning order in chaos, and dancing to a profound belief in coherence all reinforce and magnify the organic, living system metaphor of life. This imagery opens a new platform of possibility for human understanding, knowledge, and action in a complex and chaotic world.

Does the organic metaphor limit the view of complexity thinkers in the same way that the *life is a machine* metaphor limited the view of Newtonian physics advocates? If so, then the organic metaphor, instead of being a platform for really new thinking, traps the thinker into reducing everything to the organic worldview. Organic thinkers face the dilemma of reproducing the very thing they resist. Adaptive systems are not necessarily adept; human agency, if purely organic, ultimately collapses into an accommodating mode of action with the rest of nature. Stacey understands the dilemma, and still supports an adaptive mindset. My puzzle for organic thinkers is this: What is the downside of the organic metaphor? What parts of life can it not handle well?

Ethics was the second topic that I raised during my work with the Complexity Consortium. Is there a place for ethics in applying complexity and chaos theory to leadership and organizations? Again, I was taken aback by many participants' resistance to the deeper questions of ethics as worthy of attention. They seemed to want to focus on living processes and eschew ethics that might act as a formal restraint on the dynamism of connected interaction. "Complexity just 'is,'" they seemed to say. "Do not go to ethics and wrestle with 'ought.' There is no simple path from 'is' to 'ought.' Is and ought are separate realms, and one does not generate the other."

Talk about values was tolerated because values appeared diverse and flexible. Ethics appeared formal and uncompromising. My argument that ethical principles were inherent in the process of showing up and engaging in life made little sense to most participants. In addition, in complexity theory, great value is placed on diversity—of people, cultures, and systems. The concept of *universal ethical principles* appeared to be a threat to this deeply held value. Yet complexity advocates support the concept of ecological sustainability and respect for all parts of the system. A passion for justice, for the fair treatment of all people and parts of nature, and for constructive and creative adaptive work to make the system whole lurks just beneath the surface. Maybe a fear of form makes them prefer to avoid calling these implicit values *universal ethical principles*. The traditional skeleton of ethics has become arthritic and the inherited principles too rigid for a complex, dynamic world.

However, ethical reflection and principles do not have to be understood as external to human engagement with life. In my view, the principles are inherent in the engagement of diverse people. The principles tied to each zone metaphor, when linked together and coupled with the criteria for authenticity, form what I think are universal ethics discerned from within the human enterprise itself. That is, they are implicit from within, not from on high. At a deeper level, they are not even commands. They are expressions of what is already inherent in human action itself. Sacred history, freedom, justice, participation, caring, and responsibility are not imposed abstractions. They are the principles that inform, support, and release the human spirit in the cosmos. To counter or ignore them is to destroy humanity and ravage nature.

Perhaps the organic metaphor itself creates limits to perceiving ethical principles. Notions of emergence, of new realities arising from complexity, fight against the perception of ethical principles that purport to control behavior. Yet the whole point of utilizing the chaos and complexity framework in relation to human beings and their organizations is to propose specific approaches to life, framed from within the organic, living-systems mindset. Does it go far enough to grasp the depth and breadth of the human enterprise? Can the organic metaphor probe the full human condition?

Wheatley collapses human beings into the organic natural system; we are one part of nature. Stacey connects us, too, yet also distinguishes us from, other living systems. Fritjof Capra appears to vacillate, advocating our deep connection to ecology yet contrasting the self-consciousness of human beings and the consciousness of animals. In my view, the living-systems frame is necessary yet insufficient to a full grasp of human life. Using only one metaphor limits our framing. Ironically, those who apply chaos and complexity theory to human life, while explicitly challenging the Newtonian worldview as excessively limiting and restricting our understanding of the world, are themselves proposing a restrictive perspective.

Life is a living system. Human beings are living systems *and much more*. Let me repeat my question: If *life is a living system* is a metaphor as *life is a machine* is a metaphor, what are the limitations? This is something we must discuss to understand fully this or any metaphor for life.

If the attempt to discuss ethics created unease at the complexity conference, my introduction of the third topic created bewilderment. I asked questions about evil. Stunned looks spread through the room. Evil is an alien concept to a world seen through a living-systems metaphor. We need to ask: Does nature contain evil? Or are only human beings capable of evil? If nature can be evil, finding our spiritual home in the web of life may not offer comfort to our deepest spirit. If evil is only human, then the organic metaphor severely limits our inquiry and struggle with the realities of atrocities, like the Holocaust or the war in Kosovo.

The concept of complex adaptive systems making up the world seems empty of serious content when the threat of meaninglessness and despair rips to the heart of any implication that order can come out of chaos. In the presence of evil, no matter how far we step back to search for attractors, none readily emerges. We face the stark reality of disorder and real chaos. The biblical world of Job is not desired, yet it overwhelms us and raises the most fundamental questions about the nature of the universe, the existence of suffering, and the human predicament. Zone 3b inquiries do not go and cannot go where the world is unknowable and, at times, savage. It is leadership in Zone 6 that lives not at the edge of chaos but in its very midst. Ethics are necessary yet not sufficient to survive and thrive in Zone 7. This reality opens the next puzzle.

Polarity and Paradox

An amazing phenomenon is occurring in the business literature. Collins's new study on leaders living a paradox reinforces the focus. Books on polarities and paradoxes are popping up all over the place. I used to think that paradox was the province of philosophy and theology. Now the ideas are penetrating the business world. The story at the beginning of this chapter illustrates the point. Why this new attention to polarities and paradoxes? M. Scott Peck (1997) offers this provocative thought:

> I believe that those who subscribe to the notion that there are easy answers—a single reason for everything—actually promote simplism and intellectual bigotry. I have found, in my wide travels, that wherever I go such bigotry is the norm rather than the exception. If we assume that there is a reason for everything, naturally we go looking for *it*—and dismiss all other possibilities that potentially conflict with *it*—when we should be looking for *them*. . . . To think and act with integrity requires that we fully experience the tensions of competing thoughts and demands. It requires that we ask the crucial question: Has anything been left out? It requires us to look beyond our usually simplistic illusions and assumptions to try to discover what is missing. (pp. 57, 59)

Consultants at PricewaterhouseCoopers came to a similar conclusion after they interviewed senior executives about the most knotty management and leadership issues they faced. The consultants found that "managers are pushing technique and theory to an extreme, when what they need is a better synthesis of facts and ideas, a better integration of seemingly conflicting concepts—and better balance." They found that managers "achieving the highest levels of performance do so through deftly *balancing* the conflicting demands or 'tensions' created by the paradoxes inherent in developing, operating, and continuously transforming any large enterprise." And they concluded that to manage chaos and complexity, managers must engage in "managing paradox itself" (Price Waterhouse Change Integration Team, 1996, pp. 6–7).

A Polarity Example

Let me illustrate with another story. I was presenting a leadership seminar to a regional educational association. They had wanted to practice using the authenticity action wheel, so I administered the wheel instrument to get a reading of their collective perceptions of their organization. Almost to a person, they agreed that the two critical issues for the association were "mission" and "structure." My next question was obvious: "What is your mission?"

"We are here to serve children," was their reply.

The answer surprised me, after I thought about it for a minute. I said, "Really! If that is so, what are you doing here? Why are you not with the children? I don't think what you said is the total truth. Aren't you here to both serve children *and* serve your members?"

Quiet swept over the room. Then I reflected out loud: "The genius of organizations is to live a polarity identity. The challenge is to figure out how to embrace two conflicting truths simultaneously and fully, and thereby embody the deep wisdom of the polarity." Later I learned the members had just emerged from a reinventing process in which the organization had shifted from a member-focused to a child-focused mission. At the deepest level, they knew this shift, while absolutely necessary, was still inauthentic. They had to figure out how to structure themselves to serve both constituencies simultaneously and fully. The one hundred members at the seminar spent two days struggling with the polarity. Finally, they saw nowhere to go if they were to be authentic.

Regional associations now own a paradoxical commitment—serve children *and* members. The association is now working to embrace the paradox and serve both groups fully. Their current struggle is to build an infrastructure that arises authentically from the paradox. For example, most of the organizational structure was committed to members, to teachers. Now the organization had to figure out how to deal with teachers who were not serving children well. Peer review, already underway in initial planning, was affirmed. If poorly performing teachers hurt children's progress, educational associations must set up methods to improve their performance or terminate their employment. Paradoxes are not easy to live or to lead. Yet, when affirmed, the truth of both sides carries the day. Soon the vision will become the identity.

Consider this example from the business literature. In *The Discipline of Market Leaders*, Michael Treacy and Fred Wiersema (1995) identify three options for market focus—operational excellence, product leadership, and customer intimacy. They suggest that a business asks for trouble when it tries to emphasize all three or even two of these approaches equally. Yet the polarity dynamic/form seems present here. Operational excellence places form over dynamic; product leadership reverses the order by placing dynamic over form; and customer intimacy places form and dynamic side by side. I have worked with some businesses that have lived the paradox in accepting this polarity and focused on all three approaches. Are there tensions? Absolutely. However, the executives knew that all three approaches were present and must be connected. Operational excellence acts as a reliable foundation of reliable delivery of product or service. It goes after larger market share (Zone 3). Product leadership pushes the boundaries of possibilities. It goes after opportunity share (Zone 5b). And customer intimacy engages customers in emerging relationships. It innovates (Zone 6). If an organization is to be robust for the long term, all zones deserve attention. Organizational leadership tackles the challenge of integrating each of the parts into a workable whole without destroying the parts, thus engaging paradoxically with another polarity—part/whole.

Distinguishing Polarity and Paradox

The concepts of paradox and polarity are often used interchangeably. However, leadership can benefit from understanding the distinction between them. Polarities focus outside of the player, identifying opposing forces that are interconnected and never disappear, such as part/whole, inside/outside, and over/under. The deep truth rests in the idea that polarities exist, are real, and never disappear. They are worthy of leadership attention. Anyone who focuses on one half of a polarity is certain to experience arguments on the other side. For example, if you focus on color consciousness, it is guaranteed someone will argue for color neutral. President Clinton erred by putting only color consciousness people on the racism taskforce. The other side surfaced, challenging affirmative action and worrying about playing a victim card. The President could have put both sides of the polarity on the taskforce. Let the fight be inside the group.

Paradoxes are more difficult to define. Paradoxes engage us in the very act of experiencing them and thus trigger a reaction immediately. For example, if I say, "I am lying to you now," what does that trigger in you? You are experiencing the contradiction as you hear it. It grabs you and will not let you go.

Polarities offer more possibilities of dispassionate reflection and thoughtful action. As we shall see, there is a way to lead in and through polarities. In contrast, paradoxes demand action, penetrate one's inner being, and, at times, drive one crazy. It is no accident that the leadership literature, while using the word *paradox*, really means *polarity*. We will focus mostly on polarities until the last zone. Then we will experience the insanity of paradox. Now let us examine each term in more detail.

Barry Johnson (1992) offers the clearest definition of polarity that I have found: "A polarity is the possession or manifestation of two opposing attributes, tendencies or principles that are interdependent. They identify a relationship that is ongoing and raise issues that do not go away" (p. 81). A polarity is not a simple either/or dilemma or decision. A choice between McDonald's and Applebee's for lunch is not a polarity because once the decision is made, the issue goes away. Nor is a polarity a continuum. It is not solvable by spacing options out on a line and making the optimum choice. Polarities affirm the full truth of both sides simultaneously. Nor is a polarity a compromise. It is not some of one side and some of the other. Are you sort of a team member and sort of an individual? No, you are fully a team member and fully an individual at the same time.

Because polarities cannot be resolved, because we cannot dismiss one side or meld the two sides into something new and comprehensive, they can only be managed. The contrary pulls and pressures never cease. Leadership lodges in finding ways to affirm and live both poles fully and simultaneously. This is no small feat because it involves living the paradox that results from accepting the polarity.

Quinn and Cameron (1988) have assembled the most provocative and difficult text on the topic of paradox. It is upon their work that Stacey (1996) launched his discussion of this phenomenon. Quinn and Cameron describe a paradox as a real or apparent contradiction between two claims that are equally thought through and believed truth. One side or the other standing alone creates no problem. Place them side by side, and they represent contrary or contradictory claims. So far this sounds like a polarity. Then the authors move onward into the often-used historical example of a paradox, that of the liar, studied by the Megaric philosophers around 400 B.C.

If someone says, "I always lie," how are we to understand this statement? It seems both true and false.

There are three criteria for a semantic paradox. First, any paradoxical statement is self-referential. It is true to itself. "This is a sentence" is an example. Second, the statement is contradictory. For example, "This sentence is written in Chinese." And third, the logic leads to a vicious circle: "Never say never." "I am lying." "Please ignore this statement." "The following statement is false. The preceding statement is true."

No wonder no one wants to deal with paradoxes. They drive us crazy when we try to unwrap the logic buried in them. Most religions rest on paradoxical principles—yin/yang, God as other/God as present, Jesus as fully God/Jesus as fully human.

Paradoxes are not ironies. Irony occurs when unexpected or contradictory outcomes arise from an event. It is ironic, for example, that federal agencies that President Reagan tried to disband now occupy the building named after him. Paradoxes are not aberrations or discontinuities from past patterns. Nor are they dilemmas that reflect uncertainty over which of two or more attractive (or unattractive) alternatives should be chosen. Nor are paradoxes reducible to conflicts that perpetuate one alternative at the expense of others.

Much of the writing on framing and reframing mentioned in Zones 5b and 6 offers skilled approaches to addressing a number of apparent polarities. I am more taken by the fact that at the deepest level, the issues do not go away. Johnson and Stacey understand that reality and I agree with them. Thinkers in the Far East are inculcated with both/and thinking. We in the West are just beginning to understand the power and insights for business and other organizations that learn to embrace polarity and paradoxical thinking.

Leading Through Polarity

What does it take to lead through a polarity? With the help of Johnson, I have identified twelve steps.

1. Identify the polarity at issue. For the educational association, the underlying polarity was other/self. For many people it is individual/team.

2. Frame the pros and cons on each side of the polarity, using a matrix like that in Figure 31.

Write the terms of the polarity in the narrow horizontal boxes on the matrix. For the educational association it was advocacy of children (other) on the left-hand side (L), advocacy of members (self) on the right-hand side (R). It does not matter which side gets which half of the polarity. Then fill in the four quadrants with the minuses and pluses—L+, L–, R+ and R–. If educational associations focus just on children, what is the good news and what is the bad? If they focus on members, what is the good news and what is the bad? This method reduces tension and gets all the arguments on the table. The association members came up with twenty statements per quadrant. It was the best work I had ever seen in framing a complex issue.

3. Figure out which lower (bad news) quadrant is most problematic for your organization. The regional education association had been responding to the downside of member advocacy. The organization was perceived as too self-serving, ignoring kids, defending bad teachers, etc. When the polarity in question is individual vs. team (part/whole), most organizations are worried

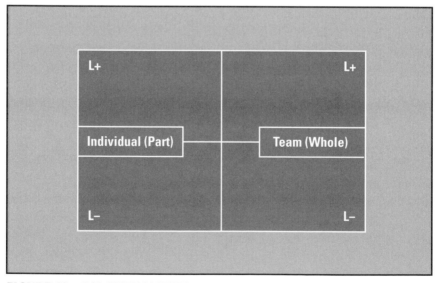

FIGURE 31 · POLARITY MATRIX

about the downside of focus on the individual: too many silos, not enough communication, etc.

4. Identify the upper (good news) quadrant that the organization is moving toward to address the concern. It is usually on the diagonal from the bad news quadrant. The education association was moving from the downside of member advocacy to the upside of children advocacy.

5. Understand the dynamic of the infinity loop (Figure 32). The issue raised by a polarity never goes away. If we begin in the lower right quadrant of the matrix, the solution goes to the upper left. Soon someone will wonder why we're paying so little attention to the view on the right. Now the issue drops down to the lower left. Then we look for the solution in the diagonally opposite quadrant. And guess what—soon the issue will drop down again. The pattern is that of the symbol for infinity. It never ends; there is no ultimate solution.

6. Keep your managerial and leadership attention above the halfway line; it's best to minimize the downside of the infinity loop.

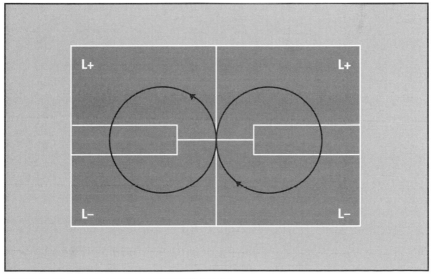

FIGURE 32 • POLARITY INFINITY LOOP

7. *To lead and manage, anticipate the necessary move to the opposite quadrant above the line.* If you are building a strong team, focus on the individual. If you want to be open, admit you are closed. If you want to compete, stress cooperation on rules of engagement. If you want to serve children, organize to strengthen teachers to do so. I challenged the regional educational association to affirm both sides of its polarity. It was shifting back and forth in an either/or rather than a both/and mode.

8. Understand your own bias. Which side do you personally like?

9. Acknowledge, deeply understand, and own the downside of your favorite side.

10. Grasp the truth of both sides of the polarity. Nondefensive framing releases a group's energy so members can listen to each other and connect on critical issues.

11. Do not attack the weakness of the side that is not your favorite.

12. Build action plans to accomplish the truths of both sides. This educational association now struggles both to serve and to discipline teachers so that children are better served. It makes sure due processes are enforced so that arbitrary use of power is contained and challenged.

Leading in Paradox

Now let us shift to paradox. Stacey (1996) links paradox with creative thinking. He reports on a study of fifty-eight famous creative artists and scientists, including Einstein, Picasso, and Mozart. They shared a common pattern: all breakthroughs occurred "when two or more opposites were conceived simultaneously, existing side by side—as equally valid, operative and true." The research concluded: "In apparent defiance of logic or physical possibility, the creative person consciously embraced antithetical elements and developed these into integrated entities and creations" (p. 66).

Paradox forces people to think differently. The worlds understood in Zones 6 and 7 are upon us. A different meaning of dialectic is upon us. Debate separates us, dialogue connects us, and dialectic unites us within opposition. Imagine being a vice president of creative paradox. The more I work with professionals like lawyers, clergy, doctors, business executives, labor leaders, and team leaders, the more I think they are all centers of creative paradox. They all live at polarity intersections. They must serve clients and their business simultaneously. It is a profound leadership challenge and puzzle. Executives live at the intersection of part and whole. They exist to build an enduring organization that simultaneously secures a growing return on investment for stockholders, fulfills expectations of the workforce, serves the community, and delivers a reliable and high-quality product or service to the customer. These parts and the whole are equally important.

As one moves through Zones 5b, 6, and 7, polarity and para-doxical thinking find their home, although they are present in all zones. The quick fixes of Zone 2 no longer work. System focus and identity guidance fail to grasp the depth of the contradictions because of Zone 3's deep belief in natural harmony, connectedness, and coherence. Political engagement often falls prey to either/or think-ing—ups vs. downs. Leadership thats sets direction does not like paradoxes. The conflicts curtail acting toward a unified vision. It is not until the world is unknown and unknowable that the deeper real-ities of contradiction can be faced and owned.

Parker Palmer knows that such contradiction is not accidental. In *The Promise of Paradox* (1993), he reflects on the source of paradox:

> The contradictions of life are not accidental. Nor do they result from inept living. They are inherent in human nature, and in the circumstances which surround lives. We are, the Psalmist says, "lit-tle less than God" but also "like the beasts that perish" (Psalms 8:5).
>
> Our highest insights and aspirations fail because we are encumbered by flesh which is too weak or too strong. When we rise to soar on wings of spirit, we discover weights of need and greed tied to our feet. The things we seek consciously and with effort tend to evade us, while our blessings come quietly and unbidden. When we achieve what we most want, our pleasure in it often fades.
>
> These contradictions of private life are multiplied over and over when we enter the world of work and politics. Here are a thousand factions competing for scarce resources. Here is a realm where val-ues cancel each other out: How, for example, can we simultane-ously have freedom and equality?
>
> In this arena vision yields to compromise, the law of collective survival. This is a self-negating world where even our finest

achievements often yield negative by-products: Medical science lengthens human life only to increase starvation in some societies and draw out the agonies of aging in others. (p. 17)

It is relatively easy to find guides and gurus to take us through the processes of managing and leading polarities in Zone 7, including some I have already mentioned here: Quinn's *Beyond Rational Management* (1988), Quinn and Cameron's *Paradox and Transformation* (1988), Handy's *The Age of Paradox* (1994), Palmer's *Promise of Paradox* (1993), O'Neil's *The Paradox of Success* (1993), and Fletcher and Olwyler's *Paradoxical Thinking* (1997) all offer sage advice and hands-on suggestions. The best at distinguishing is Smith and Berg's *Paradoxes of Group Life* (1987). Palmer is the most theological and a provocative read. O'Neil's work is more personally directed, focusing on what happens when winning at work means losing at life. Handy raises issues located in both organizations and the larger society. The question remains, Are polarities and paradoxes the same? Most of these authors use them interchangeably. I think they are connected, yet differ as stated earlier.

Anticipatory wisdom helps leaders listen to stirrings that may be weak and understated. Polarity thinking sharpens our sensibilities to these stirrings. Leadership grounded in a polarity mind-set gets there first. It is sagacity in action. To attend to one half of a polarity or seek an either/or solution to a polarity perpetuates inauthenticity. So the next time someone comes into your space, asking you to make an either/or choice on a polarity, here is what I suggest you do. Listen. Repeat the call to choose. Identify the polarity. Raise both arms over your head and while you are lifting them say "Yes!" in a firm and commanding tone. Should we concentrate on team building or focus on individual development? Both hands up.

Polarity thinking is a core competency. Rarely does it show up on leadership skill lists. Paradoxical living is even harder; we experience it in the next zone. Now we can explore shadow as a subset of polarity. It will tilt us toward paradox.

Shadow

"It was night in some unknown place, and I was making slow and painful headway against a mighty wind. I had my hands cupped around a tiny light which threatened to go out at any moment.

Everything depended on my keeping this little light alive. Suddenly I had the feeling that something was coming up behind me. But at the same moment I was conscious, in spite of my terror, that I must keep my little light going regardless of the dangers" (Carl Jung, *Memories, Dreams, Reflections*, quoted in Smith, 1989, p. 25).

This statement introduced the concept of shadow to the psycho-analytical community. Carl Jung was one of the earliest analysts of paradox and reality. He explored shadow, placing it at the center of the human condition. Shadow is created by light. Go into a window-less room, shut off all the lights, and you see absolutely nothing. There has to be contrast for there to be perception. Without light, there is no shadow; without dark, there is no shadow. It is only because of dark that light is perceived as light. Shadow lives at the edge of light and dark, making the perception of both possible.

Jung's dream of the candle is a powerful metaphor. Fear of shadow never leaves us as long as we cling to light. Our desperately preserving the flame on the candle guarantees that the fear of the shadow will accompany us wherever we travel.

Shadow as just described is a valuable concept, yet the term carries much additional baggage. Historically, shadow has carried frightening, negative implications. Shadow has related to fear and anxiety and even evil. Moreover, as a psychological as opposed to a sociological category, when it appears in the leadership literature it is connected to the individual leader rather than to leadership more generally. Zaleznik and Matsushita's *Learning Leadership* (1993), for example, links leadership with power. It tells stories of individuals who abuse power, reporting on the negative shadow of well-known leaders.

Because shadow has been linked so strongly to the negative and to the individual person, I proposed and have been using the term *stirrings* as an alternative. This term is an attempt to embrace both the negative and positive aspects of shadow and the individual and relational aspects of people engaged in reflective inter- and intra-dependent action. The polarities and paradoxes embodied in the zone framework apply here too. There is no negative without posi-tive; there is no individual (part and self) separate from relationships (whole and other).

It should come as no surprise, moreover, given the infinity-loop dynamic built into polarity and paradoxical thinking processes, that the preoccupation with the negative and individualistic side of shadow in the business literature is now also giving way to a positive and relational view. Two authors stand out—Ralph Stacey (1993) and Gerard Egan (1994). Stacey highlights the positive aspects of shadow while Egan includes both the negative and positive.

For Stacey, as organizations move farther from agreement and certainty, novelty, surprise, and creativity emerge. No formal bureaucracy can cope with the complexities of life just through rules and regulations. Informal networks are needed and are created to make things happen. It is the informal system, which "operates without the approval of the legitimate system," that he calls the shadow system (p. 379).

There is always the polarity tension between form and dynamic, between Zone 3a and Zone 3b and the zones beyond. Bureaucracies make order of diversity and thereby restrict diversity. While some people find comfort in job definitions and role responsibilities, others resent the limitations and external control. Power issues thus arise, value questions and questions of credibility emerge, and skill training may limit rather than enhance coping with the unforeseen. The request for clearer rules and regulations, even job descriptions, may dampen novelty and increase inefficiency rather than encourage creativity and effectiveness.

Bureaucracies are not good at coping with ambiguity; nor are they good at coping with complex, unstable situations. Hence, the members of the organization self-organize, while appearing to live by the rules and regulations. They collude to create a "mock" bureaucracy (Stacey, 1993, p. 380) that gives the appearance of order and rationality and avoids conflicts that would occur if the self-organizers explicitly took on and challenged the formal status quo and power of the system.

Creating Ownership (Zone 4) captures much of the richness of self-organizing. Persuasion, negotiation, bargaining, and influence rather than command and control flourish in the shadows. Networks thrive as the downs cut across boundaries to make things happen in the ups' world of established order and legitimacy. The voice of the downs is often in the shadows.

Stacey believes that shadow networks are always triggered by some defect in the formal system. And the shadow system is the source of change in the formal system. A new alignment or formal system better fitted to the realities it faces emerges. Stacey observes, "Another way of conceptualising the informal organisation is to think of it as a 'community of practice,' that is, a spontaneous grouping of people who carry out the same task and use their social network to learn informally from each other" (p. 382).

Institutionalized power, or "upness," often seeks to control, if not totally wipe out, self-organizing, which is often depicted as disobedience and rebellion. Threaten the legitimacy of the top, and the top oppresses the bottom. That, of course, further ignites social movements and causes. More insidious is the institutionalization of inauthenticity. Phony empowerment language seeks to give the appearance of belonging and participating but in fact disguises the reality of command and control. *Dilbert*'s laser beam on inauthenticity exposes such incongruities and gives glimpses into the reconfiguration of organizational life that occurs: covert politics take over.

In order to give the appearance of inclusion, negative worker feedback is suppressed and those who give it are marginalized in the hope that morale will be sustained. In fact, the information leaks out anyway. When a manager is fired, the act is portrayed as a resignation and a party is held to sing praises. Is the reality known? Of course. Buy-in is equated with ownership, then when it doesn't happen the naysayers are negatively evaluated—in private, of course. Win-lose situations are set up, and listening is turned into the technique called active listening—say back to the person, in different words, her or his thoughts and feelings, to her or his satisfaction—without really listening or caring what is being said. Managers blame workers or colleagues for defensiveness, claiming it is just part of human nature. When managers use the control model to respond to defensiveness in the organization, strategies are often employed that result in the opposite effect. Writes Stacey:

> Managers struggle to deal with strategic issues. They end up preparing long lists of strengths and weaknesses, opportunities and threats that simply get them nowhere. They produce mission statements that are so bland as to be meaningless, visions not connected to reality, and long-term plans that are simply filed. Or then may decide on an action and then not implement it. (p. 394)

> Managers collude in this behavior and refrain from discussing it. They then distance themselves from what is going on and blame

others, the chief executive, or the organisational structure, when things go wrong. (p. 395)

They look for solutions in general models, techniques, visions and plans. All the while the real causes of poor strategic management— the learning process itself, the political interaction and the group dynamic—remain stubbornly undiscussable. (p. 397)

Egan offers a broader reading of shadow. For him, "the shadow side consists of all the important activities and arrangements that do not get identified, discussed, and managed in decision-making forums that can make a difference. The shadow side deals with the covert, the undiscussed, the undiscussable, and the unmentionable. It includes arrangements not found in organizational manuals and company documents or on organizational charts" (p. 4). In organizational settings, shadows lurk in the background of decision making, reflecting issues that are not formally discussed but are outside ordinary management intervention and often "substantially affect both the productivity and quality of work life in the company or institution" (pp. 5–6). Thus shadow is both negative and positive.

Examples are numerous. The bribery going on behind the scenes in the Olympic International Committee in the late 1990s was negative shadow at work. The manager who hires a relative who has few emotional competencies triggers a negative shadow: employees recognize the person's incompetence but are afraid to confront the boss. Nevertheless, many shadow activities are ethical and add increased value to the organization. For example, workers recognize a boss's ineffective behavior and subtly surface the issue to the public. Egan's book is filled with examples and hands-on activities to address and release the positive shadows in organizations.

Egan understands that shadow-side realities affect everyone. Not only leaders and managers must deal with them. We must all take responsibility for addressing them in particular situations and in ourselves. What does Egan have to say about leadership and shadow? He urges organizations to define and live a revamped image of leadership. It is not headship; it is everywhere and it links to results. He comments, "Any definition or model of leadership worth its salt will emphasize the role of leader as a creator and promoter of the preferred culture" (p. 117). As a creator of culture, the leader can use the power of symbolic acts to make dramatic and lasting imprints.

Egan tells a story about how Lee Iacocca was honored for his part in saving Chrysler from economic disaster. The workers had assembled for a pep rally at a plant. The plant manager gave a short speech and handed Iacocca the keys to a beautiful car sitting on the plant floor.

> Iacocca looked at the key, looked at the car, then said to the plant manager, "I can't take that car." A hush went over the place and the manager, obviously nonplussed, stammered, "But, sir, it's yours, it's a gift, you have to take the car." "Oh, I'll take a car all right," the chairman said, "but give me the next one that rolls off the line." In an instant everyone understood that every car that rolls off a company assembly line should be fit to present to the chairman. (pp. 116–17)

This example used in the context of tapping into the organizational shadow amused me greatly because when I was working in Detroit with the auto industry, I had heard a similar story that made an opposite point. In the late sixties Chrysler executives were advised never to let employees know which car was to be theirs. If they knew which car was to be a company executive's, the workers would build a car that looked great on the outside but would emit strange noises when driven. The assemblers, out of anger and frustration, would leave loose bolts where they would rattle when the car rumbled over the highway. Symbolic actions can cut in both directions.

Egan advocates that leaders translate values into specific terms and live them every day. No inauthenticity. Let workers know which values are acceptable and which are not, and demonstrate what those values look like when incarnated. Asking employees to take risks, even to be courageous, and then punishing them if they "screw up" invites *Dilbert* in with gusto. Managers must develop the competencies to live the preferred culture every day. "Large consulting firms like McKinsey are receiving more and more requests from companies to help them with culture change because the managers of these companies are not *adept* at it," writes Egan (p. 117, emphasis added).

Negative shadows dampen authentic action; positive shadows quicken it. Shadow is ever present as long as there is light and dark. What one does with a shadow depends on the meaning one imputes to the shadow. Shadow is the form of what is behind the scenes; stirrings are the dynamic manifestations of the shadow quickening the impetus for increased stability and/or change. Shadow is one half of a polarity; it is a trigger into living a paradox. With change, we can have development.

Developmental Theory

Configuring a zone model of leadership requires both distinguishing the zones from each other and connecting them to each other. The connections must be such that all the zones are always potentially present in any given moment. During any day, leadership may be called to address all seven zones. The connections also allow the zones to be sequential and to build upon one another. The question that arises is, If all the zones are potentially present, how can they be developmental as well? If we are engaging in leadership in Zone 4, are Zones 1 through 3b behind us and Zones 5 through 6 in front of us? Or are the zones all around us, with any one of them liable to stir at any time? How do we construct a map or model that manages the polarity sequence/simultaneity?

Of the topics discussed in this chapter, developmental theory is by far the most puzzling for me. It is not enough to make choices if we do not have a comprehensive frame that can frame even that which is unframable, like Zone 6. Leadership confronts a tough reality in Zone 7b—*accept the puzzle; avoid the muzzle.* In other words, don't deny the polarity, or mystery. Speak the truth about it and live into it.

Developmental theories face at least four challenges:

- Define the parts of the scheme. In this model I used the term *zone* to distinguish the parts.

- Define the whole, which provides the frame for the scheme. I used participation in, and proximity to, actual chaos as the fundamental frame and used the two variables of agreement on direction and certainty of outcome as the axis on which the zones are plotted.

- Define the connections and drivers among the zones. Positive and negative stirrings serve this purpose, as do polarities.

- Decide whether the developmental model implies that some stages or, in this case, zones are somehow more desirable than others and thus should be targets toward which to strive, or whether each stage or zone is a treasured foundation for the next. Zones combined with stirrings connect these two choices and affirm the foundation model.

In Chapter Two I discussed some developmental models linked to leadership. However, to explain the distinctions and connections in my model I have drawn on other schemes.

One useful concept is that of *holons*, or organized systems. A holon is both part and whole at the same time. As Ken Wilber (1996) describes it:

> It has to maintain its own wholeness, its own identity, its own autonomy, its own agency. If it fails to maintain and preserve its own *agency*, or its own identity, then it simply ceases to exist. . . . This is true for atoms, cells, organisms, ideas.

> But a holon is not only a whole that has to preserve its agency, it is also a part of some other system, some other wholeness. And so, in addition to having to maintain its own autonomy as a *whole*, it simultaneously has to fit in as a *part* of something else. Its own existence depends upon its capacity to fit into its environment, and this is true from atoms to molecules to animals to humans. . . . If it fails at either—if it fails at agency or communion—it is simply erased. It ceases to be. (pp. 21–22)

Each zone can be thought of as a holon. Every zone is both a whole and a part at the same time and must maintain both. Another feature of holons added a further insight for the model. Holons build upon each other. If a holon is not strong, it will collapse on the one supporting it: "If a holon fails to maintain its agency and its communions, then it can break down completely. When it does break down, it decomposes into its subholons: cells decompose into molecules, which break down into atoms, which can be 'smashed' infinitely under intense pressure" (Wilber, p. 22).

The concept of the holon supports my idea that each zone, as both a whole and part, can be a secure foundation for the one that builds upon it, and that if a zone is shaky, it will collapse back onto the zone that supports it. One goal embedded in the developmental model is ensuring that each zone is vibrant and robust, and can serve to launch leadership into the next zone.

Another concept that helps us picture how the zones function both distinctly and in a linkage is that of the *meme*. The term was coined by Richard Dawkins ([1976] 1989) from *mimeme*, a "suitable Greek root," to describe "a new kind of replicator"—something akin to DNA for achieving evolutionary change. "Examples of memes are tunes, ideas, catch-phrases, clothes fashions, ways of making pots or of building arches. Just as genes propagate themselves in the gene pool by leaping from body to body via sperms or eggs, so memes propagate themselves in the meme pool by leaping from brain to brain via a process which, in the broad sense, can be called imitation" (p. 192). A zone acts like a holon. It also acts like a meme. It has skills and ideas and cultural content, and that content evolves into new content for the next zone. Ideas are not only passed on; they change and then change again.

Moreover, the evolutionary change may be considerable. Wilber suggests that evolution may be seen as a "wildly *self-transcending* process: it has the utterly amazing capacity to go beyond what went before. So evolution is in part a process of transcendence, which incorporates what went before and then adds incredibly novel components. The drive to self-transcendence is thus built into the very fabric of the Kosmos itself" (p. 23).

Cowan and Beck (1996) define some interesting and very large memes and locate them historically. For example, they identify a meme they call SurvivalSense; its content deals with staying alive through innate sensory equipment, and they suggest that it arose some 100,000 years ago. A meme they call KinSpirits deals with blood relationships and mysticism in a magical and scary world and evolved 50,000 years ago. The three most recent memes they identify are HumanBond (well-being of people and building consensus get the highest priority; 150 years old), FlexFlow (flexible adaptation to change through connected, big-picture view; 50 years old) and GlobalView (attention to whole-Earth dynamics and macro-level actions; 30 years old) (p. 41). To some extent these large, developmental memes, from earliest to latest, match up with the zones as they develop from the knowable world to the unknowable.

Cowan and Beck (1996) are polarity thinkers. "Self/other" and "inside/outside" set the boundaries for the development of the memes they define. Imagine a pendulum swinging between self and other, or me and we. We think of self, then of other; we go outside, then inside. As we go back and forth, however, our ideas change. Concern for self begins selfishly and increasingly gets less selfish; concern for others becomes individualistic and personally more meaningful. Because there is change, this polarity dynamic, this back-and-forth movement, begins to form an ascending spiral. (Barbara Marx Hubbard also employs a spiral model of development in her *Conscious Evolution* [1998].)

This idea of spiraling upward out of the movement between polarities is useful for suggesting both continuity and change, as it does in this description: "There is a theory that history moves in cycles. Like a spiral staircase, when the course of human events comes full circle it does so on a new level" (Basil Blackwell, quoted in Cowan and Beck, 1996, p. 25). Cowan and Beck also describe how Clare Graves, professor of psychology, has sought to construct a human developmental system in which human beings are seen to emerge and unfold in an "oscillating spiraling process" marked by "progressive subordination of older, lower-order behavior systems to newer, higher-order systems as man's existential problems change" (p. 28). Human beings are not static. They forge new systems, yet the old ones remain. The rules of engagement change in each new system, yet there is no final state to which all human beings must aspire, because values and modes of life differ widely. And "an individual, company, or an entire society can respond positively only to those managerial principles, motivational appeals, educational formulas, and legal or ethical codes that are appropriate to the current level of human existence" (p. 29).

Although I have not shown the zones spiraling in my zone map, this kind of upward progression that builds on and retains the old while adding to it and becoming new is the way in which I envision the connection and movement among the zones.

This continuous process suggests that we are engaged in what is known as "the social construction of reality,", that is, activity in Zone 6. John Busch and Gladys Busch (1992) point out the realities and dangers here, observing that "if one accepts the social construction of perceived reality, one cannot know the absolute truth of the material world" (p. 242). This is, of course, worrisome. Can we reasonably base any action on meaning we have created? If there are no absolutes for truth, is there any escape from relativism? Busch and Busch point to something similar to process wisdom as an answer:

> Instead of worrying about finding some criteria to establish beyond any doubt that we have found the truth, we can merely seek higher levels of confidence in what we suspect is the truth. By constantly trying to raise our confidence in what appears to be the truth, we feel increasingly comfortable acting on this presumed knowledge. . . . Confidence also increases with how the theory or fact meshes with the theories and evidence from other scientific disciplines. . . . An integrated understanding demands an integrated perspective. (pp. 242–43)

This continuous process is reflected in general in the way each zone builds on the next and in particular by the fact that each zone contains its own authenticity criterion. Each zone emphasizes a different standard of truth, and adds that standard to all the standards of the previous zones, in the drive to "raise our confidence in what appears to be the truth." The authenticity criterion for leadership in Zone 7b is configuration. Among other things, this criterion challenges anyone who would build a comprehensive map for himself or herself or in concert with an organization to question its pattern and assembly. Hence in this chapter I am trying to sort out the theories that inform and challenge the zone leadership map.

We can think somewhat further about the way the zones are different yet connected by examining the way polarities and paradox and the authenticity criteria shape the stirrings that move us onward.

Wilber (1996) tells "an old joke about a King who goes to a Wiseperson and asks how it is that the Earth doesn't fall down. The Wiseperson replies, 'The Earth is resting on a lion.' 'On what, then, is the lion resting?' 'The lion is resting on an elephant.' 'On what is the elephant resting?' 'The elephant is resting on a turtle.' 'On what is the . . . ?' 'You can stop right there, Your Majesty. It's turtles all the way down'" (p. 20).

No matter how far down or up we go, we always find holons resting on holons. Observes Wilber, "At no point do we have the whole, because there is no whole, there are only whole/parts forever" (p. 20). Having no point of wholeness can be scary. An endless process of part/whole polarities does not comfort those seeking an anchor point of total stability, perhaps in a holistic creator God and a holistic end to life in a literal heaven or hell or the metaphorical equivalent. (I address this issue in the last chapter.)

The leadership zone map differs from the models of Kohlberg and of other developmental theorists who want all humans to move from stage to stage. Do not remain a low-level moral reasoner, implies Kohlberg (1980); travel to higher levels and leave the lower levels behind. That is the goal of moral education—become a high-level moral thinker and actor. In the zone map, however, we cannot abandon any zone. We must make sure each zone is and will remain a solid platform for the newer platforms.

Newtonians highlight form; chaos and complexity thinkers stress dynamics. If, for example, command and control reemerges in a disguised form as self-directed work teams—a buffalo in goose's clothing—it will trigger self-organizing, a stirring. Leadership in part describes the process of being aware of the zone-stirring linkage, of the polarity of the solid ground of the zone that stirs beneath our feet, and responds adeptly to address the solidity and the stirring at the same time. All the zones are necessary; the stirrings signal issues in the previous foundational zones or invite us to construct the next zone. The experience of chaos can so threaten and terrorize us that we revert and self-destruct. It can also press and invite us to co-create the next paradoxical relationship.

In the zone framework, the propellant for change lives partly within the polarities. Each polarity is a unit in itself and also opens inquiry that thrusts us to the next polarity. Here's a review of the zone polarities. Recall that the three polarities of Zone 7 are emphasized in all the other zones.

Zone	Polarity
1. Serving the Past	Stability/change
2. Building Core Competencies	Potential/actual
3a. Designing Sustainable Systems	Form/dynamic, emphasis on form
3b. Affirming Shared Identity	Form/dynamic, emphasis on dynamic
4. Creating Ownership	Conceal/reveal
5a. Setting Direction	Ends/means, emphasis on ends
5b. Anticipating Change	Ends/means, emphasis on means
6. Creating Meaning in Chaos	Seriousness/playfulness
7a. Making Wise Choices	One/many
7b. Probing Deeper	Part/whole
7c. Living the Promise	Inside/outside and on to paradox

To illustrate, Serving the Past treasures stability as an anchor of life. Yet it also considers change. Its positive stirrings tell us not to let the anchor tie us to the dock but to use it like a sea anchor, stabilizing us and allowing us to move ahead at the same time. Thus the zone has an internal polarity or life of its own. However, responding to the Zone 7 polarities, it also presses *outside* of itself, opens up *many* options, and invites a new *whole* arena for action.

Once Zone 2, Building Core Competencies, emerges, it emphasizes the polarity between potential and actual. The potential in this zone is all the talents and skills awaiting development and use. The more they are fully practiced and others are discovered, the more the core competencies come up against limits. The positive stirrings in the zone, the part, see the connection to the *whole* system, where one set of core competencies is insufficient for the demands of *many outside* complex world systems.

And so the story unfolds. Zone 3 takes on life. Forms get constructed; parts get connected. Then they begin to seem rigid. Positive stirrings quicken the move to a more dynamic system. The attention to one structure now shifts so we attend to the many parts that form what we now see as a living system. That dynamic system surrounds and includes the outside as well as the inside of the emerging new system. And the process continues.

One way to characterize the postmodern age is to contrast it with the age that accepted Cartesian dualism. Descartes split subject and object, the mind from the world. Thus a person could map the world with objectivity; she or he was not part of the world being mapped. Self/world was not perceived as a polarity; it presented an either/or choice. Knowledge was independent of the knower. What was known stood on its own ground, objectively distinct from the knower or the process of knowing. Today, although acknowledging the limitations of this seventeenth-century worldview and thinking that many things are relative, we tend to exclude from that relativity the self that is thinking about itself. The world may shift but the self as a reflective entity persists. Not so, says Wilber (1996). In the postmodern view, thought is not just a reflection on reality but part of reality itself. "In short," observes Wilber, "thought is itself a movement of that which it seeks to know. It's not that there is a map on the one hand and the territory on the other—that's the nasty Cartesian dualism—but rather that the map is itself a performance of the territory it is trying to map" (p. 65). Meaning is created (Zone 6); life is art; map and mapper are not distinct.

For Wilber, the task of philosophy "is not simply to clarify the maps and correct their deviations from reality, but to elucidate these deeper currents from which thought couldn't deviate even if it wanted to!" (p. 65). Drawing on the thoughts of Zen philosophy, Wilber proposes a deeper sense of reality that is nonnegotiable. It just is. Although this is taking us into Zone 7c, I will introduce it here:

> In Zen there is a saying, "That which one can deviate from is not the true Tao." In other words, in some ways our knowledge is indeed a matter of correcting our inaccurate maps; but also, and at a much deeper level, there is a Tao, a Way, a Current of the Kosmos, from which we have not, and could never, deviate. And part of our job is to find this deeper Current, the Tao, and express it, elucidate it, celebrate it.
>
> And as long as we are caught in merely trying to correct our maps, then we will miss the ways in which both correct and incorrect maps are equally expressions of Spirit. (pp. 65–66)

It is no accident that I labeled Zone 1 and Zone 7 with "Serving." They connect. Zone 1 anchors in the past, Zone 7 in the present. More on this later. We have explored how polarities frame critical dimensions of each zone and the links between the zones. Likewise, we have seen how leadership transforms polarity into paradox, having the courage to embrace opposites fully. However, behind both polarity and paradox hovers the pervasive stirring to act with authenticity. The demands to find and use standards for the true and the real never disappear, even when denied and discounted.

Here is a review of the authenticity criteria by zone. Again, the criteria in Zone 7 cut across all the zones.

Zone	Criteria
1. Serving the Past	Correspondence
2. Building Core Competencies	Consistency
3a. Designing Sustainable Systems	Connectedness
3b. Affirming Shared Identity	Coherence
4. Creating Ownership	Codetermination
5a. Setting Direction	Convergence
5b. Anticipating Change	Conveyence

Zone	Criteria
6. Creating Meaning in Chaos	Co-creation and connnectedness
7a. Making Wise Choices	Congruence and comprehensiveness
7b. Probing Deeper	Configuration
7c. Living the Promise	Confirmation

These authenticity criteria frame the essence of each zone and also help to trigger movement from zone to zone. Let me illustrate. Zone 1 roots in the richness of history; leadership action meets the test of correspondence, objectively matching up with the factual realities of the past. Zone 2, in contrast, is not past-oriented. Its uniqueness abides in consistent delivery of products and/or services. Likewise, Zone 3a is judged by the extent to which it exhibits effective interconnectedness of the parts, not by the specific delivery of particular skills and talents.

By the time we get to Zone 7, a new set of standards is the primary frame for leadership action. Now each zone is understood as a part of a larger whole. Thus the Zone 7 authenticity criteria can be emphasized in all the zones. Congruence and comprehensiveness are really the practice/theory polarity in motion. Pay attention to the part and the whole at the same time, linking them as leadership practices Making Wise Choices. Configuration presses for theory construction that enriches the practice of everyday life. Confirmation, which we have not explored yet, invites living the deepest, most difficult, yet most hope-filled aspects of leadership.

Ultimately authenticity can never be avoided. Yet we live in avoidance even as we struggle with the reality of what we're avoiding. It is this disconnect, this inauthenticity, that propels action toward authenticity. Escaping the true and real is a short-term strategy. Ultimately authenticity wins out—if not in our lifetime, then in the next generation. The stirrings are all about us, awaiting our listening and leadership. They invite, call, and quicken a shift. If there is too much focus on the parts, our need to be authentic prods us to focus on the whole. If there is too much focus on the inside, authenticity quickens us to look outward. If there is too much oneness, the impetus to find the many is at hand. Authenticity is ever present, providing the impetus for the full expression of each zone on its own within the whole and for the creation and construction of the next zone.

As I present this developmental material to groups, I am often asked if zone leadership equals personal leadership development. I mentioned this earlier. Let me revisit it now in this context. This is a difficult question because there is no leadership if persons do not embody it. However, my answer is both no and yes. They are not the same and they are related. I am trying to show how leadership itself shifts as different realities emerge. Each zone therefore requires a different expression of leadership. And since all the expressions of leadership are important and necessary to address the differing realities, the process of development differs from many psychological development schemes that go from the individual's immaturity to maturity.

Leadership is a set of actions in the world. It is not reducible to persons, professions, or organizations. Yet in this book I link personal, professional, and organizational realities without reducing leadership to any one of them. No one always exhibits leadership, no role or function always requires it, and no organization always justifies, supports, and encourages it. Leadership is a choice, both reflective and, at times, spontaneous. Persons, professions, and organizations move in and out of leadership every day.

This book defines leadership by worldly realities. It explores what is going on and what actions to take. To know what is going on for leadership requires self-knowledge, role and function astuteness, and organizational savvy. Hence, the questions at the end of each zone. They provide initial assessment of the three links.

Therefore, leadership is not reducible to personal development, professional/executive development, or organizational development. Yet all three have their bearing on the living out of leadership every day. The goal of this book is to grasp deeply the breadth and depth of leadership and link it inside, in the job and the organization or community.

Any process that can transcend and include can also repress and destroy. Evil is an ever-present threat to global enhancement. Each new zone not only confronts grave problem; it also creates them. A developmental process that is defined as continuous and evolving raises profound questions: Are we now at the end of the enlightenment period? Is a new worldview on the horizon? Is life unfolding in a new way? Is leadership again shifting in practice and theory?

Could we be poised to destroy ourselves through biological terrorism or attempts at achieving genetic supremacy or just by drowning in information? Is zone movement inevitable? We thought so in the nineteenth century—just before we blasted ourselves with two world wars, the Great Depression, and the Holocaust. Today, ethnic cleansing dominates our consciousness. Terror haunts us. Have we advanced beyond Job and his fight with God in our understanding? We continue to ask, What is really going on?

ZONE IDENTIFICATION AND LEADERSHIP QUESTIONS

Zone 7b addresses the tough leadership challenges of thinking about theory and frameworks. Check out these questions to assess how well your organization and community are dealing with this zone.

1. How sturdy is my organization or community in this zone?

    •   Do we have lively discussions of frameworks and theories so we can understand what is going on?

    •   Do we discuss and assess metaphors for use?

    •   Are complexity and chaos theory part of our assumed culture?

    •   Do we discuss and embrace polarities and paradoxes?

    •   Do we give any attention to shadow thinking?

    •   Do we give any attention to organizational development theory, stages, and processes?

    •   Does the organization have a polarity-based mission?

    •   Are positive shadows adding value to the organization? If so, how?

```
10 |  |  |  |  |  |  |  |  |  |  0  |  |  |  |  |  |  |  |  | 10
Very Sturdy                                              Shaky
```

2. Where is my organization or community currently focusing its leadership attention?

   • Do we need theoretical underpinnings for the work we do and the relationships we develop?

   • Do we attend to this zone sufficiently or is our attention more on concrete problems and issues?

```
10 |  |  |  |  |  |  |  |  |  |  0  |  |  |  |  |  |  |  |  |  | 10
Excellent Fit                                              Misfit
```

3. Am I prepared to probe deeper?

   • What do I think of the strengths and weaknesses of the organic, living-systems metaphor?

   • Do I recognize polarities when I see them? (Can I name a few?)

   • Do I think I can lead through a polarity? (How am I doing it?)

   • Is my daily work living at the center of creative paradox? (How so?)

   • Am I in touch with the negative and positive shadows of my organization? (What are some and what am I doing about them?)

   • Do I sense any stirrings among the shadows? (What are they?)

   • What does my leadership look like from the midst of shadows?

   • Does developmental theory inform my thinking? If so, how? If not, why?

   • What do I think of the analogies with memes and holons? Do they help me see how the zones are both distinct and connected?

   • Am I intrigued with the new realities and worldviews emerging today?

   • Where do I think this talk of spirituality in the workplace and its links to leadership is going to take us? Is it worthy of inquiry?

```
10 |   |   |   |   |   |   |   |   |   |   0 |   |   |   |   |   |   |   |   |   | 10
Ready to Exhibit Leadership                              Not Prepared at All
```

ZONE SUMMARY

Like the other subzones of The Promise of Authenticity, Zone 7b focuses on fulfillment of action as leadership seeks to bring together the best thinking to configure the field of leadership, both in studies and engagement. Leadership now attends to Probing Deeper and struggles with some of the deepest quandaries in the field. Probing Deeper lives the polarity of this zone—part/whole. As we struggle to make sense out of life, to know what is really going on, we face fitting the parts into a greater whole. Do we ever totally get there? No. Is it worth the commitment? Yes. However, the yes is not an easy yes. It takes courage sometimes to probe part of the puzzle and match it with other parts. We often fail to see the emerging picture until the last piece is positioned. Intellectual breakthroughs usually require persistent and thoughtful inquiry. It takes passionate, intellectual leadership. Yet, we trust the promise. Inquiry delivers success and satisfaction.

We explored four topics deeply—complexity and chaos theory, polarity and paradox, shadow, and developmental theory. Each of these topics is rich in content and significance for leadership. Chaos and complexity thinking makes possible an inquiry into the power of metaphors and how they might open the way for understanding organizational and personal dynamics. Polarity and paradox admit some problems cannot be solved. The leadership challenge is to hold many truths side by side at the same time. Shadows take leadership behind the scenes to figure out how to address the negative, destructive forces and release the positive, creative forces. Developmental theory, the toughest of issues in leadership thinking, seeks to build a comprehensive map that unites sequential stage theory and simultaneous experiences of all the stages—without allowing the map itself to limit the stages individually or collectively.

Without leadership as Probing Deeper, an organization will never understand "learning as a way of being," the state Peter Vaill invites us to engage with. Authenticity in this zone sets yet another standard—configuration. Parts and whole must be configured or a map for leadership of the organization can never be created. It is fine to have unexplored portions on the map. There may even be places we cannot get to. They may be opened to us when we least expect to explore them.

Authenticity is still our guide in Zone 7b; however, we have a new metaphor to add to the metaphor for Zone 7a. In the previous zone, life was a polarity. In this zone, life is a paradoxical puzzle. No longer is it enough to understand two interconnected truths that persist and connect. Now leadership seeks to live the shift from debate to dialogue to dialectic. The first separates, the second connects, and the third transforms the connection into an ongoing relationship that never departs and must be addressed. The puzzle offers the inquiry no rest.

Each of the umpires grasps a critical aspect of truth. Umpire one understands Zones 1 and 2. Umpire two understands Zones 3 and 4. And umpire three really grasps Zones 5 and 6. Premodern, modern, and postmodern thinking all contribute to our understanding of the world and ourselves. Leadership in Zone 7b tries to get all in together. It goes a long way. However, the map is not complete. There are still stirrings.

ZONE 7B DEFINITIONS

Leadership: Probing Deeper
Authenticity criterion: Configuration
Metaphor: Life is a paradoxical puzzle
Core ethical principle: Authenticity
Polarity: Part/whole

STIRRINGS

The positive and negative stirrings focus on some large questions in this zone. Does leadership thinking have to take us to these abstract places? Does consideration of leadership really take us to the difficult questions of terror and hope, evil and God? And if it does, are there any answers to these questions? Life is a mess—at times a vicious mess. It is indeed a polarity. To say there is order in chaos may give us little comfort. Must we just cope as best we can, depending on our loved ones and friends, even on social causes, for our meaning and hope? Yet there is certainly much discussion about spirituality these days. Is that perhaps an avenue of investigation?

Negative Stirrings

Listen to this voice reflecting negative stirrings:

> Is spirituality a cover for religion? Is it a cover for ethics? Is it a cover for the common good, whatever that might be in a world of radical diversity? Wilber certainly advocates the organic metaphor writ large. I wonder if that perspective really offers deeper, theological answers? Wilber seems very Eastern. Where does Western theological thought enter the picture?

Recently I was given a copy of *Business Week*. I could hardly believe the stories described in "Religion in the Workplace" (Colin, 1999).

Let me read you a section:

> The big splash at the Young Presidents' Organization powwow in June at Rome's palatial Excelsior Hotel wasn't a ballroom seminar about e-commerce juggernauts or Y2K blowups. Instead, the buzz at this confab of some of the world's youngest and most powerful chief executives was about the shamanic healing journey going on down in the basement. There, in a candlelit room, thick with a haze of incense, 17 blindfolded captains of industry lay on towels, breathed deeply, and delved into the "lower world" to the sound of a lone tribal drum. Leading the group was Richard Whiteley, a Harvard business school–educated best-selling author and management consultant who moonlights as an urban shaman. "Envision an entrance into the earth, a well, or a swimming hole," Whiteley half-whispered above the sea of heaving chests. He then instructed the executives how to retrieve from their inner depths their "power animals," who would guide their companies to 21st-century success.

> Just one of the questions this raises is whether whites are distorting native sacred processes.

> What is really going on? I've read that there's a God Squad. Taco Bell, Pizza Hut, and Wal-Mart subsidiaries are hiring chaplains who

can, army-style, deliver any religious view you want. I wonder if this religion and spirituality in the workplace is just a U.S. phenomenon or worldwide? I was in Amsterdam, Edinburgh, and Manchester recently and raised these issues. All the executives, with two exceptions, did not connect with the theme.

Yet, I am still deeply disturbed by the avoidance of evil in our thinking and in leadership studies. Too much of leadership thinking sidesteps the toughest issues. Maybe it should, because there is no way to address evil that both makes sense and can be included in leadership thinking.

The more I think about these issues, the greater my despair. Not only is there no comfort in finding order in chaos, there is no meaning in chaos either. Evil destroys meaning; it destroys life. I feel helpless. Leadership is not up to the challenge. Life just goes on.

We participate in such small ways that we leave few, if any, fingerprints. We are all so finite, so limited, so small in the universe. No wonder leadership thinking does not go here. There is no "here" to go to.

Positive Stirrings

Yet, even here there are positive stirrings:

Yes, at times I feel despair. Yet at other times I am filled with hope. I want to ground my life in something other than my own mind. It is not enough to create meaning if the meaning comes solely from my head. There are profound questions I want to address and consider. I know this takes us to a very contentious place—theology and God-talk. Yet I see no real alternative if we want to face the toughest personal, social, and global issues. I know I am a co-conspirator in perpetuating evil; I also know I am a co-creator of goodness. I live the paradox every day. Spiritual forces may be real; do they have any character? I am searching for language and sensibility that can confirm my hope and faith in the future. My being is at stake. I wonder too about that fourth umpire. He promised to show up. I wonder what he is about.

In what do I ground my life? In what do we ground our lives? I believe that Making Wise Choices serves the promise of authentic practice. I also believe that Making Wise Choices serves the promise of authentic thinking. Is there still one more place to go? What does it really mean to serve the promise? What is the ultimate promise?

Welcome to Living the Promise.

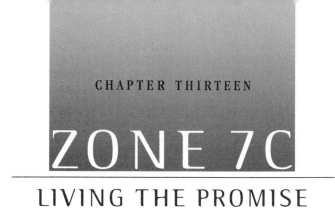

ZONE 7C

LIVING THE PROMISE

SERVE THE BEST; FACE THE REST.

Opportunities to serve come from unexpected venues. I met Jack Fortin when I led a leadership seminar for the St. Paul Area Chamber of Commerce. Jack was director of Wilder Forest, a retreat center for youth and adult leadership development. We immediately bonded and later worked together on a couple of projects tied to his center.

Independent of my emerging friendship with Jack, I had been part of a conversation with a couple of friends who were reflecting about seminary life. They were bemoaning the fact that leadership is not taught in seminaries. Pastors, priests, and rabbis concentrate on Biblical studies, their faith's history and perhaps the history of other faiths, contemporary theology, philosophy and ethics, homiletics or preaching, and liturgical functions such as worship services, marriages, funerals, and pastoral care. There is nothing about leadership, yet clergy are ordained and launched into the world where their primary function is to lead congregations. I myself had been to seminary in the 1960s. My experience was similar.

No leadership taught in seminary education . . . I decided to do something about it, and had no idea what to do. A stirring caught my spirit. I knew philosophy, I knew theology, I knew leadership studies. I had led a social movement. I had led an organization. I had taught leadership for thirty years. I was a natural to do something. What? I had no clue. When Jack Fortin became a candidate for the board of directors of Luther Seminary in St. Paul, I shared my thoughts about the lack of leadership training in seminaries. If he got appointed, he said, he would link me up with the president of Luther Seminary and see what might happen.

Jack received the appointment. He set up a meeting for me with David Tiede, the seminary president. It turned out that Luther Seminary, led by David's passion and vision, was committed to placing leadership at the core of its academic curriculum. Over the previous year, the faculty had written its mission (which we now know as its identity statement): "Luther Seminary educates leaders for Christian communities, called and sent by the Holy Spirit, to witness to salvation through Jesus Christ, and to serve in God's world." One of the things I said to David was that leadership was not in the mission statement. Leaders and leadership were not necessarily the same. The seminary had chosen the positional view of leadership over the "everywhere" view. It had chosen the individual view over the relational view, although seminary theology is highly relational. After I sketched the eight choices, the same choices I presented here in Chapter One, David wanted me to work with him and the school.

"So," he pondered out loud, "how much will you charge us for your consulting help?"

Without thinking, I said, "Nothing. I will serve free for a year." I was just as stunned by my response as David was. I had never committed myself for such a long period of voluntary service. I realized that I did not want money to interfere with my potential contribution. Then I thought, "Maybe David can help me in my own faith growth." So I asked him. I told him that I had dumped much of my traditional faith over the years and, now in my sixties, was struggling to figure out what I really believed and trusted. What promises in life were worthy of faith? David offered to be my guide in faith matters, as I was his in leadership. Authenticity filled the room. We were open, honest, and straightforward. No games or negative shadows lurked in the hallways.

I never cease to be amazed by turns of events and the impact of unlikely connections. The work at the seminary is some of the most exciting I have ever done. My friendship with Jack continues to hum and will endure. My relationship with David is building wonderfully well.

CORE IDEAS

If you thought leadership as Probing Deeper was provocative, at times overwhelming, welcome to Living the Promise. I have saved the most difficult and rewarding inquiry for the final zone. This zone is not just about intellectual mapping; it is about living one's deepest commitments every day, everywhere. It is living a paradox, not just a polarity. Hence the title for leadership—Living the Promise. I like the word *live* for its double meaning. As I live, it can be lively. What a stimulating connection of experiences. *Live* as a verb, as in the leadership title, resides, dwells, embodies. *Live* as an adjective glows, carries interests, is alive. In this zone, both fit.

The new authenticity standard informs and guides *live*. Confirmation verifies, ratifies, and strengthens whatever is at hand. Thus, for leadership as Living the Promise, it incarnates the promise. The challenge awaits us—what promise is worthy of confirmation? In what should and can we ultimately trust? The metaphor *life is a welcoming promise* shapes this zone. Having faith that the promise is really welcoming must be based on some idea or experience. That question takes us to the most difficult place—evil.

Three questions will guide our quest in this zone: What does spirituality really mean? What is evil? And what can leadership do to live fully in a world of both evil and good? This search will press the borders of leadership studies and hopefully will make profound sense to you as you live and lead every day. See Figure 33, on the next page.

Religion

Newspapers across the country reported in September 2000 the Vatican claim to religious superiority. R. Jeffrey Smith of the *Washington Post* gave this front-page report:

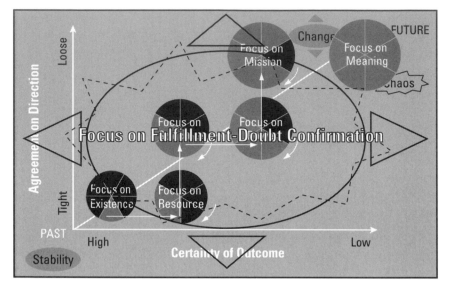

FIGURE 33• ZONE 7C: GROUNDED HOPE

A new Vatican declaration issued Tuesday says only faithful Roman Catholics can attain full salvation from earthly sin, and that other beliefs—including Protestant Christian ones—have defects that render them inferior.

The goal, according to a top Vatican official, is to combat the "so-called theology that Roman Catholics are on a par in God's eyes with, say, Jews, Muslims or Hindus."

The statement drew statements of dismay from other religious groups, with whom Pope John Paul II has sought to establish more peaceful and cooperative links over the past two decades. (Reprinted in *St. Paul Pioneer Press,* September 6, 2000, p.1)

Later, the pope affirmed the report. He played down the superiority claim, stating that he agreed to the necessity for faith groups to assert their central beliefs. Many religious groups claim certainty of truth, even superiority of faith. Southern Baptists are in the same struggle today.

Thus, probably not too many people would want to participate in a religion-and-the-workplace seminar, yet hundreds will show up to discuss spirituality issues. There is a deep belief in many people that religion separates us and spirituality unites us. Religion is often understood in popular parlance as an institutionalization of dogmatic beliefs, narrowly defined values, expected behaviors, liturgical practices, and ancient historical roots. Recently I read a bumper sticker that said, "If you want a country based on religion, move to Iran."

Spirituality

Many authors in leadership studies today embrace spirituality. For some, it's a few words in the last chapter of their book; for others it is central to their thesis. It should come as no surprise that the definitions of spirituality are as diverse as those of leadership. We have more bricks in the brickyard and no building in anyone's mind. My first challenge as a mapper is to order the schools of spirituality in leadership studies, so we can see the pattern. With the map before us, we can then go to the second and third questions about evil and hope.

Spirituality Versus Religion

Spirituality, in contrast to religion, is seen as more this-worldly and grounded in everyday experiences, and is understood as inviting an inclusive mindset. In a recent study of spirituality among middle-aged Americans, Wade Roof (1994), a religion professor at the University of California at Santa Barbara, reported, "In its truest sense, spirituality gives expression to the being that is in us; it has to do with feelings, with the power that comes from within, knowing our deepest selves and what is sacred to us, with, as Matthew Fox says, 'heart-knowledge'" (p. 9).

For most advocates of spirituality in the workplace and in life in general, especially those who are suspicious of religion or who think *spiritual* is a code word for religion, making a distinction between religion and spirituality is crucial. However, we should also be aware that separating the two within any one person may not always be possible. Religious folks talk about the spiritual; so, too, do humanists. No one comes to the spiritual table as a blank historyless tablet. Ask a humanist about her or his religious roots, and you might be amazed at what has been preserved and what has been dumped along the way.

I will be suggesting that some fundamental concepts from religion serve the concept of spirituality. We do not need to have a particular religious view in order to be spiritual; we can embrace theology to help us understand that in seeking spirituality we are seeking something transcendent. First I will outline three other views of spirituality, each of which tells us something important about spirituality in relationship to leadership. Each falls short of being a complete definition in itself. I will return to this topic later.

I do not plan to exhaust the list of authors who address the issues. Rather, as a mapper of ideas, I will offer snapshots of the major camps or schools of thought. I have selected thinkers who, at some level, tie spirituality to leadership. Although each author tends to focus on his or her own view as though it were a full representation of spirituality in relation to leadership, we will see that it is possible to take a more inclusive perspective, understanding each view as a part of a yet more comprehensive picture.

Spirituality Equals Making Meaning

At a fundamental level, spirituality equates with making meaning. All human beings under all conditions make meaning out of life. Jewish writer Viktor Frankl (1963) came to this insight when he battled to come to terms with his imprisonment in a death camp in Nazi Germany. Out of this soul-wrenching struggle, he concluded that he was in charge of making meaning of life, no matter what atrocities life presented. He realized that we seek to understand, explain, and integrate into our larger experience everything that happens to us.

Bill George, CEO of Medtronic, in the foreword to *The New Bottom Line: Bringing Heart and Soul to Business* (Renesch and DeFoore, 1998), advocates a highly general understanding of spirituality in this vein, commenting:

> We are all spiritual beings, composed of minds, bodies, and a spiritual side, whether we acknowledge this portion of ourselves or not. . . . [Tom] Peters cites Frederick Taylor, one of the founders of the science of industrial engineering, for bringing "human freedom" to the workplace. In fact, Taylor's efforts did more to dehumanize the workplace by utilizing workers' physical skills but not their minds. . . . To ask employees only to utilize their minds and bodies, while not acknowledging the power of the spirit which resides in every person not only diminishes their individual gifts and contributions but it limits their ability to contribute fully to their work and their organization. (p. vi)

George concentrates on meaning making, and his reflections anchor in postmodern understandings of spirituality.

In *Spirituality and Society* (1988), David Ray Griffin offers a very broad definition of spirituality connected to meaning making. He says that spirituality refers to ultimate values we hold and meanings we make that may be otherworldly or this-worldly; spirituality may or may not involve passionate commitment to those values and meanings. Spiritual does involve the "Holy" in whatever way *holy* refers to that which is deemed ultimately important. It could be sex, power, or success. Everyone embodies spirituality, even if it is nihilistic or materialistic. Of course, for some reflective souls, *spiritual* is a more restrictive term centering upon finding ultimate meaning and rejecting power, pleasure, and possession as unworthy of ultimate significance in life. In Griffin's societal context, *spiritual* refers to "a person's ultimate values and commitments, regardless of their content" (pp. 1–2).

All human beings make meaning. It has been suggested that some other animals like chimpanzees and dolphins do as well. However, meaning making is more a floor than a ceiling for understanding spirituality. It begins the discussion.

Spirituality Equals Belonging

Current research on vibrant, growing religious congregations suggests that their growth has very little to do with beliefs, homogeneity of members, or particular sacred histories. Instead, it roots in creating a tight definition of membership. Those congregations that presuppose that people are members in good standing, as many mainstream denominations do, are getting smaller. Those congregations that are blossoming are those that intentionally create a sense of connectedness and coherence. There are entrance criteria, tasks to accomplish, or classes to take before the new member and the existing congregation can feel coherence and connection.

Religious congregations are certainly not the only sources of communal fellowship. For an increasing number of people, the workplace has become the primary source of community (Conger, 1994).

Two related ideas permeate the studies on spirituality in the workplace. First, workers feel disconnected from the workplace culture, and second, they seek affiliation and organizational and system inclusion. They want to shift from employee to member and experience the sense of belonging to a larger whole. They are the market that Cress targets in his chaplain rental business, described in Chapter Nine.

Ken Blanchard (1998) roots much of his current thinking in this view of spirituality. He ventures forth ever so briefly into God-talk as a challenge to personal egoism, and he proposes the HELP model: humility, excellence, listening, and praising. He writes:

> Spencer Johnson and I emphasize in *The One Minute Manager* that the key to developing people is to catch them doing something right, so you can pat them on the back and recognize their performance. Nothing motivates people more than being caught in the act of doing something right. . . . To me, our spirituality goes with us into the workplace. If we take and accept the love that is there for us, we can be so much better at caring for, listening to and helping others as well as ourselves. (p. 43)

Michael Hammer (1997) also concludes his thoughts on a spiritual note:

> The recent spate of books and seminars on "workplace spirituality," despite their often superficial and sometimes ludicrous content, bespeaks a longing for transcendent meaning in our daily lives. In our secular age we may no longer see our work as service to the Divine, but we can see it as service to humanity. It is in this sense that John Martin, CEO of Taco Bell, tells his people that serving the customer "has nobility." Serving the customer is not a mechanical act but one that provides an opportunity for fulfillment and meaning. (p. 268)

Senge (1990) uses the term *spiritual* a couple of times to refer to a sense of belonging and to being grounded in values, vision, and purpose (p. 223).

Rarely, if ever, do discussions that equate spirituality with belonging ask what spirituality might mean when we confront ugly, disgusting, terror-based places. They advocate for leadership that has an uplifting, inspiring side. They do not wrestle with concepts of evil or destructive shadows. Not to address the negative is to trivialize the positive.

Wheatley (1996) advocates the most inclusive belonging available to human beings, apart from explicit God-talk. She suggests belonging to the universe, nestling in the coherence of life, finding comfort in the deep belief that there is "order in chaos." Capra (1996) resides here as well, grounding life in "deep ecology." These authors find hope flourishing within this organic, living-systems metaphor. The discoveries of science are seen to justify a belief in this belonging and this metaphor. However, does science offer enough deep meaning that the most difficult questions of destruction, greed, and human terror can somehow be addressed and integrated? I think not.

Spirituality Equals Values and Ethics

In arguing for his view of stewardship as personal accountability and self-direction, Peter Block (1993) defines spirituality as "the process of living out a set of deeply held personal values, of honoring forces or a presence greater than ourselves." Spiritual participation is available to all and is more likely to be experienced as governance systems share power. The goal of stewardship with such spirituality is authentic participation. It is not "using participation as a means of getting people to adapt more cheerfully to their helplessness" (p. 48). A force greater than ourselves does not necessarily mean a transcendent force or God. It may mean any outside reality, most often a larger sense of humanity.

Many other authors build on and go beyond belonging to connect ethics and values with spirituality and leadership. Common values and principles are seen to sustain and enhance a lively sense of integrity and grounding. For example, Tom Chappell, president of Tom's of Maine, addresses this question in *The Soul of a Business: Managing for Profit and the Common Good* (1993). Here, as in Renesch and DeFoore's *The New Bottom Line* (1998), "soul" stands for values and ethical principles that justify and engage one's life in the workplace.

In the organizational and leadership literature, when spirituality appears as a topic of inquiry, it usually links to core or shared values. Senge discusses "core values" (those tied to the business), while most of the authors in *The New Bottom Line* push toward "shared values." When the focus is on shared values, the attention usually turns to the inside of the leader. To be spiritual, leaders must live those personally embraced shared values every day, deeply within their souls.

Three other works are helpful if you are interested in ethical reflection and action as part of leadership. The most thoughtful and provocative is Clarence Walton's *The Moral Manager* (1980). The other two are Tom Rusk's *The Power of Ethical Persuasion* (1993) and

Mark Jacob's *Reality Leadership* (1997). The latter focuses on character formation, a term I expect we will hear much more about in the future.

Although often emphasizing values and ethics, very few writers on spirituality press for a definition of a universal ethic. Core values are the easiest to define and make operational. Shared values can be empirically identified by surveys, and one hopes enough common ground will be discerned to move forward collectively. It is much harder to discuss values or ethical principles that cut across all cultures. We are so aware of diversity that unity escapes our attention. When I suggest the idea of a universal ethic, a palpable anxiety sweeps the seminar room. The fear is that any group that considers a principle to be universal will try to impose it as the only truth or God's truth and use it to justify a new millennium of oppression.

Hence, we have the battle between the universalists and the relativists. While seemingly in opposition, surprisingly they do agree on one deep issue: fear. Relativists fear that any universal claim to ethical principles will become the cover to repress dissent. Universalists fear that if we embrace relativism, we will lose the intellectual leverage to declare an action unethical and wrong. Whoever is in power will set the ethical and cultural standards of behavior. Of course, there is extensive history to justify both fears.

Nevertheless, Rushworth Kidder (1994) suggests that there are some values that everyone shares. He traveled around the world, interviewing men and women of conscience, reporting these shared values: love, truthfulness, fairness, freedom, unity, tolerance, responsibility, respect for life (pp. 18–19). Twenty-four diverse yet thoughtful reflectors all agreed on the values themselves and believed they were important for everyone. Kidder suggests that these values form the platform on which to build an enduring and thriving human-inhabited planet. However, Kidder is aware of the limits of his study, which was based on interviews with only twenty-four people and did not include a scientifically controlled sample. And he knows this is not *the* code of ethics; it is *a* code. Nevertheless, his work does offer a challenge to those who say universals are impossible to discern empirically.

Since this chapter concerns spirituality and leadership, and not ethics per se, I will not venture into a full inquiry into ethics.

However, more attention is being given to ethics in leadership, in part as we all seek things that can unite us in our rich diversity, so I will briefly outline my own approach to a universal ethic. Kidder interviewed people and offered conclusions from an investigative, empirical, inductive method. Others try deductive methods, using logic or historical revelation. Kant, Plato, and many theologians travel this road. My approach seeks to identify universal ethics by a core-value methodology.

First, one has to establish what business we are in as human beings. It will come as no surprise that my answer is *authenticity*. In my earlier work I justify authenticity as the one fundamental aspect of all human beings, even when it is challenged, refuted, or negated by lying. The centrality of authenticity is affirmed even in refutation. To argue against it is to want to be listened to, therefore to be taken seriously, therefore to be believed, thus to be authentic. Authenticity is self-referential. To reject it is to affirm it in the very act of rejection. For a lie to be believed, one has to believe in the authenticity of the liar. Authenticity is presupposed in all we do, even as we negate it. Hence, our stirrings as our world changes are rooted in the quest of and for authenticity.

However, it is not enough to presuppose that authenticity inhabits all actions. We also have to ask, What keeps it alive and vibrant? The answer is the core ethical principles, which support and perpetuate authenticity. Each zone is guided not only by all the authenticity criteria and by one criterion in particular. It is also guided by a number of ethical standards and by one standard in particular. The following list shows the core ethical principle that is emphasized in each zone and also the action that derails that principle:

Zone	Principle	Derailment
1.	Sacred history	Elimination (genocide)
2.	Freedom	Exclusion (discrimination)
3a.	Justice as fair inclusion	Double standards
3b.	Justice as constructive inclusion	Rigidity
4.	Participation	Oppression and abuse
5.	Caring as sharing	Discounting
5b.	Caring as listening	Ignoring
6.	Responsibility	Abdication
7.	Authenticity	Inauthenticity and evil

Thus each zone embodies its own core principle, and the derailment of that principle is, along with the polarities, part of what triggers the stirrings that invite leadership to the next zone. I suggest that these core values linked to authenticity may be a foundation for a universal ethic. In addition, there is the deeper movement of the totality of the authenticity criteria—authenticity itself. Authenticity is a dynamic process, one that cannot be totally articulated in words and images. It is experienced every day in life. That is, it is one thing to discuss being true and real inside ourselves and outside in the world; it is quite another to live it and experience the profound nature of its reality.

Spirituality Equals Theology

Meaning, inclusion, and values and ethics all offer foundations upon which to erect faith and hope. All are necessary, yet all are insufficient when confronted with the twin realities of evil and despair. Meaning-creation, although it does open us to the spiritual question "What is life ultimately about?," is not enough to explain the significance of spirituality. Having a sense of belonging to something is as critical as creating meaning. Whether that inclusion connects us to each other, a community, a nation, the globe, or the universe, the longing for linkage runs deep in the human spirit. Belonging certainly offers proximate, temporary comfort. Yet the stirrings do not cease. Is there more to life than science's vision of universal ecological connectedness and diversity? Shared values and ethics carry the foundation deeper. Not only are we participants in the universe but our meaning is grounded in a nameable set of values, ethical beliefs, and commitments. Life is about such things as love, justice, and freedom. Finding a common ground and binding us to it with passion and hope is what life is about. God or no god, our meaning is grounded in living our ethical principles every day, in our toes. Hence, leadership lives the promise.

Before we proceed, let me offer a few defining words about theology. Is *theology* a code word for religion? For some, theology is the study of the nature of God and religious truth. In this volume, I am separating theology from religion, at least in concept. Theology does indeed ask the ultimate questions about life, pointing to God as the most fundamental reality behind the inquiry. Religion usually offers answers about God more than quickening the inquiry into God. Can religious groups support probing, provocative questions? Certainly. Adult classes occasionally push faith boundaries, asking very difficult questions without easy answers. Then congregational members go to the worship service where answers are presupposed, and usually clarified. Some clergy probe tough questions. Others announce truths.

The reason I want to separate theology from religion is to open the most inclusive inquiry possible. All human beings wonder about tragedies, particularly if they hit close to home. They do not all go to the same place for hope and coping. I want this book to invite all human beings to join with me on the search. To me, the deepest quest is a theological quest. It takes us to the most fundamental place to deal with whatever happens in life. Leadership study does not go there. It ends with spirituality. I want to challenge that boundary. Leadership as Living the Promise is relentless. It addresses the deepest stirrings.

The stirrings do not cease. The questions persist. Can commonly held values, as they are lived every day, offer solace and hope when we are confronted with the reality of evil? Shock, cynicism, fear, and despair are constantly hovering around our desperate struggle to find order in a seemingly capricious world. Someone's youngest child has just been killed in a car accident, run over by a twice-convicted drunk driver. Ethnic cleansing is still being pursued in Eastern Europe. Children are dying every day from starvation. Vicious racism and deadly hate crimes seem on the increase in parts of the United States. Terrorism is a palpable threat to safe and secure life. Religious faiths that pride themselves on uniting people often condemn and exclude nonbelievers. None of this makes ultimate sense. There is no apparent order here. Terror and chaos are always nearby, just waiting to intrude and destroy what we cherish. Meaning-inclusion and values are not enough when we face tragedy, suffering, and despair. They are insufficient resources when we are pushed to the point of madness. It is then that thoughts of a divine being, or creator, surface at a deeper level.

The biblical Job is not alone in confronting God. We all do it when we ask the ultimate agonizing questions about the meaning of life. Is there any aspect of life worthy of our faith and sufficient grounding for our hope? This is the fundamental spiritual question.

It is the question of God. It is the theological question that we all face at the heart of leadership when tested to our limits. Ethics and values do not address the questions of cynicism and hope, despair, fear, and confidence. For leadership to embody and embrace the darkest secrets of life and remain engaged, the most disturbing and profound inquiry into evil and God awaits our truth seeking.

Where one goes with the God question can be as diverse as where one goes with leadership. In Zone 7, these kinds of questions are paramount for leadership because this zone confronts the most comprehensive issues and concerns. As I have said, very little writing in the organizational or leadership literature explores the God question directly. Instead, the authors take the routes outlined.

Maybe the challenge is so profound that the language to address the toughest of issues facing the world and ourselves escapes us. Maybe we are too terrified of the answers to be willing to ask the questions. The challenge is to our *being*, not just our "doing" or "having." Or maybe we are unwilling to admit that we too are capable of causing others to suffer. If a few human beings could pull on brown shirts and black boots to herd other human beings into the cattle cars headed for Dachau or Auschwitz, what guarantee do we have that we could not, would not, do the same, even if it is a different act toward a different group of humans? It is far more comfortable to pretend we are different than to confront the possibility of evil in ourselves. Hitler is not alone out there. We all have a piece of Hitler within us, if Hitler is an image of evil.

If we desire to make wise, adept choices by listening to our and others' stirrings we will have to listen to the deeper spiritual questions that are finding voice in organizations—questions often disguised in safe terms yet pointing to the most perplexing and persistent issues of the human quest. Wise leaders ignore them at their own peril and at the peril of the organization. Ursula King (1997), professor in the Department of Theology and Religious Studies at the University of Bristol, reflects the stirrings well, pointing out that "spirituality has become a universal code word to indicate the human search for direction and meaning, for wholeness and transcendence. In contemporary secular society spirituality is being rediscovered as a lost or at least hidden dimension in a largely materialistic world" (pp. 667–68).

In the workplace, focusing on spirituality, even theology, does not just go to organizational, professional, and personal problems that can be addressed in the other zones. All of those kinds of ideas are behind us. Now the questions go to places much more difficult to address. To embody this process, a group of us linked to Luther Seminary and the University of St. Thomas have convened a gathering of CEOs to wrestle with God @ Work. The cohorts will meet four times this year (2001) for four hours per session and one overnight retreat to probe the deepest issues. Some want to examine religion at work, others want shared values discussions. Still others want to explore the connection of God-talk with mergers, firing, and other everyday organizational issues. "What does Sunday have to do with Monday?" is being asked in many ways. A few push the boundaries even farther. They want to confront their own fears, despair, and, at times, hopelessness. They see the connection between who they are and what they do every day, inside and outside the workplace.

All of these topics will be addressed. Participants will bring real cases to the table for reflection. Peer wisdom will fill the room as they share their core beliefs and insights. For me, the critical issues are faith, hope, and courage as they confront fear, cynicism, despair, and evil. This is not a fit-it mentality. It is an inquiry into the deepest, most troublesome, and most hope-filled and promising reality open to us. What follows is what I will bring to the table. I will not always speak and instruct. I am a co-inquirer, committed to authenticity. For example, if someone surfaces hiring and firing, in my mind, I go to Zone 2. Information is there to act authentically. If the struggle focuses on labor/management fights, I go to Zone 4. That is how this procedure works. I want the participants to explore and get there themselves.

One more example can illustrate how the authenticity criteria work. I was asked if I thought the election for the presidency of the United States was authentic. The questioner was probing the character of the two candidates. Since elections are about power, representation, and voice, the question of authenticity travels quickly to Zone 4. As we shall see, there the issue is participation and ownership. The authenticity criterion is co-determination. So, to determine the authenticity of the election, one must assess the extent to which the election process represented many voices and whether the voting mechanics actually worked to ensure that all voters were heard. Problems surfaced in both arenas—in the many voices dampened and excluded in national debates and in the alleged sidetracking of people of color and others in Florida through ballot tabulation.

Spirituality, Theology, and Science

One way to look at the tale of the three baseball umpires who each proposed a different way of knowing reality—describing the way reality is, interpreting it the way one sees it, and creating it in the way one names it—is as a capsule version of premodern, modern, and postmodern thinking. It also suggests the history of the debate between science and theology.

For much of human religious history God (or gods) and science were not truly separable. The earth was the center of the universe; the how and why of what constituted reality were, ultimately, theological questions with theological answers. With the growth of physical, or natural, science as a formal field of inquiry with its own modes of evidence and thought, the two became separate; the alliance split. One did not need a God perspective to understand how the world worked. As science matured and grew in power, stature, and impact, references to God receded into the background in the scientific literature.

We enter the world of the second umpire—life is not described the way it is but is interpreted the way it is seen and pictured—as theories such as the big bang theory begin leaving room for diverse interpretations of the meaning of creation. One way to view this is that the laws of physics replace the need for God as an organizing force and principle behind the cosmos. Thus the late Carl Sagan, astronomer and atheist, concluded there was "nothing for a creator to do," and thus any thinking person was forced to admit the "absence of God" (Woodward, 1998, p. 48).

For many in the scientific community, faith is still a very separate and private matter, not to be discussed with colleagues and often kept a secret because of the disdain and conflict that would surface if the topic were introduced in a scientific discussion. In contrast, the same discoveries can suggest there is design and purpose to the universe. "Evolution, say some scientist-theologians, provides clues to the very nature of God. And chaos theory, which describes such mundane processes as the patterns of weather and the dripping of faucets, is being interpreted as opening a door for God to act in the world" (Woodward, 1998, p. 48).

Certainly there seems to be a stirring. The view that life is a machine conveys a spiritual emptiness and, for some, despair. Are human beings no more than parts of that machine? Are we just rolling the rock up the mountain, over and over again, with no deeper purpose or importance?

The ancient unity of science and faith—which grounded both Islamic belief that mathematics offered a glimpse of God and Aquinas's use of Aristotle's perspective on nature to uncover the divine plan—fell apart when Copernicus, Galileo, and Newton confronted deeply treasured beliefs about the natural universe and collapsed God to first cause only. Descartes's "I think, therefore I am" split subject from object, observer from observed, exchanging relational perspectives for either/or thinking. Darwin added evolution, countering the idea that human beings come directly from God—no, they come directly from apes.

Einstein complicated the problem further in 1916 by challenging the neat orderliness of Newton's worldview. Instead of furthering the divorce between theology and science, he opened a new possibility of partnership. Later in his life he reflected, "Science without religion is lame. Religion without science is blind." The dialogue was enhanced in 1948 when George Gamow came up with a generally accepted model of the big bang, a theory that opened a space for a creator, and it was also enhanced by the developing theories of quantum physics, including the discovery that light is both wave and particle, which legitimated paradoxical thinking in faith traditions. Affirming that Jesus is fully man and fully God is not as strange as skeptics believe. Science thinks the same way. Note, however, the huge shift in source of legitimacy that has occurred. In the premodern period, theology justified science. In the modern, it has been just the reverse—science sets the frame to legitimate theological inquiry. In 1992 Pope John Paul II apologized for the Roman Catholic Church's condemnation of Galileo. Four years later "he endorse[d] evolution as part of God's master plan" (Woodward, 1998, p. 51).

Woodward sums up the current state of the science-and-theology debate:

Now, at the end of the millennium, religion and science are beginning to talk, though neither answers to the other's authority. John
Paul II consults with his Pontifical Academy of Science—most of
whom are not Catholic. Philosophers of science examine the often
hidden assumptions on which scientific theories rest. Confronted
by dimensions of the world no scripture has encoded, theologians
are discovering a God who resists domestication into any single theory of how the world works. And at the center—still—are flawed
and fragile human beings trying to understand a universe that has
the uncomfortable feel of a home away from home. (p. 52)

If you want to enter the conversation, I suggest Edward Wilson's
Consilience (1998) on the empirical side. He is an admitted reductionist, believing firmly that natural science's quest for fact and theory is the baseline of knowledge. Faith and religion may offer comfort and hope; however, they have no empirical grounding. Science
does. Sacred traditions (Zone 1) are fine. Just remember, he says,
"that our strength is in truth and knowledge and character, under
whatever sign" (p. 271).

On the other side, I suggest Houston Smith's *Beyond the
Post-Modern Mind* (1989) and *Forgotten Truth* (1993). For Smith,
reductionism is the enemy. Collapsing spirit into materialism destroys
the basis of hope and global possibility. Explaining reality by revert-
ing to atoms and molecules and other subparts misses the essence
of life. Evolution, which Wilson affirms, Smith critiques with great
passion.

Stephen Jay Gould's reflections on the dialogue capture the parallel inquiries of science and religion with a playful reference to a
Christian hymn:

Science covers the empirical realm: what is the universe made of
(fact) and why does it work the way it does (theory). The magisterium of religion extends over questions of ultimate meaning and
moral value. These two magisteria do not overlap, nor do they
encompass all inquiry (consider, for example, the magisterium of
art and the meaning of beauty). To cite the old cliches, science gets
the age of rocks, and religion the rock of ages; science studies how
the heavens go, religion how to go to heaven. (1999, p. 6)

John Polkinghorn's *Quarks, Chaos and Christianity: Questions to
Science and Religion* (1999) also seeks to offer both sides without collapsing one into the other. Yet he comments: "In their search for
truth, science and religion are intellectual cousins under the skin"

(p. 100). What he doesn't explore or identify are multiple criteria of truth.

The danger for spiritual life and leadership, struggling with the ultimate questions of hope and despair, is to lock itself into one metaphor. If that metaphor is rooted in the natural order, it should come as no surprise that the possibility for full appreciation of humanity's connection to the universe will be reduced. Neither the view that life is a machine nor the view that it is a living system plumbs the richness of the human condition and spirit. Much of pre-modern thinking lived the gift and machine perspectives on life. Modern thinking shifted, seeing life in terms of living-systems and ups-versus-downs metaphors. Postmodern thinking pushes the boundaries by viewing life as a journey, as art, and beyond.

Now let us return to the second topic: evil.

Evil

The headline grabbed my attention—"Pure Evil." Ethnic violence in an Indonesian region of Borneo Island had claimed hundreds of lives since it began in early March 1999. Malay and Dayak fighters had driven thousands of Madurese immigrants out of their villages. E-mailing his family in Minnesota from the Sambas region of Kalimantan Barat (West Borneo Province) of Indonesia, Paul Geary (1999), a medical missionary, related his experience with this violence:

> Dear family: I am undone. I am feeling empty, without a compass. I know that God is sovereign, in control, and so I am praying and crying, calling out to Him for mercy, as are all of us in this Christian community. All day long, every day since the evil began March 17, the few public buses that still are running pass by on the main road with men on the top, waving various body parts of Maduras who have been hunted and killed that day. . . .

> On Sunday morning, after the worship service, I made a plea to the church elders to become more involved in the conflict, in Christian ways, telling how Christians in other times had responded; specifi-cally telling about saving Jews under Hitler, and Hutu Christians standing up for Tutsis in Rwanda. They listened politely, but said nothing and disbanded without responding or making any addi-tional plans. Perhaps I had little idea how involved they already were, and what risks they were already taking. (p. A23)

If we could be confident that life was fair and human beings and nature itself were continually improving, there would be no grounds for despair and cynicism. During the nineteenth century there was the palpable sense that life was good and improving. The coupling of scientific breakthroughs and Western dominance linked to notions of evolution and development convinced many people in the West that natural forces justified hope. Human beings and societies were evolving and life was improving.

On reflection, we can see the naïveté of this view. The lenses used to cast such a perspective were possessed by those in power or those benefiting from that power. Little was heard from the "downs," oppressed and exploited by racism, sexism, or nationalism. Yet there was that supposed, empirically grounded hope that any problem could be fixed by the joint applications of science and human will. Nature was ethically neutral and human beings essentially good. Material-based optimism was real and a belief held by millions, especially in the West. The East, in contrast, was reluctant to buy into the mechanical worldview yet was very aware of the material successes generated in the West and political eminence that followed. Follow the money and the power. The West was competent, successful, arrogant, and smug. Leadership, locked into a positional, paternalistic mode, trivialized the past (seeing it as a limit to the future), commanded and controlled the present, and sought to determine the future.

Hubris, selfishness, domination, and exploitation were real, yet masked by the visible success. Many human beings thought they were God or God's surrogates. Others acted as if they were beasts, playing out the worst of human possibilities. Then we experienced World War I, the Great Depression, and World War II. Evil reemerged as a category to be confronted. The atrocities occurring could not be reduced to natural explanations, causal laws, psychological behaviorism, or sociology. Why would human beings commit genocide when the survival instinct was the most fundamental biological imperative? Why would white people oppress people of color? Why would men oppress women? Why would nations dominate other nations? Such things had been going on for hundreds of years. How could they have happened again in our time of scientific sophistication and patriarchal goodness?

Is evil somehow connected to our arrogance and/or raw impulses? If we human beings are neither God nor nature, who then are we? What is the paradox? Why such suffering and anguish? Is there any credible hope for humanity and the globe given the twin dangers of the heights of hubris and depths of selfishness? What does wisdom look like in the face of our naïveté about our true condition? Is God the source of evil? Whatever the source of evil, what are we to do as we stare into its ugly and devastating face? In our understanding are we really any different from Job, who finally confronted God directly about evil?

Evil is a name we should not put to things easily or quickly. It should be reserved for the most terrible, most atrocious human actions. For Paul Ricoeur, evil opens a most profound inquiry. In *The Symbolism of Evil* (1967), he analyzes how the experience of evil questions both the origin of the world and its ending. This most difficult and troublesome predicament that we face makes us ask, "Why?" Ricoeur, a phenomenologist who maps the breadth and depth of the human experience, finds that people have developed four different core explanations for evil.

The first explanation is that the existence of evil coexists with creation. God struggles creatively and continuously with chaos. Evil equals chaos, and salvation equals creation. The heart of life itself is struggle.

The second explanation affirms that creation was already completed before humankind fell and evil came into the world. In this view, salvation is the concern of human beings facing human-created evil. Thus the creator rests on the seventh day and the work of salvation persists to the "final day." Creation is good, the fall is bad, and this battle to achieve salvation constitutes the struggle of humanity.

The third explanation goes beyond the creation drama and the concept of the fall. It recognizes the kind of inevitability portrayed in ancient Greek tragedy. Think of Oedipus. If the oracle at Delphi told you that you would kill your father and marry your mother, would you fight with older men and then date older women? Witness the Greek play, and you know evil is coming like an unstoppable train. It is not the fault of anyone in particular. No one is to blame. It just happens. The fall in effect plays itself out over and over in the world. Salvation cannot be forgiveness or remission of sins when there is no choice of action. Salvation then itself is tragic. It consists, writes Ricoeur, "in a sort of aesthetic deliverance issuing from the tragic spectacle itself, internalized in the depths of existence and converted into pity with respect to oneself. Salvation of this sort makes freedom coincide with understood necessity" (p. 173).

The fourth type—the myth of the exiled soul—divides human beings into soul and body. Instead of focusing on the body, this framework attends to the soul, which experiences evil because as long as it is living in the body it is exiled from its creator. At times the exiled soul and fallen human being unite into one myth. Ricoeur thinks that the biblical myth links more closely to the chaos and fall perspectives than to the exiled soul perspective (p. 174).

The explanations suggest that the experience of evil is unavoidable and also that it challenges any mundane meaning. It triggers the most profound questions about the beginnings, endings, and purposes of human life. However, it does not necessarily require a theological term like *God* to address them. So it is not uncommon to read a newspaper article on some human catastrophe that refers to the evil of it without any spiritual connection. Take the tragic case of ethnic cleansing in Yugoslavia. Theological inquiry stands apart from the report of the evil of the events. My sense is that evil implies at least some human intent and participation, whether willing or not. Hence, human will enters the discussion and thus raises questions about the ultimate will or purpose of the universe or God in respect to human beings. That is, the worst of human conditions raises questions about the best of human prospects. Even if one believes there is an ultimate theological purpose to reality that operates in and through life, one can still experience despair. Maybe the despair is even more intense if one's trust in ultimate goodness and control slams up against the worst of human violence and tyranny.

Paul Geary's anguish overwhelmed him. He lamented: "I don't feel that I can trust myself anymore to say and do things that are wise, or that truly represent the heart of Jesus, and the interests of the local church. We are planning on leaving here tomorrow, flying out of Pontianak, the provincial capital. There, already 12,000 starving Maduras have gathered, fleeing the unfolding horror. Perhaps this is a place of ministry; I don't know anymore what to do" (1999, p. A23).

Evil makes a mockery of the ethical principles I identified earlier. If one believes in any ultimate purpose or meaning in the universe, evil evokes the most profound and devastating questions—Why this, why now? What is really going on? These questions predictably occur for leadership once leadership, as a subset of life, confronts the full range of human and ecological issues, as it confronts the paradox of life and death.

In the theological literature, in contrast to the literature of spirituality and of leadership, the responses to questions of evil are as diverse as the religious traditions that stand behind them. For some, evil does not ultimately exist and thus expressions of pain, suffering, and devastation, while real, do not express the deeper reality of the universe. Participation in that ultimate reality positions one for whatever happens in this life. Others see a constant battle between good and evil, between God and the Devil. Faith trusts in the ultimate victory of God over the Devil, but the Devil (and therefore evil) is real and apparently the victor over us in this life. The afterlife promises, however, to right the wrongs of evil's victories. Still others believe evil is real and can be confronted and overcome in this life by faith and living in the spirit. Finally, some put their faith in spiritual healing, meditation disciplines, or prayer for divine intercession as a means of coping.

Perhaps the constant in all this is that when we are in the midst of terror, of real chaos, of outrageously destructive human actions, we long for the certainty that what is happening makes ultimate sense, can be explained, and can be fixed. We want certainty in a world so profoundly uncertain that it challenges every belief. Metaphorically, at least, we want to see the face of God, to be assured that our situation is survivable. The zones behind us are always clearer than the zone we are in. So perhaps, we rarely if ever see the face of God. As our thoughtful pastor, Reverend Dan Little, framed it, we see only the "backside" of God. Only by trusting the wisdom of the past do we find the courage to endure the tragedy of the present and find hope for the future.

Application

Evil makes no rational sense yet arises in any reflective understanding of leadership. It raises the most difficult issues for anyone seeking to address evil deeply within his or her personal life and without, as he or she engages others to address it. Leadership is not reducible to strategies by positional figures seeking results embodied in a personal or organizational vision. Nor is it reducible to ethics. When the stirrings invite us to Zone 7c—Living the Promise— leadership depends upon embracing courage and faith. Denial and despair, even fatalism, prevail in our spirit as we seek to live a created meaning that makes no enduring sense and, at the same time, to trust that others and ourselves can get through chaos. Hence, leadership is Living the Promise.

Leadership in this realm builds on all the other zones, yet our stirrings ask us to seek more. What is that *more*? I have found three texts insightful as at least guides if not full answers. They reflect the polarity of 7c—inside/outside. Let me introduce them to you and then add my own reflections. The first invites us to seek inside ourselves, the second outside, and the third in a different place. It will explore the backside of God. I then offer a fourth perspective.

Inside

Two authors you have already met—Bolman and Deal—illustrate the first approach. Their widely used volume *Leading with Soul* (1995) explicitly links leadership with spirituality. They recount the story of Steve and Maria. Steve, a senior executive with an impressive track record, at fifty loses his sense of identity. He has lost his zest for life; he has become a cog in the organization. He is encouraged to meet with Maria, an advisor, to help him reconnect with his deepest inner self.

As the story unfolds, Steve initially does not know how to deal with Maria. He is the traditional "buffalo" leader, in charge of the organization, smart, strategic, and savvy. Maria asks him about his spirit, his heart, his inner self. He is used to dealing with his outer self. Maria terrifies him, yet he is aware that maybe she is on to something. His first tendency is to reject her as naive, out of touch with the hard realities of organizational life. He thinks their first meeting is a waste of time. He is a doer, not the feeler she challenges him to be. He is running a business, not a church or social club.

The story traces their journey as Maria encourages Steve to wrestle with his deepest ethical principles and his relationship with life.

Steve finally learns that spirit is not reducible to techniques. Rather it is an authentic expression of his being. Leadership is less doing than being. It is leading with soul.

Then a tragic sadness enters the story. Maria has cancer and is dying. Steve has to face the impending loss of his beloved mentor; again, denial is useless. Near the end of the story, Steve has just participated in a company event in which he was not the leader. The members of his organization had put it together. He has finally learned he is not the sole source of vision, nor is he sole leader. He has let go so others can soar. Steve was to close the event with a few prepared comments, but his address followed a profoundly moving video presentation made by young people from around the world, and he found he was all choked up. He could not deliver the prepared text. Over the phone, Maria asks him what he did. "I talked about you," he says.

> I was bone honest. Told them the truth. When I first came into this job I wasn't ready. I didn't know it at the time. John [his boss] did. He put me in touch with a wise and wonderful person. My spiritual guide. She taught me that leading is giving. That spirit is the core of life. Helped me find my soul. Then I said to the audience, "All of you have been my teachers as well. Together, we're finding our company's soul. We're building an uncommon spirit. One seed, many plants, a shared dream."
>
> Silence on the other end of the line. He knew she was crying. So was he. (p. 137)

Bolman and Deal press the spiritual journey deeply inward. A mystical sense of wonder and awe provides the foundation for leadership in a world in which we face many hard truths, including our death and that of our loved ones. This does not mean that leadership loses itself in tragedy. Ego is no longer the issue. Love for others is central. We deepen our commitment to center ourselves in spirit and to face whatever happens. Leadership leaves a legacy for others to carry forth. Stewardship partners with spirituality, and together they form the crux of leadership. (If you want to probe more deeply into the inner side of faith from a woman's perspective, I recommend *The Feminine Face of God*, by Sherry Ruth Anderson and Patricia Hopkins, 1991.)

Outside

I deeply appreciate Bolman and Deal's work. I have taught seminars centered on their text. Yet there is a stirring in me. I feel the need to go more deeply into what leadership does when faced with the real despair of evil. Roger Gottlieb takes us there in *A Spirituality of Resistance* (1999), one of the most challenging inquiries into faith and evil I have ever read. He does not seek to get beyond evil. He embraces it and then finds spiritual peace in the resistance to it. In other words, it is not enough to go inward. One must also go outward into the world and, while living in the midst of evil, act courageously. Gottlieb believes in peace. Peace, however, comes not from transcending the dark realities but from resisting them:

> I am writing about the struggle to find a spiritual heart in a dark time: a path whose authentic essence is the honest recognition of—and opposition to—brutal and sacrilegious desecration of the earth and all who dwell upon it. It is about the attempt to bring into being a personal identity that takes past and present forms of social evil seriously and knows that it is living on an earth scarred by unjustified and irrevocable loss. As other spiritual paths may center on love of God or systematic prayer, on meditation or revelation, this one is bound by responsibility to protect the earth. In this path, spirituality and resistance to the destruction of life—human and nonhuman alike—are inextricably connected. It is, we might say, a spirituality of resistance. (p. 2)

There is no peace without resistance. Evil is real; it is present in the world. To live on the earth is to experience it. To avoid asking the authenticity question—What is really going on?—offers only escape into avoidance and denial. Both states of mind perpetuate the very evil that one is escaping.

There are proper roles for detachment and acceptance. What, however, if those acts ignore the deeper issues? Often we hear stories of how people coped with terrible events and realized unexpected positive outcomes. We are invited to focus on the blessed outcome, and downplay the evil of the event. Massachusetts General Hospital medical staff who have taken chaplaincy courses offer spiritual healing to people facing death. This is certainly leadership in a difficult arena. However, if a person is dying as a result of having been tortured by a hate gang, such healing is far from confronting all that needs to be faced.

Although Gottlieb is not a traditional, faith-based believer, his religious—in this case Jewish—roots inform his view of how we should live. For example, he argues that "doing the will of God necessarily includes a response to what is going on around us. That we comply with religious rules is not enough. The general idea is often expressed by the notion that God asks us to engage in 'Tikkum Olam,' the 'repair of the world.' The cosmos, in this view, is unfinished and imperfect. God left its defects for us to remedy. If we fail to do so, our spiritual destinies are incomplete" (p. 27).

Avoidance and denial both sidetrack and derail resistance, hence they undermine spiritual peace. They leave us with an unease, a stirring, that something very important is happening. For instance, how can we manifest authentic gratitude for the good in our lives if we are avoiding or denying the evil that others are going through? "Compassion, humility, integrity, equanimity, and all the rest require as a bare beginning that we be able to confront the truth" (p. 38).

Results from resistance are not guaranteed. The outcome of the journey is unknowable. Nor does resistance ensure inward peace. It does however build the platform for spiritual peace. The explanations for evil that Ricoeur found opened questions but also hopes for the beginning and end of life. For Gottlieb, who does not trust in any saving grace, there is no stopping evil unless human beings do it. True happiness and true goodness come from total investment in combating evil.

This resistance must be rooted in an understanding of social justice, not just compassion, and must be linked to an understanding that evil imbeds itself in both social and natural systems. Both human and nonhuman aspects of life always flood the radar screen. Thus to resist "is to oppose superior and threatening powers, in a context of injustice, oppression, or violence" (p. 165). Gottlieb's focus is outward, on the derailing of justice and ecology by human destructive action.

Once one goes down this path, as Gottlieb knows, all kinds of troublesome issues arise. How does one know what to resist and what to let pass? Are all kinds of resistance justifiable? Cannot hatred and anger, which often accompany evil, come to inhabit the resister too? Might not the us-versus-them mentality that is being resisted also overtake the resister? Looking back to the metaphors for the zones, it seems Gottlieb's analytic home rests in the view that life is a living system and his resistance home takes its force from the view that life is ups (evil) versus downs (resisters).

Yes, we might hate the oppressors and yet come to embody the worst of them even as we resist. However, that hate and anger can be a wake-up call for deeper self-awareness, Gottlieb argues. Embrace the anger, own it, and move through it. Can we forgive the oppressors? "To begin with," suggests Gottlieb, "to authentically forgive someone, we must have, at the least, some sense of rough equality with him or her. The powerless do not truly forgive the powerful if the latter have all the guns and police on their side and the former have nothing but the pain" (p. 176). How do downs become equal with ups? The religious way is to imagine a God who is all-powerful and who rights injustices in another life. Gottlieb, however, is committed to the vibrancy of the earth, not a vague hope of heaven. So what is left? Resistance.

> In resistance we fully sense our own strength, value, and ability to act. In resistance we get beyond the hopeless passivity of victimhood. Only then can we honestly see the folly of having our minds dominated by bad feelings toward another. We can then view the guilty with true compassion, since compassion will not be a mask for our own paralysis or impotence. We can forgive the evildoers when they have been rendered powerless, or at least can let go of our hatred, because we ourselves have achieved a sense of our own moral and spiritual force. . . . Without resistance, forgiveness becomes too much like surrender, too much like forgetting all the victims, too much like an evasion of fate. (p. 176–77)

And what is the check or limit on arrogance? Are not the downs morally superior to the ups? Gottlieb reminds us that all of us have the potential to participate in the perpetration of evil. Thus no one is superior to anyone else.

Gottlieb believes we are called to serve this earth. Such service is at the heart of his spiritual peace. Service undergirds the necessity for wise, adept choices and incarnates as resistance. I admire his insights, and I have lived from the same beliefs in my lifelong commitment to eliminate racism. As a matter of fact, much of what I know about leadership firsthand stems from my ongoing resistance. Yet I am not satisfied. Stirrings still ripple in my core. Is it really possible to sustain spiritual peace by resistance? Is serving the earth enough? Is it possible to go inside and link mind and heart? Is it possible to go outside and resist evil directly? Is it possible to embrace both fully and still serve? What is worth serving? And what, if we serve it, will happen to the world and to us?

Servanthood

The person best known for relating leadership to servanthood is Robert Greenleaf. He opens a third option for defining and finding spirituality in leadership. When he published *The Servant Leader* in 1970, he pressed the boundaries of leadership as no one else had. We are just beginning to catch up to his spirited lead. For Greenleaf, great leaders are servants first. That is their key to greatness. Serving joins listening and prophecy. Leadership does not bring all the answers to the table. It is rooted in the wisdom of the past and spurred by wisdom and mystery in the present. It involves continual choices, matching the best of knowledge and experience to current reality. In part, hope stems from natural servants "listening carefully to prophetic voices that are speaking now. They are challenging the pervasive injustice with greater force, and they are taking sharper issue with the wide disparity between the quality of society they know is reasonable and possible with available resources, and, on the other hand, the actual performance of the whole range of institutions that exist to serve society" (p. 3).

What makes leaders worthy of following is their commitment to service. Leadership faces the most difficult realities and still engenders hope. In this Greenleaf is similar to Gottlieb. Where he differs is in his deep belief in living paradoxes. The world is full of contradictions. Leadership understands that behind many of them are deep, abiding polarities that do not go away. Greenleaf believes in order and creation coming out of chaos. He believes in individual and community, reason and intuition, comfort and dismay, and many more such polarities. (p. 6)

The term *servant-leader* is itself a polarity in most people's minds. Moreover, Greenleaf makes the servant-leader travel first to the servant side of the polarity. Servanthood diminishes one's need for power, ego satisfaction, and material rewards. Careful listening and seeking ensure that others' needs, interests, and aspirations come first. The test of one's effectiveness as a servant is that those being served become "healthier, wiser, freer, more autonomous, more likely themselves to become servants" (1970, p. 7). And those who are "the least of these" also benefit—or at least are not further diminished and deprived. Maybe servant-leadership is behind Collins's (2001) discovery of humility and fierce resolve.

John Poupart, founder of the American Indian Policy Center, made a similar point when explaining the meaning of "elder" to me (personal communication, September 10, 1999). One is an elder only when labeled so by others. To promote oneself as an elder is clear evidence one is not. The status must be ascribed, not self-proclaimed. Leadership flows from service, not the reverse.

Does leadership as service guarantee results? No. Leadership requires continual questioning and choice. Continue the course or change direction are always the options. Search for the nobler alternative. Not the noblest, since that is never known for sure. This perspective does not sit well in most organizations. Looking for results, executives will embrace authenticity only if they believe it will lead to predictable outcomes. In my view, authenticity goes way beyond everyday results. It is not reducible to a skill set or an individual philosophy. It is much more profound. It addresses who we are—our being. There is a challenge here for followers too, to identify the authentic servant leader. The results that emerge may or may not be what they anticipated.

For Greenleaf, servant-leaders not only serve first, seek, and listen; they also articulate compelling visions that are grounded in ethics and stretch toward currently unattainable futures.

Servant-leaders do not blame or shame. They are often silent, listening for stirrings. They know when to engage and when to disengage. They are not trapped by current circumstances—they have exit cards. They also do not reject, but accept and empathize. They accept what life brings as a gift, whether it was wanted or not, and seek to understand the lived experience of others. Servant-leaders certainly challenge others and guide them. They do not, however, reject them.

In addition, "the leader needs two intellectual abilities that are usually not formally assessed in an academic way: he needs to have *a sense for the unknowable* and be able to *foresee the unforeseeable.* This is partly what gives the leader his 'lead,' what puts him out ahead and qualifies him to show the way" (1970, p. 14). Thus three decades ago, Greenleaf saw the importance of grasping patterns and discerning insights that penetrate to the heart of an apparent mess that I associate with Zones 5b and 6. "The wise leader," suggests Greenleaf, "knows when to bet on these intuitive leads, but he always knows that he is betting on percentages—his hunches are not seen as eternal truths" (p. 15).

Servant-leaders also ground themselves in ethical reflection. A small ethical misstep today can create a huge ethical calamity in the future. Foresight informs present decision making; ethical consideration offers criteria for priority setting. Yet awareness of this sort is not a source of solace, says Greenleaf. In fact, servant-leaders are not seekers after solace. They "have their own inner serenity" (p. 20).

Greenleaf's insights about that serenity and about leadership in general root deeply in his respect for the Quaker heritage. Nonviolence, the equality of all human beings in spirit, and the confrontation of oppression with truth and servanthood all lodge in the Friends' rich and profound past. For the Friends and for Greenleaf, coercive power only strengthens resistance. Here he differs from Gottlieb. Yet like Gottlieb, he is clear that one must be close to both the terrors of evil and the goodness in the world to be fully human. A servant-leader lives the paradox between the two every day. Serenity rests in faith that goodness will ultimately prevail. This perhaps echoes one of Ricoeur's four explanations of evil and salvation.

Greenleaf does ground his hope in faith as trust. And this faith opens theological inquiry:

> It may not be possible to find a basis for all people of widely varying beliefs to work together toward a "good" society, but it is hoped that enough of them can find common ground to give the culture more solidity and resiliency than it now seems to have. What is required is that enough people who hold differing beliefs can accept a common definition for religion as is suggested here: any influence or action that rebinds or recovers alienated persons as they build and maintain serving institutions, or that protects normal people from the hazards of alienation and gives purpose and meaning to their lives, is religious. (1998, p. 121)

Who, then, is the enemy? "It is not 'evil' people. Not stupid people. Not apathetic people. Not the 'system.' Not the protesters, the disrupters, the revolutionaries, the reactionaries" (p. 34). Granted, without them life might be easier. However, eliminating them will not fix the problem, argues Greenleaf. The real enemy, he suggests, is fuzzy thinking on the part of good, intelligent, vital people, and their failure to lead, and to follow servants as leaders. Too many settle for being critics and experts. There is too much intellectual wheel spinning, too much retreating into "research," too little preparation for and willingness to undertake the hard and high risk tasks of building better institutions in an imperfect world, too little disposition to see "the problem" as residing *in here* and not *out there*. *In short, the enemy is strong natural servants who have the potential to lead but do not lead, or who choose to follow a non-servant*. They suffer. Society suffers. And so it may be in the future. (1970, p. 35)

LIVING THE PROMISE

Bolman and Deal ground their spiritual hope in the human heart. They go inside. Gottlieb grounds his spiritual hope in resistance. He goes outside. Greenleaf embraces the paradox of grounding hope both inside and outside. I propose taking another step: building on all three of these ways of living the spirituality in leadership. I will be more explicit about the basis of faith and grounds for hope.

The more I reflect on authenticity the more profound the connection I try to make between my own life experiences, faith, and hope. Authenticity tells me that paradox is central in life. It also tells me to have reservations about paradox as a metaphor for life. Yes, life is a paradox, and life is more than a paradox. Life is grounded in authenticity—that which is ultimately true and real, both inside and outside. As much as I would like to have one metaphor of life, I can't. Authenticity will not let me. Just like the question I asked the believers of the living-systems metaphor in Zone 3b, "What is the downside of your metaphor?" so the question haunts me. Yes, life is a paradox. Yes, life is more. The other metaphors are also insightful. A deeper reality will not be exhausted by one metaphor, no matter how inclusive.

What then is worthy of our trust and hope? What promises deserve our passionate commitment and faith-filled service? What is balm for our cynicism, despair, fatalism, and disconnection from life? What never lets us avoid and deny that which is the most difficult to face? What quickens our spirit and invites us simultaneously to go deeply inside and expansively outside? What is behind and within all that is, carrying global life forward with possibilities, including possibilities for disaster and evil? In other words, what is God?

Humans' concept of God has varied over the centuries (see, for example, Karen Armstrong's *A History of God*, 1993). I see God as the ultimate mystery of the universe. God reveals God's reality throughout creation by the invitation to trust the promise of authenticity. That which is true and real inside and outside all aspects of life is that which will prevail. How can authenticity not prevail? When we express authenticity thoughtfully and courageously, the core ethical principles express themselves at the same time authenticity plays itself out. And as human beings act, even when they act in spite of or contrary to authenticity, as I argued earlier in discussing ethics, the presence of authenticity is ever at work.

Many roads open pathways to authenticity. For some it is disciplined practice, for others revelation, for others service. Regardless of how we get in touch with authenticity or how authenticity gets in touch with us, the engagement is ongoing and forever challenging. We may believe there is an escape. There is none. At worst, avoidance, denial, cynicism, fatalism, and despair derail us. Such derailment can create the most devastating of consequences. Evil is the ultimate product of derailment. Yet eventually authenticity persists. It is always there for us. It is the promise to be lived. Leadership lives the promise of authenticity.

In Chapter Two I offered two grids that illustrated distinctions between authenticity and inauthenticity. Let's look further at them on the next page (Figure 34). Authenticity is more than sincerity. We all know persons and groups with wonderfully pure intentions who have no grasp of what it means to translate sincerity into integrity. One can be sincere and sincerely wrong. Furthermore, we sometimes do not tell the truth when we believe we are, and there are those very difficult situations in which authenticity requires us to lie. Protecting others from abusive or even deadly enemies, for example, may require this of us.

Authenticity also goes beyond integrity, beyond walking the talk. Being true and real inside is no guarantee that one understands how the world works. Authenticity requires both knowledge of the world and the wisdom to act in it. If a person distorts what is going on in

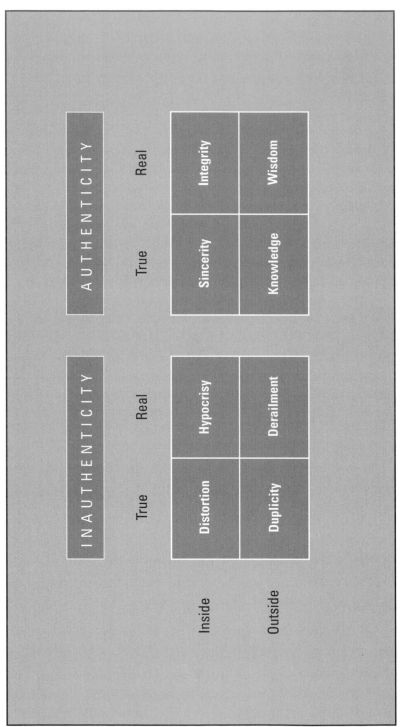

FIGURE 34 • INAUTHENTICITY VERSUS AUTHENTICITY

the world and acts accordingly, the consequences can be terrible not only for the recipients of the action but also for the person taking the action. I mentioned this earlier when discussing Hitler as a leader. If we claim another is inferior, we are simultaneously saying we are superior. As we lie about others, we lie about ourselves. Hitler's lie about Jews devastated them. It also devastated Hitler and his followers who sought to live that inauthenticity, that evil. In the long term, when authenticity faces evil, authenticity wins. Inauthenticity, intentionally or unintentionally, distorts what is true and real inside and outside, which results in both hypocrisy and duplicity. This derails authentic human action. Yet it never does so forever. What is true and real will ultimately emerge and persist.

Authenticity, as I have described throughout this book, expresses itself in many different yet related forms. Each new expression builds on the previous one and the expressions are cumulatively present as one moves through the zones. This process circles back on itself repeatedly. As we make headway on one zone's issues and shift to another zone, the new zone opens other serious issues. Resolution of our problems is never just a breath away. Zone life is ongoing and never complete. Yet, as authenticity appears, we experience it, rejoice in it, and celebrate it. The taste of authenticity confirms its worth. Do we ever experience the full expression of authenticity? No. We participate in it partially as it invites and calls us to deepen our commitments and faithfully serve with trust-based hope. Confirmation hopes for correspondence.

The Backside of God—Confirming Authenticity

When we are in the midst of chaos and devastation, the past looks clear and sensible, the future unclear, even senseless. Yearning for order and meaning, we want to know that whatever is worthy of our faith and belief is present to inform, support, sustain, and encourage us. We want to see the "face of God" directly. Yet we can't. The mystery is too overwhelming, the situation too intense, to yield a clear view. Where can we go?

Whenever we are living and leading in the middle of a zone, that zone confuses us profoundly. We cannot see it clearly from the inside. Not much makes sense. We know the stirrings are real, although we are not always sure of the truth behind them. That is why a wavy line has surrounded each zone as it first appears on the zone map. In Zone 7b, the wavy line surrounds the whole set of the six zones from Serving the Past to Creating Meaning in Chaos. In Zone 7c (Figure 33), the wavy line has become a line of sharp angles, more explosive, more threatening, more ominous. Everything is at stake. We are unsure what is required by authenticity. The standards that arose in the past are now clear, but the current struggle is mystifying. God's face is not apparent. Where can we go?

One morning I was sitting in the congregation of the Westminster Presbyterian Church, anticipating a good sermon because of my past experiences with Reverend Dan Little even though the sermon title, "The Backside of God," had no immediate importance for me. So I listened, somewhat disengaged. Suddenly I was caught up in the sermon; it was deepening my understanding of God and leadership. Sometimes, as Harlan Cleveland once said to me, leadership is caught.

Dan Little came into this congregation as an interim pastor after it was learned that the former two lead pastors were having an affair with each other. Betrayal and disbelief shattered the congregation. Nearing the end of his nearly yearlong tenure, Little was probing the meaning of leadership in times of uncertainty and chaos. He reflected on Moses's leadership challenges as described in Exodus 33: 12–23. Moses asks God who will be sent with him as he leads the people from Egypt. Moses desperately wants some hard facts or correspondence to something objectively trustworthy. Finally, seeking this proof, he says to God, "Let me see your glory."

God responds, "'I myself, will make all my goodness pass in front of your face. And I will proclaim the name of God in your presence, that I show favor to whom I show favor. That I show mercy to whom I show mercy. You cannot see my face, for no human can see my face and live.' And God said, 'Here is a place next to me; station yourself on the rock, and it shall be that, as my glory passes by, I will put you in a cleft of the rock, and screen you with my hand until I have passed by. Then I will remove my hand, and you will see my back. But my face shall not be seen.'

"What good is it to see God's back?" asked Little of all of us. The question made my mind spin as I recognized the link between the backside of God and the backside of authenticity. When evil surrounds us, when all promises are broken, when nothing seems worthy of trust and belief, where can we go? In what can we trust with faith? We are offered the circle of wisdom, the *promise* of authenticity. We have wisdom from the past; we know authenticity has been present in the midst of tragedy in the past even as we experience alienation, abandonment, and terror in the present.

We are still challenged and invited to confirm what is authentic and to acknowledge and resist what derails authenticity and its principles. When we are living faithfully in evil situations, the commandments that set moral boundaries transform into commitments, confirming the promise of that which is true and real inside and outside. The paradox engages us.

Imagine yourself rowing a boat. Your back faces the future. The sight of where you have been keeps you on course. We can back into the future with the wisdom of sages and gurus who have tested the promise of authenticity in the most devastating and joyous of circumstances. Trust tested wisdom and tested principles of authenticity implicit in all we do.

We struggle to confirm what we have known while we are in the midst of what is unknown and unknowable. We trust that the past lessons of authenticity will persist and open even deeper wisdom as we look back on the current situation. The wilder the storm, the greater the requirement for the sea anchors. The authenticity of the past is our sea anchor for the present and the future. Sages confirm the promise of authenticity when in total chaos, fear, and despair. It is their gift. Our challenge is to receive it and act on it. The circle of wisdom is the circle of authenticity, of fulfillment awaiting the next test of its confirmation.

Authentic wisdom differs from conventional wisdom. The latter consists of commonly shared or accepted views, the taken-for-granted perspectives that are often offered as advice. In the most turbulent contexts, conventional wisdom often proves inauthentic. It offers formulas that do not reflect the deepest struggles or the profoundest devastation. "Find friends and trust them" may work in most situations, for example—however, what if it is your supposedly trusted friend who is the betrayer?

Authentic wisdom—the backside of God—offers no easy answers or solutions. It does tell us to confront what is true and real inside and outside, to embrace it all with the confidence that authenticity will prevail. Live in and through the paradox.

Being Led by Authenticity—the Fourth Umpire Shows Up

We exhibit leadership in and through authenticity as authenticity simultaneously leads us. Do science and religion have to be at odds? No, not if both are committed to knowing and living that which is true and real. Science, religion, and spirituality at their most faithful are committed to authenticity. And any derailment is equally serious for each.

If authenticity is cast as pure ideas, like Plato's concept of essence, it misses the reality of everyday life. If it is cast as the details of particular cases and instances, it misses the larger realm of possibility. We not only face the polarities of past/whole, one/many, and inside/outside but also are challenged to live the paradox of despair and hope.

The three umpires we met in the Introduction are all correct, yet each errs in thinking that only one view can reflect the total truth. Let's now invite a fourth umpire to the table. He listens to the others' comments. Then he reflects:

> At times, we call it the way it is. Then again, at times we call it the way we see it. And there are also times where the way we call it determines the way it is. Each view is appropriate in particular circumstances.
>
> I have a different view. *I call balls and strikes as I serve the promise of baseball.* Sometimes I get it dead wrong. Sometimes I don't see clearly. And, sometimes, when I make my decision, I wonder what I am doing. I never give up my belief in baseball as worthy of my commitment. Baseball is my game, and I confirm its importance every time I take the field.

The fourth umpire understands confirmation as a standard of authenticity. Only by our living the promise of authenticity every day is that promise real for us. Confirmation unites what is inside and what is outside. This umpire trusts the game.

A Definition of Leadership—the Long One

In this section I offer a definition of leadership that fully transcends all the zones yet simultaneously applies fully in each one. In it I seek to practice the final authenticity criterion—confirmation. Test it.

Check it out. Question it. Is it true and real for your personal experience and the experience of others in this world of chaos, great change, stability, and variety? This long definition is as follows:

> Leadership is wise, adept choices by persons who singularly and collectively respond to and/or anticipate stirrings, embrace the challenge, and courageously and faithfully serve the welcoming promise of authenticity.

Let me briefly explain each element.

Wise. Choices are wise when they integrate our reflections on experience, theory and frameworks, the testing of ideas, feedback from friends and critics, and constant learning, and when they clarify and affirm our ethical and spiritual core. They reflect our trust in the backside of God.

Adept. Choices are adept when they reflect astuteness and flexibility. We make adept choices when we are centered and living at the intersection of humility and engagement, avoiding both arrogance and adaptiveness.

Choices. We make a true choice when we own the responsibility of decision making without blaming the past, the system, or others, and when we see multiple options, not just dichotomous either/or thinking.

Persons, singularly and collectively. We understand that individuals make a difference yet rarely does leadership center on just one person. Groups and teams also make wise, adept choices.

Respond to and/or anticipate stirrings. We listen to the voices inside and outside that tell us they are aware of inauthenticity, voices that tell us we need to shift attention and take appropriate action to be authentic again. The stirrings may be loud; they may be very quiet. Leaders who wish to have anticipatory wisdom learn to hear the quiet stirrings earlier than others do.

Embrace the challenge. We face the uncertainties of life, confront and resist evil, live in the midst of real chaos, and admit and own the despair and fears that are palpable in everyday life.

Courageously. We take risks for a worthy, virtuous cause or circumstance with no guaranteed outcome.

Faithfully serve. Through the way we live we confirm our abiding confidence that hope is grounded both outside and inside our personal or communal life. The challenges are real and ultimately addressable.

Welcoming promise of authenticity. That which is true and real inside and outside us is worthy and deserving of commitment and service. We experience the "really real" every day even though we do not experience it fully. The welcoming promise of authenticity is confirmed only as we trust in and live out the promise every day. It is welcoming because it stirs us, invites us, scares us, and ultimately enhances us. We live the paradox.

A Definition of Leadership—the Short One

The definition can be refined down to this essence: *Leadership serves the promise of authenticity.* Leadership chooses, probes, and lives the promise every day, everywhere, all the time. All the other parts of the definition stand on this foundation. The spirit and wisdom of authenticity and the experience of inauthenticity engage all of us to face the possibility of our own leadership in many worldly contexts.

In that service to the promise, leadership presses into the future, lives in the present, and directs action into the past. As leadership, guided by authenticity, opens inquiry into life, it also opens the possibilities of solving some problems that are, in fact, solvable. In those cases, leadership transforms into management.

Leadership awaits our authentic action. Authenticity/God is always present.

ZONE IDENTIFICATION AND
LEADERSHIP QUESTIONS

1. How sturdy is my organization or community in this zone?

    - What kinds of discussions do we have about spirituality in the workplace?

    - Do our spirituality discussions imply a particular religious belief?

    - Has the terror of evil ever invaded the workplace?

    - Do we have much discussion, implicit or explicit, about authenticity?

    - Do we have confidence that authenticity ultimately wins?

```
10  |   |   |   |   |   |   |   |   |   |   0   |   |   |   |   |   |   |   |   |   |  10
Very Sturdy                                                                    Shaky
```

2. Where is my organization or community currently focusing its leadership attention?

   • Are the earlier zones demanding attention?

   • Is the stirring in this zone so quiet that hardly anyone hears it?

```
10  |   |   |   |   |   |   |   |   |   |   0   |   |   |   |   |   |   |   |   |   |  10
Excellent Fit                                                                  Misfit
```

3. Am I prepared to live the promise?

   • Have I struggled with my own deepest faith issues?

   • Do doubt, faith, and humility inform my life?

   • Do I see any connection (and if so, what is it) between sacred days (Friday, Saturday, and/or Sunday) and the workplace?

   • Have I ever experienced evil? What did I do, and how did I cope?

   • Do I go inward, outward, or to some other place in response to theology and evil?

   • What is it like to go there and live there?

```
10  |   |   |   |   |   |   |   |   |   |   0   |   |   |   |   |   |   |   |   |   |  10
Ready to Exhibit Leadership                                   Not Prepared at All
```

I hope you have completed your assessments for each zone. If you want to display them on one page, go to the Appendix, where I will offer some advice based upon your scores.

ZONE SUMMARY

Zone 7c targets ultimate reality, what is in and behind meaning and the basis for fulfillment. It builds on the other zones, embraces all of them, and adds to them the struggle with the most difficult paradoxes in life. Spirituality is currently hot in leadership studies. For some it means making meaning out of life's most painful and puzzling problems; for others it equates with belonging, ethics, and shared values. A universal ethic for a diverse world can be constructed by linking the human business of authenticity with the six supporting core principles outlined in the six earlier zones.

In the terror of evil, leadership confronts the reality of doubt, fear, cynicism, fatalism, and despair. It struggles by grounding hope in something that endures. In what can we trust? The promise of authenticity. The fourth umpire understands that the secret is serving authenticity. Only in service to the fundamental call of life can other human and global activities persist and thrive. Leadership is a wonderful phenomenon that is available in all of us as we listen, assess, and act authentically in any reality that comes to us or that we help to create.

As we confirm authenticity in our belief and action, it confirms us. It welcomes us as a promise. In some way it is like a marriage. Who knows what will be the result of the vow? One makes a promise and seeks to serve it. Hope builds on the faith that the authenticity is a secure and solid platform. Is the marriage guaranteed? No, of course not. We all falter. No one is perfect. Yet living in accord with the welcoming promise of authenticity does guarantee that whatever happens will be the best for that circumstance. Even divorces can be authentic. To go one step further, confronting evil can be authentic as evil confronts us with the potential ultimate negation of faith itself. The paradox of good and evil, as experienced, takes us to a deep place of life that goes way beyond thinking. It involves living authentically every day.

Living a promise opens us up to a world of unknown, even unknowable, realities. It is not just realizing potential while keeping roots in the past, which is the way many people like to think about the future. Promise invites a future we have little clue about. It requires a proactive leap into the future with only the promise that authenticity will prevail. Is there any certainty? Yes, the certainty of authenticity. Is there any security? No. For this reason, the heart of leadership beats with courage and faith. To live the promise confirms in our experience every day the grounds for hope for another day, for another millennium.

Zone 7c lives the inside/outside polarity. It confirms both. Going too far inward will trigger a movement outward and vice versa. As we saw in the last chapter, one quickens the other. One goes inside to prepare to come out and goes outside to discover context for what is within. This zone goes from polarity to paradox, from what is knowable and manageable to what is livable.

While the most comforting zone, it is also the most terrifying. With only tastes of the richness of what is true and real, one commits to and confirms faith in authenticity itself. It is a radical act of faith in an unseen promise. The terror is that the promise may prove not to be real. The faith is that the promise will be kept.

ZONE 7C DEFINITIONS

Leadership: Living the Promise
Authenticity criterion: Confirmation
Metaphor: Life is a welcoming promise
Core ethical principle: Authenticity
Polarity: Inside/outside and on to paradox

STIRRINGS

At the end of the zone map there are stirrings that can move us beyond the map. What is a promise? It is a vow, an assurance that what is proposed will occur. Promises can propose terrible as well as glorious outcomes. Evil as well as goodness can be promised. What, then, is a welcoming promise? What are we being welcomed into? What are we likely to experience? Is it worth the belief and the required action? A restiveness is in the air. Leadership commits to a welcoming promise with no immediate guarantees of outcome yet trusts that in some way something positive will eventually occur. We wonder and ponder. What is really worthy of our ultimate trust?

Negative Stirrings

The negative stirrings in this zone tell us things like these:

> Betrayal looms as a real possibility. Evil is real; it does not ever seem to disappear. It just assumes different faces at different times. Maybe resistance is enough. Maybe finding comfort through inclusion with friends, even the universe, will be enough. Sharing values might carry us forward, but religion makes me nervous. It is too narrow, too ritualized, its history tied too much to the support of the very evil it is supposed to fight.

> I am not sure there is any secure place to go, any solid foundation upon which I can build my life and practice leadership. Maybe leadership does not need a faith base. Maybe it rests on the human creativity and courage that is spurred by events. Secular humanism is not that bad. As a matter of fact, I would trust an authentic humanist before an inauthentic faith-based person. Who is really trustworthy anyway? Greenleaf (1970) suggests that wisdom is knowing the difference between servants who lead and leaders who may or may not serve.

> Friends and colleagues have betrayed me before. Maybe I am just an existentialist, coping with the ambiguities of life and fumbling through the calls the best I can. I know I am cynical about a lot of life. Betrayal does not scare the "hell" out of me—it puts "hell" in me.

> Not only have I been betrayed, I have betrayed others. I'm lost and frightened. What a foundation to lead from! The rhetoric of welcoming promise may be hollow rhetoric. Maybe I ought to retire early and withdraw from anything contentious.

Positive Stirrings

Welcome to the real world of faith and doubt. They go hand in hand. If the outcomes of faith could be proved, there would be no need for faith. Only struggle, as part of personal and collective leadership, moving through the dark night of the soul, can offer light. We are not called to be perfect. We are called to be authentic. To be authentic is to admit that we are both inauthentic and authentic. We are not called to be God. We are called to know who we really are and to admit it. As human beings we are part of nature and transcend nature as we think about our place in it. No one view of life can grasp the totality of the human experience.

After all this struggle, I have finally figured out who I am. I am a secular theologian! Authenticity really is my foundation, a base accessible to all. As I become more secular, more this-worldly, I become more theological. I too have experienced betrayal both as receiver and doer. I have spent thirty years fighting racism, sometimes with little sense of progress. I have thought of giving up, of retiring and playing with no serious consequences. Except there are and I can't and won't.

I am ready to go deeper. Someone suggested I go on a five-day silence retreat. As a flaming extravert according to my MBTI results, I was terrified. I went and lasted three days.

I'm sixty. Life is just beginning to unfold in some new ways for me. I'm excited. I'm ready to see what life offers. A friend told me the word *religion* came from *religio*, meaning "that which binds." He said it was different from faith *pistas*, which means "relationships." I was deeply intrigued.

Then I was stunned when a friend gave me a book by Parker Palmer. Entitled *Let Your Life Speak* (1999), it summarized on one page my life quest. It stirred me so much that I quote it all the time. Let me share it with you.

> The God I know does not ask us to conform to some abstract norm for the ideal self. God asks us only to honor our created nature, which means our limits as well as potentials. When we fail to do so, reality happens—God happens—and the way closes behind us.

> The God I was told about in church, and still hear about from time to time, runs about like an anxious schoolmaster measuring people's behavior with a moral yardstick. But the God I know is the source of reality rather than morality, the source of what is rather than what *ought to be*. This does not mean that God has nothing to do with morality: morality and its consequences are built into the God-given structure of reality itself. Moral norms are not something we have to stretch for, and moral consequences are not something we have to wait for: they are right here, right now, waiting for us to honor, or violate, the nature of self, other, world.

> The God whom I know dwells quietly in the root system of the very nature of things. This is the God who, when asked by Moses for a name, responded, "I Am who I Am" (Exodus 3:14), an answer that has less to do with the moral rules for which Moses made God famous than with the elemental "isness" and selfhood. If, as I believe, we are all made in God's image, we could all give the same

answer when asked who we are: "I Am who I Am." One dwells with God by being faithful to one's nature. One crosses God by trying to be something one is not. Reality—including one's own—is divine, to be not defied but honored. (pp. 50–51)

I am stirred to go deeper, broader, and hopefully wiser into the "isness" of life. Authenticity is already here in its fullness. I'm ready for my next experience, whatever it is. My hope is grounded even if I do not have all the answers. Who does?

Relationships are the foundation of leadership. Without them, servanthood sinks into quicksand and hope dies the death of despair. So what is worthy of our trust, in what do we ground our meaning? I know that *Making Wise Choices serves the promise of authentic practice. I know that Probing Deeper serves the promise of authentic thinking.* Now I trust that *leadership serves and lives the promise of authenticity itself.*

SELF-ASSESSMENT

OF ORGANIZATIONAL ZONE AND LEADERSHIP READINESS

In this appendix, you can review your self-diagnosis from each zone. Transfer your assessment marks from Zones 1 through 7 to the following chart.

Zone 1	Zone 2	Zone 3a
1._____	1._____	1._____
2._____	2._____	2._____
3._____	3._____	3._____

Zone 3b	Zone 4	Zone 5a
1._____	1._____	1._____
2._____	2._____	2._____
3._____	3._____	3._____

Zone 5b	Zone 6	Zone 7a
1._____	1._____	1._____
2._____	2._____	2._____
3._____	3._____	3._____

Zone 7b	Zone 7c
1._____	1._____
2._____	2._____
3._____	3._____

You have assessed where your organization is sturdy and where it needs attention, where the organization is currently focusing its attention, and the extent of your preparation and willingness to lead in that zone. As you step back from the book, you have in front of you a picture of your whole organization or a part of it, or some aspect of your community. You also have a reflective appreciation of your personal and professional ability to lead.

Any score higher than 5 that points to a weak area deserves attention. If the organization is sturdy in a zone, make sure it remains so. If it is shaky, with a 6 to 10 vote, it is in trouble, requiring leadership. The same is true of the other two broad areas of focus. This assessment can be a guide for your own leadership development, both personally and professionally.

REFERENCES

Abrahams, J. (1995). *The Mission Statement Book: 301 Corporate Mission Statements from America's Top Companies*. Berkeley, CA: Ten Speed Press.

Anderson, S., and Bryson, J. (1998, February 15). "Applying Large-Group Interaction Methods in the Planning and Implementation of Major Projects." Unpublished manuscript. Reflective Leadership Center. Available: sanderson@hhh.umn.edu or call 612-625-5888.

Anderson, S. R., and Hopkins, P. (1991). *The Feminine Face of God*. New York: Bantam Books.

Anderson, W. T. (1990). *Reality Isn't What It Used to Be: Theatrical Politics, Ready-to-Wear Religion, Global Myths, Primitive Chic, and Other Wonders of the Postmodern World*. San Francisco: Harper San Francisco.

Argyris, C. (1996). *Overcoming Organizational Defenses: Facilitating Organizational Learning*. Upper Saddle River, NJ: Prentice Hall.

Argyris, C., and Schön, D. A. (1996). *Organizational Learning II: Theory, Method, and Practice*. Reading, MA: Addison-Wesley.

Armstrong, K. (1993). *A History of God*. New York: Ballantine.

Atkinson, T. (1995, September). "Embracing Stability." *Training*, p. 106.

Bank, D. (1999, March 2). "Upstarts Succeed Where Microsoft Fails: Charging Fees for Internet Transactions." *Wall Street Journal*, p. A3.

Barker, J. (1992). *Discovering the Future*. New York: Morrow.

Barshay, J. J. (1999, November 14). "Feeling Groovy." *Minneapolis Star Tribune*.

Begley, S. (2001, May 7). "God and the Brain: How We're Wired for Spirituality." *Newsweek,* pp. 50–57.

Bennis, W., and Mische, M. (1997). The 21st Century Organization: Reinventing Through Reengineering. San Francisco: Jossey-Bass.

Benveniste, G. (1994). *The Twenty-First Century Organization.* San Francisco: Jossey-Bass.

Berman, M. (1996, Winter). "The Shadow Side of Systems Theory." *Journal of Humanistic Psychology, 36*(1), 28–55.

Black, E. (2001). *IBM and the Holocaust.* New York: Crown.

Blanchard, K. (1998). "The Spiritual Workplace." In J. Renesch and B. DeFoore (Eds.), *The New Bottom Line: Bringing Heart and Soul to Business.* Pleasanton, CA: New Leaders Press.

Blanchard, K., and Johnson, S. (1985). *Leadership and the One Minute Manager.* New York: Monroe.

Blank, W. (1995). *The 9 Natural Laws of Leadership.* New York: AMACOM.

Block, P. (1993). *Stewardship.* San Francisco: Berrett-Koehler.

Block, P. (1987). *The Empowered Manager.* San Francisco: Jossey-Bass.

Bolman, L. G., and Deal, T. E. (1995). *Leading with Soul.* San Francisco: Jossey-Bass.

Bolman, L. G., and Deal, T. E. (1991). *Reframing Organizations: Artistry, Choice, and Leadership.* San Francisco: Jossey-Bass.

Boyett, J., and Conn, H. (1991). *Workplace 2000: The Revolution Reshaping American Business.* New York: Dutton.

Branch, S. (1998, June 8). "Where Cash Is King." *Fortune,* pp. 201–210.

Briner, B., and Pritchard, R. (1997). *The Leadership Lessons of Jesus.* Nashville, TN: Broadman & Holman.

Briskin, A. (1996). *The Stirring of Soul in the Workplace.* San Francisco: Jossey-Bass.

Broder, E. (1998). *The Below-the-Belt Manager: This Book Shows You How to Make Your Employees Sick with Fear in as Little as 30 Seconds!* New York: Warner Books.

Brooks, R. (1999, January 7). "Unequal Treatment: Alienating Customers." *Wall Street Journal,* p. A1.

Browne, M. (1996, May 12). "Era of Heroes, Now Past, Spawned the Likes of Admiral Byrd." *Minneapolis Star Tribune,* p. A22.

Bryson, J. (1989). *Strategic Planning for Public and Nonprofit Organizations.* San Francisco: Jossey-Bass.

Bryson, J., and Crosby, B. (1992). *Leadership for the Common Good.* San Francisco: Jossey-Bass.

Buckingham, M., and Coffman, C. (2001). *Now, Discover Your Strengths.* New York: Free Press.

Buckingham, M., and Coffman, C. (1999). *First, Break All the Rules.* New York: Simon & Schuster.

Buckman, J. (1999, August 29). "Is 'Six-Sigma' Improvement System for Mere Mortals?" *Minneapolis Star Tribune,* p. D5.

Bunker, B. B., and Alban, B. T. (1997). *Large Group Interventions: Engaging the Whole System for Rapid Change.* San Francisco: Jossey-Bass.

Burns, J. M. (1978). *Leadership.* New York: Harper Colophon Books.

Busch, J., and Busch, G. (1992). *Sociocybernetics: A Perspective for Living in Complexity.* Social Systems Press.

Capra, F. (1996). *The Web of Life.* New York: Anchor/Doubleday.

Cashman, K. (1998). *Leadership from the Inside Out.* Provo, UT: Executive Excellence.

Chaleff, I. (1995). *The Courageous Follower: Standing Up to and for Our Leaders.* San Francisco: Berrett-Koehler.

Chappell, T. (1993). *The Soul of a Business.* New York: Bantam.

Cleary, T. (1992). *The Book of Leadership and Strategy: Lessons of the Chinese Master.* Boston: Shambhala.

Cleveland, H. (1995). Foreword. In W. Reckmeyer (Ed.), *Leadership Readings.* Stanford, CA: American Leadership Forum.

Cleveland, H. (1985). *The Knowledge Executive.* New York: Dutton.

Colin, M. (1999, November 1). "Religion in the Workplace." *Business Week,* pp. 151–157.

Collins, J. (2001, January). "Level 5 Leadership: The Triumph of Humility and Fierce Resolve." *Harvard Business Review,* pp. 67–76.

Collins, J. (1996). "Aligning Action and Values." *Leader to Leader,* Drucker Foundation and Jossey-Bass, pp. 19–24.

Collins, J. C., and Porras, J. I. (1994). *Built to Last: Successful Habits of Visionary Companies.* New York: HarperCollins.

Conger, J. A. (Ed.). (1994). *Spirit at Work: Discovering the Spirituality in Leadership.* San Francisco: Jossey-Bass.

Conger, J. A., and Benjamin, B. (1999). *Building Leaders: How Successful Companies Develop the Next Generation.* San Francisco: Jossey-Bass.

Conger, J. A., and Benjamin, B. (1996). "Leadership in and of Demographically Diverse Organizations." *Leadership Quarterly,* 7(1), 1–19.

Covey, S. (1990). *The 7 Habits of Highly Effective People.* St. Louis, MO: Fireside.

Cowan, C., and Beck, D. E. (1996). *Spiral Dynamics: Mastering Values, Leadership, and Change.* Cambridge, MA: Blackwell.

Coy, P. (1999, June 7). "Exploiting Uncertainty: The 'Real Options' Revolution in Decision-Making." *Business Week,* pp. 118–124.

Crosby, B. (1999). *Leadership for Global Citizenship.* Thousand Oaks, CA: Sage.

Crosby, P. (1997). *The Absolutes of Leadership.* San Francisco: Jossey-Bass.

Davis, D. (1998). *Klan-destine Relationships: A Black Man's Odyssey in the Ku Klux Klan.* Far Hills, NJ: New Horizons Press.

Dawkins, R. ([1976] 1989). *The Selfish Gene.* New York: Oxford University Press.

Denison, D. (1997). *Corporate Culture and Organizational Effectiveness.* (2nd ed.). Denison Consulting.

Denison, D., and Mishra, A. (1995, March–April). "Toward a Theory of Organizational Culture and Effectiveness." *Organization Science,* 6(2),184–185, 204–223.

De Pree, M. (1997). *Leading Without Power.* San Francisco: Jossey-Bass.

Drath, W., and Palus, C. (1997). "Making Common Sense: Leadership as Meaning-making in a Community of Practice." Greensboro, NC: Center for Creative Leadership.

Dreher, D. (1996). *The Tao of Personal Leadership.* New York: Harper.

Eden, C., and Ackermann, F. (1998). *Making Strategy: The Journey of Strategic Management.* Thousand Oaks, CA: Sage.

Edmunson, C. (1999). *Paradoxes of Leadership.* Available from CEdmunson@webindustries.com.

Egan, G. (1994). *Working the Shadow Side.* San Francisco: Jossey-Bass.

Eoyang, G. (1997). *Coping with Chaos.* Cheyenne, WY: Lagumo Corporation.

Fairhurst, G., and Sarr, R. (1996). *The Art of Framing.* San Francisco: Jossey-Bass.

Fish (1998). Video. Burnsville, MN: ChartHouse International Learning Corporation.

Fisher, R., Ury, W., and Patton, B. (Eds.). (1983). *Getting to Yes.* New York: Penguin.

Fletcher, J., and Olwyler, K. (1997). *Paradoxical Thinking.* San Francisco: Berrett-Koehler.

Forscher, B. K. (1963). "Chaos in the Brickyard." *Science, 142*(3590), 339.

Frankl, V. (1963). *Man's Search for Meaning.* New York: Washington Square Press.

Franklin, R. (1998, November 12). "Daytons Reveal Decision to Cap Income: Extra Money Will Go to Charity." *Minneapolis Star Tribune*, pp. A1, A15.

Frieberg, K., and Frieberg, J. (1998). *Nuts!: Southwest Airlines' Crazy Recipe for Business and Personal Success.* Austin, TX: Bard Press.

Ganzel, R. (1998, December). "What's Wrong with Pay for Performance?" *Training, 35*(12), 34.

Geary, P. (1999, March 28). "Pure Evil." *Minneapolis Star Tribune*, p. A23.

George, B. (1998). Foreword. In J. Renesch and B. DeFoore (Eds.), *The New Bottom Line: Bringing Heart and Soul to Business.* Pleasanton, CA: New Leaders Press.

Gergen, D. (2000). *Eyewitness to Power.* New York: Simon & Schuster.

Gibb, R. (1997, March). *Systems Model of Organization.* Unpublished manuscript.

Gleick, J. (1987). *Chaos: Making a New Science.* New York: Penguin.

Goleman, D. (1998a, November–December). "What Makes a Leader?" *Harvard Business Review*, pp. 93–102.

Goleman, D. (1998b). *Working with Emotional Intelligence.* New York: Bantam.

Goleman, D. (1995). *Emotional Intelligence.* New York: Bantam.

Gottlieb, R. (1999). *A Spirituality of Resistance.* New York: Crossroad.

Gould, S. J. (1999). *Rocks of Ages.* New York: Ballantine.

Greenleaf, R. (1998). *The Power of Servant Leadership.* San Francisco: Berrett-Koehler.

Greenleaf, R. (1970). *The Servant Leader.* Indianapolis, IN: Robert Greenleaf Center.

Griffin, D. R. (Ed.). (1988). *Spirituality and Society: Postmodern Visions.* Albany: State University of New York Press.

Gross, B. (1998, November–December). "The New Math of Ownership." *Harvard Business Review*, pp. 68–74.

Hagberg, J., and Guelich, R. (1989). *The Critical Journey: Stages in the Life of Faith.* Dallas, TX: Word Publications.

Hall, B., and Ledig, B. (1990, February). "Values, Ethics, and Efficiency: A New Approach to Organizational Development." *Values Technology*, pp. 144–53. (Graduate Division of Counseling, Psychology, and Reeducation, Santa Clara University, Santa Clara, CA).

Hamel, G., and Prahalad, C. K. (1994). *Competing for the Future.* Boston: Harvard Business School Press.

Hammer, M. (1997). *Beyond Reengineering.* New York: Harper Business.

Hammonds, K. H. (1996, September 16). "Balancing Work and Family: Big Returns for Companies Willing to Give Family Strategies a Chance." *Business Week,* pp. 74–80.

Handy, C. (1994). *The Age of Paradox.* Boston: Harvard Business School Press.

Harvey, E., and Lucia, A. (1997). *144 Ways to Walk the Talk.* www.walk-thetalk.com.

Harvey, J. (1974). *The Abilene Paradox: The Mismanagement of Agreement.* New York: AMACOM.

Havel, V. (1985). *The Power of the Powerless.* New York: Sharpe, Inc.

Hawken, P., Lovins, A., and Lovins, L. H. (1999). *Natural Capitalism.* Boston: Little, Brown.

Heerman, B. (1998, March). "Spirited Teams." *Executive Excellence,* pp. 9–10.

Heider, J. (1985). *The Tao of Leadership.* Atlanta, GA: Humanics New Age.

Heiman, S. E., and Sanchez, D. (1998). *The New Strategic Selling.* New York: Warner Books.

Hersey, P. (1984). *Situational Leadership.* New York: Warner Books.

Heuerman, T. (1999, April 13). *The Jazz Musician.* Available via e-mail at tomheu@aol.com.

Hillman J. (1996). *The Soul's Code: In Search of Character and Calling.* New York: Random House.

Hirsh, S., and Kise, J. (2000). *Introduction to Type® and Coaching.* Palo Alto, CA: Consulting Psychologists Press, Inc.

Hoffman, W. (1999). *ABC's of Communication.* St. Paul, MN: Daybreak Publishing.

Hubbard, B. M. (1998). *Conscious Evolution: Awakening the Power of Our Social Potential.* Novato, CA: New World Library.

Imparato, N., and Harari, O. (1994). *Jumping the Curve.* San Francisco: Jossey-Bass.

Jacob, M. (1997). *Reality Leadership.* Indianapolis, IN: Performance Press.

Jacobs, R. (1987). *Real Time Strategic Change: How to Involve an Entire Organization in Fast and Far-Reaching Change.* San Francisco: Berrett-Koehler.

Jones, D. (1999, July 21). "Firms Aim for Six-Sigma Efficiency." *USA Today,* p. 2B.

Jones, L. B. (1995). *Jesus as CEO.* New York: Hyperion.

Johnson, B. (1997). *Polarity Management.* Amherst, MA: HRD Press.

Kao, J. (1996). *Jamming*. New York: Harper Business.

Kaplan, R., and Norton, D. (1996). *The Balanced Scorecard*. Boston: Harvard Business School Press.

Kauffman, D. (1981). *Systems 2: Human Systems*. St. Paul, MN: Future Systems, Inc.

Kauffman, D. (1980). *Systems 1: An Introduction to Systems Thinking*. St. Paul, MN: Future Systems, Inc.

Kellerman, B. (1986). *Political Leadership: A Source Book*. Pittsburgh, PA: University of Pittsburgh Press.

Kelley, R. (1992). *The Power of Followership*. New York: Doubleday/ Currency.

Kidder, R. (1994). *Shared Values for a Troubled World*. San Francisco: Jossey-Bass.

Kiersy, D., and Bates, M. (1984). *Please Understand Me*. Del Mar, CA: Prometheus.

King, U. (1997). "Spirituality." In J. Hinnells (Ed.), *A New Handbook of Living Religions*. New York: Penguin Books.

Kleiner, A. (1996). *The Age of Heretics*. New York: Doubleday/Currency.

Kohlberg, L. (1980). *Moral Development, Moral Education*. Birmingham, AL: REA.

Kotter, J. (1990). *A Force for Change: How Leadership Differs from Management*. New York: Free Press.

Kouzes, J., and Posner, B. (1996). *The Leadership Challenge*. San Francisco: Jossey-Bass.

Kouzes, J., and Posner, B. (1993). *Credibility: How Leaders Gain and Lose It, Why People Demand It*. San Francisco: Jossey-Bass.

Kragness, M. (1994). *Dimensions of Leadership Profile: An Approach to Understanding and Developing Effective Leaders*. Des Moines, IA: Carlson Learning.

Land, G., and Jarman, B. (1992). *Breakpoint and Beyond: Mastering the Future–Today*. Champaign, IL: Harper Business.

Langreth, R., and Lipin, S. (1998, February 24). "SmithKline Breaks Off Talks with Glaxo." *Wall Street Journal*, p. A2.

Lebow Company. (1995). *The Shared Values Process Operating System*.

Leonard, D., and Straus, S. (1997, July–August). "Putting Your Company's Whole Brain to Work." *Harvard Business Review*, pp. 111–121.

Lippitt, L. (1998). *Preferred Futuring*. San Francisco: Berrett-Koehler.

Lombardo, M., and Eichinger, R. (forthcoming). *The Leadership Machine*. Prepublication edition, Lominger Limited, Inc.

Losada, M. (1998). "The Complex Dynamics of High Performance Teams." *Meta Learning*, pp. 1–16.

MacArthur, J. (1997). *The Power of Integrity: Building a Life Without Compromise.* Wheaton, IL: Crossway Books.

Maccoby, M. (1976). *The Gamesman.* New York: Simon & Schuster.

MacKenzie, G. (1996). *Orbiting the Giant Hairball.* New York: Viking.

Manning, J. (1998, October 2). "Heart Revolution." *City Business,* pp. 1, 45.

Manz, C. (1988). *The Leadership Wisdom of Jesus.* San Francisco: Berrett-Koehler.

Martin, M. (1986). *Self-Deception and Morality.* Lawrence: University Press of Kansas.

Martinski, N. (1998). "Twenty-Five Ways to Retain Your Best Employees." Chicago: Lawrence Ragan Communications, Inc.

Maynard, H. B., and Mehrtens, S. E. (1993). *The Fourth Wave: Business in the 21st Century.* San Francisco: Berrett-Koehler.

Medtronic. (1998). *1998 Annual Report.* Minneapolis, MN: Author.

"Meet the Man Who Determines Where Southwest Lands." (2001, May 6). *St. Paul Pioneer Press.*

Mills, W., and Associates. (1998). *StarMap System Strategy Map.* Loretto, MN: Author. (William Mills and Associates, 6810 Greenfield Road, Loretto, MN 55357.)

Mintzberg, H. (1994). *The Rise and Fall of Strategic Planning.* New York: Free Press.

Moore, G. (1999, October). "The Anatomy of Failure." *Red Herring,* pp. 86–94.

Munsey, B. (Ed.). (1980). *Moral Development, Moral Education, and Kohlberg.* Birmingham, AL: Religious Education Press.

Nanus, B. (1992). *Visionary Leadership.* San Francisco: Jossey-Bass.

Neff, T., Citrin, J., and Brown, P. (1999). *Lessons from the Top: The 50 Most Successful Business Leaders in America—and What You Can Learn from Them.* New York: Doubleday.

Nohria, N. (1996). "From the M-Form to the N-Form: Taking Stock of Changes in the Large Industrial Corporation." Working Paper, Harvard Business School.

Ogilvy, J. (1995). *Living Without a Goal.* New York: Doubleday/Currency.

O'Neil, J. (1993). *The Paradox of Success.* New York: Putnam.

Oshry, B. (1999). *Leading Systems: Lessons from the Power Lab.* San Francisco: Berrett-Koehler.

Oshry, B. (1986). *Possibilities of Organizations.* Boston: Power and Systems, Inc.

Owen, H. (1992). *Open Space Technology: A User's Guide.* Potomac, MD: Abbott.

Palmer, P. J. (2000). *Let Your Life Speak: Listening for the Voice of Vocation.* San Francisco: Jossey-Bass.

Palmer, P. J. (1993). *Promise of Paradox.* Potter's House.

Palmer, P. J. (1992, March–April). "Divided No More: A Movement Approach to Educational Reform." *Change Magazine,* pp. 10–17.

Peck, M. S. (1997). *The Road Less Traveled and Beyond.* New York: Simon & Schuster.

Peters, T. (1994). *The Pursuit of Wow!* New York: Vintage Books.

Petersen, J. L. (1994). *The Road to 2015: Profiles of the Future.* Corte Madera, CA: Waite Group Press.

Polkinghorn, J. (1999). *Quarks, Chaos and Christianity: Questions to Science and Religion.* New York: Crossroad.

Prahalad, C. K., and Krishnan, M. S. (1999, September–October). "The New Meaning of Quality in the Information Age." *Harvard Business Review,* pp. 109–118.

Price Waterhouse Change Integration Team. (1996). *The Paradox Principles.* Burr Ridge, IL: Irwin.

Quinn, J. B. (1980). *Strategic Change: Logical Incrementalism.* Burr Ridge, IL: Irwin.

Quinn, R. (1988). *Beyond Rational Management.* San Francisco: Jossey-Bass.

Quinn, R., and Cameron, K. (1988). *Paradox and Transformation.* Cambridge, MA: Ballinger.

Reingold, J. (1999, November 15). "In Search of Leadership: A Talk with Headhunters Turned Authors Citrin and Neff." *Business Week,* p. 176.

Renesch, J., and DeFoore, B. (Eds.). (1998). *The New Bottom Line: Bringing Heart and Soul to Business.* Pleasanton, CA: New Leaders Press.

Ricoeur, P. (1967). *The Symbolism of Evil.* Boston: Beacon Press.

Rifkin, J. (2000). *The Age of Access.* New York: Tarcher.

Rifkin, J. (1998). *The Biotech Century.* New York: Tarcher/Putnam.

Roof, W. (1994). In J. Conger (Ed.), *Spirit at Work: Discovering the Spirituality in Leadership.* San Francisco: Jossey-Bass.

Rosato, D. (1998, February 23). "Today's Issue: Putting Humor to Work in the Workplace." *USA Today,* p. 5B.

Rost, J. (1991). *Leadership for the Twenty-First Century.* New York: Praeger.

Rusk, T. (1993). *The Power of Ethical Persuasion.* New York: Viking.

Schwartz, P. (1991). *The Art of the Long View: Planning for the Future in an Uncertain World.* New York: Doubleday/Currency.

Schrage, M. (1995). *No More Teams.* New York: Doubleday/Currency.

Seagrave, S. (1995). *Lords of the Rim.* New York: Putnam.

Senge, P. (1990). *The Fifth Discipline.* New York: Doubleday/Currency.

Sennett, R. (1998). *The Corrosion of Character.* New York: WWNorton.

Smith, H. (1993). *Forgotten Truth.* San Francisco: Harper San Francisco.

Smith, H. (1989.) *Beyond the Post-Modern Mind.* Wheaton, IL: Quest Books.

Smith, K., and Berg, D. (1987). *Paradoxes of Group Life.* San Francisco: Jossey-Bass.

Stacey, R. (1996). *Complexity and Creativity in Organizations.* San Francisco: Berrett-Koehler.

Stacey, R. (1993). *Strategic Management and Organisational Dynamics.* London: Pitman Publishing.

Stacey, R. (1992). *Managing the Unknowable.* London: Pitman Publishing.

Stanley, P., and Clinton, J. R. (1992). *Connecting.* Colorado Springs, CO: NavPress.

Star Power. Simulation. Simulation Training Systems, PO Box 910, Del Mar, CA 92014, 619-755-0272.

Stayer, R. (1990, November–December). "How I Learned to Let My Workers Lead." *Harvard Business Review,* pp. 2–11.

Terry, R. (1993). *Authentic Leadership: Courage in Action.* San Francisco: Jossey-Bass.

Terry, R. (1975). *For Whites Only.* Grand Rapids, MI: Eerdmans.

Tevlin, J. (1998, March 20). "Professional Loudmouth Is in Demand." *Minneapolis Star Tribune,* pp. D1, D8.

Thompson, D. (1998, February 1). "Befriending the Enemy." *St. Paul Pioneer Press,* p. A4.

3M, (1999). "Innovation through Interaction." 3M Tech Forum brochure.

Toffler, A., (1991). *The Third Wave.* New York: Morrow.

Treacy, M., and Wiersema, F. (1995). *The Discipline of Market Leaders.* Reading, MA: Addison-Wesley.

Vaill, P. (1998). "The Unspeakable Texture of Process Wisdom." In S. Srivastva et al. (Eds.), *Organizational Wisdom and Courage.* San Francisco: Jossey-Bass.

Vaill, P. (1996). *Learning as a Way of Being: Strategies for Survival in a World of Permanent White Water*. San Francisco: Jossey-Bass.

Vaill, P. (1991) *Managing as a Performing Art: New Ideas for a World of Chaotic Change*. San Francisco: Jossey-Bass.

Van De Haijden, K. (1996). *Scenarios: Art of Strategic Conversations*. New York: Wiley.

Ventura, J. (1999, November). Interview. *Playboy*, pp. 55–66.

Vincenti, L. (1994, May). "Sowing the Seeds of Success." *Venture Capital Journal*, p. 42.

Waldrop, M. M. (1992). *Complexity: The Emerging Science at the Edge of Order and Chaos*. New York: Simon & Schuster.

Walton, C. (1980). *The Moral Manager*. New York: HarperCollins.

Welles, E. (1997, November). "Chaplain to the New Economy." *Inc.*, pp. 68–77.

Wells, B., and Johnson, D. (1998). Rules for improvisation. Unpublished list. Wells Humor Organization, 1624 Market, Suite 301, Denver, CO 80202.

Wheatley, M. J. (1992). *Leadership and the New Science: Learning about Organization from an Orderly Universe*. San Francisco: Berrett-Koehler.

Wheatley, M. J., and Kellner-Rogers, M. (1996). *A Simpler Way*. San Francisco: Berrett-Koehler.

Whetten, D., and Cameron, K. (1998). *Developing Management Skills*. Reading, MA: Addison-Wesley.

Whyte, D. (1994). *The Heart Aroused*. New York: Currency.

Wilber, K. (1996). *A Brief History of Everything*. Boston: Shambhala.

Wilson, E. O. (1998). *Consilience: The Unity of Knowledge*. New York: Vintage Books.

Woodward, K. (2001, May 7) "Faith Is More Than a Feeling." *Newsweek*, pp. 48–58.

Woodward, K. (1998, July 20). "How the Heavens Go." *Newsweek*, p. 52.

Woodyard, C. (1999, July 27). "In-house Travel Bookings Boost Budgets: Eliminating Middleman Flips Trend." *USA Today*, p. 7B.

Youngblood, M. (1997). *Life at the Edge of Chaos*. Dallas, TX: Perceval.

Zaleznik, A., and Matsushita, K. (1993). *Learning Leadership*. Chicago: Bonus Books.

Zohar, D. (1997). *ReWiring the Corporate Brain*. San Francisco: Berrett-Koehler.

INDEX

action: appropriateness of, 11–12; causes of, 93; centeredness of, 291–292; features of, 3–4, 48; importance of, 3; leadership and, 5

action wheel: components of, 3–4; illustration of, 4

adaptation, 146–147, 210–211

adeptness, 304–309, 392, 417

agreement: definition of, 43–44; present and, 46

Anderson, Sherry Ruth, 403

Argyris, Chris, 273

Aristotle, 93

Atkinson, Tom, 74

attractors, 341

authenticity: avoidance of, 370; centeredness as standard for, 269, 291; co-creation as standard for, 269; codetermination as standard for, 186, 216–217, 393; comprehensiveness as standard for, 303–304, 310; confirmation as standard for, 416; confirming of, 413–416; congruence as standard for, 303, 310; consistency as standard for, 90–91, 102–103, 112, 132; convergence as standard for, 223, 228; correspondence as standard for, 83; criteria, 59–62; definition of, 5–6; description of, 2–3, 16–17, 389; forms of, 413; fulfilling of, 51–52; inauthenticity vs., 411–413; leading by, 416; pathways to, 411; polarities of, 60–61; promise of, 415, 418; sincerity vs., 5, 60; wisdom derived from, 415–416; in Zone 1, 82–83, 369; in Zone 2, 102, 369; in Zone 3a, 369; in Zone 3b, 369; in Zone 4, 186, 369; in Zone 5a, 223, 228, 369; in Zone 5b, 247, 263, 369; in Zone 6, 269, 294, 370; in Zone 7a, 370; in Zone 7b, 370; in Zone 7c, 370

authoritarianism, 188

Barker, Joel, 246

Barlow, Ed, 229

Bates, Charles, 57

Bennis, Warren, 316

Benveniste, Guy, 147

Blanchard, Ken, 386

Block, Peter, 187, 192, 195–197, 387

born exclusive theory, 313–314

Bossidy, Larry, 122

bounded rationality, 109

Broder, Eric, 188